# SOLDIER
## BLUE

The people who fought in that war and know what it was like are in their twenties and thirties. Soon at least some will be writing their memories, autobiographies, reminiscences. Then the truth about the War will be exposed, and there will be two versions, the official histories and the truth.

**Doris Lessing,** *African Laughter*

A true war story is never about war. It's about sunlight. It's about the special way that dawn spreads out on a river when you know you must cross that river and march into the mountains and do things you are afraid to do. It's about love and memory. It's about sorrow. It's about sisters who never write back and people who never listen.

**Tim O'Brien,** *The Things They Carried*

# SOLDIER
## BLUE

Paul Williams

davidphilip

For
Shelley Davidow
Lina (Cavedaschi) Williams
And in memory of Bernard Hugh Williams
(1931–2007)

First published in 2008 by David Philip Publishers
An imprint of New Africa Books (Pty) Ltd
99 Garfield Road, Claremont 7700, South Africa

ISBN: 978-0-86486-714-8

Editor: John Kench
Typesetting and design: Matthew Ibbotson @ PETAL**DESIGN**
Proofreader: Glynne Newlands

Printed and bound by Pinetown Printers

# CONTENTS

**Acknowledgement**

My thanks to the Poultry group in Oregon (Bette, Caroline, Judith, Molly and Ursula) for their support.

**Disclaimer**

Although this is a memoir and strives to give a 'true' account of the narrator's life, certain events, characters, and characters' names have been changed/blended together to protect identities, and to telescope history into manageable proportions. As Azar Nafisi says in her Author's Note to *Reading Lolita in Tehran*, 'The facts in this story are true insofar as any memory is ever truthful'; that is, all history is fictionalised, second-hand, and transmuted by the act of writing into the language of myth, dream and metaphor.

# INTRODUCTION

## 3 SEPTEMBER 1978

The Air Rhodesia Vickers Viscount *Hunyani* banked to the left and bumped lightly through the cumulonimbus cloudbank on its ascent from Kariba. In five minutes, flight RH 825 was already out of sight of the control tower, speeding into the haze of a September African evening. The only evidence of its passage was a brown smear across a tawny sky. The cicadas began singing in the grass lining the runway, and the airport prepared to close for the night.

The fifty-four passengers in their window seats watched the sky turn to gold over the Kariba Dam. Hippos made ripples in the shallows. But soon the plane was in unfamiliar territory – the inhospitable brown quilt (it was the end of a dry winter) of the Urugwe Tribal Trust Lands, a great sward of what white Rhodesians called 'terrorist-infested' land.

Captain John Hood turned off the No Smoking sign, and most of the passengers lit up their Madison or Embassy cigarettes, filling the cabin with smoke. They were already thinking of getting back to the bright lights of Salisbury (Did Gran know to meet us, or will we have to take a Rixi Taxi 60666 again?), but some were reminiscing about the weekend in Kariba – Caribbea Bay, the cruise, the honeymoon, last night's party, lights sparkling on the waters from Lake View Inn.

A bang shook the aircraft. It lurched to one side, plunged into a giant air pocket and spun ninety degrees, east to south. The two newlyweds clutched each other and stared out of the starboard window. Flames and smoke poured from the first engine. A metal fragment thunked past. The plane shuddered again, and the second engine burst into flames. Black smoke rushed past the window; intense heat radiated through the thick glass into the cabin. One man drew the blinds. "Put your head between your knees and hold your ankles," another told his wife. The No Smoking and Fasten Seat Belt signs blinked on, and the two air hostesses rushed to the front of the plane.

The pilot's first words to the control tower were jumbled. "… I can't… They're going like fuck…" But there was no doubt about his next message: "Mayday. Mayday, Rhodesia 825. I have lost both starboard engines. We are going in."

Hood aimed for what looked like a flat cotton field and tried to level the unruly beast. The two pale air hostesses followed procedure, checking that everyone was strapped in, but the passengers would not sit still. One man stood to fumble with a window. (What was he thinking? Was he hoping to jump out?) Another man staggered drunkenly down the aisle demanding a fire extinguisher. "Brace yourselves for impact." *Kopjes* scudded past. The fuselage and wings brushed the tops of the trees, and the ground sped by. As the clumsy pterodactyl touched down in an open area the size of a large stadium, the wheels bumped gently on the grass, taxiing smoothly, and it looked as though they might make it. Hearts soared. There was a God.

But the pilot didn't see the donga – an irrigation ditch more than six feet deep and wide, bisecting the makeshift landing ground. The Viscount hit the ditch at 120 miles an hour, cartwheeled on impact, and exploded. The front end of the plane burst into flames, killing the pilots, the crew and the front thirty-four passengers instantly. The wings broke off, and the fuselage blasted across the countryside. The back end of the plane continued ploughing the field, scooping dirt and shooting flames back into its tail.

Then the tail section tore off, and the eighteen people at the back were saved from the inferno. They were flung out of their seats, thrown upside down, and showered with dirt and metal fragments. The hull of the plane was now alight, and fire spread to the surrounding dry bush, ate up the acacia trees and raced to consume much of the surrounding countryside. The plane had scorched a path through the field fifty metres long.

Only eight of the fifty-six survived. When soldiers discovered the wreckage two days later, they found the burnt limbs and black torsos of the crash victims. Seventy-five metres from the tail wreckage (which still clearly showed the thin Air Rhodesia bird emblem), they found the bodies of ten more passengers, lying

face down, pocked and riddled with bullet holes in their backs. At least three of
the bodies had been repeatedly bayoneted after death.

★   ★   ★

At six o'clock on that same
evening, a twenty-year-old
white Rhodesian soldier
sits on his arse on the banks
of Lake Kariba, skimming
stones into the weeds
that choke the lake front.
Crocodile eyes watch him
across the surface of the
water, and hippo noses
blow bubbles at him. His
weapon, an FN automatic,
lies unloaded at his side.
This is a 'terrorist' area, but
he doesn't care any more.
Despite everything, it
has always been this way:
he is on a ball in space,
turning slowly, going
nowhere. There will be
no final confrontation, no
resolution, just the wind
in the grass of a soon-to-

be-extinct country. His life and his death have both passed him by.

   He watches a white egret perch on a dead treetop sticking out of the shallows.
The scene is idyllic: golden ripples surround him; the sunset yawns across the sky;
the cicadas pulse. But he is not fooled. Kariba is a lake that was made by flood-
ing the plains, drowning the trees and animals, and displacing the tribes along its
banks. Dead, dead, dead, he thinks: all dead.

In his head, he can still hear the roar of the Viscount taking off at Kariba airport, and when he closes his eyes he can still see the image of its vapour trails and the glint of its fuselage in the red sun. He should be aboard RH 825 on his way home. But no, here he sits in 98 percent humidity, in 40 degrees of heat – waiting. He watches the plane as long as his mind's eye can follow it, until it disappears gently in the dark night and becomes a star in the dusk, and the sound of its engines turns into screeching cicadas in the reeds.

His story began innocently enough, but even in the beginning he sensed foreboding, futility, ineptitude. His parents had gone out to Africa, taking him with them on their adventure. They went to make something of themselves. But the seeds of his destiny were already sown in their smallest gestures, hesitations and doubts.

# CHAPTER ONE

# IAN SMITH AND
# THE THOUSAND-YEAR REIGN

*My family in Salisbury, Rhodesia, 1963*

When my parents decided to go to Africa in September 1958, they didn't know they were stumbling into the beginnings of a civil war that would spiral into political madness, and end in economic ruin and poverty. They didn't know that their only son would be coerced into fighting in the war. Nor did they know that in the early hours of the new millennium, they would have to flee the Dark Continent, leaving their house, car, servant, bank account and forty-six-year-old suntan.

No, in 1958 they believed the stale propaganda that was still being disseminated, albeit in an embarrassed way, by the British government – that the Federation of Rhodesia and Nyasaland (as it was then called) was a healthy animal, a thriving outpost of the Commonwealth Empire, another Canada, Australia or New Zealand. The fact that Southern Rhodesia was still a colony meant nothing to my parents. They had enthusiastically celebrated Ghana's independence in 1957, admitting that they had no idea what they were celebrating, but the jubilance was infectious. My parents were neither racist colonisers, rabid capitalists nor ranting missionaries. They had no business in Africa, and were, I now sadly conclude, simply naïve. But by committing themselves to settling there, Africa became their problem, and mine. And Africa did not tolerate naiveté.

They arrived in Rhodesia, the story goes, with a pram full of saucepans, a few shillings jangling in their pockets, and an optimistic trust in a benevolent universe, that things would somehow work out. That's how they tell it, anyhow. I have to admire them for bravely tearing the umbilical cord of family tradition. No Williams had ever set foot out of England before, and most of them had never ventured out of Norwich. If Norwich was good enough for my grandfather, my uncle said, it was good enough for him.

I didn't want to go. Or let's say, I wouldn't have wanted to go, if I had had a choice. But I was only three months old at the time. I was not consulted. I would like to have grown up in England, eaten sandwiches on a warm train, rocked through the countryside of cows, sheep and green hills, watched the 'Flowerpot Men' and 'Muffin the Mule' on TV, read Enid Blyton's *Folk of the Faraway Tree* and *Noddy in Toyland*. But my parents had other plans.

Let me introduce them: Bernard Hugh Williams of Old Catton, Norwich, Roman Catholic, graduate of Strawberry Hill Catholic College, and Lina Cavedaschi, now Williams, Italian, from Parma, Italy, brought to England after the war as a reward for helping the Partisans against Mussolini (or so they said – I suspect that she was told this so that the raw wounds of Italian fascism would not smart her in post-war Britain). Newly married and living in South London, they had seen a film of blue skies and smiling colonials in a place called Southern Rhodesia.

Deceived by the British government, who knew damn well the Federation was falling apart, they were sent as gullible Brits to pretend they were living in an extension of England, sans snot. For Rhodesia, promised the film, was a paradise of blue grainy skies and green vegetation, clear flickering air, mountains, gurgling streams, crime-free cities. But this film failed to show the five million brooding, dispossessed Africans in the townships and Tribal Trustlands. It failed to sweep its 16-mm Beaulieu camera lens up North, where the British Empire was cracking and crumbling in Northern Rhodesia and Nyasaland. Instead, the film focused on a smiling, black 'delivery boy' on a bicycle, ringing his bell at the gate of a large house. This house could be yours; that 'madam' could be you, Lina; and that man caressing his Lion Lager on his *stoep* could be you, Bernard.

And who could blame them for wanting that? In 1958 they were living in Austerity Britain, in a caravan, for God's sake, on a mouldy, squelchy Kingston estate. Maybe they would have liked to think of themselves as imperialists (making a better world for themselves), or missionaries (making a better world for others), but they never thought of themselves as susceptible victims of an outdated image of Africa.

I have no recollection of the *Cape Town Castle*'s voyage from Southampton to Cape Town, the dramatic arrival at Table Bay, the awe with which these Brits gaped and gawked through the town, the dismaying train trip up through the Transvaal and Botswana, through deserts to the back of beyond, with scrawny picanins running alongside the train yelling at them as if they had left something behind.

Finally, they arrived at Salisbury Station, which to their relief looked like Surbiton Station back in Surrey (a blackened brick model, with London Bakery nearby), steel passenger bridges over the tracks (made in Birmingham), black porters, a tearoom, and a black Bentley in which they were escorted through the town to their residence.

"It's just like England!" The only difference was the naked blue sky, so blue as to make the pale northern sky of England look white, the heat visibly shimmering on the red corrugated roofs of the low government buildings, the emerald green grass growing untidily through every crack in the road, and the palm trees in a line down the Causeway. The road we are driving on, the driver said, was once a river, and was the first path the pioneers had trotted and splashed through to Fort Salisbury to set up the Union Jack in Pioneer Square, announcing the 1890 occupation of Mashonaland.

The films were right about the weather. The sky was a lonely blue, with no protective guard against infinity. You felt as if you were on a ball in space, turning slowly, going nowhere. The sense of purpose in England, its smugly ordered history, with a BBC commentary to guide you through the low clouds of depression to those metaphysical mountains of meaning – there was none of that in

Rhodesia. Here, you were alone. The Milky Way was a band of milk splashed across the night sky and the city lights did nothing to it, except for the pearl of great price, as my father called the Pearl Assurance building in First Street.

Salisbury, the capital city, named after the Prime Minister of England in 1890, was where we settled. Yes, we were settlers too. Settler in any African language is a nasty word – one settler, one bullet, as they used to say. Dust settles over everything. It's insidious; once it's settled, you can't get it off. But we thought of it as a good word. We've come to settle; we're not going to take the gap at the slightest disturbance, like they did in Kenya or Zambia.

Rhodesia is different from all the other colonies in that here people settle. It's our home; they don't understand that, do they? We came to settle. We settled three generations ago; we came just as the African was arriving from the north, just as the Matabele had settled earlier. You can't give the land back to the original inhabitants: there are no original inhabitants. There are no expats here, only Rhodesians who have been on the land for generations. To settle also means to tame, to conquer, to civilise, as in we've settled the unrest, calmed it down, stroked Simba till he purred.

So we settled easily: glorious sun, dark shadows, thunderstorms, white kingdoms of solid clouds, every day a celebration from riotous birds at five a.m. to the orange sunset theatre at six p.m. and the stars heavy in the Milky Way all night. Life in Rhodesia was ripe fruit falling into our hands.

Our country was named after Cecil John Rhodes who, as our teachers explained, had sailed like Columbus across the seas to discover a new world. After extracting all the mineral wealth out of South Africa, elbowing his way into governorship of the Cape Colony in the 1880s, he set his sights northward. He had a dream: to conquer the whole of Africa, to paint the map British-red from the Cape to Cairo. Due to ill-health and the shortsightedness of the Crown, however, he only managed to get as far north as this small country. In his honour, a statue of him was erected on the main street of the capital city, Salisbury, on Jameson Avenue. The statue was made of copper, so in the subtropical African weather, it quickly turned bright green.

Most of the whites who populated this new country had been lured from England, Scotland, Wales and Ireland to wrestle farms out of rocky red earth, to

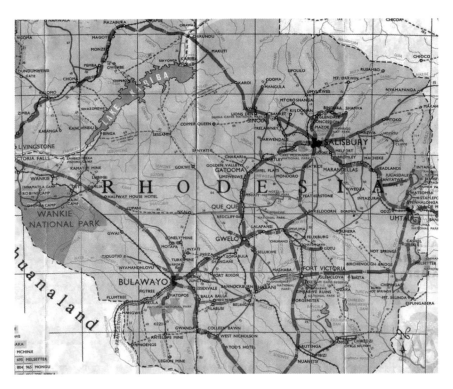

leech and export copper, tin, coal, asbestos, and to build a neat, two-hundred-thousand-strong civilisation.

Some of them were descendants of the first few pioneers who trekked up with the pioneer column in 1890. The core of the new Rhodesian spirit – doctor, lawyer, baker, candlestick maker – arrived at a low, unimpressive *kopje* on 12 September 1890 and surveyed the swampy Makabusi and Marimba marshland around it that was to be called Fort Salisbury. "All is well," the leader of this pioneer column, Colonel Pennefather, reported. "Magnificent country. Natives pleased to see us. Everything satisfactory."

He thundered down the *kopje*, splashed across the Causeway, set up the Fort and planted a Union Jack in the mud of what was to be Pioneer Square, later to be surrounded by the *Rhodesia Herald* offices, Meikles Hotel and the Anglican Cathedral. For seventy years, the country flew the Union Jack and unashamedly proclaimed itself to be a British colony, for the betterment of all its peoples and for the glory of Christian Western Civilisation which had now been brought to shine in the Heart of Darkness.

By the 1950s, however, the British had changed their minds about colonising Africa, declaring that it was no longer decent to spread Western Civilisation in this way. Under pressure from writhing black populations, the British apologised and made unobtrusive gestures of withdrawal, magnanimously giving the Africans their continent back with a timid smile, the teeth falling out one by one:

> *Ghana 1957*
> *Nigeria 1960*
> *Kenya 1963*
> *Malawi 1964*
> *Zambia 1964*
> *Rhodesia?*
> *Mmm? Well…*

The Williams family were settled into Government housing at Francis Flats, the cheap housing in Belvedere. My room was in a dark brick second-floor flat with a window facing a jacaranda tree – the wonder of wonders – purple bells as flowers, those pods as large as my arm, gnarled and curly, with black seeds the size of tadpoles. We were welcomed by our neighbours, who relished our arrival, and brought us tea and biscuits, and stories, and tips on how to live here. My father had a lot to learn. The Kloppers, a couple who had lived here forever, it seemed, became our self-appointed mentors and guides to Darkest Africa.

If I could have remembered arriving, I would have been able to judge better what was in store for me. Those Africans lurking on the sidewalk, glowering at us but collapsing into subservience when we greeted them, those haughty white policemen with brown batons in leathery pouches, those empty blue skies: they would all have told a story. That Pearl man on top of the building, steel girders making up his body, legs and arms, a glass white light bulb the size of a hot air balloon for a head, turned on at night so that it beamed a ghostly light into the darkness of our small city: this, too, should have warned me.

My first memory is a stark image of the white bars of my cot, a square, mauve-wallpapered room, and a window with sunlight pouring in, beckoning me out of the shadows. I was trapped. However big I felt inside, I was barred in this cot, this box room, by my inability to speak, and that light shaft just outside my reach. I pushed my way out of the cot, so the story goes. I wiggled the bar loose and backwards, nappy first, crashed out into the bare room onto the floor where my parents found me crawling up to the windowsill.

I am also told that I waved goodbye to my mother every morning as she guiltily drove off to work, and, once she had gone, crawled to the chocolate bar on the tea tray which was my reward and her recompense. I remember the black, shiny, puffy arms of the nanny, large Annie, yanking me off to play and sitting in the shade of the *msasa* tree, knitting with other loud nannies while we squirmed and squealed as a mass of three-year-olds, bullied and biting and playing in the empty carports of Francis Flats.

But I really only remember from about the age of four onward, and I only remember insignificant fragments of my life *in media res*. Salisbury (pronounced Strawberry) was an established fact, and I was swimming in its current. This was a thriving new city, with clean streets, empty of people. We had a Consul, and at the Caltex garage I was given a sheet of paper with pictures of all the cars on it, so I could tick them off as I saw them on the road. Three Rovers, five Renaults, a Mini Cooper and, look, an MG. Our neighbour was a Mrs Renault, like the fox in the fairy tale, but she had a bubble car, a three-wheeler, which fared badly in the torrential rains and red floods of mud on the Causeway. I confused Armstrong the astronaut with another neighbour called Armstrong and also a man on TV who pulled a truck with his teeth. It worries me how trivial these memories are. I didn't remember anything important, like the time I was lost and then found in the servants' *kaya*, eating *sadza* with them, to the wrath of my parents.

I didn't know about the riots in the townships, the break-up of the Federation which had brought us here in the first place, or the crisis when my parents almost returned home with a pension, but then bravely stuck it out. I didn't know about the fear that oozed out of the white population at the break-up of the Great

British Empire, the surrender of power, the flight of whites, and the triumph of independent dancing Africans in certain countries to the north of us. I didn't know that our own country was heading for a crisis, because it refused to join those other independent countries, and tried to turn back the clock.

I do have a persistent memory of adults crossing their legs and frowning about politics. Politics was a big word. While I played, they sat on verandas in wooden chairs watching red sunsets, while servants brought Lion Lagers on tin trays, and the women bustled in the kitchen, directing the cooks to make dinner. The men talked. Smith, Smith, Smith this, Smith that, until I learned through repetition that Smith was some sort of god, some saviour who would rescue this country and stand up to the corruption of the rest of the world.

The rest of Africa, Mr Kloppers informed my polite parents, was a nightmare of chaos and barbarity. Look at Idi Amin! Look at the Congo! Look at Guinea! Instead of feeling nervous about living on the same continent as these people, we were made to feel proud that we were the one country standing against this type of Africanisation (a dirty word, I gathered by the way Kloppers pronounced it). And Smith was our Sisyphus, he said, who could roll the rock of decay and mould up the hill. A rolling stone gathered no moss, I knew, so it must be a good thing. Mick Jagger and Ian were both rolling stones.

"Come on," my father the naïve settler would laugh, "it can't be as…"

"Bad as that?"

Mr Kloppers, backed up by the vehement nodding of his wife, who finished your every sentence, gobbling it up before you could get it out, like some competition she won every time, was grimly serious.

"It can and it is," he said. "They are a nation of destroyers. They'll wreck anything they lay their hands on."

"Who?" I said.

"Never mind, Paul." My mother was afraid that the Kloppers liked their children to be seen and not heard. But Mr Kloppers gripped my shoulders to drive home the lesson I had to learn.

"Kaffirs," he said. "Kaffirs."

The lesson: there were two types of people on earth – us and them, white and black. We were the good guys who brought Light and Civilisation and the Protestant Work Ethic. The Kaffirs were the chaff of society, the Black Sambos who were funny by very nature of their blackness: the garden boys, the cooks, the workers on the back of trucks, the nannies – 'them'. They were stupid; they were hewers of wood and drawers of water, as it said in the Bible. They worked well only under supervision. You could take the African out of the bush but you couldn't take the bush out of the African. They were children. They were not capable; they stank; they were hung like…

"He's only seven, Henry…"

But if they were Kaffirs, what were we?

"Whites…"

"We're Aryans…"

"Oh, don't start your Aryan nonsense again, Henry Kloppers, you sound like Adolf Hitler. And you're offending Lina. She helped the Partisans in Mussolini's Italy."

But I knew who the Aryans were. They were a carbreaker's yard on the industrial side of town, on the Beatrice Road, a delicious five acres of wrecked cars, where you could wade through piles of debris and pick up aerials, mirrors, sumps, radiators, heating units, alternators – whatever you needed for your car. My father and I spent many a Saturday morning sauntering through the labyrinth of twisted metal, naming cars, ruminating on how they had crashed: "Look, it must have rolled at least twice – the driver's side is gone, poor soul."

'ARIANS' was painted in black on the concrete Durawall in large rough letters. I imagined there was a Mr Arian, who had started the business, collecting wrecked cars, eyes widening with delight whenever he heard the screech of brakes and the thud of metal against metal, rubbing his hands as he started up his diesel towing truck, with 'ARIANS' painted in black on the side, to remove the offensive wreckage and extend his empire. I could think of no better career. I wanted to be an Arian.

There was no war yet, only unrest. Sleeplessness: true to the word, the townships exploded at night while we were sleeping in our quiet white suburbs. The kaffirs were unhappy about something, but nobody knew what it was. They didn't like the lot God had apportioned them, perhaps.

But Kloppers held a much simpler theory. Kaffirs were only good at wrecking things. "Let's see how they can wreck a perfectly good country like Rhodesia. They've done a pretty good of job of Uganda, Nigeria, Ghana…"

After all, in the countries to the north of us (that was his biggest argument), they were starving. They had no *sadza* or *nyama*, they had no jobs. They were ruled by dictators who killed and slaughtered, to whom they submitted and at whom they ululated in praise. We, on the other hand, had a happy, British-style civilisation where everyone had their place and if they accepted it, would live happily too. Those qualified to rule ran the economy so everyone had something to eat, and those who hewed wood and drew water did so to fulfil their own virtue.

It was a watertight argument. We (I mean Kloppers here) had proof, absolute proof, of how African democracies didn't work. Africa was a black hole that sucked everyone into its void if you let it. But Ian Smith, smiled Kloppers with a Colgate ring of confidence, ushering him into every conversation, the saviour that he was, ah, Ian Smith could hold back the forces of darkness.

So who was this Ian Smith, the Prime Minister of the self-proclaimed rebel-rogue-state, Republic of Rhodesia? He was a true Rhodesian, a descendent of Rhodes, or so people claimed. He wasn't much to look at, with a drooping eye and a long nose, crooked teeth and a crew-cut, often caricatured in the newspapers. But he was a tough cookie. When the British called for elections to vote for a majority rule government, which of course would be black (there were only two hundred thousand whites in a population of four million), he refused, saying that blacks weren't responsible enough to run a country. Not yet. His proof was evident: all the newly independent countries of the north – Tanzania, Zambia, Ghana – were corrupt, one-party communist dictatorships. All this calling for one vote, said Kloppers, meant one vote, once. And he grimaced at us, daring us to unravel his cryptic statement.

So Smith took matters into his own hands. In 1965, he decided that what was planted here, the dream we had fought for and built on foreign soil from 1890 on, was going to continue beyond the sunset of the British Empire. Never in a thousand years, said Smith, would we let this become another African casualty of corruption and power and terror. American-style, he declared u.d.i. (Unilateral Declaration of Independence), vowing to keep Rhodesia in the hands of civilised men for all time and to remain true to the vision of its founder. He severed links with the crumbling British Empire and set up a new flag, the Green and White, to replace the colonial one.

On that day we sat gathered around the television after supper, having been warned that the Pry Minister (as I called him) was going to say something important. My father stretched his feet up on the couch; the cats lazily stretched out on the carpet; my mother clanged and banged dishes in the sink to the tune of my father's, "We have a servant to do that, Li, come and settle down." And at eight o'clock, we sat in stunned awe, or was it shock, as Smith dropped his 'ings' and squinted his way through the grandiose speech that would change our lives and plunge us into a fifteen-year war.

"We may be a small country," he said, "but we are a determined people who have been called upon to play a rôle of worldwide significance. We Rhodesians are rejectin' the doctrinaire philosophy of appeasement and surrender. The decision we are takin' today is a refusal by Rhodesians to sell their birthright. And, even if we were to surrender, does anyone believe that Rhodesia would be the last target of the communists in the Afro-Asian bloc? We are strikin' a blow for the preservation of justice, civilisation and Christianity; and in the spirit of this belief we are this day assumin' our sovereign independence. God bless you all."

None of us really knew what it meant. It felt noble and grand to do what America had done two centuries before us, but my father had slightly dampened my patriotic enthusiasm by interjecting words throughout the Pry Minister's speech like "Christ Almighty!" and "Now we're really in the shit."

Personally, I was not actually living in Africa yet. I lived in Enid Blyton's Toyland. I wanted a fusion of England and the USA where red, red robins went bob-bob-bobbing along, where there was snow, where you had to post early for Christmas, where you could sell lemonade on the street. I didn't like this raw green-and-red, tooth-and-claw, brutish life we lived.

But I did like the milkman who pushed a metal cart every morning at six and deposited two clinking glass pints of milk on our doorstep, the silver caps in tiger stripes of black and gold. I did like the blue skies, the tropical thunderstorms, the large green man, Rhodes, our Father and Founder, keeping guard in the middle of the city. And I did like our new house.

When I was five, we moved from Francis Flats to the housing provided for civil servants, in a poor, white, high-density area called Mabelreign. It consisted of thousands of small, low-cost, concrete-block 'as-is' houses in bubbles of cul-de-sacs, in streets running north to south and avenues from 1 to 100, where each white family had a quarter-acre plot of land, a brick house with mud splashed three feet up against the black paint, a garden, trees, a greenway of jungle with snakes and *chongololos* and chameleons for children to play with, a garage, a swing, a ditch to protect us from the summer storms, and white working class neighbours from Manchester, Liverpool and other (I'm quoting Kloppers) God-forsaken places.

Mabelreign had originally been a 1,500-morgen farm north-west of the city centre, claimed by the pioneer settler Kermode, whose surveyor renamed the land after his sweetheart Mabel (may she rule forever). It was filled with immigrants from all over the world, from South Africa, from newly independent African countries to the north, from Europe, from Australia. Each house had a servant's room at the bottom of the garden called a *kaya*, in which lived one male black servant whose job it was to clean the house, weed the garden, and wash dishes.

Sing to the tune of 'Edelweiss':

> *Mabel-reign, Mabel-reign, every morning you greet me;*
> *Small and white, clean and bright,*
> *Bless my homeland forever.*

I remember our first servant. He arrived like an alien from another planet. Take me to your Master, he asked me, so I ran back into the house to get Mom. I had never been up close before to these intruders, because they were not allowed in our white city except to work. They had to live in the Tribal Trust Lands and the satellite townships from where they had to commute to work. So we never saw much of them except in their functions as servants, cooks, gardeners and nannies.

A very black, shiny-skinned man, quiet, humble, nervous and sweating, he asked for a job by pleading with his hands together, saying he had to support a large family in the township and that he could do "anything". He held in his hand what he called a *situpa* or reference. My parents hired him and he moved into the *kaya* that night, with no belongings at all, except what we gave him: some crates for tables, an old mattress and blanket for a bed. His wages? Five pounds a month, plus free food and lodging. Did he also have a family? I asked my parents. Yes, but they weren't allowed to stay with him in white areas. They lived in a house the other side of town in a place called Harari.

His name was Linksome. He taught me how to whistle through my teeth, how to pretend to throw bricks at people but harmlessly drop them behind me, how to plant and grow maize in the back garden, and how to burp loudly while drinking a Coke. Linksome called me "master", and when it was time for me to go to school, he sat me down on a rock in the greenway and gave me a long, passionate lecture about the merits of my privileged education system. I was lucky, he told me. He had never been to school, which was why he was only a houseboy. Did I want to end up as a houseboy?

I didn't like the idea of school. I did want to be a houseboy, or else a black policeman like the one who helped kids across Latchmore Road. Or better still, a rubbish bin collector, like those loud black men who rode on the sides of trucks and whistled to stop and hoist up huge clanking silver cans from each house. You didn't need school for that. I begged to get rides on the trucks and help them, but was never allowed.

Surprisingly though, Linksome could write. I still have my Mickey Mouse Fun Book on which I practised my first words, KOOB NUF ESUOM YEKCIM, on the inside front cover. The page also contains the word 'Ringson' over and over again, in large looping writing, which puzzled me for a while, until I realised that this was what the houseboy had written at my encouragement.

Linksome's skin was black, but curiously, it was reflective of white light, as if it had been polished. I watched his skin in won-

*With Linksome in the back garden*

der as the kitchen light mirrored itself on his forehead. He was a cheerful fellow, always grinning and smiling and laughing, and obeying commands wordlessly, until I realised that words bounced off him, especially bad words, like kaffir and stupid hout and lazy munt. They didn't go inside him at all.

Of course one servant wasn't enough. He had a friend who was hungry – that man sitting in the ditch, who became, for free lunch and tea, the garden boy. He was a fifty-or-so-year-old black man with a white bristly beard, a Jed Clampett hat, a stoop of deference and gratitude, a skin that was cratered with the eternal bombardment of insults like one of Jupiter's moons, and a white grin, who twirled his hat and clapped his deformed, gnarled hands.

"I can do anything, baas," he said. We already had a houseboy. But the garden, this quarter acre of river mud and clay and trees, of rotten avocados, sugarcane, guavas and fruit flies, spoke loudly. After all, we had two rooms in the kaya. My mother was too busy with her new job at the Petrol Rationing Office (we were short of petrol because those Bloody Brits had imposed sanctions on us) to work in the garden.

He started immediately, after a paint can of sweet tea and a slice of thick bread. He drank the paint can to the dregs, smiled and said, "Aah, sorry, *baas,*" when he saw I was scrutinising him, fascinated at this raw man from the bush. He called himself – thumping his chest – Magadzwe, but we couldn't say it, so my parents called him Johnny the garden boy and he seemed happy with that.

And here began my new career aspiration. I wanted to be like him; I wanted to be, as I announced proudly to my parents one breakfast, a Kaffir.

"Don't use that word, Paul," said my mother. "It's not nice."

The first African word he taught me was *chelogue.* When I asked what it meant, he pointed at the crotch of his stitched-up khaki trousers. "That is your *chelogue.*" So my name for him from that day forward was Chelogue. He looked like a *chelogue* to my seven-year-old imagination, wrinkled, ugly, unsightly. A *chelogue,* so my mother told me, was a boy's secret, not to be revealed to anyone.

So too was our gardener. He collapsed into cringing humility whenever white adults were around, but was loud, arrogant and obnoxious when they weren't. He was wary with me, because he knew that I knew his secret. Chelogue, the wrinkled dusty organ of a person who sat and listened while he weeded the garden invisibly, as I played Thunderbirds or Batman around the adults. He listened, plucking weeds, a crouching gnome-man watching us watching him watching them. Chelogue – the secret worm that destroyed the rose.

"How do you spell *chelogue*?"

"No," said Chelogue, "you don't spell it, you say it."

Confident that my parents did not know what a *chelogue* was, I asked them how it was spelled. Maybe he meant a *chongololo,* that six-inch shiny black centipede that appears after the rains?

"Who told you about a *chelogue*?"

I pointed dumbly at the weeding, wrinkled ball in the luminous green garden.

"Don't listen to him, Paul. He should be working instead of filling your head with nonsense. I'll dock his wages."

God made people in a hot oven out of mud, he told me, and baked them brown. All the people on the earth were brown, but He thought of one final improvement: make them white. He told his animals to send the message: humans were invited to bathe in a magic pool to turn them white. God sent the cheetah to Europeans, the fast-footed hare to the Asians, but to the Africans, he sent the nervous chameleon. The Europeans arrived first and washed in the pool, diving and swimming, until they were completely white. By the time the Asians arrived, the pool was murky brown, but they still bathed in it and turned a pale yellow. But the chameleon took so long to get to the Africans, that by the time they got to the pool, it had all but dried up, and all that was left was enough of a puddle for them to dip the palms of their hands and the soles of their feet.

"Where are you from? Which TTL?" I asked innocently one day.

"No, I'm from heeya," he said, pointing to the ground he had recently mashed and weeded. "My father was here before the whites came."

Before the whites came, he said, it was paradise. No one owned anything; we were one. We were the blue dome of sky, the chinkling pebbly rivers of Nyanga, the scraggly msasa trees clutching whispered spells from the wind, the roar of *mosi-oa-tunya.* We lived in peace and serenity.

Then one day people without knees arrived and squatted on our land. At first they did not bother us, merely scrabbled for shiny stones in the ground. But then the Iron One called Lodzi made a strange request. He wanted the land we were sitting on. We laughed. You cannot buy the land. It's like the air we breathe, the water we drink. But while we were laughing, he took it. We were driven off like cattle. Then he took the rivers, so we could no longer drink. He took the sky and filled it with clouds of brown so we could not breathe. And with his white magic, he caused drought here, and made it rain in his countries far away. He tilted the earth so that the rivers sloshed away from us. The clouds were sucked up by his cloud machines in the northern lands, leaving us high and dry, so the seasons changed. We had floods, then drought, then starvation.

What were we to do? To stay on the land, we now had to work in the sky-devouring factories, the river-blackening mines. So, with the rivers dammed up, the sky brown with smoke, the air noisy from machines and the tak-tak of the machine guns he brought, we lost our spirits.

"So who were these evil people-without-knees?" I asked. "Who was this Lodzi? Did you throw him out?"

"It has begun," Chelogue said. "For a long time, the people were asleep, but now they are waking. They will throw the kneeless people out, and will have the land back again. Again it will be paradise, clean blue skies, clean rivers and proud spirits."

He laughed a smoker's cough (for he rolled about ten newspaper cigarettes during each story) and puffed thoughtfully, as if the stories were sucked through the smoky red tube between his lips. The smoke he exhaled was the telling of it, and his cough was the bitter moral.

Before the white people the ancestors lived here. The ancestors were dead people, still alive somehow (like zombies or vampires), watching over us, helping, disapproving, squabbling, and crowding from some vantage point where they could see us. The ancestors had warned people to wake up when the kneeless people took over the land, and two of their leaders were captured and hanged on a tree in Seventh Avenue, the one leaning over the road. Kneehanda and Maholo were their names. "But," he laughed, "you can't kill ghosts."

What a load of codswallop, said Kloppers. Before the whites came, Africa was a dark continent of disease and intertribal war. The whites rescued the Shona from being slaves of the Matabele. When we arrived, the land was vacant, with the huddled Shona living in fear in stony forts in Inyanga, eating millet and at the superstitious mercy of an inhospitable universe full of wild animals, monsters and cruel gods. We saved the ungrateful Calibans from their own nightmares. We brought roads, the railway, schools, medicine and democracy.

We whites were a strange race, I learned later – people who had vital organs missing. In Hawaii, the white invaders were called "people without history" because they were unable to recite their ancestors' lineage, like all civilised islanders could; the Spanish sea pirates who invaded the Caribbean and then the Americas were heartless and soulless; the British in Africa wore long trousers which rendered them kneeless. Most colonisers were deaf and blind to local cultures and sensitivities. In their turn, too, the indigenous people of invaded lands were missing vital human characteristics: they were not reasonable creatures; they had no souls; they were incorrigible cannibals, or pagans, or had not severed their mind from their bodies, their self from the other, their heart from the land, like all good descendants of Descartes should.

The school I attended was Alfred Beit Primary. Coincidentally, this was the same school that had been used in the British propaganda film, so I could see firsthand what had seduced my parents into becoming white settlers. The school was surrounded by mulberry trees (which supplied food for our silkworms and bled purple on our fingers and lips), jacaranda trees (that rained bells of purple on the road, and could be popped if you knew the right way to do it) and poinsettia (red flowers that bled white and stung your eyes). Clean, green roundabouts welcomed parents who were dropping off kids in Sunbeams or Cortinas or Vauxhall Victors.

Trooper Thomas, we learned at school, was chased up a tree by a lion which then proceeded to eat the Royal Mail. In the early 1890s, Allan Wilson and the Shangani Patrol, a group of Rhodesian pioneers, had been surrounded in battle by fierce Matabele warriors and had all died as heroes saying the Lord's Prayer. Our Father which art in heaven, they had prayed, closing their eyes bravely while the assegais flew around them. The last man to die had managed to get all the way to the end – for Thine is the kingdom, the power and the glory, forever and ever, amen – before they killed him. It was a good story, but I could never figure out how anyone knew what they had prayed when there had been no survivors. And now, with the help of the two hundred thousand whites, Smith claimed that, like Allan

Wilson, he could stem the tide of corruption, Africanisation and communism (all synonymous) that was sweeping down from the north.

Although most whites shared his vision, the black population didn't. They wanted to vote, live or work where they chose, own land and play a part in the country's affairs. So they protested in strikes, marches, demonstrations, riots, and eventually a guerrilla war in which two main liberation armies (grandiosely acronymed ZIPRA and ZANLA, the Zimbabwe People's Republican Army and the Zimbabwean African Nationalist Liberation Army) recruited large numbers of black people and trained them outside the country to return clandestinely and fight the white minority regime, to topple it by all means necessary.

But this did not deter Smith or the Rhodesians. They saw such bad behaviour as the essential nature of the primitive African. Almost the entire white population was involved in defending the country from this onslaught from the outside, from these peace-loving ordinary African servants and peasants who had been transformed into communist terrorists, and who now wanted to destroy this white paradise and replace it with an African socialist state. More and more white males were mobilised to fight for their country and keep the invading barbarian hordes out. Rhodesia was going to survive and never give in to the trend of the rest of Africa: starvation, *coups d'état*, terror rule by a socialist vanguard party, anarchy, corruption and Idi Amin. Ian Smith, responding to one outbreak of rebellion, went on the television to speak for the white nation:

"Rhodesians understand this sort of thing. In fact, it proves how right we are in our determination to maintain high standards in Rhodesia. Those responsible for this barbaric destruction have ironically played right into our hands. What greater proof can anyone have of their lack of maturity and civilisation…? We have no intention whatever of surrenderin' our country to appease the communists. We have no intention of allowin' our country to degenerate into the sort of shambles which we see in Mozambique and Angola today. I don't believe in black majority rule in Rhodesia, not in a thousand years. Good night and God bless you all in these tryin' times."

To look at, Smith was a little disappointing. He was skinny; he Brylcreemed his thin hair over his scalp. His voice was thick and guttural, South African, not elegantly British. But when he spoke on TV, everyone listened. He made sense, was the comment everyone made.

"Have you heard the joke about the future machine?" said Colin Edkins, my eight-year-old neighbour, as we sat on the twenty-foot-high granite rock in the greenway. "Smith was worrying about the future of Rhodesia…"

"The Honourable Mr Ian Douglas Smith, if you don't mind," interrupted seven-and-a-half-year-old Douglas Pike. Arthur Kerrington, eight and three-quarters, picked a long strand of elephant grass, stripped it and placed the succulent end in his mouth. "My parents just call him good old Smithy."

"Smith was worrying about the future of Rhodesia," continued Colin, ignoring the interruptions, "so he went to consult a machine that could predict what was going to happen to the country."

9. Douglas Arnold

Paul Williams, only seven, said nothing, but stripped a hibiscus flower of its red dress and its green underwear, and then popped out its seed. Colin continued: "The first question he asked was, who will be running the country in twenty years, blacks or whites? And the machine buzzed and bells rang and lights flashed. Smith looked worried. Then at last the answer came out – whites. He was relieved and laughed. Then just for curiosity, he asked another question, how much would a beer cost then? And the machine buzzed and bells rang and the answer came out – fifty roubles."

"Well, go on," said Arthur.

"That's the joke."

"I don't get it."

"You don't get it? Well, I'm not going to explain it to you. You don't go explaining jokes. I heard it from my parents last night and they laughed themselves silly."

Here I placed a finger into the air, as if to test the wind. "It's about the communists. My dad has been talking about them too."

"The communists?"

"My Dad," said Arthur, "says that the communists are going to take over his dead body."

"Why would they want to do a thing like that?"

Colin: "Did you know that there are so many communists in China that if you shot one every five seconds, if you lined them all up and shot them, you would never get to the end?"

"Why?"

"Because by the time you got to the end, it would be years and years and more of them would have been born and grown up."

It was common knowledge: the communists were a bunch of people who lived in the East, in Russia and China mainly, whose obsession was to wreck the world. They wanted, without any motive, to destroy all that was good and pure and healthy and innocent and working well. They wanted to murder and rape and pillage. The Americans were fighting them in Vietnam; the Rhodesians were fighting them here. They had already taken over the rest of Africa to the north and had caused misery and destruction there. Now they wanted it to happen in Rhodesia as well.

**Soviet Government Statement: The Situation in Southern Rhodesia, 1965**
The colonialists have committed a new crime against the African peoples. On November 11, the racialist régime of Ian Smith proclaimed the 'independence' of Southern Rhodesia. These actions are aimed at perpetuating in Southern Rhodesia a colonial system based on inhuman oppression of the Zimbabwe people, four million strong, by a handful of racialists and on ruthless suppression of the lust [sic] struggle of this people for real independence, freedom and social justice. . .

Loyal to its steadfast policy of supporting the national liberation movement of the peoples, the Soviet government declares its full solidarity with the Zimbabwe people and again confirms its readiness to co-operate with the African countries in rendering them all-out support in their just struggle for genuine national independence.

I had no idea at the time that any 'lust struggle' for independence was countering our own inverted-commas white independence. Nothing showed on the surface, at least to me. Every Saturday morning, Salisbury bustled with white families shopping on First Street and drinking coffee at The Egg and I. My biggest problem was to find Toomer's Book Exchange, where you could buy Superman comics for a shilling, or Kemsley and Dawes, where my father ruminated over electric switches, flanges and female sockets he had to buy. To get there, we had to park on Fourth Street, next to the RF headquarters, cross Cecil Square and go down First Street, stopping at the outdoor Wimpy restaurant for a quick milkshake or brown cow.

Cecil Square, aka Pioneer Square, aka Unity Square, had blue and red and white flowers along the paths, which all met at a fountain in the middle.

I wished I could see the park from the air. It would have looked like all the butterfly flags on every government building. But in 1965, there was one change: the Rhodesian flag became three oblongs of colour, green-white-green, with a coat of arms in the middle. The Union Jack flowers in Cecil Square were dug up and the park left to grow wild. The Prime Minister had ordered it, I knew. I thought he might have the diagonal paths dug up too and made into the shape of the new flag, but they weren't. The city was the shape of the new flag though, I noticed, and you could get a good view of it from the Kopje. In the middle was a block of white, the city centre, and flanking it were two blocks of green suburbs. But spoiling the flag were the huge townships that spread out higgledy-piggledy in all directions.

The townships were rows and rows of tin-shack housing for the black servants and workers in the factories, who always had fires choking the view and grey smoke twining up invisible beanstalks into the blue skies. Not that I ever went there; my parents pointed out the townships from the top of the Kopje, at the pioneer memorial – the Kopje was the first hill the pioneers had galloped over in their column in 1890.

The Pearl Building was my favourite icon in the idealised Africa I surveyed from the Kopje. It was a white building across from Livingstone House, with the steel girder skeleton of a man holding up his huge pearly light for a head. Once we bought greasy fish and chips from The Sunflower on Jameson Avenue and drove to the viewpoint to sit in the Consul and watch the Pearl Building shine for us over the Dark Continent.

"The Pearl of Great Price," chuckled my father.

"What's that?" I asked.

"The white light of Civilisation," beamed my father, "shining its light over darkest Africa."

"Bernard," chided my mother, unsure of his irony.

"Don't take everything so seriously," he said, with the confidence of the newly arrived, unenmeshed world traveller.

On the side of the huge white bricks, I could read the words Pearl Assurance, which, according to my father, meant a pledge or a guarantee to put your heart at rest. While the rainbow was God's assurance, the pearl was Smith's.

# CHAPTER TWO

# RHODESIA IS OUR ONLY HOME

In January 1966, the year I started Primary School, a girl moved in next door. My parents invited her parents around to sit on the veranda, drink beer and talk politics. They were settling in Rhodesia after a hurried flight down the continent of Africa, from Ghana to Kenya to Zambia to God's own country. They had brought with them two children, a boy and a girl, and had moved into number 10, 32nd Avenue (we lived at number 8), Mabelreign.

The father was already dressed like a Rhodesian. He wore a safari suit, that coarse cotton outfit with matching jacket and pleated trousers, short-sleeved shirt in beige blue, tight around the arms – "comfortable," my father said, "better than a suit" – but with hairy neck showing, plus the necessary accessories of *veldskoens* (soft leather shoes) and a pack of Embassy Bonus cigarettes (26c for twenty) in the top right-hand pocket next to the leaking Biro ballpoint pen.

The woman wore a short Crimplene (equally coarse material) dress, a beehive hairdo held together with sweet-smelling lacquer, heavy teardrop earrings and make-up.

A beer was planted in each male hand, a shandy (beer diluted with lemonade) in the ladies', and the African litany began:

"Look what's happening in the Congo… I can't believe Uganda… in Ghana… Tanzania…" They were silver balls in a pinball machine that had been bumped down every country, and would spill into the sea if the Rhodesian flippers Smith and the Rhodesian Front hadn't saved them for another spin.

They brought with them a girl, about my age, and presented her to me as a companion to entertain while they talked. She plopped down on the lawn next to me and folded her legs under her, plaited her hair and grinned with dirty teeth. She wore a floral dress, so short that she could not fold her legs modestly enough under it, and she had to keep pulling the hem down to cover her thighs.

She was the first girl I had ever met. You see, I had no brothers and sisters. They all died mysteriously. My mother produced still-birth after still-birth. No one wanted to talk about it. To me, it seemed as if someone wanted to make sure I was really alone in the world. Perhaps I was a Job-type game between God and Satan to see what would happen if a sisterless boy grew up without anyone of the opposite sex except an invisible mother.

Or maybe this was how it was supposed to be. Isn't it evil (as some patriarchal religions maintain) to mix the sexes? Isn't the chemical reaction of male and female responsible for all the woes of this world? Or maybe Freud was right by suggesting that we repress our desire for the opposite sex, then take it out on the world in the form of sports, war and bad behaviour; so in order to allow civilisation and culture to flourish, the sexes must be separated. No wonder I always thought of culture as a bad thing, a mould that grows from our dirty minds.

For whatever reason, I was excluded. Whatever virtue of Western Civilisation decreed that the feminine was taboo in my life, I had few friends, only other little boys who fought and bragged and bullied in our street. I never met girls. They were alien beings, creatures who behaved differently to us, who were destined for higher things than us boys. There were some who lived on 33rd

Street, but these were always chased away when they ventured on their bikes into our neighbourhood. But now one of these aliens had come to live next door.

"What's your name?"

With a finger, she spelled the word in the dust for me: JAQI.

"Jackie?" I said. She nodded.

"That's wrong," I said. "Q always must have its friend U following it."

"Not me. I spell my name how I bloody well want."

"Jaqi, don't," said God in the form of her father, reinforcing his commandment with a *klap* on her ear. Her eyes brimming with bravado, Jaqi nudged me with a plea for help. "Can we go climb trees?"

After a nod from my mother, Jaqi and I raced from adult company to the protection of the foliage at the back of the garden. But I too was shocked at the way she defied the English language. The way things were spelled was important for me. Words had to look right. Each word had a weight, a feeling, a balance. I liked English words: heavy with an 'ea', their rhythm, the soft slide of rhyme. But Jaqi? Like that, her name sounded all jaggy and sharp and long-nosed. Her nose was long, granted, her skin a blotchy brown, her hair wild, windy and scraggly, her dress dirty and uncomfortably short, and she reminded me of the cat that lived in the neighbourhood, especially the way she climbed trees. The cat would scratch its claws out and run up a tree with ease, its ears back, right to the top. Jaqi did the same. She scrabbled ahead of me and we climbed the syringa tree, with the yellow-berried pips inside, that had grown across our whole back fence. She would monkey up and then curl her legs around the trunk like a lover – no, I would not have thought that then – like a snake entwining and entangling itself with another snake. She would go right to the top, so I could see her dress and the pink panties underneath.

Sex was one of those myths I had a hard time believing, especially as I learned it from my peers at school through guffaws and sneers. Did girls really have slits in their crotches into which *chelogues* were inserted? My friends had always mocked girls and made them pull down their pants so they could laugh at their small slits, and had told me so. But I had never seen one myself first-hand, so I assumed that they had to be horizontal, like mouths, with fleshy top and bottom lips. I also had a hard time believing, though I knew it had to be true because

Scott Galloway told me, that once you inserted your *chelogue* into the female slit and pumped vigorously, her stomach ballooned, and out popped a baby.

As far as I could see through her threadbare panties up the tree, Jaqi's genitalia were missing, which made me feel instantly sorry for her and treat her with patronising sympathy. "Why did you leave Kenya?" I said to the top of the tree, clinging on, trying not to look straight into her crotch, while she, leopard-like, lounged in the fork, gazing down at the world below, legs open for balance.

"Because of the Miao-Miaos."

"The...?"

"Miao-Miaos. You know, black gorillas."

In vain I tried to picture the species of wild animal that had chased them all the way down to Rhodesia from Kenya.

"We have Miao-Miaos here too, you know," I told her (never admit ignorance: pretend to know everything). "In the game parks." From that moment on, Jaqi was a Miao-Miao to me – she was tough, wild and climbed trees like a cat.

From that moment on, too, she was my constant companion. We climbed trees, waded through storm drains and filled every moment of those hot blue weekends of childhood. I never figured out why the boys didn't like girls or why they laughed at them. Jaqi, though, wasn't your typical girl. She was dirty and immodest. All the words girls were, she was not. Sugar and spice? She used expressions I'd never heard before, like "damn your sodomising little prick to hell," when she was angry. Or modest? She would hook up her dress to pee into the bushes or compete with me in a defecating competition over the granite rock in the greenway – and win.

And she had her own sexual counter-theory which she picked up from her school friends Bernadine Smothers and Rosemary Bezuidenhout. Her younger brother Drew, who followed her round half-naked, mysteriously wearing only a shirt and no pants, provided the opportunity to expound on her theory of sexual difference while we played in the cool shade of the greenway behind my house.

"Do you know why my brother has a willy?" she asked me. "And my Dad, too?"

I shook my head. "A willy?"

"What do you call it, then?"

"A *chelogue*, it's a *chelogue*. He said so." I pointed to the wrinkled squatter in the corner of the garden, who was picking at the weeds with a rusty iron tool, but whom I knew was listening.

"It's like Pinocchio," she said. "When he told lies, his nose grew. Same with Drew and my dad." I thought of Jaqi's dad, shouting and hitting the kids, drinking beer, with his colourful language (well, that's how my parents described it; we could hear it over the fence, though colourful is not how I would have described the expletives that pelted down over our hedge like a meteor shower). "Bad people grow willies."

She stared at the silence shrouding me, and I swallowed.

"It's true," she said, mistaking my discomfort for incredulity. "Don't you believe me?"

Was it true? I couldn't tell her otherwise; she was convinced. I suppose if you have deformed genitals, you have to make up a story that consoles you. But by humouring her, I realised that I had to start living a lie. From that moment, I could not let her know of my genetic deformity.

Now, of course, her next question was, did I have a willy? Suddenly it was time to go home. Bath-time. I beat my hasty retreat, but Jaqi followed. She never had to take baths, she said, but would like to see me take mine. My mother was not an ally. "Of course Jaqi can sit in the bathroom. Does she want to get in too?"

Shit, no, Jaqi was not prepared to go that far. But she sat on a wooden chair and I had to lie face down the whole time she was there. She was watching carefully but I never moved, even when the water grew cold, so cold I was goosy and told her to go.

"Oh, well, it's suppertime anyway," she shrugged, disappointed.

I was privileged to see female genitalia for the first time on a warm October pre-rainy-season day, the kind when the clouds heat up intolerably and you have to run through sprinklers or go to the public pools. Jaqi called me over the fence to meet her friends from school.

"Do you want to join our gang?" said Rosemary, the curly, dark, freckled Irish ball of a girl. A wispy, blonde Bernadine sat us in a circle, and Jaqi sat nervously on my left. She knew what was in store for me.

"In order to get into our gang, you all have to swear by the rudest thing you know."

"I swear sexual intermittence for ever and ever, amen," said Bernadine.

"By the tough tits of my dead aunt," said Rosemary.

"I swear by the black *chelogue* of my garden boy," I stuttered.

"By the juice of Mother Mary's virgin cunt," said Jaqi.

Rosemary nodded. "Now you have to show your wee to get in the gang. Paul first."

I modestly waived my right, so Rosemary impatiently offered to go first. She shifted her skirt and without warning thrust aside her panties with a thumb to reveal a wrinkled fold of skin which was... vertical. It was raw red, which confirmed my theory that God had circumcised her with a cosmic knife. But vertical? Bernadine did likewise, thrusting out her tongue as if exposing her genitalia was a rude, defiant gesture at the world, or at me. And dog my cats if hers wasn't vertical too. Jaqi followed suit, and I had to endure three vertical gash wounds jeering at me.

"Now you."

"Have to go," I said.

"Oh, don't worry, he doesn't have to show his," said Jaqi. "He has a small wee. It's OK."

They nodded, but with a look of suspicious dissatisfaction. Rosemary in particular wanted to make sure. But I clamped my legs together tightly.

The girls' club was a surprisingly zestful exploration of sexuality. Rosemary and Bernadine would waylay small boys, and pull down their pants to reveal their willies, often resulting in the small boy crying and running home. They terrorised the avenues after school, and taunted and teased the male population. I was doubly guilty, mocking the deformity of other boys, masquerading as an ally of the *chelogue*-less amazons, while I concealed the very *chelogue* they despised. I was the enemy within.

Despite this, Jaqi and I became comrades-in-arms. Whenever she was beaten at home, she'd arrive at my bedroom window, her face tear-stained and dirty where she'd wiped her hands, and I'd cheer her up. Her father weekly pulled her pants down, threw her over his knees and paddled her arse with his belt, while her mother would slap her across the face for her insulin, or so Jaqi said. So we'd play school, caning our toys until their backsides fluffed out, or hospital, cutting open their tummies for operations. Or the inevitable doctor and nurse, in the darkness of my bedroom, while my mother was at work, my father at school, and the houseboy sunning himself against the limed *kaya* wall, smoking Star. I would never let her operate on me (we had developed an unspoken agreement about my privacy), but she would readily pull down her pants and hoist her dress so I could operate.

"Hmm, you're wounded," I'd say, examining the vertical gash. "How did it happen?" And with the plastic scalpel, I would poke and press and probe in her wound, while she lay meek and Puritan-like for me to rub medicine and soothe her.

"It'll get better soon."

But I lived in perpetual guilt that she would discover my dreadful secret, especially when she taught me the ditty she had learned from her girlfriends Rosemary and Bernadine:

> *My friend Billy had a ten-foot willy*
> *And he showed it to the girl next door.*
> *She thought it was a snake*
> *So she hit it with a rake*
> *And now it's only six feet four.*

At school it was different. I played only with boys, of course, and while girls segregated themselves into pale, powder-puff games, we played stingers, open gates, and K.I.N.G spells king. The boys' club was a good deal easier to join. It involved proving yourself by fighting someone, or jostling smaller boys in the school corridors, or, when you grew older, going to war. At least, that's what I gathered from my parents, from friends' older brothers, and from television.

The six o'clock news not only showed the Pry Minister talking – Ian Smith, Ian Smith, Ian Smith – but sometimes the war in Vietnam where the Americans were fighting the communists. I watched men snake into muddy trenches and shoot, always getting 'inchered'. What is 'inchered'? I asked my parents. Getting hurt in battle, my tired mother would say.

"Why?"

"The communists," said my father, "want to hurt us, so we have to fight back."

"Does everyone have to go and fight in the army?"

"Yes. Communists are behind every bush, apparently, so when you finish high school, you'll go to the army. All men do."

And get inchered, I thought. My life was predetermined. I should not have dwelled so much on the pain I would feel in the army so early in life. But this was a rite of manhood, my parents insisted. Only cowards and girlies did not go to fight for what was right.

★  ★  ★

Slowly, imperceptibly, I was becoming white. And slowly, perceptibly, I was becoming male. But first, may I give you a short political contextual digression so I can step back out of the embarrassment of white malehood?

The Federation of Rhodesia and Nyasaland had collapsed because, said Mr Kloppers, the foppish Prime Minister, Garfield Todd, was too liberal, wanting to appease the African nations around him. But because the Federation – a controlled greenhouse environment in which African aspirations were supposed to be cultivated and flourish – buckled under, those aspirations became a cancerous array of political parties and sporadic acts of sabotage. Spreading this cancer (to use another of Mr Kloppers's metaphors) was the Zimbabwe African People's Union (ZAPU), mostly Ndebele, led by Joshua Nkomo. It was shortly joined by the Zimbabwe African National Union (ZANU), mostly Shona, a break-away group under Ndabaningi Sithole. After the collapse of the Federation in 1963, both ZAPU and ZANU were banned and the majority of their leaders imprisoned.

Overnight, our motherland became our mother-in-law, and Harold Wilson, the Labour Prime Minister of Great Britain, smoking his incessant pipe, arching his villainous eyebrows, became our enemy.

HAROLD WILSON: "The purported declaration of Independence by the former Government of Rhodesia is an illegal act and one which is ineffective in law, an act of rebellion against the Crown and against the Constitution, and actions taken to give effect to it will be treasonable. The Governor, in pursuance of the authority vested in him by Her Majesty The Queen, has today informed the Prime Minister and other Ministers of the Rhodesian Government that they cease to hold office. These small and frightened men are now private persons and can exercise no legal authority in Rhodesia."

But British scolding and UN sanctions had the opposite effect on Rhodesia's wellbeing. The manufacturing sector in Rhodesia, already well developed before UDI in 1965, was given a stimulus by the imposition of sanctions. The sanctions obliged Rhodesian industry to diversify and create many import-substitution undertakings to compensate for the loss of traditional sources of imports. Rhodesian processing of local raw materials also grew rapidly. Major growth industries included steel and steel products, heavy equipment, transportation equipment, ferrochrome, textiles and food processing.

Gone were Kellogg's Rice Krispies and Cadbury's chocolates, but here came Willard's chips, Honey Krunchees and Charhon's chocolates. The only faithful multinational which sustained a visible profile was the black, fizzy, caffeinated, carbonated drink called the Real Thing. After all, in the sixties, things in the townships went better with Coke, and in the seventies, it taught the world to sing in perfect racial harmony. I collected the golden stamps given at government offices (Prosper with Rhodesia), and a proud array of local products – David Whitehead cotton, Wish toilet paper (the luxury you can afford), BATA *takkies*, CAPS pharmaceuticals.

So why would any white person want to live in such a hotbed of unrest and instability? Why were we not prepared to pack up and go home when the indigenous people demanded their land back?

Because of the birds, sunrises, smells, trees, flora, fauna, the warm climate, the sunshine. Because of the red soil: you could grow anything here. Tobacco, maize, cotton, sugarcane, vegetables, sorghum, millet, rice, peanuts, fruits, cassava, coffee, tea – you were guaranteed a rich harvest every year. You could walk into the jungle at seventeen, walk out at twenty-one, and by God, you'd be rich. Because, too, of the mineral wealth: the country was endowed with a wide variety of mineral resources, including copper, asbestos, aluminium, gold, nickel, silver, tin, iron and coal. Our industrial products included iron and steel, cement, food products, machinery, textiles and consumer goods.

And because of the cheap labour. Most great civilisations are built on the backs of disenfranchised workers and slaves, and Rhodesia was no exception. Which brings me back to our servant who kept our garden free of weeds and blossoming with poinsettia, frangipani, three-coloured bougainvillea, passion flowers and roses.

Chelogue's *kaya* was out of bounds, because it was filthy and smelly, said my mother. It therefore held a boundless fascination. From the *kaya* wafted delicious smells of *sadza* cooked on an open fire in a black enamel pot. At night, I heard the hissing of his paraffin lamp, saw monstrous shadows leap out against the whitewashed wall, and when he took a shower, water splashed over the walls, and the Lifebuoy soap stung my eyes.

Jaqi and I once dared to peek in Chelogue's *kaya* when he was out to lunch down the road. While she was 'keeping chips', I pushed open the creaking green metal door to find a high bed on bricks, a small table and little else. What did he do here all day? Under the bed was a black trunk, locked. His toilet was a concrete slab with a hole in the middle, and his shower was a spout protruding out of the wall at adult head level. The walls were blackened from fires, and the roof ticked in the sun as it expanded and contracted. A small Bible lay on the table, but I didn't recognise any words.

"Shona," Jaqi murmured in awe.

"What are you doing here, you nincompoop?" I hissed. "You're supposed to be keeping a lookout…"

Too late. A heavy hand squeezed my shoulder. Chelogue. "What are you doing? I'll tell the *baas.*"

"I am the *baas,*" I said. For the first time I feared him. He was no longer a garden boy or a *chelogue* but a burning fire, with ashy grey eyes and a forged manacle grip. Jaqi squeaked out, "We came to listen to stories."

"About the ancestors."

He softened his grip and a tell-tale look into his *kaya* told me everything. He had something to hide.

Soon we were sitting on the grass behind the *kaya*, facing the greenway, chewing on dry *sadza* and listening to a tale of Chief Lomagundi, who hid his whole herd of cattle in the Sinoia Caves when a marauding tribe came to exact tax from him. Then we heard about a great kingdom, Zimbabwe, that existed here before the whites, and the Monomatapa who lived there.

"The Zimbabwe ruins?" I recognised the place. "In the Fort Victoria area?"

He nodded. "It was a great centre, a city of thousands. Before the whites came."

"Nonsense," said Mr Kloppers, that evening. "Zimbabwe was an ancient Phoenician outpost built by guardians of King Solomon's Mines. Everyone knows that. Who told you that Kaffirs built it?"

I did not reveal my source. But I was disappointed that Chelogue had found it necessary to tell me such lies. It was a sign of insecurity, I thought glumly, to insist that his tribe had built those ruins. It was obviously wrong; only a foreign civilisation would build in stone, when the local indigenous people only built in straw and mud. And every day after that, his green door was locked with the padlock, a sign that our friendship of trust was over.

★ ★ ★

The scene is a garden barbecue (called a *braai*) outside a typical white Rhodesian home. There is the quarter-acre plot, dogs racing around the yard, the glitter-blue of a swimming pool. A black servant in a white apron is bringing out trays of sausages and steaks to be cooked, and there is a brown bottle of beer in every man's hand. A blonde woman speaks directly to the camera, smiling and squinting in the sun.

BLONDE WOMAN: Rhodesia is our only home.

She gestures behind her and the camera pans across the scene. Her husband is *braaiing* the sizzling steaks with a long fork and two kids are running around the pool, screaming and splashing each other. A bikinied blonde teenager floats in the pool and waves at the camera.

HUSBAND (HUGGING HIS WIFE): We married here and our parents are here. We're buying our own home and bringing up a young family. Why should we give this all up?

BLONDE WOMAN (CONFIDENTLY): We're here to stay. That's why we're going to vote for the only party that can safeguard our future.

Two purple letters appear on the screen:

# RF

VOICE OF WELL-KNOWN TV ANNOUNCER: Safeguard your future, vote Rhodesian Front.

The advertisement played every night before the main eight o'clock news, before I went to bed, and I learned it off by heart, not just the scripted dialogue but every movement, every smile and gesture, every extraneous, inadvertent action on the periphery. Television was black and white, or rather a grey fuzzy storm of buzzing insects, but I saw everything in colour. A casual announcement by my father precipitated the crisis. The Woods were friends of theirs, he said, gesturing to the ad on the TV.

"The Woods?"

"Gerald and Nancy, and the kids…"

"Penny and Jeannie," supplied my mother.

"You know those movie stars?"

"They're not movie stars, Paul. They were just asked to help out for the campaign. Penny goes to Alfred Beit School."

That girl? The one in the bikini, waving to the camera, to me, was a twelve-year-old at our school, a real girl who cycled to school every day, past my playground, and into the cycle shed, who sat in sweaty classes at wooden desks and dipped her pen into inkwells like me? I didn't quite believe my parents, and had to verify the information firsthand.

I was at school early the next day, at six-thirty, just as the sun poured its molten gold onto the Hunyani Hills, and waited at the main roundabout bicycle entrance. Sure enough, here she came, wearing a green and white checkered dress and a mauve hat with a green striped hat-band, pedalling hard, her morning shadow a monstrous distortion of her angelic figure. I leaned on the metal post and gawked, as if I was watching TV, not realising until she wobbled self-consciously past with a frown that I was a solid presence in her world, just as she was in mine. She pursed her lips into a smile so that dimples moulded her cheeks into the TV face I recognised. In surprise at being visible, I smiled back.

That night, I lay down on the bed and my concerned mother asked me what was wrong. I was dizzy; I was weak; my heart was pumping painfully; my soul was being sucked down an enormous black hole.

"What's the girl's name?" she smiled.

Without the word to cage the experience, I was truly lost. Had I known this was only 'puppy love', or a 'crush', I would have been OK, but nothing so serious had ever happened to me before. Worse still, the gods had ordained that she was to be a prominent actress in the school.

The Standard Fives (Grade Sevens) were putting on the pantomime for Christmas 1965 and the teacher chose Her to be Sleeping Beauty, this twelve-year-old called Penelope Woods, or Penny, whom everyone called 'Shillings' for short. To explain: a penny was an inch-wide copper coin, heavy, with raised writing and a hole in the middle so you could string them in twelves. They showed antelopes standing on their hind legs, floral raised designs, and 'Federation of Rhodesia and Nyasaland' written around the edge. A shilling was smaller, silver and more desirable.

For those weeks of the rehearsals, I lived in hope of seeing her at school. I watched her every morning from the same post, until she grew to expect me, and smiled at me as she approached. "Hello, Sixpence," she called every day, and I would gawk back and grin as I marvelled at the texture of the hem of her green and white dress in the early sunlight, the way her white throat moved when she smiled, the way she lifted her fingers from the rubber handlebar grip and fluttered them in the air for me.

And every day after school I sneaked in the back of the hall to watch the Standard Fives go over their scenes. In the front row, I stared in a giddy transport of bliss, like a Medieval monk witnessing the Immaculate Conception of the Virgin Mary. The first time she walked onto the stage, she mixed up all her words. She put her soft white hand to her face; her cheek flushed red. Then she lay asleep for a hundred years, waiting for a prince to come wake her with love's first kiss.

"I love you," I whispered, "I love you, Shillings."

Tuesday afternoon, two-thirty. Mauve clouds grow in the corner of the sky, from the north, and build as I watch them. The air grows cold, birds fly fast past me, and the air is heavy with the smell of rain and red dust. The first raindrops clatter on the tin roof of the school hall and then bullet into the dry earth. It is good: these are the first rains of October, the suicide month. I take refuge on the veranda, then in the hall itself. The play cannot continue because of the noise on the roof – why did no one think of this when they built the hall? – but the rain is a catharsis after the celibacy of the dry season from April to October. Lightning cracks above us and we duck, though we are safe here. In the TTLs, they say at least one family is killed every thunderstorm, because of the granite locations, the huts exposed or the people huddling under trees. Suspicious of their government's motives, the locals will not erect the lightning rods provided by the Ministry of Housing and Development.

She sits in the front row to watch the witch's opening scene, two seats away from me. My heart beats like a prisoner hammering on the door of a cell to get out. I examine the back of her head, the way her hair shines, the way her neck tenses as she silently mouths the words for her next scene. She senses my hot stare, turns, and I am floundering in sticky emulsion, out of my depth. I shimmer a watery smile.

"Hello, Sixpence," she says brightly.

I try to steady my hands. "Hello, Shillings."

She laughs, a musical laugh, like waterfalls over delicate chinking pebbles at Inyanga, and then turns back to her script. I hold tight onto the chair. I am the rain bursting onto the roof. I am the puddles splashing up at the bicycle tyres of schoolchildren riding through me. I am the rain soaking them through, plastering their hair, licking down their faces and chins and on onto their chests. I write 'Sleeping Beauty' on my hand in the design I have seen cyclostyled on the pantomime programmes we coloured in at school. Even the words are pretty, soft letters snugly fitting into each other, the sound curving like a swing. They are spelt correctly.

I run home in the storm, in the road which is now a river, in between the ditches gurgling with blood-red topsoil. I am soaked by the time I have crossed the path behind the police station. I love it. I love her. I love being a small running white boy in shorts with a universe aching inside me.

"What's that?" asks Jaqi.

"Nothing." But I want to tell her; I am bursting into flames to tell someone. Who better than her?

"Can you keep a secret?"

She flutters dirty eyelashes at me (she has been crying again).

"What's the secret?"

"I love someone."

She doesn't blink or laugh or punch me in the gut like Nigel did at school.

"I do too," she says.

"She's a girl called Sleeping Beauty."

"Sleeping Beauty? The fairy tale?"

"She has... blonde hair."

Jaqi fingers her scraggly locks.

"She is twelve."

Her blue eyes flood with tears.

"What is it?" I say.

Jaqi stands on tiptoes.

"I'm not crying. I'm not."

"She's beautiful," I say. Jaqi smiles her gawky, toothy smile.

"You wouldn't understand," I say.

"What's her name?"

"Penny Woods. I love her."

"Oh," says Jaqi. "I also have a secret."

"What?"

"I know something bad about you."

"What?"

"*Chelogue!*"

Sleeping Beauty was, of course, the princess I had to kiss to awaken. I was the Prince who raised her after a hundred years of sleeping death in the tomb; she was the Eve who was bitten by the sharp fangs of the Witch's spinning wheel. But to Jaqi, I was Pinocchio, lying about my male deformity, a wooden boy masquerading as a real one.

On the final day of rehearsals, I trailed Penny Woods from the hall to the playground, and watched her sit to eat her Marmite sandwiches on a blue-painted bench by the fishpond. Now was the time. I strode up to her, past her, back, and then sat on the same bench, albeit at the rotting end. I had bought what was then a popular ice-cream called a Honeybeat, and loudly unpeeled its paper wrapping. She smiled. Her skin was white smooth.

"What are you doing here?" she said.

"I've come to see you, Sleeping Beauty."

She asked my name.

"Paul."

"That's a very nice name. Do you know what it means? Small."

And she laughed.

"Small?"

"Paul the Apostle," she explained. "He was Saul, a bad man persecuting the Christians, but one day he fell off his horse and a voice from heaven spoke in a bolt of lightning and said, 'Saul, Saul why are you persecuting me?' Ever since then his name was Paul and he became a good man, an apostle for Christ."

I wasn't sure how to respond to this information. She intended a hidden significance, I was sure, but I was too smitten to contemplate any interpretation at that moment. I knew, though, that I was struck by lightning, by the voice of God, by her miraculous appearance.

"Have a bite of my Honeybeat," I said, leaning over towards her. I trembled so she had to steady my hand with hers as she bit into the dripping honey and ice cream.

"Thanks," she said. Her hand touched mine. I watched her red lips part and glisten. Her hair curled and touched her face like leaves, and her soft eyes danced with starlight.

"I love you Sleeping Beauty, I love you," I said (but not aloud). Hallowed be Thy Name and the fruit of Thy Womb.

"I must go now, Paul" – a pause while she hoisted up her dress to get at her pocket – "Give me a call in ten years."

And she pressed a threepenny piece in my hand (called a 'tickey'), kissed me on the forehead, and walked away before I could ask her what she meant. My head tingled for days where she had kissed it.

The 'tickey' was a small silver coin with the Queen on one side, three assegais on the other, and 'Southern Rhodesia' written around its edge, worth thruppence. In those days it could buy you an ice cream, bus fare to town and back, a telephone call, a Coke in a bottle without deposit, or a packet of salted Willard's plain crisps (salt 'n vinegar had not been invented yet). I slept with my tickey under my pillow. How long was ten years? I would be eighteen. I would be 'inchering' people in the army, by my calculations. And she would be practising adultery (being an adult).

The play ran Thursday, Friday and Saturday, and I sat in the front row for every performance, watching the universal story of rapture and ecstasy. Sleeping Beauty, chosen to be queen, falling under the spell of the Evil One, falling asleep forever, but awakened by a magic kiss, riding off into the Prince's kingdom.

I watched Penny perform the mythical ritual spell that inevitably unravelled from oppression to freedom, from misery to happiness, from fear to love. Every night I recited the canon, mesmerised, as I would say the Holy Mass, in reverence for the very syllables of her mantra. At the end of the last performance, the audience spontaneously rose to a standing ovation, as arranged, and I clapped long after the heavy purple curtains closed for the last time. The crowd dispersed, sighing, snatching their Banda-copied programmes, remarking what a sweet show it was, and thank God it's over, now we can get back to more important things, while I sat in the empty hall until they turned the lights out.

I waited for Sleeping Beauty to come out of the dressing room, in disguise once more as a schoolgirl, never to be Sleeping Beauty again. She saw me, smiled sweetly and gave her fluttery finger wave as her parents whisked her outside into a waiting car. I followed her outside, watched her green Zephyr drive off past the purple letters of the poster from a recent campaign:

**RHODESIA IS OUR HOME: VOTE RHODESIAN FRONT**

She looked out of the back window, waving, but I was trapped behind the filmy emulsion of her eternal advert, of Disney's infernal movie. No matter how I tried, I could not stick my fist back into the real grey world again.

"I thought you didn't want to see me any more," said Jaqi. "What happened to Penny Woods?"

"She's gone, left school, to go to High School. She's... grown up."

"So we can play again?"

I played with a rage and vehemence, blaming Jaqi for the heaviness in my heart. Penny's Prince, adulthood, had come to take her away and I was one of the palace stone statues.

★  ★  ★

Meanwhile, unrest was growing in the townships, said Geoffrey Atkins on the six o'clock news. I still had little idea what was happening, except that the Africans spent their nights throwing stones at police Land Rovers, and running from smoking tear gas. They wanted to be independent, said the heavily censored Roving Report. Zambia had independence; Malawi had independence; the shiny black rulers Kaunda and Banda shook handkerchiefs and fly whisks at ululating crowds. Why then did Southern Rhodesia, the only remnant of the old Federation, stubbornly resist independence?

We had independence, said Smith. We had majority rule – responsible majority rule, which meant that the whites were the only ones allowed to vote, which meant, said Kloppers, that the troublemakers Joker Ink Homo and Rubber Dinghy Shit Hole were kept out of the race. Competing for Rhodesian independence is... Ian Smith... Ian Smith... and Ian Smith. And the winner is... Ian Smith.

The townships erupted into an ugly lava flow. But the new winning party, the Rhodesian Front, had given itself powers to deal with the unrest. For the white population, a tranquiliser-news in simple black and white; for the black population, curfews and bannings. Why they wanted to be like those corrupt dictatorships to the north, no one could understand... If they really knew...

But who were Joker Ink Homo and Rubber Dinghy Shit Hole?

★  ★  ★

*Hamba gahle, Baba Zimbabwe! Bayete*, O Matabele King. We salute you in death, as we saluted you in life. Joshua Mqabuko Nyongolo Nkomo, you were our first great leader in white-ruled Rhodesia. You were a big man, literally and figuratively, who fought against the slings and arrows of outrageous white Rhodesians for half a century. *Umdala Wethu* – our old man – you sacrificed your life for your beloved country and for the principle of majority rule.

Born in 1918 in a missionary family, you were educated in South Africa, where you were inspired by Nelson Mandela and other nationalist leaders to take up the struggle for our freedom. On return to Bulawayo in 1948, you worked ceaselessly as a trade unionist to better the lives of poor black railway workers. But for all the good work you did in the 1950s and 1960s, your organisations were all banned by the Rhodesian racist dogs.

You founded ZAPU in 1962, which was also banned immediately. You were detained for ten years by the Ridgeback Rhodesians, from 1964 to 1974, after which you took up the armed struggle. Like Mzilikazi, Mncumbatha, Lobengula and all the other Ndebele heroes you have now joined in death, you stood up to the evil system of colonialism fearlessly and with great conviction. Joshua Nkomo, you taught us black people how to hold our heads high, to value our humanity, and to measure ourselves by standards other than those of the white settlers.

Yes, we hated you, we whites, when you laughed at the downing of the Viscount. Yes, we hated you, we Shona, when you were accused of creating a Super ZAPU dissident stew. But how our hearts went out to you, we Zimbabweans, when we saw how you had to flee, how you were set up, how *gukurahundi* swept away the noble Matabele nation and you were powerless to stop the 5th Brigaders. We will never forget. And how we loved you in death, Father Zimbabwe. You are our father and we are your sons of the soil, all of us dead in mineshafts, in shallow graves, in death camps. Dead, dead, all dead, so many dead.

And goodbye to you, my trusted friend, Ndabaningi Sithole. You too are dead now, but your black shining deeds live on. You formed the ZANU (Ndonga) in1963, and fought tirelessly for African dignity and independence.

You were born in 1920 in Chipinge, and as soon as you were able, you joined the struggle for liberation. The Rhodesian government tried to squelch your gleaming voice of truth, yet you spoke loudly, your vision a shimmering beacon for us to follow. We admired your attempt to unite all liberation movements and to bury our differences, yet you were stabbed in the back by power-hungry ZEZURU leaders who trampled on you for personal gain. You stood for higher principles than the opportunists, and you held steadfastly faithful to the vision of a peaceful Zimbabwe. We loved your lips and red mouth, your smile, your sense of humour, your flexibility, your moderation. You were the first and you will always be the first ZANU DONGA. Our hearts went out to you when you were slighted in the election. You deserved more, much more – we all did. The tragedy of Zimbabwe will sit forever with us, the living, and you will watch on and judge us and see all. Give us strength. Give us power.

★   ★   ★

But according to Mr Kloppers, they were just a bunch of troublemakers, the metaphorical serpents come to seduce our black Eve into eating the apple of the Tree of Knowledge. After she ate it, she realised she was naked. But unlike Sleeping Beauty, she was now wide awake.

Inevitably, just as it appeared that Smith had saved the country from the creeping corrosion of Africanisation and stopped the onslaught of black nationalism with his bare hands, the war came to our country.

It was during a memorable sundowner session, while my father poked *boerewors* in the *braai*, and Mr Kloppers snorted at the antics of those clowns Kaunda and Banda, that the war was announced. As he has been intruding into most of the story up to this point, I had better admit it now, once and for all, that I felt utter repulsion for Kloppers and his words, as if he were responsible for my aching heart. Jaqi's expletive Dad, cradling his beer bottle, was in on it too. I hated their blasphemy, their swearing, their profane sexual references. Both were crew-cut, stocky, took no nonsense from Kaffirs and were Fact Men. My father had adjusted well, as far as wearing safari suits and drinking beer, but he never got the hang of smoking those local cigarettes all day, or using the word *Kaffir* comfortably, especially when the houseboy was mooning around the veranda collecting empty bottles and the garden boy sunning himself in the weed patch.

The war began when a group (called a 'gang' from here on) of armed insurgents, or guerrillas, or freedom fighters (called 'terrorists' from now on), crossed the Zambezi from Zambia where they had been trained to kill. They carried with them limpet mines, AK47s, grenades and various other explosive devices strapped to their backs, and stopped only to eat raw turtles they cracked on rocks. Some were eaten by crocodiles, others drowned in the river, but the survivors made their way to Sinoia, after sheltering in villages, demanding food and other favours ("You know what I mean," winked Kloppers, "but not in front of the kids"). Seven of them attacked the police station, and of course were routed, chased and all except one killed. According to Kloppers, they were fucked up badly and fled, limping back to their holes of hatred and hell.

"Jesus," said Jaqi's father. "First the Mau-Maus and now this. Settlemunt my arse."

★  ★  ★

"Is that true?" I asked Chelogue, the next day. "Are these the terrorists who have come to destroy our country, just as you said?"

He picked his teeth with a piece of dry grass. "You don't fight a crocodile by stabbing its nose with a thorn." And he laughed a hoarse cougher's laugh, scaring Jaqi and me a step back. "You have to wait until it sleeps, then you worry it constantly so it cannot sleep or rest until it gets uncomfortable. You can't kill it, but you can drive it into the sea."

★  ★  ★

Where are the animals in this story, you ask? As well as *coups d'état*, famine and political unrest, to the decadent West, Africa means animals. Even our garden was a wild, squirming, writhing, living thing. Whenever I dug in the red soil, I unearthed some strange creature, or had to avoid standing on giant snails, *chongololos*, Matabele ants (which stank if you squashed them), ant lions in their negative pyramid sand traps, chameleons, and the birds every morning when we woke.

Once a *boomslang* – brown and deadly – twirled around my arm as I climbed a tree, threatening me with a slow writhing death if it struck. A black mamba once curled its way into my father's golf bag on the veranda and ate two golf balls, thinking they were eggs. I watched Chelogue and my father pulp the head of the snake with the seven iron, and cut open the stomach with the wedge, in order to retrieve our rightful property.

We drove to the Sinoia Caves to see the bottomless blue pool where Lomagundi had hidden his cattle, and found snakes guarding the entrance. In the pool at the Caves Motel, where I played in a hall of mirrors and my parents were served Malawi shandies under a huge cassia tree on an open cement terrace, a four-foot leguan swam with me. On the way home, secretary birds and crowned cranes picked their way through water pans at the side of the Lomagundi road. At lay-byes we found duikers, kudu herds, wildebeest hiding in the savanna scrub, and we watched luminous blue jays sitting on the telephone wires. We saw crocodiles at Kariba and Victoria Falls slide into muddy swamps, dragging with them duikers, wild pigs and rabbits. Chelogue was wrong about crocodiles; they were crafty aggressors who didn't kill their victims but snatched them underwater and stuffed them into ledges until they drowned so they could eat their rotting soggy flesh at leisure. Hippos in Lake Kariba bobbed in the shallows; we saw monkeys on the overhead branches of the dirt road to Inyanga, and elephants as still as granite rocks watching our passage. Giraffes stooped uncomfortably, hyenas screeched at night, overturning our rubbish bins, and lions growled, keeping us awake.

Yes, we had wild animals. There were four million people living in a country the size of Texas, so the animals had plenty of room. But as an African, I didn't see their appeal as Europeans did. They were a threat, not an exotic attraction. Wild animals were for tourists.

No, my main concern was the animal growing inside of me. It felt – to continue the imagery – like a crocodile. It invaded my childhood games with such violence that I was frightened by it. For suddenly in the middle of pirates and robbers, I would find myself taking delight in flogging all the imaginary slaves and lashing them cruelly against a tree. I beat them until they cried for mercy, bleeding and tearful. I would imagine all the slaves in torn, skimpy clothing

– all of them girls, young girls crying out to me while I, the reckless pirate of the seven seas, whipped them again and again. Jaqi played the helpless slaves and had to remind me sometimes that it was only a game.

Or I was the slave tied to the ship's mast. Jaqi was the ship's captain and beat me mercilessly until I escaped and chased her shrieking overboard where she was devoured by sharks (played by me). Or we were both drunk pirates. We swigged imaginary jugs of rum and swayed and tottered in loud revelry on board, until we fell over each other in slumber and drunken stupor.

It was soon after the Battle of Chinoyi (as history later labelled the beginning of the war) that Jaqi's parents announced they were leaving the country and going to live in South Africa. They were fed up with the unstable political situation in Rhodesia. It was Kenya all over again. My parents tried to argue, pointing to the headlines of the *Rhodesia Herald*: 'SMITH PROMISES OPTIMISTIC PATH TO PEACE TALKS.' But they just shook their heads. "This is where the terror war starts."

"Rhodesia will never go the way those countries to the north have gone," said my father. "Look at our infrastructure; look at our economy; look at our granaries…"

"That's what we said," Jaqi's father said darkly, "about Zambia, and Congo and Kenya. And if you mark my words, you'll get the hell out of here too."

We also moved later, but into a more affluent suburb, to a better house and plot of land in Hillside, Salisbury, so that I could go to one of those good government high schools – Churchill Boys' High. Hillside was a rocky ironstone outcrop, settled in 1891 by Tommy Constable, who grew vegetables at the foot of the hill (Eastridge) where our new house now stood. It had also been a successful dairy farm, and then had been settled by pioneers who wanted to live 'out of town' on acre plots (it was only two miles from the city centre). The plots grew smaller and smaller, until it became the tight but respectable suburb of Hillside, albeit on the wrong side of the railway line.

My parents were doing well. My father was the headmaster of a government primary school, my mother worked at the Petrol-Rationing Office, dispensing petrol coupons to our faithful citizens. And the country was good for them; they were no longer wrapped around radiators in England as poor relatives. So they happily swallowed the propaganda as all good Rhodesians did, bought a brick house on half an acre for $12,000 of the new stable Rhodesian currency (one dollar equalled one British pound), employed two servants, ran two cars (the Cortina and the Datsun 120Y station wagon, assembled in Rhodesia for $5,000), and all was well with the world.

Chelogue, the friendly black servant who had been quietly pulling weeds and planting seeds, didn't stay long either. Before we made the move across town from Mabelreign to Hillside, the police arrived at our house in a big blue and white Peugeot 404 early in the morning, and crunched on the gravel straight to his *kaya*.

We stood on the red veranda in pyjamas, sipping tea and avoiding the red line of the sun that blocked our view. Chelogue's eyes were wide and white; he ran, but they caught him in the greenway and hauled him into the driveway and into the back of the car where he was, in the words of the report, 'subdued' by a white policeman's baton. A search of his *kaya* revealed limpet mines under the mattress, a cache of assorted weapons in the cupboard – AK rifles, land mines and plastic explosives – smuggled in from Zambia.

We crept around the entrance, my father asking questions, a white policeman directing operations, a black policeman securing Chelogue with clinking, glittering handcuffs, playing the cops and robbers games we had invented. We watched in wonder as a large pizza-pan limpet mine was pulled out from the mattress, boxes of bullets from the pillows, and literature (Mao's *Little Red Book* on how to attack and kill) was displayed to the commanding officer.

A communist, whispered my mother. He was a communist. The white policeman in his safari suit and short khakis called on a CB radio in the car and soon a blue Land Rover arrived for the prisoner. They carried him away like a Thunderbirds puppet whose strings had been cut, with two white policemen in the back of the cab and caged wire netting holding him so he wouldn't escape again.

He came with the gang, the Sinoia gang, the policeman said to my father. We've been tracing him for months. He crossed the Zambezi and set up a cell here in Salisbury. We searched the townships, but never suspected here, until we received a tip-off from a neighbour of yours.

My father held my mother tight. The other houseboys gathered around the ditch, and talked loudly in Shona, shaking heads, holding jaws as if their teeth ached. The last I saw of Chelogue was his defiant, raised fist thrust between the bars of the Land Rover's back window as if he were holding something tight in his hand which he refused to let go. A tickey, I thought stupidly. Or was he ashamed of his white palm that he had dipped into the puddle at the chameleon's instructions all those years ago, before the white man came? The crowd bowed their heads, avoiding the display of his fist. We watched solemnly from the veranda; I raised my hand to wave at him, but my father stiffly pulled it down. And once the van had gone, followed by flashing red lights of the Peugeot outriders, the crowd dispersed slowly as if at a funeral.

CHAPTER THREE

# THEY DIED FOR THEIR COUNTRY

*Honour Roll in Churchill Boys' High School*

*Lord, behold us with thy blessing, once again assembled here.*
*Onward be our footsteps pressing, in thy love and faith and fear;*
*Still protect us; still protect us, by thy presence ever near.*

THEY DIED FOR THEIR COUNTRY, the board announces as you walk into the foyer of Churchill Boys' High School hall. The board is three by six feet, in a glass case, higher than boy level, and the names of the dead are painted in gold with a careful hand (though if you look closely, you'll see that a stencil has been used). The first name on the left-hand column (one of six columns, as if the designer had anticipated a large number of casualties, even at this early stage of the war) is that of N.P. Cahill.

Thereafter, names are added yearly as the war froths up and over, and by the time you leave school, every month. These are our boys who have made the Ultimate Sacrifice. Derek King, who attended Churchill from 1968 to 1973, died this week In The Line of Duty; Steven Houseman died Fighting for his Country, at the Hands of Cowardly Terrorists; George Stefanopolis in

Operations against The Enemy; Tim Stevens in a Surprise Ambush in Enemy Territory.

The TV news at eight in the seventies always begins with a similar head count of the dead: Combined Operation Headquarters regrets to announce the death in action of Peter Wright, 19, of Salisbury, John Bentley, 18, of Gwelo, Phil Johnson, 21, of Mangula… But it is always followed by bigger statistics of enemy deaths. A 'gang' of three CTs (Communist Terrorists) died in contact with Rhodesian Forces; twenty TCs (Terrorist Collaborators) were also killed in a Combined Forces Operation; three TSs (Terrorist Supporters); five RTs (Running with Terrorists), three CCCs (Civilians Caught in the Crossfire), six CBs (Curfew Breakers) died in a gun battle when Terrorists opened fire in an ambush…

But in 1971, the year I began attending high school, the war was the bite of a mosquito on an elephant's arse, as they say. We now lived in the lower middle-class suburb of Hillside. Our house edged the Makabusi swampland, a wild *msasa* forest land where genuine wild animals had been planted, so we could watch zebras and duikers on weekends. I spent my first few teenage years exploring the woods on my bicycle, criss-crossing the cycle paths and frequenting a granite river beach where, it was reputed, the first white settlers bathed on weekends until one was eaten by a crocodile.

The woodlands became my sanctuary. I dragged my puberty behind me, hoping to leave it behind in the red dust I raised with the Dunlop tyres on my Raleigh Performance bicycle (assembled in Rhodesia), and hoping, too, that the celluloid wrapping around me would dissolve through my exercises of spontaneous and unselfconscious toil.

59 Hillside Road moulded itself to the shape of my soul. On half an acre, this modest three-bedroom, one-carport house of my teen years became the place that would forever feature in my dreams: the dark corridor between bedrooms, the monkey puzzle tree my father hated because of its ever-shedding needle carpet, the mango tree with its bitter-tasting leaves, the gooseberry bush with papery cages and sour fruit, two outside sinks, ironing room and long washing line where the 'boy' was always at work. The house was brick, red tiled, with three pine trees (one crow per tree), a stone wall in front (three feet high in

1970, six feet high in 1980, broken bottle-topped and electrified in 1990), a short one-mile bicycle ride to school, a walk to the Clyde shops, as well as to the Makabusi swamplands, later the Makavusi Game park, and the *msasa* woodlands (with imported animals from Wankie). Whenever I thought of home, although I had lived in several other places already in my life, 59 Hillside Road became my nostalgic soul cage.

In 1971, government schools in Rhodesia were racially and sexually segregated. Black schools were shabby, overcrowded, poorly equipped, while white schools had the best teachers, produced shiny scholars who 'went up' to Oxford, Cambridge or Harvard. White schools were modelled on the old British system, with all its neuroses and repressions, and its insistence on standards that had vanished from Britain decades ago. The English must have looked on in horror at the parody of their past in the colonies, but we were proud of our schools.

Churchill was one such 'good' school, whose express purpose, it seemed to me, was to keep boys apart from girls, so that the only relationship we could have was one of alienation, otherness and mystification. Churchill Boys' High was a hundred metres down the road from Roosevelt Girls' High and the main rule enforced was that the Churchill schoolboys were not allowed near the Roosevelt schoolgirls. A demilitarised no-go zone had been created between the schools and if you were caught trespassing, spying or trying to destroy Western Christian Civilisation by narrowing the distance between the sexes, you would be punished severely.

In the six years I toiled through high school, I learned to become one of those boys who raised their hats respectfully to every (white) adult in sight, played rugby, sweated with other boys in the gym, showered naked in steamy communal rooms and jostled others in break-time lines. I was forbidden to associate with, mingle with, talk about or even think about those thousand green-and-white blurs across the abyss.

But every system has a weak spot. After school every weekday, at precisely thirteen-o-five, streams of Churchill boys and Roosevelt girls would converge and follow the cycle path down Daventry Road to the pedestrian crossing, where they would wait for the light to change. And in those few minutes, Churchill boys and Roosevelt girls would have to bunch up close together.

The trick was to make sure you arrived there while the light was red.

My school was named after that stiff upper-lipped British Prime Minister in World War Two. The man leered at us from portraits hung high in the halls everywhere, with his supercilious snobbish look that made me feel helpless and inferior and outraged at the man's fatness and his bulldog's ugliness. He looked as if he were eating sour lemons, and the way he glared at us from up there, it seemed as if we were the pips. And as I was introduced to all the traditions in the school, I suspected that they all stemmed from this dead white male: haircut inspections, rugby matches, war cries, old-fashioned prickly school uniforms, bullying by prefects. Churchill looked on with approval at all these things with his sneer of satisfaction. And we couldn't get away from him. His portrait hung in the hall, but he also smiled with wry amusement from the mantelpiece in the deputy-head's office, coolly smoking a cigar while some poor boy was caned for long hair (touching his ears and collar), or a lost tie, or forgotten PT shorts or apathy at a war cry, or protest at bullying. And in the foyer of the hall, where we filtered out every week through a line of prefects conducting hair inspections, he (a closely cropped man himself) watched with sadistic pleasure as boys were caught.

The real Winston Churchill, I was to learn later, unlike the bull-dogged, heavy-jowled man I associated with my purple and grey school years, spent seven harrowing years in a public school, where he rebelled against the petty tyranny of the system and found himself in constant trouble. If anything, that man watching us with sullen eyes from his portrait would have been sympathetic to our plight. But we were not to know that.

Ugliness was the central tenet of the school's mission, as far as I could make out. Crewcuts were required; fringes were not allowed. Hair had to stick out like hedgehog bristles, and schoolboys had to look at all times like convicts or lunatics or hospitalised patients in preparation for lobotomies. Desperately, anxiously, I cultivated long hair in private, at weekends, grew it like marijuana, pulling it over my ears, or raising my eyebrows so that a fringe covered my forehead. I had tricks to make it look shorter in school, but it was never long enough out of school.

The closest you could get to a girl was in Room 14B on the second floor of the library block, whose large window faced Roosevelt's Eleanor Field. On Tuesday mornings at ten-thirty, in the middle of our Physics and Chemistry lesson, a girls' class streamed out of Roosevelt opposite and performed physical education stunts in the open field. From the back of the class, ensconced in a gang of grey-uniformed boys, with poised test tubes and litmus paper and propped-up textbooks that were used as screens from the teacher, I gawked for a full half hour at those delicious mythical creatures who jumped up and down, ran, cartwheeled, star-jumped and displayed their white limbs and green gymslips to the world.

The teacher commanded attention by tapping the blackboard with a large compass in the hope of getting us to attend to his cold diagrams, but had little success. I tried to take an interest, but out of the corner of my eye those pale limbs, leaping and springing, frantically urged my attention.

"You!"

"Sir?"

"What did I just say?"

"That we can see curves… We can see round, look in a straight line and see around."

The twenty other girl-watchers sniggered nervously as I was sent to the headmaster. In his office, Mr Gardini frowned at me, as did Churchill from his portrait on the wall, both disappointed and stern, as they concurred with each other as to what to do with such dissident behaviour.

"I have only three things to say to you, Williams," he said. "Restraint. Restraint. Restraint."

He strode to his cabinet, and inside, as graphically described by all who had been through this rite of passage, stood a vase of canes. Each one was designed for a specific purpose. The long yellow cane called 'Schweppes' was the most deadly. It could draw blood; it whistled through the air; it was supple and had to be replaced frequently because it often broke on the most stubborn boy's backside. Then there was the flat 'board of education' cane with slogans printed on it (this is going to hurt me more than it hurts you; spare the rod and spoil the child) – standard issue by the Ministry of Education. No one feared this cane; it was only used for minor offences as a warning and didn't hurt. But the 'birch buster' was the heaviest and deadliest, used for the most intransigent of boys, with holes drilled into it for more wind speed. I watched as he selected a smaller, newer version of Schweppes, the latest model to be broken in, by the look of things. I clenched my jaw, bent over, and gripped the worn wooden lip of his desk, where thousands of fingers had preceded mine.

Two-stroke penalty: two lessons to be learned. The pain was swift, and I had to blink hot tears back, then turn, stand and face him to receive the speech: pay homage to the god of testosterone. Punishment is good; violence is good; channel your energy into more worthy pursuits, like sport, competition, aggression and bravado. Work is work, he said, and play is play. Don't be a lady's man. Don't run after them; let them run after you.

By the early seventies, my Beloved Country was steadily plummeting into a civil war of which I knew very little. No, no, said Kloppers, Smith and the TV presenters, you've got it all wrong. It is the world outside that is decaying around us and we stand as a jewel of Africa, of morality, standards and good government. A glittering thousand-year reign had begun in 1965, a paradise which now had to be guarded on all four corners with flaming swords and torches.

In 1972, ZANLA began infiltrating the northeast of the country where the Tribal Trust Lands lay close to the border. They first had to 'soften' an area before taking up residence there, by teaching the *povo* Maoist theory, setting up local committees, training spies, organising suppliers of food and items needed for a guerrilla campaign, and planning routes in and out of the rural areas without being noticed. Once the area was mulched, they instituted an intricate system of infiltration, using local people to carry their supplies, designating places to cache arms, and conscripting goat herders as lookouts (called *Mujibas*). They travelled in units of twelve men, led by a political commissar whose job it was to create base camps over large areas in order to use the liquidity of the people. The guerrillas were fish swimming smoothly through the rivers of the people, invisible, insidious, waiting to strike.

★ ★ ★

Every school had a gang, and ours, 'The Bang Gang', was led by a pudgy bully by the name of Craig Hardy. This group of schoolboys did not conform to good Rhodesian educational standards, refused to play rugby, refused to channel its desires into such honourable activities as schoolwork, chess and the Christian Union. The Bang Gang swaggered from tuck shop to class with loose ties, fringes, top buttons undone and socks down to their ankles. The name of the gang, I discovered, referred to the act of violating, raping, deflowering a Roosevelt girl. Each member of the gang proudly displayed lists of the various girls he had 'banged', and his assessment of the performance rated from 1 to 10. 'Banged' girls, I found out, were called 'punchlines' because, I supposed, the joke was at their expense.

In reality, of course, these adventures were largely imaginary, and the gang's main activities centred on the use of the word fuck. The Bang Gang scratched it onto desks, toilet doors, walls, and pronounced it violently in the presence of Roosevelt girls. After school, they hid in bushes along Daventry Road and Nigel Philip Avenue and pounced on groups of virginal girls, chanting the expletive at them.

Craig Hardy was sweaty, witty, shaved, wore Brut aftershave, liked underground music (Black Sabbath, Grand Funk, Deep Purple), and of course, girls. He had a stash of pornography in his hat, and whisked it out every break time to corrupt wide-eyed first-formers. His purpose in life, he informed me, was to turn virgins into sluts. There were only two types of women, he said. Those who do and those who don't… yet.

My reputation as a girl-watcher and my initiation into corporal punishment earned me the type of respect a Bang Ganger should have, I suppose, because Hardy cornered me at break time that day.

"Meet the gang after school today at five past one on Daventry Road. We'll show you how to get girls."

Craig's large, sweating flesh could not be contained in neat uniforms. His shirt buttons strained and popped, his garters could not circle his calves, his trilby had been turned into a pork pie, and his tie was a string of ink and oil stains. Yet he got away with it. He knew all the prefects, and they let him pass. His hair was long, but he carefully concealed it under a purple cap during school hours. His pudgy fingers could hardly encircle a victim's neck – he was strong, make no mistake – but he could crack his knuckles, burp and eat a whole chicken-in-a-basket at Gremlin Restaurant. And he basked in the ailment that afflicted us all.

Once the gang had assembled at the school gates, we rode, an unsteady mass of bicycles, along Nigel Philip Avenue and into Daventry Road. The Roosevelt rush was over, and only a few Churchill stragglers were picking their way home over the bumps in the tar (made by the roots of regularly spaced jacaranda trees). But up ahead walked a girl in a green dress, all alone, with a suitcase banging against her legs. Her blonde hair shimmered in the dappled sun, and her willowy body danced rather than marched down the road. Hardy grinned, pointed and laid a finger to his lips. I gripped my handlebars so tightly that it hurt. When we were a few feet behind her, Hardy dismounted, puffing and sweaty already from the ride, his Brut aftershave polluting the atmosphere, and sauntered up to the girl, while we kept our distance in a mass of ticking wheels and hot grey male uniforms.

"Hello." He had to skip alongside her to keep up, panting and wiping the sweat from his brow. "Can I carry your suitcase for you?"

"Shove off."

"Let's go," I urged Wrigglesworth. But Hardy, the cool professional, whisked around at me.

"I know her game. She's playing hard to get."

The girl hurled a furious look back at me. "Leave me alone."

Hardy shook his head at Bentley in the condescending, pitying way teachers did when you hadn't done your homework.

"Let's go guys – she's green."

He mounted his bike and pedalled past her. We followed.

"Still a virgin, hey?"

At the railway crossing, Hardy wheeled his bike round in the dust and waited for us to catch up.

"We have a new member of the Bang Gang with us – Williams."

All eyes fixed on the newcomer, who wondered how he had been conscripted without ever volunteering or agreeing to anything.

"I have a proposal to make concerning his initiation." He cocked his thumb back in the direction of the girl. "You bang her."

I protested silently with a look of incredulity, but Craig was unrelenting.

"You have until the holidays. And you know the penalty for failure."

He turned his bicycle around, gestured for his gang to follow him, and they rode across the railway line, whooping at a group of girls who were standing by the bus stop on Helm Avenue.

I hoped to avoid her, but she rounded the corner before I could escape. She glided rather than walked, and her skin was so translucent that I felt I could look through at the bright African day behind her. I should now have simply cycled away. But I felt I had to make amends. I dismounted and pushed my bike alongside her, skipping to keep up with her strides.

"I'm sorry."

As there was no response, I located her name badge under the ROOSEVELT GIRLS' HIGH SCHOOL emblem on her left breast: Bianca Pennefather.

"Male chauvinist pig."

"I…"

"I'll report you for this."

"Listen, I'm not like them, I'm sorry, I'm not part of it. I just came to warn you."

"Who are you?"

"My name is Paul, Paul Cavedaschi."

Let me explain: I hated my name. My parents named me after my Uncle Paul Williams of Old Catton, Norwich, Norfolk. Why couldn't I have been named something special, like Elton John or Cat Stevens or Gary Glitter? Or Cavedaschi? My mother's name is Cavedaschi. It's Italian, but must have its origins in Eastern Europe, the *ski* softened by the Italian language's lack of harsh consonants into *schi*. It's more exotic than Williams, which must be the ho-hum name of tens of thousands of other people in this world. Paolo Cavedaschi. Or, if I was Czech, Pavel. Much better. But Bianca was unimpressed.

"Well, Paw-Paw Cavedachi, tell your friend if he ever speaks to me again, I'll… I'll…"

She transferred the suitcase into her left hand, so she could wag a finger of reprimand at me. Then she continued marching forward.

I called after her. "I meant to say, Bianca is a nice name."

"Can't say the same for yours. Paw-paw?"

"Paul. Cavedaschi. It's Italian."

"Cavedaschi?"

I cantered next to her, past the black and white Morton-Jaffray Road sign. My next tactic was the Chocolate Pop in my pocket. Although warm, it hadn't melted yet, so I offered it to her.

"And I won't bother you again," I pleaded. This stopped her. I stopped, too, panting. "Have it."

She squinted at the Rhodesian version of a popsicle, back at me with incredulity, snatched and hurled my gift into the bushes lining the path, then marched away. Before I could think of how to detain her further, she was a shimmering mirage on the other side of the railway line on Helm Avenue. I retrieved the Chocolate Pop, unwrapped it and ate it myself.

At home I tore off my uniform, choking tie, black heavy shoes, grey socks and garters, and found my cool blue denim jeans and T-shirt. I ruffled my hair, but it was still cropped and prickly from the last haircut inspection and hadn't grown at all. No one was at home, except the garden boy, snipping a hedge and talking loudly in Shona to a neighbour's garden boy two houses down.

I pressed the power button of the locally assembled Tempest stereo system and slid my latest vinyl acquisition onto the turntable: Deep Purple's *Machine Head*. Only now could I settle on the floor and spread out my homework, the Latin–English dictionary on my left, the text (*The Approach to Latin*, corrupted by vandals to *The Approach to Eatin'*), my Latin workbook in front of me, Deep Purple around me in a cloud of solace and obliteration.

*Nobody gonna take my car, I'm gonna keep it to the end*
*I love it, I need it, I want it... I'm a highway star.*

Pygmalion, I translated, was a man who hated women. He hated their wiles, their trickery and deception, their manipulations. But he loved Woman.

He had been hurt badly in his love adventures, and had vowed never to open his heart to their treachery again. So he avoided feminine company and, instead, by art, fashioned himself a statue of a girl out of ivory, white as snow, and gave her a beauty surpassing that of any woman born – and fell in love with what he had made. Using *a priori* perceptions of the ideal form of a woman, he carved a statue that looked like a real maiden whom you could believe was alive and willing to move, if modesty did not prevent her. To such an extent art concealed art. Flames of passion burned in his breast when he gazed at his finished work of art. He wanted to run his fingers over her, bestow kisses upon her, speak to her, lie beside her on the bed and shower her with love, hoping to find her warm, the ivory to grow soft and the rigidity to give way to the pressure of his fingers; to yield just as Hymettan wax when melted in the sun was fashioned into many shapes by the working of the artist's hands.

*Nobody gonna take my girl, I'm gonna keep her to the end*
*I love her, I need her, I want her... I'm a highway star.*

At the annual ceremony to Venus, he made a prayer as he offered his small sacrifice. I wish, Goddess of Beauty and Love, he whispered so that no one near would understand him, that my maiden, I mean my work of art, would move and breathe, that you would breathe on her and make her real, a real woman. At that very moment, the flames rose and crackled as if in response, and the stern statue of the Sea Sperm, Mother of all feminine virtues, smiled down on him as if she had heard him. At home, he lay beside his statue in bed and caressed her, as was his usual custom, but this time, his touch was reciprocated. The hard marble softened and warmed in his fingers and responded to his gentle manipulation. The woman rose up and her white hair fell like silk onto his face, her mouth curling into a smile.

"Pygmalion," she purred, "your wish is granted."

*Nobody gonna take my hair, I'm gonna keep it to the end*
*I love it, I need it, I want it...*

★ ★ ★

And it came to pass, in those days, that a certain man rose to prominence, mission educated, a good Catholic, thick 'Brains' glasses, a Shona man called Robert Gabriel Mugabe who, after studying in South Africa and Ghana, returned to Rhodesia in 1960 as a committed Marxist with a mission to train guerrillas and to swim like a fish among the people; for which purpose he joined the NDP, which later became ZAPU. He formed the rival ZANU, was detained with other nationalist leaders in 1964 and remained in prison for ten years, split ZANU, and on his release, resumed leadership of ZANU and left Rhodesia for Mozambique to lead the Chinese-financed ZANU military arm, ZANLA. Then, when ZANU allied itself with ZAPU as the Popular Front (PF), fighting with ZIPRA, he reformed the party into a revolutionary guerrilla army determined to topple the illegal, racist, white-supremacist Rhodesian regime by any means necessary.

## CONFERENCE COULD LAST MONTHS, SAYS SMITH

**PARLIAMENT STRUCTURE DISCUSSED**

*Wednesday 21 January 1976*

*Political Reporter, Ronald Golden*

THE resumed Constitutional conference between the Government and the Nkomo African National Council yesterday discussed the structure of Parliament, a joint Government-ANC communique said afterwards.

We whites were not to hear of Robert Mugabe until much later, the contenders for political supremacy at this point being Ian Smith and Joshua Nkomo, often caricatured in newspaper cartoons as having endless discussions about settlement. Thank goodness Smith and Nkomo were politicians, quipped Vic Mackenzie the cartoonist. What if they were parents? In one cartoon, Ian Smith is dressed as a father, Joshua Nkomo as the mother, and the dismayed daughter is Rhodesia: "It's going to take your mother and I [sic] two weeks to decide if you can have the car tonight," says Ian Smith in the cartoon.

★ ★ ★

And speaking of Catholics, did I mention that I was, by virtue of my Italian ancestry, a good Catholic boy too? Every Sunday I went to Mass; every Saturday night I knelt in confession to purge me of any venial sins (I have been thinking unpure thoughts, father; impure thoughts, my son?; yes, father, I have been polluting myself every night; say three Hail Marys and five Our Fathers and don't do it again); every Saturday morning, my zealous semi-practising Catholic parents sent their son to Catechism classes at the Our Lady of the Assumption Church in Rhodesville, a suburb within cycling distance of home. For a time, I even wanted to be an altar boy – I liked the robes and the incense and the ceremony and the candles – but for Churchill boys, such a vocation was frowned upon. It was a matter of attitude: a Churchill boy had to be sceptical, cynical and rebellious, not holy or spiritual, or conscious of the dancing numinous world just out of reach of our yearning senses.

My father, too, was increasingly sceptical, and widened cracks in my naïve child-like faith early in my teenage years by asking questions of my mother like, "Do you really think that that man over there" – pointing in the direction of Rhodesville – "can mumble a few words over a piece of bread and magically turn it into the body of a man who died two thousand years ago?" But in 1971, I was still in the everlasting arms of the Church, and every Saturday, with a handful of pre- and post-pubescent boys, dressed in silky robes, in the holy dim light from stained glass stations of the cross, I practised serving at the altar, swung incense and learned my rosary.

One blue-lit Saturday morning, the silence of God was shattered by a thudding of sound waves. The altar toys reverberated, the walls shook, the candlesticks trembled, and my incense holder clattered. The two priests, one white, one black, calmly placed their Catechism books down and motioned us with the duplicate fingers of saints to trot out of the sanctuary to see what the hell was going on. Blinking into the blue sky, which was scored with frightened birds, we watched three Antichrist Alouette helicopters from The Apocalypse circling the church in the vulture patterns of mastery. Father Boniface opened wide eyes, while the white priest huddled his purple and silver robes around him in the protection of the Church. We saw his Catholic smile skewed for once, as he held us with soft, fatherly hands. But we squirmed out of his grasp and ran exuberantly to the fence: we guessed the helicopters were landing in the next field. Mother Mary's stone arms welcomed them.

Our Lady's assumption was correct. They nosed down, proboscis first, then bounced on under-inflated rubber tyres on a bald patch of earth. Before the rotors had stopped, soldiers were pouring out of the open doorways of each chopper. Stretchers were lowered, then humped across the field to the hospital. A soldier in a blue beret yelled, "Get a fucking move on, you wankers," as he ran alongside the stretchers, while other soldiers spidered outwards and crouched in shooting positions around the machines. We hung onto the fence, our fingers knotted in the mesh, while the priests coaxed us from behind: "Come, children, come back."

"Casualties," murmured Todd.

"Terrorists," said Colin.

The priests shrank back and shook their heads. We hung onto the fence in awe of our new gods in uniform, rifles slung carelessly over shoulders, webbing tied around them in wreaths. One soldier lay close to the fence so we could call to him.

"Yes," he grinned, "we *dondered* them."

Another soldier walked over to us. "We gave them a *skrik, jong*."

"Who? Who?" we yelled.

"The terrorists."

"They sneaked across the Zambian border."

"Training camps."

"Did you get them?" said Turkington, the boy next to me.

"Yes, we got them." And we laughed like crows.

"Come in, boys, please." The priests flapped their silk wings in distress.

★  ★  ★

I find her injured on the road. I help her up and she gratefully leans on me, her doe-eyes moistening with love, her arms tight around me. At home, I dab her wounds, soothe her, and her irony is washed away with her pain. She kisses me.

At night, while my parents watch the news at eight, I walk slowly around the garden, watching the Southern Cross and hearing the cicadas and the frogs in our pond. Paul, I hear from the bushes. She is in half shadow. I had to find you, she says. I've been thinking about you, and I wanted to apologise. She presses me against the wall and kisses me.

At the rugby matches we are forced to watch and cheer on every Saturday afternoon – "*Chasawakka wa wa wa!* Who wins? We win! Who's we? Churchill!" – I slip behind the stands to find her sitting in the cool shadows.

"Bianca?"

"I came to watch my brothers play," she says, "but I'm bored stiff. I'm so glad you're here."

"I know a place to go," I say. "Come." She stretches a hand and we escape through the back hedge into the bower of bougainvillea where Churchill boys go to smoke or sleep between classes.

And so on… such are the fantasies of a white Rhodesian school boy in the early seventies. I want, want, want so much. Some crime was being committed against me, to deprive me of my soul. The universe had conspired to wound me with this flaming ache that sucked at me and made me need, desire, yearn for Something. And capricious Fate had determined that she would be my tormenter.

★  ★  ★

Mr and Mrs Kloppers still lived in Mabelreign, but visited regularly. Today they had 'popped in' after a morning in the Farmer's Co-op. Mr Kloppers began the conversation by hurling the *Rhodesia Herald* down on the garden table. 'STRIKE AND YOU GO TO JAIL', was all I could read, because he was banging the paper with his hand, and picking it up repeatedly to fling it down in emphasis.

"What's this country coming to?" he said. "It's getting as bad as Britain, with all its strikes and unrest." My mother poured out cups of tea. My father took his cup and sipped loudly, staring into the bushes. Kloppers indicated with a finger where my mother should place his tea. "Smith takes no nonsense from cheeky *munts*," he continued, easing himself into a chair. "He's already put the striking bus drivers in jail. That should..."

"... teach them to strike," said Mrs Kloppers.

"What was the problem, anyway?" my father ventured.

"Ag, there was no problem, they were just being cheeky. But Smith... aah, Smith..."

Here my father wore his stern political expression and crossed his legs.

"Smith knows how to handle blacks," said Mrs Kloppers.

"There are plenty of other Africans who need jobs and would willingly have theirs," said Mr Kloppers. "How can they complain? At least they have jobs. There are hundreds of thousands, millions, who don't."

"One thing I can't stand," said Mrs Kloppers, "is an ungrateful *munt*." She pronounced the word with relish, as if she were disposing of a sack of manure that she had been carrying grudgingly around for many years.

"What's the strike about?" asked my father, leaning forward to read the newspaper, but Kloppers whisked it away, clattered his cup onto the saucer and smacked his lips.

"Bernard," he said. "You have to treat Africans like children. As Rhodes said, they can't think for themselves. You have to do all the thinking for them. You have to act the father-figure, guiding them gently, punishing them where they go wrong, rewarding them when they do good..."

"What *is* a strike?" I asked.

No one knew I had been listening. I was thinking of the way the policeman struck Chelogue with his large baton when he was taken away.

Kloppers waved the question down. "Rhodes said it, Smith said it, I say it. They must know their place."

"But Smith may be making things worse..."

I watched Kloppers's Adam's apple bulge. I also saw the knowing look he gave his wife. The secret was out, then. My parents were not the faithful followers of Ian Smith they were commanded to be. Ian Smith, of course, was supposed to be every white family's hero. His portrait was suspended on every lounge wall: Smith in his younger RAF days, before his eye drooped, but with his chin proudly sticking out in the Mussolini tradition, as if he were displaying the merits of a new brand of razor in some advertisement. His hair was also fanatically short and plastered down with Brylcreem. There were many similar portraits in those seedy barber shops you found in back streets with red and white poles outside.

But my parents had no such portrait on their wall. They did not participate. I was ashamed of them; they were still oddballs who hadn't adapted well, and still voted (so they told me) for another party, a minority who opposed Smith and appeased the *munts* and wanted to settle and integrate. I could have told them that they didn't stand a chance. In every election, Smith won, white hands down, every seat in parliament.

And why not? The country was doing well economically, in spite of UN sanctions. We produced everything we needed, we fed five countries around us, we had raised the standard of living of Africans so that, per capita, Rhodesian Africans earned more than any black independent country in Africa. In fact, they earned more now than they ever would after independence in this country. They should have been grateful in anticipation. But, sighed Kloppers, they were still unhappy.

I wished I had had Chelogue to speak to about it, but our succession of garden boys, cooks and houseboys had been rapid, none staying long, one preferring a 'man's job' in the mines, one fired for drinking and diluting our whisky piss-white, another disappearing in the night with most of our cutlery, the washing off the line and my father's Kodak camera. Our current houseboy, Wonderson, the tall Malawian, told us that his country was terrible under Banda and that everyone there came to work here. Malawians, said Kloppers, made good servants because, as illegal immigrants, they couldn't cause any trouble without being deported. Malawi under Banda, said my father, was an absurd place; women could only wear long dresses, men short hair, under a strict Puritan code. And Zambia? Mrs Kloppers snorted in derision at the mere mention of the country's name. Northern Rhodesia, corrected Kloppers. It will never be called Zambia in my presence. A chaos of corruption and economic graft. Rhodesia? A shining example of economic growth, zero national debt, zero inflation, zero corruption and zero tolerance.

"You compare the two and tell me what you see, Bernard. Then come talk to me about your liberal ideas."

★ ★ ★

"So how's it going, Williams? Banged her yet?"

I was hauled before Craig Hardy in the lighting room, the dark space that was occupied by privileged fifth formers (how he, a Form Two, had managed to wriggle himself into their exclusive club, I don't know), plastered with naked *Playboy* centrefolds and smokes and contraband – a pair of girl's panties they had found on the road, a used *frikkie* on the wall, also found on the road, and photos taken by the man himself, of dark shapes through the bathroom window of Jane Bartow's house.

"She called me a male chauvinist pig," I said. "She's going to report us."

Hardy scratched his head. "Your first mistake," he said, "was to let her open her mouth. Women…" He rolled his eyes the way his paternal elders had passed down to him, then grabbed me by the throat. "You know the rules, Williams. There's no going back now. You have until the holidays. And if you don't…"

Without warning, he banged my forehead with his, pushing me so I fell back against the wall. The bell rang and the gang dispersed for Maths. But Craig held me back. "Here," he said, "you have this." It was a photo he had taken of a girl's legs. The photographer was shadowed in the photo, and here I saw Hardy's outline, a large, pitiful creature, a victim of desire, trapped in his longing for the Other, and unable to attain it.

Desire makes you grow crooked and perverted. How could you grow straight in such circumstances? Sex was such a monster in our lives. It occupied us all day, all night, in and out of class, and Craig Hardy was injected, it seemed, with a double dose of the disease. In Puritan, Western Civilised Rhodesia, we clothed our naked desire in uniform behaviour. The headmaster called us gentlemen, and referred to our objects of desire as "those ladies at our Sister School". They were scrubbed of sexuality, and it was inconceivable that they should ever desire sex. Marriage was the only respectable cage for all those anarchic desires.

The storm drain running alongside Daventry Road was a metre wide and half a metre deep to cope with the torrential rain storms that battered the city from November to March every year. An alternative to the cycle path, it provided boys with a primeval pastime – mud walking. I was not exempt from this regression. After school one day, after a storm had attacked, I threw down my bike, kicked off shoes, put prickly socks and garters into my suitcase, and waded up to my knees through the chocolate mud. The slime squelched between my toes in unexpected sensuality. I pasted mud onto my face in ritualistic patterns; I bathed my arms up to the elbows. I smeared mud on an imaginary giggling girl who waded with me in the ditch. Then my foot crumpled on a sharp object and my baby toe snagged on a hook of some sort. I panicked, slopped out of the mud and fled to the bank, the thing holding on with its teeth. A snake? A *boomslang*? A thin animal? A blob of primeval black tar with a tail?

I let the mud dry itchy on my legs in the sun and sat on the storm drain's concrete slab, washing the thing in a puddle. The tail was a coarse black string or waxed elephant tail. Hanging from the string was a black fist carved from ebony. The fist gripped the string and was severed at the wrist. At first I assumed it was a hand in hitchhiking pose, the fingers curled in, the thumb protruding. But why a black hitchhiking hand? The severed wrist made me think of more sinister meanings: the hand was grasping onto the string desperately, for life, for salvation, as it had grasped onto me, but the owner – the wearer – had cut off the black man's wrist and left the plea dangling on him still. Or, like in the Arabian tale, this was the grasping hand that wouldn't let go and burdened the wearer for life. Whatever it was, it was a talisman, a sign of some sort, and I wore it around my neck all the way home, letting it bounce against my breastbone.

Suddenly, there was Bianca with two friends, chatting, laughing, strolling drunkenly, zigzagging on the path, singing, 'Mamma mia, here we go again, my my, how could I forget you!' But my face was streaked, my hands brown. I had to avoid her. She couldn't see me like this! I cycled past her, but she saw me, I know, because they stopped singing and burst into laughter. I didn't dare turn my head, but sailed on, cursing the gods, cursing the black fist which had muddied me like this and made me unfit for her presence.

In English classes we read George Orwell's essay, 'Shooting an Elephant', but at fourteen years old I missed the whole point of it, which was, I suppose, to critique colonialism and the position of the white man in a sagging British colony. The British education board must have planned O-Levels with Rhodesian whites in mind, to show us the error of our ways, yet we read about ourselves without recognition. In History classes, we spent a year studying Nazi Germany, their propaganda, the fallacies of basing ideology on the myth of racial superiority; we wrote passionate essays about the evil Nazis and how gullible the Germans were to be taken in. Imagine, they had concentration camps in their own country and did not know it; imagine being deluded into thinking the world is as your government tells you it is!

Who was in on the conspiracy? Did our teachers all know? Were they demystifying subversives, trying to get us to see, or were they in the same box, blindly seeing mirrors and thinking the reflections were other people? In Africa, in the middle of a civil war, with the country in a terrible crisis, we learned Greek Mythology, Medieval English and Latin; we sang in a choir; we played bagpipes and drums and dressed in kilts. We chanted conjugations and danced declensions, divided the world into Masculine, Feminine and Neuter. *O Me Miserum*! I shall have been loved (future passive perfect). *Bianca est puella pulchrissima*. And saw the world through a glass, darkly.

Oh, sure, we did read *The Man and His Ways*, a pamphlet about 'the African' and his quirky customs (When an African walks into your office, you will think him rude because he will immediately sit down in your best chair. In African culture, he is being polite, trying to put himself lower than you). We thought this book trivial and funny, reflecting our parents' attitude to African culture, which was deemed worthless and irrelevant, a joke.

I watched diligently every school day at lunchtime as I rode home on the current of grey and green. I dawdled and scuffed my feet up and down Nigel Philip Avenue and Daventry Road. And I saw her, often, with her suitcase, walking down the road. I dared follow only at a distance. Under the pretext of a bent mudguard, a loose suitcase, a slack chain or a lost hat, I tore past her, then stopped to act out my charade, stooping to fix my bicycle, sneaking glances at her as she, obliviously innocent, passed by. She had grown so large in my mind, that I did not know how

I would ever be able to speak to her again.

Nevertheless, I did. I was riding my bicycle down Daventry Road and she was ahead of me, alone, her suitcase assaulting her legs. She stared ahead at the flashing red man, aware that she was being watched. I prayed the light would not turn green.

"Bianca. I'm Paul… Cavedaschi. Remember?"

"How could I ever forget a name like that?" The light flashed orange and cars stopped, waiting for us to cross.

"Bianca…"

"That's my name – don't wear it out." A smile cut dimples into her cheeks. "See you, Paw-paw Cavedaschi." She walked across the pedestrian crossing, then looked back to see if I was crossing too.

"Cavedaschi? Where on earth did you get a name like that?"

I had no idea why I did not follow her that day. Instead, I watched her escape across the mirage of a railway line, through the pathway between the two bent *msasa* trees, and onto Helm Avenue until she was a green speck in my eye.

That night in bed, the scene replayed itself in numinous colour. At the point of hesitation, my True Self took over the narrative. I follow her home; she leads me into an empty house. "My brother doesn't come home until four and my parents work," she says. "This is my room. Can you help me with this…?"

I unhook the green dress at her neck, and she slips off her clothes.

"There," she smiles, "that's better. Now you."

My parents sat on the veranda to discuss Ian Smith, but with increasing gloom. The Kloppers had come to visit. They were still thinking of 'taking the gap' and leaving Rhodesia, but now their destination was Australia.

"Australia? I thought you were going to South Africa."

"South Africa has…"

"Had it," completed his wife. "Just like Kenya, and Northern Rhodesia, and this country."

"When we lived in Northern Rhodesia," said Mr Kloppers, "we knew it was time to leave when we saw cheeky *munts* on the road, hitching." He nodded, interpreting my parents' bewildered look as one of utter incredulity. "*Munts* – hitching on the roads – from white people. Can you imagine it? *Haugh*."

My mother shook her head in sympathy.

"You know when a country has had it," continued Kloppers, "when you see those buggers with their thumbs out on the road, large as life."

"Hard to believe," said my father, hiding his mystification.

"And now what do we see in this country?" A dramatic pause while he looked at me, a schoolteacher asking his pupil a question. I shook my head, gave a little shrug of the shoulder. "*Munts... MUNTS* – hitching, hitchhiking on the roads. I nearly ran one over the other day. He was practically standing in my way, thumb out, grinning at us, demanding..."

"And South Africa," said Mrs Kloppers. "For years, every April, we have been going on holiday to South Africa. Not once has this happened, has anyone done that..."

"But this year..." frowned Kloppers ominously. He stuck his thumb up in the air, waggled it, and shook his head in unfathomable gloom, lips pressed tightly together. A silence. "That country has had it, mark my words."

# CHAPTER FOUR

# THE WHITE GODDESS

**GHANAIAN HEAD OF STATE:** Let our brothers in Zimbabwe and Zambia take one white Rhodesian each and they will be liquidated in a matter of days.

**IAN SMITH:** I have no objection to majority rule as long as this is responsible majority rule. I am opposed to majority rule based on one man, one vote. We have always had majority rule in Rhodesia.

**ABEL MUZOREWA:** The people's struggle has been ceaselessly waged since 1890. We challenge the people of this country to come out of the current political dream world by realising that what has been called 'peace' and 'happiness' and 'good race relations' are, in fact, repressed fear, restless silence, forced tolerance and hidden hatred.

**NDABANINGI SITHOLE:** We intend shooting our way back into Zimbabwe until majority rule is established in our country.

**IAN SMITH:** I don't believe in black majority rule in Rhodesia, not in a thousand years.

**KENNETH KAUNDA:** Before Zimbabwe is free, there is going to be a bloodbath in that country.

**IAN SMITH:** Majority rule has been the ultimate goal of Rhodesia since 1923, but progress cannot be measured by a clock or a calendar but by achievement.

**ABEL MUZOREWA:** We have no choice but to attempt to change the present system through a violent revolution.

**ROBERT MUGABE:** The armed struggle shall continue until total power is transferred.

**IAN SMITH:** If we were to give way now, it would not be to majority rule. It would be to a Marxist indoctrinated minority.

★  ★  ★

My mother, being Italian, mixed her metaphors. You didn't get up at the crack of dawn or at sparrow's fart, according to my mother, you got up at the crack of sparrow. And if my father couldn't trust Ian Smith as far as he could throw him, if he wouldn't touch him with a barge pole, and if he was as slippery as a bar of soap, my mother "wouldn't trust him with a barge of soap".

My father, being British, had risen to the respectable position of Headmaster at a government school, Prospect Primary. His job was to maintain standards of behaviour, discipline and civilisation, and to make sure that white Rhodesians got the best goddamn education in the whole world. But even this did not redeem him in the eyes of his peers. My parents, I knew, were Kaffir lovers, 'liberals', because they didn't vote for Ian Smith.

Black people didn't get away with it either. You couldn't work for the white man without the same kind of guilt forcing you to justify your mundane existence. No one was innocent by virtue of being black. You were *zvimbwasungata*, stooges, sell-outs, puppets. If you worked with the white man against the African cause, you were a *mutengesi* (literally, a trader). But of course it wasn't that simple.

All nationalist party division members were stooges of the white man, except the division to which you happened to belong yourself. When ZAPU and ZANU split in 1963, Sithole and Mugabe were denounced by Joshua Nkomo as stooges who had sold the country to the Americans. Sithole became a sell-out when Mugabe split the party. Abel Muzorewa and Sithole were white puppets who negotiated with the white man. And any black man who helped the Rhodesian security forces, or worked for the white government, or co-operated with the white regime in any way was *chimbwasungata*, 'a chained dog' or 'running dog' of capitalism and imperialism. The imagery was animalistic; blacks were dogs, whites were capitalist pigs, and if we weren't careful, we would be swallowed up by the great big Russian bear.

I liked the puppet image. Since Jaqi, I had likened myself to Pinocchio trying to be a real boy, but getting caught up in the lies and tangled strings of his society. One day, like black people, I would be free to move as I wanted to, not at the whim of some puppeteer who controlled me from above. But at the time, I was a teenage conformist who feared disruption of the status quo. It was only much, much later that I discovered civilisation to be a disease, an empire built on sand, and culture a green mould growing on white bread.

Two men sit on the veranda, caressing Lion Lager bottles, snacking on a spread of biltong and salt 'n vinegar chips, and watching the sunset over the city.

"What are we fighting for? How can you ask that question, Bernard? We're fighting for a way of life."

"But what is so bad if an African family moves in next door? If an African boy enrols in Churchill school?"

"Bernard, Bernard, Bernard. You're thinking that the only difference is skin colour. You're thinking of a middle-class black man. There is no middle-class black man."

"Before Smith took power, there was one growing. He destroyed it. There were black MPs in parliament, for God's sake. A black middle class was growing. We should allow one to grow again. Let society find its own level. The middle way, that's what I say."

"If you stand in the middle of the road, you'll get run over, Bernard."

"It's not worth dying for."

"You haven't seen what happens, have you? Have you ever lived in Uganda? Sierra Leone? Suburbs that were once like this are rubble."

"It won't happen here."

"Gangs driving with machine guns through sewers that were once streets."

"That would never happen here. Rhodesia has a good infrastructure. You can't compare it to those countries to the north of us."

"Do you know what your son's school would be like? Would you want him to go to a school where their standards prevail? Where they wipe their snot on the back of their shirt sleeves? And Roosevelt? Where they leave abandoned babies in their dormitories, stand on toilet seats to do their business? Is that what you want?"

A man stands at the podium, huddled against the cold of exile, drinks a glass of water.

"What are we fighting for? For the dignity and worth of each individual, irrespective of race, colour, creed. It is a principle we are willing to die for, and one for which many have paid the ultimate price. The armed struggle is not something we have entered into lightly. But if your life is not valued as highly as a white man's dog, if you need a *situpa* to move from one part of your country to the other, if your first name is Kaffir and your second name Boy, if you are unable to walk on the same pavement as a white man without him spitting at you, if you have to toil on the stolen land of your ancestors to make the white man rich, if you are forced to work in the white man's mines, gardens, factories, if no one will listen to your peaceful demonstrations and pleas for humanity, if you cannot vote or have any say in the destiny of your people, if police brutality is the order of the day, if you cannot look yourself in the eye, then and only then will you understand what we are fighting for."

I had to carry the sad burden of having liberal parents. How could they not vote for Ian Smith? Hadn't they learned? Grim-lipped neighbours had now taken it upon themselves, as if Rhodesian civilisation depended on it, to put my parents right. I remonstrated with them, too; even showed them the Albert Schweitzer quote we had laboriously copied down from the Geography teacher's board:

> *There is something that all white men who have lived here, must learn and know; that these individuals are a sub-race; they have neither the intellectual, mental or emotional abilities to equate or share in any of the functions of our civilisation.*

I was a racist. The word did not exist then, not in Rhodesia; but my world view had been constructed on the premise that whites were right, Britannia ruled the waves, that Rhodesia saves and Zimbabwe ruins. My world was black and white.

All that was good came from white civilisation. All that was bad came from Africanisation. I was a self-righteous teenager, and to me my ideas were obviously, self-evidently true. All my friends and neighbours, the government, all Rhodesians knew that we were doing the right thing, that this was how things were. Even black people knew which side their bread was buttered. All except my dense parents. No, for them, the world was grey. They voted for a small minority group who wanted 'dialogue' (sneer!) with terrorists (double sneer!), who wanted, as Kloppers said, to give the country away, all that we had worked hard to achieve here in ninety short years of civilisation, to the 'bloody Kaffirs' (laugh in scornful derision).

Stubbornly, they refused. And Kloppers refused to let them refuse: it was imperative for all white Rhodesians to think the same. Otherwise the whole edifice would fall on top of us.

★   ★   ★

Enter Miss Botha, our English teacher, who believed that literature could save the world.

"We left off, boys, where Theseus, king of Athens, had conquered the Amazons and brought home the queen Hippolyta and her beautiful daughter Emily. Translate Chaucer's description into modern English. Memorise for the exam. Literature is life, boys; literature is life."

> *Her beauty would shine brighter than the lilies and flowers,*
> *And you could not tell which was lovelier,*
> *The hue of the roses or her face,*
> *The sun on the dewy grass,*
> *Or her yellow hair,*
> *Which hung a yard down her back.*

Emily, according to *The Modern Chaucer*, was an Amazon princess, from the land where women ruled, brought into subjection and submission in Athens. Theseus had also taken two prisoners, Palamon and Arcite, and from their prison cell they could watch Emily walking about in the garden every day. Palamon thought she was the goddess Venus, because she was too beautiful to be human, but Arcite in his lust saw her as very human, and his only thought was of enticing her into "c... c... carnal relations" (Miss Botha's words).

"Carnal relations! Carnal relations!" whooped Craig Hardy at break time.

But I held the image of Emily in my hands in an invisible golden chalice.

"Holy, holy, holy!" I prayed.

★  ★  ★

Enter, too, Mrs Scholes, the school librarian, who prowled her twenty-shelf library on the second floor of the Science block, lying in wait for boys who showed the slightest interest in books. I was a victim as soon as I expressed interest in goddesses of ancient mythology.

"That's the reference section... No, don't go there, you'll find nothing you want in History. Literature is the 800s. Tell you what, I'll look it up for you... there's a book called *The White Goddess* by Robert Graves. I'm sure we have it..."

"The White Goddess?"

"The test of a poet's vision," she quoted with quivering eyes closed in ecstasy, "is the accuracy of his portrayal of the White Goddess and the island over which she rules."

"Which island?"

She didn't know, but sent me off to the reference section with slips of paper on which she had scribbled six-digit numbers. I began my quest by entering the labyrinth at *The Scarlet Letter*: 'A'. After Aryanism came...

ATLANTIS: A counter-civilisation to Aryanism, based on intuition and the seven senses of mysticism. Atlantis was a continent which attempted to conquer the Mediterranean world, but had been defeated by Athens. In about 1450 BC an eruption of the volcanic island of Santorini (or Thera), and the ensuing tidal wave, destroyed this civilisation. It threatened the patriarchy of the West because it was associated with other mythical counter-civilisations, such as the Amazons, where women ruled.

AMAZONS: A mythical race of female warriors ruled over by a queen, Hippolyta, who despised men and bred only girls for war and the chase, motivated by her desire to avenge her rape and the abandonment of her sister Antiope by Theseus, king of Athens. The goddess of the Amazons was Artemis who practiced chastity and despised men's domination over women. The punishment for seeing the goddess naked was to be turned from the hunter into the hunted.

ARTEMIS: When I found this illustration in glorious colour, I thought I had found what I was looking for. Here was Artemis being watched by a man in the bushes. She was bathing in a pool, naked, and her body was so sensuously drawn, with water dripping off her breasts, that I wondered how it had been allowed in the library. After all, the penalty for Actaeon, the man in the bushes, was to be turned into a wild animal. I traced the drawing (no photocopies in those days), following those sacred curves with a trembling pencil, afraid that I might grow horns myself.

"Found it?" Mrs Scholes peered at me over moon-rimmed spectacles which were chained to her ear with gold links. "No?" I concealed the picture as best I could it with a hunched body. My tie lolled onto my traced copy. She slammed a large, hardcover book on the desk: *The White Goddess* – Robert Graves.

"I can't say I can make any sense of it, and no one else has ever taken it out of the library, but I'm sure this is what you're looking for. I've checked it out already for you."

"Thank you, Mrs Scholes."

★ ★ ★

Enemy number one was Robert Mugabe. I had never even heard of him, but in 1975, while my parents and I attended the Rhodesville Catholic church, he was hiding out in the parish house nearby.

Robert Mugabe, detained since 1964, was released in 1974 to negotiate a settlement and to heal the rifts between ZANLA and ZIPRA, and reluctantly he began talks. 'TERROR WAR OVER', the *Rhodesia Herald* headlines read, and my father delightedly thwacked it onto my bed at 6 a.m. in the morning.

"Perhaps you won't have to go to the army after all."

But Mugabe was secretly plotting in a mission house outside Salisbury to fight a more intense war, and when the Smith security began to close in and arrested his comrade Nyagumbo, he slid into the warm hands of the Catholic Church. He walked into Rhodesville, past Bianca's house in Moon Crescent, up the main road crossing Jameson, and was ushered into Father Da Silva's sanctum, talking with him in hushed tones. Black men were invisible, so even if we all saw him there, we would not know we had seen him. I attended a youth club at the parish house every Friday night while a bespectacled, fifty-year-old man with a grizzle of white hair hovered in a back room, pushing glasses onto his nose in what would later become a familiar gesture of our President on the eight o'clock news. I may have even seen this cheeky Kaffir looking at me, as if we both knew we knew we knew. But I didn't know. While we were attending Sunday services, he had been planning a guerrilla war. While we were sipping tea after Mass one Sunday, he was fleeing the country in the back of a truck. And while we were watching Miss Roosevelt contests one evening, he was walking into Mozambique to set up the new ZANLA guerrilla army.

★ ★ ★

Bianca Pennefather and I remained at a critical distance. I watched her walk home but I dared not speak to her again, no matter how Craig Hardy and the Bang Gang prodded me. The deadline passed, and I was unpunished. The year passed, and still the Bang Gang talked of large slag heaps of girls they had banged, and how I was failing in my duty as a gang member.

"Have you banged that virgin yet?" Hardy asked me.

"I'm working on it."

"If you don't do it soon, not only will you be out of the gang," he said, "but I'm going to grab her for myself."

"I swear I'm working on it."

Hardy grabbed me by the collar. "So am I. And I've made progress."

"What do you mean?"

But Hardy was all winks and mysterious sneers. He passed me a photographic grey shadow.

"What's that?"

"It's her," he said triumphantly. "On the john. See, through the window.

I managed to get one of her." I looked but saw only grains of black and white. "Here," he said. "Here, her legs, the pink panties at her ankles."

The others crowed. "How, Craig, how?"

"No flash, unfortunately. I know where she lives. I followed her home one day and was nearly eaten by the bloody dogs."

On the path, a girl walked ahead, blonde hair a yard long (well, six inches maybe) swinging behind her, that green garden of a dress with all its folds and hills and valleys, ivory white legs, glistening with sweat caught in rays of sun. I skidded my tyres to a stop and watched her from the distance of twenty-five feet. Her head was down. She didn't see the line of boys blocking her way. She banged into them, dropped her suitcase and stumbled. They mumbled exaggerated apologies and nodded their heads like feeding pigeons. A bicycle tyre jostled her suitcase (sorry, sorry), burst it open, and scattered its contents over the path and verge. (Oh, dear, oh, sorry.)

Hardy, the gallant hero, dismounted, picked up the books and packed them into her suitcase. The other boys collected pencils, ruler, compass, files. She nodded in confused gratitude. Hardy touched her on the elbow to escort her, hoisted up her suitcase, and skipped alongside her as she picked up her former gait, the other boys cycling off at a frantic sign he made behind his back. My worst fears were confirmed. But I had seen something they hadn't.

I waited a full minute, listening to the jacaranda seed pods crack and burst in the trees, before walking my bike up to the spot where she had been waylaid. Here. I crouched to tie my shoelace. Yes. Half hidden in a bougainvillea bush by the side of the path lay a pink file, flung wide out of her suitcase.

I picked up the file and read the cover: GEOGRAPHY – BIANCA PENNEFATHER, 3A1. Inside, I found numerous teapot-shaped maps of Rhodesia, one overlaid with the Inter-Tropical Convergence Zone, another in colours representing maize, cotton and tobacco, another demarcating the Highveld, the Midlands, Lowveld and the Great Dyke. Bianca Pennefather, I said. The sound was a soft wave rippling onto a shore, the 'B' breaking open a vessel of perfume which flowed outwards, as the mouth widened to pronounce the 'IA' the 'N', the echo

'CA' a double wave of delight. Bianca Pennefather.

★  ★  ★

I carried the file pressed to my chest on the way to school the next morning, though it could have fitted in my suitcase strapped to the carrier of my bike. I walked into my class form room with it, but before I could hide it, Craig Hardy lunged at me.

"Time is running out," he warned. "The end of term is coming soon."

"How many days?" called Burnett, behind him.

"How many points? How many points?" Wrigglesworth held up fingers and hands.

"Have you banged that virgin yet?"

I held the file close to my chest so they would not see her name. Hardy folded his arms. "Too late. I've already asked her to the school dance."

"What?"

He smirked. "I spoke to her brother, the prefect. We set it all up."

I tightened my grip further. "What do you mean?"

"I take my sister to the dance, he takes his. Then we swap. At the school dance, I bang her outside in the bushes. You lost out, Paul."

Her brother, Luke Pennefather. Of course. The prefect with the shiny blond hair, the immaculate, handsome, carved face, the Christian who was earmarked as head boy, who did everything right, played first team rugby, soccer, basketball, tennis. Luke Pennefather.

I had no time to lose. Meet her today after school, wait at Roosevelt gates until she comes out. Give her the file and begin a conversation. Warn her of Hardy's intentions. But that old ninny-woman Fate had other plans. School was cancelled that day. A thousand boys arrived for classes, but before the end of the first period, our class teacher (named Tickhead by his merciless pupils) broke the news.

"Keep quiet, boys," he said in his harassed way, stroking his beard. "I'll tell you what's happened. Mozambique has declared war on Rhodesia."

"War?"

"We might all be mobilised immediately," he said (meaning himself, I suppose, for we were too young to be conscripted). "But Mozambique couldn't raise an army to match ours in a thousand years." He recited this Smithism in a half-hearted way, trying to laugh, but looking very white. The hubbub in the class rose as the words sank in.

It had happened before. Just a year or so ago, Zambia had declared a state of war with Rhodesia, so Smith promptly closed her borders, and when the Zambians complained that their food aid was not getting through any more, he commented:

"The pathetic wailin' of the Zambian government rin's a particularly hollow note."

And now Mozambique was sealing us off. Tickhead placed a portable Supersonic radio on the front desk, and we huddled around, listening to the radio broadcaster who was reading in his usual deadpan, nasal tone:

"Mozambique has not declared war on us. They don't have the gall. They have merely declared a state of war, meaning that they have stolen all our assets in the country and closed their borders to us. This is an empty threat to make Rhodesia panic. It makes no difference, because Mozambique is sending terrorists into the country anyway. It means though that our only ally is South Africa and on all other sides we now face the communist onslaught. But does this mean that we are going to give in to terrorism and corruption, to dictatorship and slavery?"

"Digging their own graves," smirked Hardy. "They can't feed themselves like us." And he patted his stomach. The radio voice droned on.

"Hasn't the world learnt from World War II? Are there only Chamberlains left to appease the forces of evil and compromise with communists? No. There is one Churchill left – Rhodesia. We alone are prepared to stand against the onslaught of terrorism and the decline of Western standards and Christian values. We will take no nonsense. We will show no mercy to the enemy. We will show our strength, we will stand tall with the truth upon our side."

Ian Smith himself spoke next. After clearing his throat, he expressed disappointment and dissatisfaction with the breakdown of the so-called Geneva peace talks because of the intransigence and pigheaded stubbornness of the so-called Patriotic Front. He had bent over backwards to meet the demands of the so-called black leaders of the country (I had yet to see this party trick, which

Smith assured the public he performed often at conferences), and if that wasn't enough, the so-called Free World seemed to be supportin' the so-called freedom fighters and gangin' up against them. A glob of reporters was heard in the background, clamouring for his attention. "But the newspaper yesterday stated…" In the silence I could almost see Smith smile and wave his hand: "Don't tell me you believe everything you read in the liberal press?"

★   ★   ★

I was outside by ten o'clock in the morning, waiting in ambush by the Churchill gates for Bianca to pass. I assumed that the Roosevelt girls would be released at the same time, so I sat on the low granite wall next to the pedestrian crossing where a prefect wearily raised his hat to every passing car as he let schoolboys cross the road. Yes. Roosevelt girls began pouring out of the gates in a trickle, then a stream, then a green flood.

I waited for an hour. Still no Bianca. Stragglers dragged satchels, but no prim girl ported a suitcase. I jumped onto my bicycle and rode down Nigel Philip, past Benwell field, turned right at Clyde Road and rode hard up to Clyde shops. I couldn't see her on any of the roads fanning out from Roosevelt. I'd have to think of another strategy. I rode furiously past Spencer hostels, past a group of girls whom I had seen pass me earlier. I jumped a red storm drain and landed hard on my tyres, then crossed into the Clyde shops.

Three girls crouched in conspiracy at Clyde Café: a redhead, a brunette and a blonde. And there she was. A Morris Minor was parked next to the café. That's how she had escaped my dragnet. I coasted across the Mobil garage forecourt, skidded past the Morris Minor, propped my bike against the curb in front of them, and walked nonchalantly through the café door. The file was in my suitcase on the bike carrier. Through the shop's windows, obscured by piles of Surf, Omo and Lifebuoy soap, I contemplated my plan. The girls were seated in two wrought-iron chairs, and Bianca was perched on the table, swinging her legs and eating an ice cream.

"Yes?" The Greek shopkeeper watched me with narrowed eyes.

"A Coke and a packet of salt 'n vinegar chips, please." I paid him ten cents (we had gone metric in 1970, and had expunged all images of the Queen from our currency), took the drink and crisps, thought frantically. With a swig for courage, I walked outside, set the drink and packet on the next table, took off the suitcase, took out the file, calmly walked up to Bianca and gave it to her.

"This…"

She stopped swinging her legs. The girls stopped talking.

"I found this on the path. You dropped it."

"Oh," she said, rescuing the file with her free hand. I held her gaze long enough to colour her cheeks red. A pop of saliva burst out of her slightly parted lips. "I thought I had lost this."

The girls eyed me critically. I was interrupting something important. I offered the drink and crisps as an apology, and the girl with short red hair and a running nose took a crisp; the other girl shook her head with not-so-subtle disdain. Bianca pointed to her ice cream. Did she mean, "No, I've got this," or "Do you want some?" It was a Green Mamba – white soft-serve ice cream coiled on a cone covered with green flavoured-sugar dots. It was supposed to look like a snake with its tail up, head in the cone, but she had already licked one side of green away.

"How did you know it was mine?" said Bianca, placing the file on the table and tweaking one eyebrow at me.

"Your name is inside. Thank goodness girls have name badges."

She licked the ice cream, and her left eyebrow arched in acknowledgement of the allusion to our earlier meeting. I dived for the Coke again, to buy time.

"This is Paul, by the way, Paul Cavedaschi."

The brown-haired girl spluttered into her hand and nudged the red one.

"Cavedaschi. Is this the guy…?"

Bianca kicked out her left foot at the girl's shin.

"This is Sue and Angie." She pointed to the brunette who was wearing a badge: BIANCA PENNEFATHER. Bianca's name badge read SUE WHITE.

"Just to throw them off the scent," said the red-haired girl.

"Thank goodness girls wear name badges," said Bianca in what I could only take to be mockery. I smiled with thin lips.

"You know him?" The red-haired girl pointed a bony finger at me. "Why not ask him?"

Bianca frowned.

"No, really, listen," the girl insisted. Again, she pointed at me. "Do you have a partner for the school dance?"

"The Churchill dance?"

"Bianca has to go. And she doesn't really know anyone she can ask…"

"She doesn't want to go with her brother."

Bianca kicked at her again. "Sue."

I nodded warily, suspicious of the flippant, breezy tone, and aware of Bianca's embarrassment.

"Spell it out for him."

Bianca sighed. "Do-you-want-to-go-to-the-dance-with-me, Paul Cavedaschi?"

I took a slow swig of Coke. "I suppose. OK."

The red-haired girl spread out her hands in the air as if carrying a large parcel. "Problem solved."

"Can you pick me up, 7 Moon Crescent, just off Jameson?" said Bianca.

"I don't have a car."

"7 Moon Crescent," said Bianca, talking to me as if I was hearing impaired. "Eight p.m., Saturday?"

"If you don't mind walking?"

"Bianca," said Fran. "Tell him about your parents."

Bianca shook her head.

I placed the empty bottle back on the shop counter, crunched the packet of uneaten crisps into my pocket, and walked to my bike. "7 Moon Crescent," I said as I mounted. "Eight p.m., Saturday."

Bianca held up the file in lieu of a wave, then turned to the other girls.

"Your brother will absolutely kill you when he finds out," said Sue.

"So the Portuguese packed up and left, just like that (snap fingers). They had had enough of colonies, and all the trouble they caused, and had not made good returns. They left Mozambique in the hands of FRELIMO, a gang of terrorists who would make short shrift of the population and the country's assets. Angola was a bloody mess, and now Mozambique – those troublesome natives wanted a Marxist government (shake head). Well, let the buggers have it. We haven't invested much here anyway. We've extracted a few minerals; we've taken what we want."

"And Zambia?" (raise eyebrows)

"It's turning into a good example of what would happen here in Rhodesia if the *munts* ever took over. Corruption is the order of the day. Kaunda has had elections once or twice, yes, but opposition parties are banned and burned and branded traitors. Make it a one-party state and have done with it. All this democracy nonsense is a Western invention. It doesn't work in Africa. And look, they're already starving. They nationalised the bloody copper mines; now they don't function. The kwacha is not worth the paper it's printed on."

But we are also besieged. Zambia is to the north and west. Mozambique is east. The oil pipeline from Beira travels through Mozambique to reach us. We have no port. We have no allies around us, only South Africa to the south. Beitbridge is our only contact with the outside world.

# CHAPTER FIVE

# THE ILLUSION MONGERS

Gamma was not his real name, but that's what we called this archetypal weedy, spectacled boy all through school. Gamma was the victim of a group of smart Alecs in class who called themselves 'The Illusion Mongers'. Whatever they concocted, he believed. They systematically created an illusion around him by pretending he was a strong bully who was the terror of the school. They pretended to fear him, and feigned agony when he rabbit-punched them.

And Gamma took it all at face value. If they told him that the prettiest girl in Roosevelt was in love with him, but was too shy to ever admit it, he believed them. If they told him that he was a genius, and that the teachers were too stupid to understand his great intellect and therefore gave him bad grades, he believed them. So Gamma to his surprise – a thin, weak boy with spots and gawky, uncoordinated movements – found that he was strong, handsome and popular, and all through school puffed himself up with pride, believing their picture of him.

I stumbled upon the Illusion Mongers at work one break time in the muddy playground on a rainy December morning. Gamma had been primed to fight Craig Hardy. By the Bengal-juice sellers (those black men with bells and white berets and tricycle carts stuffed with dry ice and chocolate milk), a tight, male circle had gathered. Gamma circled the school bully with arms out, making stabs into the air with his white, clenched fist. Hundreds of goading boys cheered and encouraged him. Hardy, between laughs, cringed in fake cowardice, and when Gamma ventured a tentative blow to his shoulder, fell violently backwards, screaming in agony.

"I wasn't using my full strength," Gamma warned Hardy. "Now you buck up or I'll really hit you."

"No, Gamma, please," pleaded Hardy in mock terror. Gamma punched him lightly in the stomach. Hardy rolled on the ground, hiding his mirth in groans of defeat. "I give up, you win." Then the Illusion Mongers moved in, faked admiration for Gamma, felt his muscles, and asked him where he had learned to fight with such lethal effectiveness. Gamma swallowed all the ham acting. Perhaps he had been brought up on romance films and novels, and had not looked too carefully in the mirror. Without an objective reference point, he had no way of knowing the truth.

"What's the point?" I asked a jostling Illusion Monger. "Why make him out to be so good? He thinks he's Superman."

"It's an experiment. Our friend Gamma is being primed for the Great Fall."

'History repeats itself because no one was listening the first time.' These words were gouged into my desk in Room One. I didn't write them, but I'm sure the History teacher, Mr Horace, seeing me slouched on the desk during History class five times a week, thought me a sceptical critic of his rhetorical skills.

"Since Mozambique and its people have been thrown to the ravenous dogs of communism," he said, "and Portugal has washed its hands of its African responsibilities in Angola, leaving its colonies to their grim fates, the communist countries of the OAU and their paymasters in Moscow and Peking are rubbing their avaricious hands with glee. What is their ultimate goal? Wright?"

"World domination, sir."

"Yes. Considering the Southern African continent is a strategic supply route, the inevitable march down the African continent has closed Rhodesia in on all sides."

"There's someone muscling in on our territory, Paul," Hardy whispered. "Someone called Cavedaschi, a foreigner she keeps talking about."

"Cave...?"

"Cavedaschi. She's taking him to the dance, her brother says. Just wait till I find out who he is. He'll be looking through the wrong end of his arse after I get hold of him."

Mr Horace tapped Hardy's desk. "And inside our sovereign state? What strategies are employed to secure their goal of world domination?"

"Terrorism?"

"Terrorism, yes, Hardy. How do you persuade people to do what you want? You terrorise them. You force the local population into supporting your cause, using torture, rape and murder. Then they'll vote for you." He smiled as he paced his normal route down the aisle. As usual, I covered the offending graffiti on my desk with a sleeve. "Boys, their brutal campaign can make little headway because of one obstacle they have not planned for. What is that? Forth?"

"The Rhodesian army, sir."

"The Rhodesian army, seen by all as the best in Africa, is in complete control of all terrorist activity, and even uses pre-emptive strikes on training bases in neighbouring states to prevent the terrorists, before they can even think of striking at us. So can the terrorists ever win the war?"

"No, sir."

"No, they can't win the war, but sadly, the communists won't take over this country by winning a war against us. Rather, we'll be stabbed in the back by a Brutus, an erstwhile friend." He paused to dramatise the moment. "Who? Who?" Even Wright did not know this one. Hardy, too, shook his head.

"Recently, the ratchet has been tightened on Rhodesia by none other than the conniving South African government, busy shining its perfidious blade, which it is now ready to sink, with Vorster's stinking policy of détente, deep into our back. South Africa, yes."

Mr Horace, like most Churchill teachers, believed in corporal punishment. He hooked his cane on the front wall next to the blackboard, but he used it mostly on non-human animals. Crows dominated the bird life around Churchill school, though we often saw storks picking away at the worm-matted Garner and Benwell fields, and even an ibis, or a long-legged crowned crane, would grace our turf. But mostly those black and white crows, the size of large chickens, dominated the school skies. Besides terrorising little sparrows and stealing lunches from careless schoolboys, they taunted Mr Horace mercilessly by cawing, coughing and gargling outside his classroom windows all day.

"Smith has bent over backwards to try to satisfy the unreasonable demands of the West. He has opened his arms to all negotiations, but behind their treacherous smiles are the prodding fly whisks of the OAU, and the hammer, sickle and star of the communist bloc, who want Rhodesia to be, simply, a one-party communist state. And this will happen, unless…"

We were watching a large crow on the windowsill, which was peering in at the window. Mr Horace knew it was there (we noted the tensing of his neck muscles), but ignored it for the present.

"Unless…?" The crow barked at us, until Mr Horace rattled his cane at the window. Hardy raised his hand.

"We fight them."

Horace nodded. "We do what we can, boys, to stop this slow but relentless march of the terrorist nations. We disrupt the links in the Maoist chain. We eliminate their bases, we raid neighbouring countries." More crows bounce-landed on the windowsill, cawing at each other, and he lunged at them through the window, punctuating his lecture with whacks on the wall.

"The British let us down, and now the Americans (under the anti-Christ Kissinger) are selling us down the river, too. We have no friends. Yes, Hardy, we have to fight. And what has this got to do with History, you wonder? Perspective, boys, perspective. Will we go down in history as the valiant last frontier of Western Christian Civilisation?" He banged again at the crows who had picked up a Willard's salt 'n vinegar crisp bag and were tearing it apart on the ledge. "You know the story of the boy who put his finger in the dyke to stop the sea rushing into the lowlands of Holland? You are that boy. You." He pointed at us in turn: Wright, Forth, Hardy, Williams, Wrigglesworth. Hardy nudged me, about to make a lewd comment about putting fingers in dykes, but Horace was watching him, so he kept quiet.

"In a hundred years from now, will your name be written into posterity? In thirty years from now, will you be the decorated heroes who held back the tide of communism and terror in the world?"

★　★　★

In thirty years from now, this high school will be renamed Josiah Tongogara, after the high Commander in Chief of the guerrilla ZANLA fighters. The country will be at war with 'dissidents', those who oppose Mugabe's reign of terror, and the State of Emergency imposed by Smith will still be in place, this time to punish those who want to turn the clock back, not forward. Most whites will have left the country, or will have been expelled by the government, so no white boys will attend the school. No white heroes will be written into the history books. The school will be grubby and derelict, crowded with more boys than can ever be taught. They will wear parodies of the purple uniforms we wore, will still take off hats (if any) to passing adults, but sport no inky purple-grey ties, or belts, or garters. A uniform in Barbour's or McCullough's and Bothwell's will cost more than a month's salary for a teacher, so the clothing rule will no longer be enforced. There will be more important things to think of, like finding food for the boys so they do not faint in class. There will be no rebellious gangs. The enemy to buck will no longer be the collapsed system. It will be poverty, AIDS, the fear of not getting an education at all, or the fear that even the best education will not get you a job.

The weekend of the school dance brought my jangling feelings to a crescendo. I paced up and down all morning. I wrote down things to say to Bianca all afternoon. I memorised jokes in the evening and practised them on the cat, putting on a confident air, a swagger and a laugh. The cat licked her paws and settled down to sleep, twitching her ears at the consonants.

7 Moon Crescent was in a cul-de-sac off the four-lane Jameson Avenue. The house was double-storey, set back in a rambling acre of towering trees and bushes. The high wall and gate hid me from the mysteries of the Pennefather residence, and I lagged outside under a spithodia tree until it was exactly eight p.m. Then I creaked open the gate and followed the path of low lights.

On the left a pool glistened in the darkness. I briskly and loudly paced up the driveway. Two huge slobbering black dogs bounded up to me, barking and snarling at my feet. I froze. The curtains moved at the lounge window and a man's voice called out, "Pasha! Glubb! It's OK." One dog sniffed my crotch and the other growled as I nudged it away with my foot. The door handle turned and a shaft of light streamed out onto the path. "Come, come, they won't hurt you." A large man held open the door. A woman stood behind him, pushing her husband away to see me.

"Come in, take a seat. Bianca will be down in a minute."

"Paul, isn't it?"

The room was stone-floored, with a mud-stained grass mat at its centre. The furniture was dog- or cat-scratched. Pasha or Glubb leaped onto one sofa and lay there, its suspicious eyes on me. The other dog bounded through the lounge into what presumably was the kitchen, its claws sliding on the stone floors, and I heard it lap water noisily out of a metal dish which it nosed around and clanged. The father sat down next to the WRS black-and-white television, turned it down.

"So…" he clapped his hands together and smiled, "you're taking Bianca to the Churchill dinner."

"No… er… it's a… dan…"

"Dinner," cut in the mother smoothly. She frowned at me and indicated her husband with a nod of the head. "Bianca said it was a formal affair, with the teachers and everyone."

I looked carefully at the mother. Instinctively, I fashioned the mask I was supposed to wear for the occasion, cued in by Mrs Pennefather's prompts. The couch dog had now settled into licking its pink genitals.

"Where do you fellowship?" was the man's next question.

The problem with the game of saying what is expected of you, of being someone approved of, is that you have no idea what is expected of you or what will be approved of. But Mrs Pennefather came to my rescue again. She didn't even lift her head from her knitting, which she had taken up. "We go to Central Baptist usually," she said.

Fellowship. I brightened. "I go to the church on Rhodesville Avenue."

"Isn't that a Catholic church?" asked the father, frowning. "I can't recall one there."

I thought furiously. OK, Church was right. Catholic was wrong. "No, it's small. Quite small."

"A house church?"

"Yes." I stuck out my chin and pulled my tie from my throat.

"Talking of that Rhodesville church," said the father, "I've heard that the priest there is really in the pay of the terrorists."

"Really?"

"Father Cough."

"Goff, dear."

"He's on the Commission of Justice and Peace or some such nonsense – well, that's what they call it, but it's really a front for communist support. These Catholics lick the feet of terrorists and criticise whatever the government does to defend itself."

"They shouldn't get involved in politics anyway, I think," said the mother. "They've lost the truth of the gospel, that church."

I shook my head slowly, in disapproval of the Catholics. But Mr Pennefather was warming to the subject. "They're doing a series at Central this month on the Roman church," he said. "You should come, Peter, you'd find it interesting." The mother looked up at me and smiled. "They link Catholicism with the Babylonian religion in the Old Testament," he went on. "I would never have imagined it to be so evil. It's really an instrument of Satan."

"The speaker is really good too," said the mother. "A Protestant from Ireland who really knows how to fight for his faith. Not a good Baptist, I'm afraid, but still very good. He gets you all fired up, doesn't he, honey?"

"For instance," said the father, "he says that the worship of the Virgin Mary is really the worship of the Great Whore."

"George," whispered the mother.

"It's all in the Bible, Margaret. It's time people knew about the great Whore of Babylon."

A passage door opened and, as if announced, in walked Bianca. I stood.

"Hello, Paul."

"Ready?"

"Sorry to keep you waiting." She looked at her mother, then her father, then my red face. "I hope you didn't... didn't preach at him, Daddy?"

"We were having a good chat about the Counterfeit Church."

She kissed her mother tenderly, her father with a dismissive impatience, and then took my arm. "God bless, dear," said her mother, rearranging her hair. "Don't be too late."

I bowed my head, stumbled backwards to say my goodbyes, and the two of us walked into the cool night air. Bianca's father's voice boomed through the closing door. "A good Rhodesian lad."

We walked in silence for a while, except for her clicking heels on the rough tar. She looked down at her feet as she walked. Cicadas screeched, insects buzzed around the halos of the street lights and the occasional car drove past, but otherwise the silence pressed down on us. I loosened my tie, and measured thirty-five paces before I spoke.

"Maybe you should have warned me about your parents. They think you're going to a dinner."

"Dinner. Dance. What's the difference? What he doesn't know won't hurt him."

"You could have told me."

"He doesn't let me out anywhere. He made me drop Miss Roosevelt. He made me drop the Drummies. He's ruining my life. But not tonight, he's not."

The first topic was to be how beautiful she looked in that (insert colour) dress, how her hair looked good in that style (add details), how her eyes were so (blue/brown/green) etc, but my courage failed me, so I moved onto topic number two. "Isn't your brother going to the dance too?"

She turned sharply to me. "What do you know about my brother going to the dance?"

"Nothing, nothing."

"He told you." In the dim light of a yellow streetlamp, she looked like a cornered rabbit. "Shit, shit, shit."

I regretted bringing up the subject now, and didn't quite know how to respond. And I was alarmed at her language. I hadn't really thought that girls swore like this. What else didn't I know about them? Did they fart too? I wisely kept silent, and listened to her heels click until we were past the Winston hostels. She didn't want to talk about it, but three full minutes' silence made her capitulate.

"He lined me up with someone... else. Typical male, he thought I wouldn't find out." Here she gave me a wary glance. "Doesn't he think I get a say in my own life?"

The silence was uncomfortable, but I couldn't think of anything to say. Saying no or yes both seemed wrong.

"You think I'm a liar. Is that what you're trying to say? I lied to my parents. I lied to you. I lied to him. Shit, I'm awful."

"No, you're not. You're…"

"Bloody awful. And it's even more complicated. There's this other guy. Oh, I'm awful."

"No, you're not. You're…"

"Yes, I am." But she smiled as if her inner turmoil was a game she was playing for her own amusement. It was the same game my Italian mother played every time she cooked dinner for guests. "It's such a bad meal," she would say, and on cue everyone would compliment her on the excellent lasagne, pizza, ravioli or spaghetti.

We had arrived at the entrance of the Churchill hall and I escorted her past the They-Died-for-Our-Country board. I stared at all the decorations, the ribbons coating Mr Churchill's portrait, the disco's flashing lights, and the thick stout Churchill boys, accompanied by frail silky-clothed girls. At Churchill school, your prestige was graded by the beauty of your girlfriend. I hustled her past classmates who whistled. "Ten! Ten!"

"A drink?" I pointed to the back corner by the foyer, where the sign DRINKS had been painted in large uneven letters on an asbestos board. The school grounds keeper (who was called the 'Boss Boy' and kept control both of the gardeners, who invisibly picked at weeds all school-day long, and those who swabbed the decks of the classrooms and corridors after school hours) wore instead of his servant's uniform, a suit and tie, and over this an apron. He stood by a zinc bathtub of ice, filled with Cokes and Fantas and Sparletta Cherry Plums, which he would fish out on demand for the schoolboys. He had been placed strategically on the side where he could not see the white girls dancing (at the request of the girls' parents). He poured us both Cokes in large champagne glasses, and smiled broadly as he recognised me out of my school disguise. "A large Coke (he pronounced it Cock) for the *Baas*'s little lady." She demurely accepted the dripping-with-iced-water glass from his hand. "Thanks, Philemon."

We sat at a table covered in a white cloth, and watched the dancing. Boys, unrecognisable in civilian clothes, twisted slowly to the music as if they were trying to get sticky gum off their shoes, and girls bounced dreamily on the same spot, moving hands and pelvises. Bianca drained the fizzy black liquid as if it were a strong cane, and smiled at me. I swigged my Coke too, cherishing the fizzy bubbles in my throat and caressing the glass as my parents did their beer glasses during political discussions.

"Shall we dance?" I took her cold, soft fish of a hand, and taking her demure look as assent, ushered her gently to the dance floor. We positioned ourselves in the centre of the wooden platform and she began to dance, or rather she moved slowly from side to side and buckled her knees every so often. All the while, she watched me with teasing, judgemental merriment.

The song was local, sung in a Rhodesian accent by Ted and Beverly Lynn. We danced. I loved her every movement, gawky though it was: the feet gliding, the hips dipping, the arms flopping, hair bouncing, her rapturous smile, her eyes fixed on me.

> *Daddy went to fight for the green and white, I won't forget that day*
> *We were down at the old drill hall, as the convoy pulled away*
> *Daddy went to fight for the green and white, we miss you all each day*
> *Tall and lean in his jungle green, we heard our Mama say*

"Paul, I can't dance to this crap." She twisted her face in distaste. "Don't they have any decent music?" We peered up at the DJ on the stage, crouched over a turntable, the record needle in one jittery hand, a torch (to see where to cue the song) in the other. Piles of LPs and singles surrounded his console, and the front of each speaker proudly announced in glittering fluorescent paint that this was 'Starlight Disco'.

> *Green and white you're flying, in the blue Rhodesian sky*
> *Green and white, you know that we all love you till we die*

That brought me to my third contrived topic of conversation, rehearsed that afternoon. "You know I've just registered for my National Service," I said. We stood still on the dance floor, while others swayed and swooned around us.

"You're going to fight for the green and white?" She cocked her thumb at the large speaker behind her.

It was the irony in her voice that perplexed me. "I'm not that enthusiastic about it myself." Her attitude was supposed to be one of sympathy (according to the scenario I had acted out that afternoon to the cat), not wry humour. We waited for the music to change – Status Quo's 'Down Down', David Bowie's 'Rebel Rebel', and Alvin Stardust's 'My Coo ca Choo'. She liked these, and danced vigorously to each with eyes closed in some self-absorbed trance-like state where her body floated in an invisible viscous substance. But when Mike Westcott's 'We are the Shumba Drinkers' began to play (*We are the Shumba drinkers, we drinks a dozen a day; we are the shumba drinkers, why work when you can play, ek sê, ek sê, ek sê, ek sê*), her lips opened in a helpless plea. "I can't dance to this."

"OK." She took my hand to lead me off the dance floor and we walked proudly through a throng of admiring Churchill peers. As we approached our table, though, her fingers stiffened. I didn't have to ask why. Craig Hardy stood at the table where we were headed, with three members of the Bang Gang leaning on the drinks counter, all of them girl-less. Hardy's eyes bulged; he couldn't believe what he was seeing. His gaze was locked onto me, as if he were taking aim to fire a deadly missile. Still more disconcerting was the paralysis I saw on Bianca's face. "Why does no one ever listen to me?" she hissed through clenched teeth.

Bewildered, I indicated our table, which was now occupied by louts and Bang Gang members. "Let's go outside," Bianca suggested brightly. I didn't protest. Her fingers still tensely gripped mine.

We sat on the grass under a dark, cool whispering tree. In daytime, this was a favourite lunch spot for seniors; now it was a holy place. The pressure of her hand did not relent, and I squeezed it back as intensely, communicating whatever meaning I could. She was, I feared, too preoccupied with a private conflict in her mind to notice my attentions, and I guessed, with sinking heart, what her conflict was. The triumph, though, was that she preferred me to him.

"You understand, don't you?" I didn't understand anything, but as long as she gripped my hand, it didn't matter. "It's a mess, as usual," she said," but I don't care. I don't care." She pushed against me, and parted her lips as she pressed her face to me. "As long as you are here with me, Paul Cavedaschi."

Without warning, she leaned forward and kissed me. I gripped her shoulders to steady her, in case she pulled away, but I need not have worried. She was glued to my mouth. She raised her soft shoulders, the ground on which her waterfall of hair rested, as she felt my firm grip on them, and sighed deeply. "Cavedaschi," she murmured, holding my face with both hands. "You silly, silly boy."

I opened my eyes to see, overhead, through wavy, dark green leaves, milky stars twinkling. Echoes of ABBA's 'Fernando' wafted out to us in pleasant dream-like memories of a real world. Her hair glinted gold and a sparkle of light in her eyes danced merrily.

"Game's up, Williams."

A shadow hulked out of the doorway and pinned us in the light. "Oh, Christ," she said, before her lips had even left my mouth.

"Or should I say, Cavedaschi." The sardonic smile of my nemesis, my Bang Gang leader, reflected red, green and yellow in the disco lights. Bianca pulled away. Two other distorting shadows stepped out of the doorway. I recognised Jones's wiry voice: "So, Paul, have you banged that virgin yet?"

The other was Wrigglesworth. "I guess he wins the competition."

Bianca squinted at the dark shadows. "What competition?"

"And his name is Paul Williams," said Hardy in a cold drawl, "not Cavedaschi."

"He made a bet with us that he could get into your pants before the end of the term."

She let my hand go and rustled her dress away from me. "Paul?"

Hardy was a leopard about to pounce on its prey. "Williams, I must say you're a smooth operator. You had her out here before the first hour."

Bianca stood. "A competition?"

"Yes," said Jones. "Williams here won… put it there, man, you're a fully fledged member of the gang." He reached out a hand, but Hardy pushed him aside. "Leave him to me." I stood, too, and walked towards Bianca, but Hardy stepped between us. "Cavedaschi, eh?"

The first blow hit me in the jaw, and I fell back heavily on the low stone wall, clutching onto ferns in the flower bed. Bianca circled us, her arms hugging her breasts tightly. "Craig Winston Hardy, what the hell are you trying to do? I told you…"

Hardy gave no sign of hearing her. His eyes were locked onto mine. He lunged at me again. I ducked and swung around the other side of the tree.

"Bianca, it's not what you think," I said, but he lunged at me again. I blocked a punch to my stomach, tried to wrestle his arm back behind his back, but he used his weight to push me down again onto the hard concrete edge of the flower stand.

"Stop it, please, please stop it." Bianca danced around the two of us, and the two Bang Gang members stood like referees, dancing too.

"So, Cavedaschi, what have you got to say for yourself?" Hardy was at me again, a sweating solid mass of flesh, smearing me against the wall.

"Craig, leave him alone. You said…"

I saw I was meant to fight back, for Bianca's sake too. I clenched my fist in anticipation of driving it into his gut, when a torch shone out onto the road and a teacher's voice cut through the tension. "What do you boys think you are doing?"

Hardy was gone in an instant. Wrigglesworth and Jones also spirited themselves away. I was left in the beam like a blind man. I recognised my Science teacher, Mr Moore, whose job it was at the school dance was to flush out couples who sneaked off into the bushes.

"It's me, Williams, sir," I called out.

"What are you doing, Williams, in the dark all by yourself? Oh, sorry, miss." His light framed her head and threw a grotesque shadow of her against the white wall. "Miss?" She held a hand over her eyes.

"Everything's all right, sir," I called out. "We were just taking a breath of fresh air."

But my breathing was heavy and fast, my heart pounding, my tie wrapped around my neck and my shirt pulled out. And Hardy was nowhere to be seen. The teacher flicked the torch onto me, slowly around the dark flowerbed, then caught Bianca again in his beam.

"Are you all right, miss?" His torch revealed the obvious truth: the distance between Churchill boys and Roosevelt girls necessary to preserve Western Christian Civilisation had been breached.

"Please go back inside, you two. I will deal with you inside."

"I'm going home," said Bianca to some higher authority in the sky. "My brother is waiting for me. He caused this mess."

"No, Bianca," I called. "Wait." But she swished her evening dress – blue silk, strapless – to the entrance of the hall. The teacher guided her into the hall with his torch beam, and then played it directly onto my face, the way interrogators do to their prisoners in movies.

"Williams, you'd better see me on Monday at the Headmaster's office at eight a.m. sharp. That clear? Now get back into the hall."

On that night, the night I walked home by myself and felt the warm wind blowing cold through me, police raided Tafara township and arrested fifteen people, the army marched into a village in Murewa and beat ten terrorist sympathisers; another army unit arrested five suspected terrorists; a group of thirty schoolchildren were recruited and forcibly marched through the night to a training camp in Zambia; a Congregational church was closed by the government for aiding and abetting terrorists; Selous Scouts infiltrated a village in Matabeleland to catch terrorists, but only succeeded in killing two children; two tribesmen who had given information to the security forces were tortured in front of their village by guerrilla leaders as an example; four land mines were laid under dirt roads by guerrillas who had carried them on their backs from Zambia; one political activist was placed under house arrest in Harari township; and three terrorists were hanged for their crimes in Salisbury Central Prison.

# CHAPTER SIX

# HOW TO BE CHRISTIAN
# WITHOUT BEING RELIGIOUS

I managed to avoid Craig Hardy for a whole year after that. He ignored me, I ignored him, and I rode home every day avoiding Bianca too. But in January of my sixth form year (how had I managed to get through 'O' Levels in such heartbreak?), on the first day back at school, there was Craig Hardy, fifth former, waiting for me at the entrance to the lighting room. I was on my way to Fizz & Cum (Physics and Chemistry). I had no retreat. I ducked past him, but a hairy arm blocked my way through the narrow passage.

"Forget her, Paul," he said. "She's a Jesus freak."

It was his act of penance, though why he should back down, I didn't know. I presented my hand, suspecting a trick, but he shook it firmly.

"A Jesus freak?"

He nodded sadly. We all knew what Jesus freaks were. One by one, comrades at our school had fallen under this spell, turning sanctimonious, clutching Bibles to their chests to read at break time, preaching at us with clichés about being 'saved', or 'born again', or 'baptised in the spirit'. With Roosevelt Jesus freaks, Hardy had often warned us, you were wasting your time trying to get into their pants: they were all virgins. And worse, once they got hold of you, they would brainwash you until you'd become a virgin yourself.

It took all my powers, all my prayers to the goddesses of antiquity, to summon up the courage to sidle next to her, dismount, and smile. "Hello, Bianca."

"Well, well, well, if it isn't Paw-Paw Cavedaschi."

We were old friends, apparently, if I was to judge by her demeanour. "C… Can I walk you home?"

"Please do, Monsieur Cavedaschi. After all these years, I still have no idea where my house is."

I took that as a yes, and she offered no resistance to my mooning along by her side. But though I was six inches from her right elbow, the ironic distance I measured was galactic. Time had healed none of the wounds I had been nursing in my heart, and none of the speeches I had rehearsed for the last year offered themselves up as introductory ice-breakers.

Nothing had happened between us – no school dance, no kiss, no hand clenching mine. I could not even tell her how many strokes I had received from Mr Schweppes for taking her outside in the bushes. Our past – my careful construction of love – had been obliterated. And she didn't look any more religious than she had before. Nevertheless, I plunged on.

"Craig Hardy tells me you have become… you are… a Kuk… Christian, a… Jah… Jesus freak."

Her cheeks reddened and I saw a chink of another Bianca. But only for a second.

"Paw-Paw Cavedachi, you are *soooo* ignorant. Do you even know what a Jesus freak is?"

I took up the challenge. "Tell me."

She rolled her eyes up at the gnarled jacaranda branch above. "Why don't you come to the Round-Up?"

"The Round-Up?"

"At Eastridge School. Saturday morning, 10 a.m."

I walked with her in silence, listening to the ticking wheels of my bicycle and the swish of her dress, the snapping jacarandas and the breathing of Africa around us. It was all suddenly glorious. I tripped beside her all the way up Moon Crescent and stopped at her gate. As she stepped through, she turned and smiled (not at me, of course, but at the SLOW CHILDREN road sign behind me), slammed the gate shut, called the horse-sized Labradors to heel as they lunged at her in greeting ("Pasha! Glubb!"), and then waved goodbye to the SLOW CHILDREN.

★　★　★

Eastridge School, at the foot of Hillside hill, was a typical government primary school: a cluster of brick buildings and large playing fields, its main feature an ugly hall with wide corridors. At the far end of the soccer field, under the *msasa* trees, I picked out the blonde hair of my beloved amidst a clump of schoolboys and -girls. But before I could make my way towards her, a hand stretched out to me at the gate.

"Carter."

"Paul Williams."

The handshake belonged to a sideburned man with toothy smile, bell-bottom jeans with flowers embroidered on the flairs, unusually long hair, piercing eyes and an American accent. "Walk with me."

He was an American. Now I was really done for.

Did I mention the infatuation I had with America – not the real America, or the Americans inchered in Vietnam, but the America of my childhood, Archie's Riverdale, Batman's Gotham City, Superman's Metropolis, *I Dream of Jeannie's* Cocoa Beach? Enid Blyton's England had long been supplanted by Hollywood's Amerika-ka-ka. In this I was not alone. Our society, both black and white, worshipped this plastic paradise. Most of our TV shows were American. And on these shows, black and white people lived together in complete harmony; ordinary people had large cars and houses; boys and girls mixed freely at school and after school, and wore jeans and sneakers, and caps backwards on their heads.

He didn't ask me what I was doing here, but simply ushered this lost sheep towards the herd. He was, I took it, the preacher man with the red Ford Mustang with the Massachusetts license plates, and this was his doughy-skinned wife saying "You're welcome" at everything people said to her.

"Sit. Sit. Here's a chorus sheet."

A line of bad guitarists strummed out-of-tune Gallo Aces and Yamaha nylon stringers, and the colourful crew sang along. I mimed the words and followed on the sheet, which was labelled 'Choruses'.

> *Boys: It only takes a spark to get a fire going –*
> *Girls (including Bianca): going –*
> *Boys: And soon all those around will be warmed by its glowing –*
> *Girls (including Bianca): glowing –*
> *All: That's how it is with God's love once you've experienced it*

*Boys: It's fresh like spring*
*Girls (not Bianca this time: she has noticed me, and red-faced, looks down):*
*You want to sing*
*All: You want to pass (pronounced American-style – 'ass' not 'arse') it on.*

Leading them was a blonde, Hawaiian-shirted boy who also shook my hand and announced himself as Luke Pennefather. After the 'choruses' (what happened to the verses?), we sat cross-legged in a circle in the shade, picked grass stems to suck, and listened to the American with the sideburns and the accent from heaven.

"I'm looking for twelve disciples. Only twelve."

He peered around at the circle of boys and girls. Across from me, the blond brother and blonde sister sat cross-legged. She smiled at a point geometrically central to the circle.

"God is calling you today. Can you hear him? Don't turn away from His voice. That small voice you hear inside your soul, in your heart, is God's voice."

And blow me down if I couldn't hear that voice calling. Granted, it was a metaphorical voice, did not speak in English, or even in words, but it was loud and insistent and emanated from the focal point of all the hot radial energy of that circle. It sprang from the tuft of Durban shade grass where Bianca smiled so intently; it spoke from the spot Luke Pennefather was thumbing on the black cover of his Scofield Reference King James Version Bible. I had always thought that God spoke in a deep masculine voice from the sky, but no: it rose from the laps of all those cross-legged Roosevelt girls in bright dresses; it vibrated from the minor chords of those Yamaha strings; it called from those white cumulo-nimbus clouds puffing up miles into the blue sky behind, ready to burst.

We are in a river, the preacher said, and all of us are going with the flow, downstream, towards a waterfall. The Christian, however, has to swim upstream against the current. Is it *harrrd*? You can bet your doggone stitched britches it's *harrrd*. It's darn well-near *impassable*. But underneath are the Everlasting Arms. Jesus has washed us clean of all sin. If we wear His garment, God will not let us drown.

"Let us pray." With all other eyes closed, all heads bowed, and her hair swinging into a fringe across her brow, I peeped at her gaping dress to see a talcum powdered bra chafing against white flesh, then, guilty as hell, closed my eyes tightly.

"Who will heed my call, says the Lord? Ask and you shall receive. Seek and ye shall find. Knock and the door will be opened unto you. Repent. Say I am a sinner; raise your hand so I can pray for you. Accept the Lord Jesus into your heart."

I didn't raise my hand. No one else did either – they were already saved, of course. They were all Jesus freaks, I realised in alarm, and the sermon was meant for me. It was all a setup. But oddly, I didn't want to escape. In fact, I couldn't think of one reason not to become a Jesus freak on that summer afternoon, when the bees buzzed and the sky thundered and the girl-smell of her perfume and the urgency of her desire to have me saved like her crashed onto me like salty waves. My walls of Jericho, Carter later told me, were crumbling.

My eyes were supposed to be closed, but I peeped through eyelashes to see God talking. I know you are not supposed to, and I felt that I was going to unmask the Wizard of Oz and find out that he was a puny man with a megaphone. But the voice did not come from the preacher at all. He was talking, yes, but his voice was coincidental. The real voice was in my blood, urging me to give in to its call. What was this booming earthquake in my soul? Who could not heed its command? I had been waiting for this voice, it seemed, my whole life. I wanted to be saved. I wanted to be edged over the Victoria Falls, wanted to abandon myself against reason to the Voice, and give this petty, trivial, lost self to whatever was outside. The voice hinted at something real, something that existed just beyond this mean, grey world.

"It may be too late when you are called to judgement and He says, 'I never knew you.'"

I tried to hold myself back, but the wishes – prayers – of the kids in this group, the sheer force of this preacher, and of course the desire of Bianca to have me here, pushed me over the edge. OK, OK. Yes, Lord, I said (not aloud, of course). I want to be saved.

"Thank you, God. Thank you, Lord."

I held tightly to the grass on both sides of me, preparing myself for whatever was to happen when you are saved. But nothing happened. I felt nothing, only relief at having given in. Maybe that is what 'saved' meant – a big relief.

It was obvious, too, that this preacher could read my thoughts. He knew what I had done. But I peeped out of the blurred bars of my eyelashes to see another hand going up. A boy across from me had heeded the call, and his hand had gone up of its own accord, it seemed, like a wisp of smoke spiralling into the sky.

"Amen."

Luke stood over the boy who had raised his hand, and placed his hands over the boy's head, as if shielding him from the bright sun. The American preacher raised his hands to the sky.

"The angels are rejoicing in heaven for you, Brian. Can you hear them?"

I heard crows cackling on top of the corrugated iron roof, the roof itself ticking in the sun, and the wind brushing the leaves of the trees above us. But Brian was hearing angels.

Then it was all over. Legs uncrossed and backs stretched and the final strumming of major chords roused us from our trance.

"So, Paul." The preacher clapped a hand on my back. "What do you think of our little gathering?"

I knew what he was asking me. Had I acknowledged I was a sinner, repented of my sin and accepted the Lord Jesus Christ as my Personal Lord and Savior (spelled without the 'u')? I hadn't done any of that, but I had felt the heavy presence of God in the air like a band of high-pressure air, the Inter-Tropical Convergence Zone pressing on me. This God knew my thoughts, knew all about me, could see right through me. He or She or It was everywhere, in all times, knew everything, and could do anything. There was a world beyond this one, one packed with angels rejoicing, devils dragging souls down to hell, and the glow of this God's presence was a luminous lining behind the clouds, behind my thoughts, in the veins of every leaf on every tree. But I still felt nothing. Shouldn't I be leaping and dancing and saying hallelujah?

"What church is this, Reverend?"

The preacher squeezed my shoulder. "This is not a church, Paul. Church is the hardened artery, the dead form of a living God, and religion is the hard husk of the Pharisees' laws. No, this is living Christianity. We don't have a church, Paul. We *are* the Church. This is the real thing. And we're happy you are visiting us. Please feel free to join in our games and our singing."

"Thank you, Reverend."

"Steve. Call me Steve."

Soccer was the designated game for boys. Rounders was for the girls. But Bianca, perversely, tomboyishly, played soccer. She jostled Luke for the ball and took possession. Luke then demarcated the pitch and placed his flip-flops for a goal. Bianca hopped on one leg while she took off hers, placed them six feet apart, and stood between them, spitting on her hands and bouncing on her haunches, challenging anyone who dared to get the ball past her.

This is when it hit me. A tornado spun through me and propelled me into a frenetic energy that I had never known. I was never a good soccer player, but today I managed to wrestle the ball from innocent-looking Christians and dribble it towards her. She pulled blonde strands out of her eyes, danced left and right as I teased the ball with my left foot, right foot, and dribbled forward, back, with a dexterity I didn't know I had.

"Come on, Cavedaschi," she cooed, and I slammed the ball at the left goal post. She dived and embraced it as it hit the ground, and in loving mockery, kissed it. "Gotcha, my beauty."

I didn't get another chance. She threw the ball out to her brother in a hefty move that left her hair whirling and my heart spinning. I tried to tackle him, but he bulldozed past me, and switched feet so rapidly that I tripped and fell into the mud. I caught sight of her burying a ponytail into a sniggering mouth as I sat up. Luke slammed the ball into the goal, and then strode back to pull me up.

"No hard feelings."

"No hard feelings."

By the end of the game, I was weaving in and out, passing, tackling, sweating and enjoying myself. She was omnipresent, watching from her vantage point as goalie, and I was always aware of her eyes, her crouching stance as she waited for my next attack. But after fifteen minutes, Steve Carter, the referee, blew his plastic whistle and, after a short prayer where he asked God to bless us and go with us and keep us safe until next weekend's Round-Up, dispersed the gathering and sent us home.

Bianca retrieved one of her flip-flops (we called them slip-slops – those blue BATA plastic moulds we all wore since childhood as standard foot garb), but before she could reach the other, I dived on it in mock replay of her goal-saving skills, and hugged it to myself. "Gotcha, my beauty." I kissed the imprint of her toes in the mud-scored grooves, and when she lunged at me, held it high above her, dancing above her shrieks. She grabbed at it, fell, and we tumbled into a tangle of arms and legs. "Give, give, give," she said. I held the blue rubber oval out of reach so she had to tickle me to get it.

"Sis," called her brother from the edge of the field. "We have to go."

A purple thunderstorm loomed in the west – a real one, not the one in my heart. I surrendered the slop, went with her to the bicycle shed, and we walked our bikes down a road smelling of the promise of heavy rain. Birds flew frantically past us over high treetops as the bicycle wheels ticked in time with each other. Her brother wheeled his bike next to the boy who had become a Christian.

Cars were few and the roads were deserted, thanks to sanctions and pass laws. There was no litter, either – everything was used and used again, nothing was thrown away. Behind us a group of three walking virgins linked arms and in step marched along singing, "A hat, a coat, an umb-a-rella, a hat, a coat, an um-ba-rella," then switched to ABBA's 'Mamma Mia': "Here we go again; how can I forget you…", then collapsed onto each other in giggling heaps.

This is it, I thought. I am in the centre of my life, in the centre of the universe. The presence behind, around, in me was a whispering voice, nudging me with an invisible finger. You are my chosen son, in whom I am well pleased. So this is what it felt like to be saved. It was a biological event, as if someone had stirred up the chemicals in my brain, and pumped pheromones into my pulsing veins.

"Are you Swiss?" I asked her. "You're so blonde."

"Swiss?"

"Why do Swiss cows wear bells?"

"I don't know."

"Because their horns don't work."

She pinched my arm. "I'll take that as a compliment."

We stopped at the junction of Hillside and Helm Avenue. The marching girls turned right, waved goodbye, and the other stragglers climbed straight up the hill. We veered left toward the railway line. This was where we had to part. Luke waited for us further up the road, fortunately still in earnest conversation with the new convert, gesticulating with his hands to emphasise the importance of the new path his convert was to lead. But Bianca was not ready to let me go. She held the handlebars of my bike and steered me backwards against the light post.

"What colour are your eyes?" she asked.

"What colour are yours?"

"Muddy grey." We locked eyes and I stared into her soul. I saw fairy kingdoms; I saw dancing goddesses; I saw reflections of a brown-haired, gawky teenager with pimples and crew-cut hair.

"Blue. Your eyes are blue. What about your hands?"

"They're white."

"Silly." She held them, feeling their texture. I had to hold my bike between my legs so it would not fall. "I mean, are they cold or hot?"

"Yours are cold, cold, cold, like ice."

"Cold hands, warm heart," she said. I held hers tightly, ostensibly to clinically gauge her temperature, but savouring the texture of her slim fingers and the nails that had been trimmed neat and close like a boy's.

"I would rather you were hot or cold," she said. "If you are lukewarm, I will spew you out of my mouth."

"Sis?" Her brother beckoned impatiently, against a background of blue-black cumulonimbus towering above us. She did not flinch, her eyes locked onto mine, her hands clamped onto my baby fingers.

"When will I see you again?" I stuttered.

"Next weekend, you bozo, at the Round-Up."

"Of course, of course."

The rain broke while I was coasting down the hill into the dark, warm wind. Lightning crackled above me and Thor hammered at the glass prison of the sky dome. This is what my life was for, I thought. This, this, this.

★ ★ ★

We saw the planes fly over, but we didn't know what they had been doing. A few boys out in the street cheered as the two Hawker Hunters ripped through the sky, leaving shit-coloured trails behind them.

Rhodesian Intelligence had become aware of a main ZANLA base in Mozambique. Nyadzonya Base housed as many as five thousand ZANLA guerrillas/insurgents/terrorists/gooks/freedom fighters, a treasure chest for the digging Intelligence pirates. So the Rhodesian forces (RLI, SAS, Selous Scouts et al) planned their attack. Aerial surveys provided maps of the area, captured terrs gave information about where everything was, and what it was, and we were ready.

It was called a 'flying column': eighty-five black and white soldiers, dressed in FRELIMO uniforms and carrying 20 mm aircraft cannons, medium and light machine guns, and a captured Soviet 12.7 mm heavy machine gun, would drive ten Unimogs and four Ferret armoured cars disguised as FRELIMO vehicles. FRELIMO (Frente de Libertação de Moçambique, or the Liberation Front of Mozambique) was the political party ruling Mozambique.

We knew (well, the Rhodesian Central Intelligence Organisation knew) that the guerrillas mustered for parade at 08h00 every morning, so they were to attack ten minutes later. On August 9, at midnight, the 'flying column' crossed the Mozambique border, passing all the sleeping/deserted/saluting FRELIMO guards on the way. The column bivvied at the Pungwe River and moved into the camp at 08h00. The six ZANLA soldiers on guard duty dutifully waved the fake FRELIMO convoy into the compound. The white Rhodesians, wearing ski masks to look black, reportedly gasped in amazement at what they saw as they surrounded the parade ground with their vehicles. Here was the largest concentration of bloody gooks they had ever seen, and for the Guinness Record book, the largest concentration of enemy insurgents any Rhodesian would ever see throughout the entire war – approximately four thousand.

"*Zimbabwe tatona*," shouted one of the disguised Rhodesian soldiers. "Zimbabwe is liberated!" The crowd began cheering, converging on the vehicles, and singing. More guerrillas streamed onto the parade square, and squeezed around the vehicles.

Then the Rhodesians opened fire. The 81 mm mortar section fired into the crowd at its maximum rate, machine guns tak-takked, until all were killed. One hundred and fifty of those who fled faced death from the machine guns on the Ferret armoured cars which had blocked the escape route, and another two hundred drowned in the river trying to escape. Rhodesian soldiers received minor gunshot wounds. After forty-five minutes, the Rhodesians withdrew, blew up the Pungwe bridge behind them, and fled.

On their way home, they got lost and were directed by a friendly FRELIMO soldier on a football field. All looked good for the Rhodesians until two of the vehicles stalled and the FRELIMO soldier noticed a white man in the back of one of them. Their cover blown, the Rhodesians had to fight their way out, killing more people and calling on the Hawker Hunter jets to escort them back home safely. Thus began the pre-emptive strikes, in which Rhodesia would invade neighbouring countries and destroy what they said were terrorist bases.

All I can think of now is the last few minutes of those thousands killed. "What? We are finally free? Zimbabwe is liberated?" Were those their thoughts, those who had fled, or had actively joined the liberation struggle, or who had been taken at gunpoint to fight for the terrorists? Now the nightmare is over. Zimbabwe is ours. Only one more river to cross, and we're home. We've reached the Promised Land. Is that what they thought as the bullets ripped through them, and they saw their illusions shattering around them? It's the Rhodesians, others must have screamed, and some fired back. Some still pushed forward, singing, We're free, we're free, we're free at last.

★  ★  ★

By Monday morning, the spell had still not worn off. My pulse was fast, my senses were strong, my mind a joyful flowing river. Was this the God of Abraham pulsing through me, the God who flooded the world, who parted the Red Sea, who sent His only begotten Son to die for me on a tree?

In my Bianca-drenched euphoria, I did not know any better. I picked out the tattered Bible from my parents' bookshelf and began to read from page one. 'In the beginning, God created the heavens and the earth'. According to Steve, this Bible was supposed to speak to me, or rather, God was somehow supposed to speak through the Bible. "Speak to me, Lord." I flipped the pages to the Song of Solomon, closed my eyes and placed a finger in the middle of the page. "A bundle of myrrh is my well-beloved unto me," I read aloud. "He shall lie all night betwixt my breasts."

I needed some help here. And who better to turn to than Luke Pennefather

himself? He was a prefect, but he was also a Christian brother. At school, during break, I intercepted this purple-jacketed prefect as he strode importantly
across the quad.

"Paul? No, no. That's not a real Bible – it has the Apocrypha in it. God won't
speak through that. Use this, my old King James. See here, where I've marked
passages from Bible study. Start there. I've earmarked it. Psalm 22. John 3:16.
Romans 12."

The gleam in his eye told me that he was also basking in this huge presence,
that we were brothers, members of a secret society, and together we comprised
the Bride of Christ, which meant that I was now wedded to his sister. So through
break time, under the shade of a *msasa* tree, I read the words he had underlined
for me. "God so loved the world that he gave His only begotten son... I look
up to the hills, from whence cometh my help... Though we see through a glass
darkly, one day we shall see face to face..."

And now for Bianca herself. We met at one-fifteen at the pedestrian lights, as
if prearranged. I was a new person; she could not ignore me now. And Praise the
Lord (I had to get used to this new terminology), she didn't. She welcomed me
warmly, with a smile. She talked breezily of her morning at Roosevelt, how they
had had a hem check today, where the dress mustn't show more than three inches
above the knee, see; and I looked scientifically. She got away with wearing earrings
today and no prefects noticed, and she was never going to wear the regulation
green underwear they were supposed to have. She didn't own any of that stuff.

She was self-assured, smug about her position at the centre of the universe,
but was no longer playing a game with me. I had broken the code.

"Why didn't you tell me?"

"Tell you what?"

"About... Jesus." The word 'Jesus' was difficult to say. It had been worn as
smooth as the word 'fuck' by my friends at school ("Jesus Christ, it's hot in
here! Christ, she's gorgeous! Jesus-fucking-Christ!"), and to use it non-ironically
seemed childish. Her reply was hidden in the strands of blonde hair that covered
her red face.

"To tell the truth, I was... I was embarrassed. I know the Lord says that whoever denies him, He will deny on that last day of judgement, saying 'I never

knew thee.' I'm awful. Will you forgive me?"

I stroked the hairs on her arm. "Yes."

Her breasts squished against me, her arms pressed in the small of my back, her lips moistened my neck, her leg wrapped around my leg, and the green buttons of her dress dug hard into my chest.

The church was called Hillside Non-Denominational Fellowship, and met every Sunday in the lounge of the Pastor's home. He drove his red Ford Mustang, with the Massachusetts license plates, a sticker adorning the chromed bumper – 'Wise Men Still Seek Him' – and his wife served us what she called 'subs' with a sweet, welcoming smile. The youth group met on Friday nights, while Wednesday night was Bible study. Every break time, we boys met to pray, under the leadership of prefect Luke Pennefather. At every opportunity we linked arms to pray and, when the Roosevelt girls joined us on Wednesday afternoons, held hands to supplicate and give thanks and further forge our spiritual ties to Our Heavenly Father. The bubble of joy inside me (which John called the Holy Spirit) grew until I was swimming in what could only be described as ecstasy (a chemical mixture of love, joy, desire and intoxication). And every meeting, she was there to smile and pray and touch (hands only).

"Luap," she said, one day. "Your name is Luap Smailliw. And so I'm going to call you Smiley, a better name than Cavedaschi, for sure."

'Acnaib Rehtafennep' didn't quite have the same ring to it, so I stuck to calling her Bianca. However, my new name meant a lot. I was no longer the Saul who persecuted Christians but the Paul who fell off his horse at the voice of God. I was Smiley the Jesus freak, not the rotten paw-paw dripping with carnal desire. I was Martin Luther breaking away from the Mystery Babylon Religion. I was justified by faith, not works. At every meeting, we would sing 'choruses', sit in a circle and pray for each other, we brothers and sisters in the Lord. The Reverend Steve would speak and God would thunder through him. Afterwards we would 'fellowship together', which meant we would flirt casually, using metaphor and innuendo to disguise our burning attractions – well, speaking for myself – my burning attraction to this Goddess who was now allowing me to talk to, touch, admire, covet and pray over her.

"I want twelve," Steve reminded us (the "I" being God). This time I put up my hand when he made the 'altar call' and was gratified to see Bianca clasp her sister Alison's paw and thank the Lord. I had to go public; it was only fair. "Hallelujah," murmured Luke, who after the meeting prayed over me with hands protecting me from Satan's slings and arrows. "Thank you for Thy sheep, Father, which hath returned to the fold."

The debate about which language God spoke (was it Arabic as the Muslims insisted, or Latin or Greek or Aramaic?) was over. God spoke, I discovered, in King James English, and I soon learned to address Him and others in the holy language of the Book too.

"The angels are rejoicing in heaven," said Steve. "Can'st thou hear'st them?"

I could this time. I could hear them, all of them, from Gabriel down, in the sweet breathy voice of Bianca's laugh. I could feel their presence in every cell of my body.

Steve recited a verse, which was mine to keep. "Fight the good fight of faith, lay hold on eternal life, whereunto thou art also called, and hast professed a good profession before many witnesses." I didn't know what it meant, but I suspected it was a dig at me for not putting my hand up the first time.

You are going to do great things, my son. Great things. God has recruited you to fight in His army. He has chosen you to be one of The Twelve. The Twelve, I learned, was one of God's instruments of manifest destiny, an idea Steve propounded. God chose certain people to fulfil His Will, sometimes groups of people, sometimes races of people, like the Jews, like the Americans, like the... wait for it... Rhodesians. Steve had been told in a dream that he was to go to Rhodesia to train twelve young people who would have a special role to play in God's unfolding plan to hold back the forces of Satan until the End Times.

So now I was one of the Chosen Twelve: Luke Pennefather, Philip Colquhoun, Frances Johnson, Wendy Starr Jameson, Alison Burnett, Desi Harris, Richard Willoughby, etc etc... and last but not least, Bianca herself.

But it was a serious business. The devil was seeking whom he might devour, so we had to keep a sharp lookout. It was all a conspiracy, apparently – ten men, the Illuminati – ruled the world under Satan's guidance, among them the Anti-Christ Kissinger, Sadat, U Thant, the European Union and the Oppenheimers. It was all there in Revelations for those who had the eyes to see. And what made us swell with pride was that Rhodesia was the fulcrum on which the world turned.

★ ★ ★

In the seventies, most Protestant churches, like most other institutions, were segregated. Far from being a transcendent, God-centred force outside space, time and history, the Rhodesian church was a superstructure that grew upon the cultural bases of racism, xenophobia and myopia. Of course I was not to know this, but the church had religiously reflected its colonial culture since its introduction into the Dark Continent in the 17th century. Even before mission stations, chapels had been built on top of slave-holding stations. As Ngugi wa Thiong'o once said: "The missionaries asked us to close our eyes and pray, and when we opened them, our land was gone."

So God was a white, male Rhodesian with a Rhodesian accent – no, wait, didn't He have an American accent? I am not sure what the black churches did with this. Most of them, I think, preached endurance and denial of this unjust world in the hope of a better one to come. Come to think of it, Christianity lent itself more easily to the dispossessed. After all, rich white people can't squeeze through the eyes of needles. The poor are blessed, not the rich, and if you wanted to be a Christian, surely you were meant to sell everything you possessed and give it to the poor? But of course we had different Bibles to our black brethren. Our Bible preached American concepts of individual empowerment and abundant enrichment. Our Bible told us that if we had enough faith, we could move mountains.

The Catholics were an entirely different kettle of fish. They spearheaded the Justice and Peace Commission to dig up the dirt (I mean, investigate human rights abuses) in Rhodesia. Bishop Donal Lamont, the leader of the JPC, insisted that the church should assist the liberation forces in their struggle for equality and human rights for all. Although priests and nuns should be non-violent and peaceful, they should not collaborate with an oppressive regime which tortured and murdered its own people. In 1976, the Rhodesian government arrested, imprisoned and then deported Donal because of his refusal to report 'terrorists' who had paid him a visit on his mission. On 11 August that year, Lamont wrote an open letter to Ian Smith:

*In a state which claims to be democratic, people are restricted or imprisoned without trial, tortured or tried in camera, put to death by secret hanging, and justification for all this barbarity is sought by you in the name of Christianity and of Western Civilisation and for what you call the 'maintaining of Rhodesian standards'... No wonder the oppressed people, made marginal to society in their own country, have welcomed and continue to welcome those they call freedom fighters, and whom you call terrorists... If intensification of racial hatred, widespread urban guerrilla activity, increased destruction of property and fearful loss of life are to be avoided, if the whole of the subcontinent of Africa is not to be engulfed in a cruel war, you must without delay change your present tragic course of action.*

★ ★ ★

"What are the desires of your heart? The Psalmist tells us that we can have them. Do you believe that? Let's read."

Steve had been to Bible School in New Jersey and when he preached wore a huge football sweater with the letters NE (North-Eastern) sewn on it in purple. This was one of the Americanisms we loved about him. We also loved the word 'sweater' – better than a namby-pamby 'pullover' or 'cardigan' or 'jersey'. From now on I would wear sweaters. Steve also caressed a leather-bound Bible with his name embossed in gold lettering on the front. But it was his accent that got to us most of all. He took our ordinary, flattened Rhodesian pronunciation and imbued it with a magic and power of the New World that lit up our path to enlightenment. We also loved the way he preached from his armchair in the lounge of his humble Hillside Gardens flat, while we squatted on the floor at his feet.

"Delight thyself also in the Lord, Psalm 37, verse 4 reads, and He shall give thee the desires of thy heart."

Here, he would turn to his pale American wife, the proverbial ideal wife, who sat demurely on a kitchen chair by the door, her eyes fixed on him in radiant heavenly transport, her hands placed in her lap. "God has the person for you. You're each a half created for another half. Don't go trying to get the wrong half. God will bring you together."

"How do we know which is our other half?" asked Allison. "I thought it said in the Bible that God helps those who help themselves." The congregation, all eleven of us, sniggered.

"He will let you know in His own time. Delight in the Lord and he will give you the desires of your heart. It means, don't even think about it. He'll take care of it all."

After the meeting, his wife served tea and what she called cookies, which were in reality undercooked doughy biscuits with too much sugar and too many gooey chunks of Charhons chocolate. While we chewed, Steve announced our first mission.

"Your task this week is to preach the Good News to your friends at school. Think of someone, pray for them, then approach them and share with them God's word."

The only person I could think of sharing anything with was Craig Hardy but it was a preposterous idea, so instead I picked a spotty, glass-eyed boy whose nickname at school was 'Hedgehog', and pinned him down at Monday break time to tell him of the Four Spiritual Laws. He listened politely and then told me that he was Jewish.

I had done my duty, but I knew this was a cop-out. God insisted that I had to witness to Craig Hardy. Yes, Smiley, you have to stop being a coward and face up to your past. What will happen when you are in heaven, and he calls up from hell, remonstrating, "Why didn't you tell me about Jesus?" So, after school, I knocked on the lighting room door. And there was Craig.

"Hey, Wily Willy, how's it hanging?"

"I'm a Jesus freak."

"Fuck right off." He punched me in the guts. "You dog, Williams. Is that your ploy to get girls now?"

"No, no." I tried to explain. This was true conversion. I had found the secret to the universe. I had been chosen. I had been blind, but now I saw. I was Born Again. Saved.

"You? A Jesus freak?"

"I'd like to invite you to our fellowship, Hillside fellowship. On Saturday we have a Round-Up. Would you like to read this pamphlet telling you about the Four Spiritual Laws?"

"Fuck off."

I read the Bible every day during what was called a Quiet Time to let God speak to me. He didn't speak with a literal voice, as He did in the old days, but through the Bible, that hodgepodge of letters and histories which had been amended, translated, added to and taken away from. In total disregard for how the meaning of words changed over the centuries, we knew that what had been written thousands of years ago was how God spoke to us.

You had to take the Bible out of its historical context in order for God to speak. It was like a horoscope. You randomly placed your finger in the pages of the Bible, and let the Holy Spirit guide you. Or you could read a chapter of Solomon's Proverbs every day. So if today was the 31st, you had to read Proverbs 31, and God would tell you what you needed to know for that day. Like so:

> *When one finds a worthy wife, her value is far beyond pearls.*
> *Her husband, entrusting his heart to her, has an unfailing prize.*
> *She brings him good, and not evil, all the days of her life.*

At home I had more success in 'witnessing', not in converting anyone, but in airing my views. As good Catholics, my parents were concerned about Hillside Non-Denominational Fellowship. Wasn't it a mortal sin to reject the Holy Church and her teachings for some cultish Protestant heresy?

"But don't you see, the Catholics have got it all wrong," my arrogant teenage whine insisted. "You can't use works to get to heaven – they are filthy rags before God. It's all in the Bible, if you only trouble yourselves to look. Romans 5 plainly states that we are justified by faith, not by works. But the Catholics won't let you read the Bible for yourself."

"Religion," my father replied, "is the best business in town, biggest lie in history."

"But this is not religion. The Bible says…"

My father turned out to be a bigger sceptic than I thought. His good Catholic upbringing apparently had turned him away from the One True Church and he was bitter about all forms of religious experience. "Well, if it keeps you out of trouble. But don't come home any more spouting that religious claptrap to me."

On Friday, we shared our missionary attempts to 'witness'. I had to admit failure, as did most. Luke had managed to get the Head Boy to accept a copy of the Four Spiritual Laws, but had to retrieve it from the rubbish bin afterwards. Some of us had been mocked. Like me, Clive Harris had also been punched in the guts. To my surprise, Steve regarded failure as OK, and even considered it to be a good thing. If we suffered hardship for Christ's sake, apparently, then it was called persecution, and we were closer to God for it. So I didn't feel too bad about not converting Craig Hardy.

Our next task had been to bring all our rock records to the meeting. Puzzled, I thought we were going to have a dance party, but that thought soon withered, as Steve called them vinyl relics of our dark past. You don't put new wine into old bottles, he said, do you? Of course not. Lucifer is the god of Rock 'n Roll, he said, and he uses music to destroy the youth of today.

Luke brought *Sweet Fanny Adams*, a heavy metal (or the seventies equivalent) album by the British group, The Sweet, dressed in drag on the cover. I brought Deep Purple's *Machine Head*, and Bianca brought *Slade's Greatest Hits*, which she swore contained subliminal messages if played backwards. Her favourite Slade song, 'My friend Stan', actually meant, if you listened closely, 'My friend Satan'.

"Luke wanted me to bring my ABBA records too," she said wistfully. "But I can't believe they are the work of Satan, even if they give money to the terrorists."

We spent the evening in Steve's kitchen, melting the records over baking pots, and turning them into flowerpots and vases. We chanted "Get thee behind me, Satan," as each record melted.

★ ★ ★

One Sunday a greasy photocopy (or Photostat, as we called it then) was passed around a tongue-clicking, head-shaking congregation before the sermon. The note, purported to have been found on a 'dead terrorist', revealed the enemy's poisonous ideas and his plans if he were ever to come to power.

*MANIFESTO*

*1) As everything shall belong to the state,* ZANU *will provide free transport, free medical treatments and houses.*

*2) All children from the age of seven shall undergo military training as well as the principles of Socialism.*

*3) ZANU government shall be quite aware of people who have lived luxurious lives and acquired money, expensive furniture, houses, shops and cars at the expense of the suffering masses of Zimbabwe. ZANU shall demand a fully detailed explanation of them.*

*4) All land belongs to the people. ZANU will not tolerate any private land owner-ship, regardless of race, colour or creed. ZANU shall introduce mass collective farming, and every son and daughter of Zimbabwe shall compulsorily be called upon to work in such fields.*

*5) ZANU regards the church as the imperialistic instrument of colonialism and assuch all churches will be turned into barracks, concentration camps and dancing halls. Furthermore, all those associated with churches will be brought before a military tribunal.*

> *Long Live ZANU!*
> *Long live ZANLA!*
> Pamberi ne Socialism!
> Pasi ne Capitalism!

What concerned Steve the most was the future of the church if these Marxist Communist Terrorists were ever to take over the country. God Forbid! Would we be persecuted like those in Communist China? Would we have to go underground? Would some even have to die for their faith? And how prepared were we to die for our faith, Steve asked? How committed to God were we?

Craig Hardy owned a red 1969 Mini Cooper, though how he fitted into the car is still a mystery to me. His arrival was always announced by the engine coughing and spluttering into parking places at school, at the Gremlin Restaurant – and at Eastridge School. For my foolish attempt to bring him into the fold had, like his car, backfired. In the middle of a Round-Up, or Bible Study, or flirtatious soccer game, we would be interrupted by the fart of a Mini engine and the dust of a wheelie as Craig Hardy skidded into the parking lot.

Flash would go his telephoto-lensed camera as Bianca stretched up to spike a volleyball, or bent down to pick up the soccer ball, or hoisted up her dress to get at her handkerchief. Glint would go his rearview mirror, hiding the dark shadow of a fifth-former in the front windscreen. Only later did I understand the extent of his obsession, when he surrendered to me his spoils from those last years at school. His school cap was inscribed with her name: Bianca; Bianca; Bianca. The lighting room was splattered with her photos; her phone number was tattooed onto his wrist; his journal of Daily Sightings was fat with tiny writing, describing when and where he had seen her, what she was doing, and how much of her white flesh she had revealed to him that day. The photographs, as I rifle through them today, are greasy, faded, well thumbed, in different sizes – black and white, colour, unfocused, close-ups, long shots – and are all pictures of a plain blonde girl in her teens.

Here is one of her at the holiday Round-Up, leaning forward, eyes closed in prayer, her hands supplicating God, her blouse open at the front so that the photographer can feast on the white-capped breasts in the shadow of her dress. Her hair is golden, covering her face. She looks sixteen. Here is one of her walking with a large suitcase down a jacaranda avenue of purple bells. Again her face is covered with her hair, and she is striding fast so the photo is blurred, her arms and legs splayed in gestures of fear or haste. Here is another, of her sitting on what looks like a toilet – yes, 'Shanks' is written clearly on white porcelain – her dress pulled up, her face absorbed in a *Betty and Veronica* comic. The photo is framed by a bathroom window, and is obscured by out-of-focus hydrangea leaves, as if the photographer were crouching undetected outside. Here is one of her smiling at the camera. She is marching in a green and white uniform, with a mace, furry boots, pom-pom hat, in a line with five other similarly dressed girls. She looks fourteen. In the background, I see blurred cars, jacaranda trees in blossom, and the purple letters RF written on the side of a low white building.

Craig was the watcher, the voyeur, the outsider. I, on the other hand, in only a short few months, had been catapulted into the centre of Biancadom. I learned to play the guitar and was soon leading choruses, singing Alleluia and praying in public. I led the youth group, led the games, and gave short devotionals after each Round-Up.

Every school day, girls from Hillside Non-Denominational Fellowship (Wendy, Sue, Sharon, Debbie and Jennifer) would gather outside my front gate to ride to school with me, and we cycled together, chattering, telling jokes, praying, sharing what God had told us that morning in our quiet times. Here was my missing family. I was no longer an only child. It was a pity, I thought, that Bianca lived on the other side of the railway tracks (the good side), but I made sure I walked her home after school each day.

And Craig Hardy, if you are watching from your Mini, I want you to know something. I want to add as a postscript this Catch 22: these girls were now my sisters, and carnality in any form was forbidden. Verily, Verily I say unto you, Jesus had said, you cannot enter the kingdom of heaven unless you become 'as a child'. And of course, the only way to become 'as a child' was to obliterate your sexuality. With Steve's guidance, we reverted to our pre-sexual innocence. We became silly, childish, childlike pre-adolescents in sinful teenage bodies. Sex was the enemy, and with the voice of Serpent Satan creeping in, we had to be vigilant at all costs. The sins of the flesh had to be denied, purged and repressed.

Did it work? Not really. All night, my unconscious ate away at me, manufacturing erotic images, turning innocent encounters with sisters-in-Christ by day into lustful thoughts and violent deflowerings by night. I prayed hard in the morning for God to forgive my weakness. The spirit is willing, I pleaded, but the flesh is weak. And the voice of my friend Satan whispered to me, tempting me, mocking me, in Craig Hardy's voice: You're only here to get girls. You're not a Christian. You're a wolf in sheep's clothing. Get Thee behind me, Satan, I told him, I am purified by the Blood of the Lamb.

And the red Mini Cooper would not go away. It showed up at the most unexpected places: half hidden in willow trees at the end of Moon Crescent; at the pedestrian crossing, barring any passage for cyclists, forcing her to squeeze her breasts against the driver-side window to get past; or lying in wait at Clyde shops, in case we happened to meet there for an after-church ice cream treat.

★ ★ ★

And so it went: my sixth form years were spent in constant hope, in radiant company. I had left behind the dark days of the Bang Gang, the gawky adolescence of a squeaky voice and gangly legs, and moustached upper lip. Every Wednesday (Bible Study), Friday (The Twelve) and Sunday (church) was spent in ever-spiralling circles upwards. I grew intellectually, spiritually, emotionally. Steve assured us that as Christians, if we studied the Word of God and put Him first, we would know more than our teachers.

And it was true. In those years, Steve crammed into our heads much more than we learned at school. We soon felt we had surpassed our clumsy colleagues at Churchill and Roosevelt. I sailed through 'M' Levels and mock 'A' Levels without effort, and never wanted these school days to end. Our world was a hermetically sealed bubble of love, ecstasy (the heavenly kind), truth and extended childhood innocence.

But I knew it was coming to an end. I had kept the knowledge away from me for so long that when it happened, with the swiftness of a dark summer thunderstorm, I was taken completely off guard. My childhood ended with a letter in a brown envelope stamped in black – ON GOVERNMENT SERVICE – with my name and address unevenly typed in the cellophane window.

*111563N \ 156*
*NATIONAL SERVICE ACT 1972, NOTICE OF CALL-UP FOR PHASE I SERVICE*

*You are hereby notified in terms of section 10 of the National Service Act, 1972, that you are required to report to Llewellin Barracks at 0900 on 5th January 1977 for intake 156 for Phase I training.*

*NOTICE: Failure to report for your medical examination or Phase I training in terms of the above is an offence punishable by a maximum fine of $1000 or imprisonment for a period of two years or both.*

At once the voices began in my head, bringing back the fear that had plagued me since seeing 'inchered' soldiers in Vietnam and that I had skilfully suppressed in the last two years. You have to survive in the bush without food and water. You learn how to live on berries and plants. You cut off heads of enemy terrorists and use them to play soccer, with their dismembered limbs for goalposts.

Don't cut your hair before you go; they'll cut it even shorter if you do. Get as fit as you can; you have to run for days with large packs on your back. Don't take anything with you; they make you run with your suitcase up and down the parade square. Take everything you can; you'll need Kiwi polish to 'bone' your boots, you'll need your own sheets and toothbrush and razor, because the issued items are for inspection only. Don't volunteer for anything; if you say you play the piano, they'll make you carry a piano around. Volunteer for everything; it shows you're willing and you won't get picked on. It's good for you, it'll make a man of you; it'll fuck you up for life, ruin your career. Don't bother trying to get fit before you go. You mustn't stand out. They want you to act as a team. And get a haircut, man. You can't waltz in there looking like a hippie…

But then the voice of God spoke to me again, calming me, reassuring me that it was all right: here is my only begotten Son, in whom I am well pleased. And the hymn we used to sing at Churchill in morning assembly came back to me. The words were written by hand on a rolling paper screen on either side of the stage: 'Fight the good fight with all Thy might. Christ is Thy strength and Christ Thy right…'

★ ★ ★

How was the war going, anyway? Fine, said the media. Can't complain. In fact, we're coping just fine with the new anti-terrorist strategy called COIN (Counter Insurgency Operations). Having removed the water and fish from the terrorist, we can now pick him off as he traverses the countryside, like a flea off a hairless dog. Here's how it works. The Army cross-grains the countryside looking for tracks. They ambush infiltration routes, they use Fire Force (a 911 service using helicopters, back-up vehicles and support troops). It is an impressive tool. But we don't stop there. SAS cross the border to find incoming groups and supplies, while the new and highly secret Selous Scouts begin to develop the art of pseudo-warfare, using disguises to penetrate ZANLA groups and eliminate them or to guide Fire Force to them. So the buggers have nowhere to turn, even in their own bases.

★ ★ ★

7 Moon Crescent, Greendale, Salisbury. I braved the dogs, calling them "Pasha! Glubb!" in imitation of her sweet tone, and they stared at me puzzled, and snarled less. The pool in the garden was bright green and teeming with frogs. The bushes were untrimmed, the house earth-red up to its windows where rain had splattered. The path was overgrown with weeds.

The door handle turned and Mrs Pennefather, beaming, ushered me in. "Bianca is doing her homework," she said, "I'll call her."

Bianca walked through the door, cheeks flushed, harassed, in green uniform and bobby socks. We sat in the dining room, at the table, within sight of her parents. She slid a record on the turntable, ABBA's *Greatest Hits*. "I don't care," she said, "they still play good music." And to the sound of 'Hole in my Soul', we talked. The record was, of course, white noise so that we could have privacy from the ears of her parents, though I was now a fully approved Brother-in-Christ.

I pulled out the call-up papers and she read them in detail before looking up. She looked me in the eye, about to smirk and quirk her eyebrows, and make some witty comment about the Green and White. But when she saw that I was performing this gallant deed (being called up) solely to win her affection, she placed a hand on my arm and let it rest there.

"Will you be all right? You will write to me, won't you?"

"If you'll come and see me off at the station…"

In a spontaneous and completely unrehearsed gesture that I had been practising all day, I pulled the black fist out of my pocket and placed it in her hand. "I wanted you to have this, to… remember me…"

"What is it?" She ran her fingers over the smooth texture of the clenched fist, the protruding thumb and the rough elephant skin tail, trying to hide her bewilderment, or amusement. "Thank you."

The phone began to ring (and if you remember those loud rings, and those empty corridors where the phone sat on a small table to echo insistently, you'll know that you could not talk over it). "I'll miss you, Paul," she said, squeezing my fingers. "I'll pray for you every night."

Now was my chance for one final plunge before time ran out. I would invite her out, to a movie, to dinner at Guido's, or Jameson's. I would declare my love for her once and for all. But her father's voice called across the house.

"Bianca. Phone for you. It's Craig."

Her cheeks reddened, and she tossed her head as if to say, why is he bothering me now? Or, Dad, I'm the middle of something important here. Or rather, I wished that was what she meant. Instead she clasped my hands even tighter.

"Guess what?" She spoke with the radiant eyes of the Holy Spirit. "Craig Hardy has become a Christian too."

# CHAPTER SEVEN

# A MAN AMONG MEN

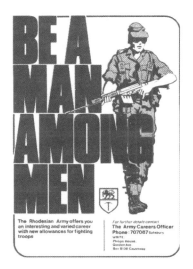

The Rhodesian Army offers you an interesting and varied career with new allowances for fighting troops

For further details contact
The Army Careers Officer
Phone : 707087 Salisbury
WRITE:
Phillips House,
Gordon Ave,
Box 8138 Causeway

Let's face it – I was a vomit-yellow coward. All that propaganda and brainwashing still could not convince me that I had to lay down my life for my country. In my pre-Christian days, I had played Donovan's 'Universal Soldier' and Dylan's 'Masters of War' enough to know that I was being used as a patsy to fight for other people's selfish interests. I was a dispensable pawn in the hands of global powers. And though I had made flower bowls of those records in Pastor Steve's wife's oven, and now believed that I was fighting to preserve Western Christian Civilisation and stemming the tide of evil, I still didn't want to go. I didn't want to put my eighteen-year-old life in danger. I didn't want to go through basic training to be brutalised and institutionalised (words I had read in books and that I little suspected already applied to me). I didn't want to leave my cosy home and girl-scented neighbourhood that was only now beginning to blossom into some sexual coherence. I didn't want to get my hair cut again.

Throw out fear, said Steve in his sermon. Get thee behind me, Satan. Say it aloud, Paul, whenever you feel afraid. God will be there to protect you. Gird your loins with truth; have on the breastplate of righteousness; take the shield of faith to quench the fiery darts of the wicked; wear the helmet of salvation and brandish the sword of the spirit. And the shoes? Forget the shoes.

Not that the elders of the church were a good example. As I discovered later, the Deacon of the church high-tailed it out of Rhodesia as soon as he got his call-up papers, to become a successful Baptist minister in Dallas, Texas. Steve Carter, exempt from call-up to active duty, became a Chaplain, but left when the war reached the Salisbury suburbs, taking his wife back to Plymouth, Massachusetts, from whence they came. Luke Pennefather, to whom I looked as a model of Christian submission to God's will, was suddenly 'called' to North-Eastern Bible School in New Jersey, and was out of the country before you could say Jesus Effing Christ.

But these good men still insisted that I go fight to preserve Christian civilisation. They had launched many other schoolboys into the war, with Bibles and promises of God's speed and victory. And so, resigning myself to the inevitable, I began training on rainy December mornings, running down the thunderstorm-backdropped lanes of Hillside and Eastridge. My heart pounding, my senses heightened, I tried to stem the panic of the voices in my head. Didn't I want to be a hero, like David in the face of Goliath, or Samson in the temple? When they cut his hair, he lost his strength, and here was I, shorn and emasculated since high school. I tried to masculinise myself, harden my heart and aspire to war and soldiering, to inchering people. But please God, I want to be somebody: a poet, an artist, a writer, a film maker, a musician, anything, but not a soldier. Not one of those Vietnam Americans who crawl in steamy jungles on their stomachs shooting and killing and inchering people.

Two years back, when I had had to register for call-up at sixteen, my parents, in a gesture of panic, realising that I was going to be sucked down the plughole of a vicious war not of their choosing, offered to send me out of the country to England, but I was sufficiently propagandised that it was out of the question. What would I do in England, I had asked, with my palms outstretched in righteous indignation? I grew up here. My family is here. Rhodesia is my home. What would I do in rain-sodden England anyhow?

★ ★ ★

It was all very logical. In order to maintain decent Rhodesian standards of Christianity and Western Civilisation, it had become necessary to imprison people without trial, torture them, try them *in camera*, put them to death by secret hanging, and disenfranchise the entire black population. In order for our democracy to flourish, we found it necessary to intensify racial hatred and engulf the whole subcontinent of Southern Africa in a major conflict, take away civil liberties, gag the press and expel all foreign dignitaries who disagreed with us. And it had become necessary to plunge all Rhodesian citizens, black and white, into this hot cauldron of a war, to bring this great country tumbling down on top of us all. In order to save the country, we had to destroy it.

So at six o'clock on 5 January 1977 (twenty-five degrees centigrade, rainfall 20 mm), earnestly clutching his call-up papers in his hand, Paul Smiley Williams joined the throng of three hundred eighteen-year-old white males on Salisbury Station to catch the Bulawayo night train. The Churchill pipe band marched up and down the platform in kilts providing background music to his heroic departure, the Pearl man on the Pearl building beamed his white light of civilisation outward, and the sign above platform one beckoned him to his destiny: Heany Junction – Llewellin Barracks.

Rhodesia's rail system was limited to articulated Garratt steam locomotives, and it was one of these which was to transport him to Dante's Inferno. While the rest of the world had shelved their steam trains for more modern diesel and electric locomotives, Rhodesia (because of sanctions and the Wankie colliery) had reintroduced these Victorian monstrosities.

Along with the others, to the "Oyl Aboyd" of the train engineer, I was vacuum-sucked up the steps, down a metal passageway, into a six-bunked passenger carriage, and hurled against a red leather seat, my head pressed against the dirty headrest. I peered through a greasy window at three hundred reflections of myself surging forward to our fate, and then shut my eyes. It was too late. There stood my parents, my mother a nest of teary wrinkles ("Hope he gets some sleep; he'll have to be up at the crack of sparrow tomorrow") and my father, tall and lean with his chin jutting out ("Who would have ever thought that our son…?").

But lo and behold, between the bristly brown heads, the smell of smoke and coal and the wailing chanters, an apparition of blonde hair and blue eyes weaved through the crowd, pushed its way to my carriage and raised its face to the window.

Her eyes were brimming with sincerity, her hand submissively pliant in my hands. With her head to one side, as if she had practised this gesture in the mirror, she pulled a pink envelope from a pocket and poked it through the window slot. I grasped at it, touching her cool fingers for a second that would be revisited a thousand times in the next six weeks.

"Oyl Aboyd!" The guard blew a long tired blast on the whistle, and the train responded, lurching forward. Her lips moved in speech. The glass was grimy, and I could not hear her words, but the gesture was spontaneous: she raised a hand and waved, twiddling three fingers. Behind her, my parents waved too.

"We're proud of you, Paul."

"Don't forget to write."

The platform slid back, the earth lurched under me and spun slowly towards Heany Junction. I stared into the dark night for a while, then closed my eyes, to find the after-image of Bianca in negative on the insides of my eyelids. I watched the wispy hair blowing gently in her face for a long time, until she faded. I held the pink envelope up to the carriage light and breathed in its hint of perfume. Then I placed it in my jeans back pocket, lay on the top bunk bed and jiggled to the train's rhythm, trying to sleep. Through the night, an ivory white image of Bianca remained.

The irony, of course, is that three years from now, I would not have had to fight at all. From 1972 until 1978, war was the status quo, and my military service a normal rite of passage. But unknown to me, as early as 1977 the regime was beginning to crumble; by 1978, Smith had been strong-armed into settlement; in 1979, he set in place a moderate ('puppet') black government, which collapsed within six months; and by 1980, the war, the regime, the thousand-year reign was all over. My class-mates in intake 155, 156, 157 would take the brunt of the war in casualties, but by 1979, conscription would end and the 'terror war' would be over.

Three years from now, the wet street my parents were now crossing to get back to their cars would no longer be called Railway Avenue, but Kenneth Kaunda Avenue, after the Zambian president who assisted our enemy ZIPRA in the war. Those three hundred families sending their boys to fight against ZANLA's Robert Mugabe, public enemy number one, and now driving back to their white, middle-class suburbs in Hillside, Greendale and Eastlea, would soon have to drive across Robert Mugabe Way and onto Samora Machel Avenue to get home.

And if we were to squint myopically even further into the future, say twenty-five years from now, we would see those same parents smiling with cynical satisfaction at the confirmation of their worst fears and direst predictions about African majority rule. See how these neat roads have degenerated into potholes – this is the Africa up north Smith was warning us about. We were right! Smith was right! The same trains would leave from the same station, but the sidewalks would be lined with war-maimed beggars. Large black families would wait patiently in long queues with plastic bags, goats and chickens, for delayed, overloaded trains; the lavatories would overflow with sewerage; litter would plaster the fence in a solid wall. In twenty years' time the signs Robert Mugabe Way, Kenneth Kaunda Avenue and Samora Machel Avenue would be gone, stolen for use as coffin handles for the many AIDS victims, and eventually the train itself (yes, the same Garratt articulated loco) would stop running because amateur panhandlers would undermine the tracks on the way to Bulawayo in a vain search for gold. And Mugabe, in his drive for total control, would implement draconian measures of repression: detention without trial, torture, disenfranchisement. In order for his socialist state to succeed, he would find it necessary to intensify racial hatred and engulf the whole subcontinent in a major conflict, take away civil liberties, gag the press and expel all foreign dignitaries who disagreed with him.

But not now. Not yet. In 1977, the war was still smouldering, and I had to live through this slow-burning chunk of history.

The train arrived at Heany Junction at five in the morning and disgorged its passengers, who walked in *guti* – that warm, misty drizzle – towards the line of camouflage-painted Bedford trucks through muddy red earth, clambered on and sat in obedient lines down each middle bench. I fingered the pink envelope in my back pocket as the trucks drove in slow convoy down riveleted roads, passed under an arching sign over the road – Llewellin Barracks – and parked in a line on a tar road.

So here was the famous Llewellin Barracks we had spent the six years of high school anticipating, repressing and sublimating. It was an old airfield with long stretches of tar and concrete, airplane hangars, and towers at each end of the field, a series of prefab buildings squatting in low lines like chicken coops, and rows of jeeps and trucks, all painted a seasick greeny-brown. An oblong human machine, with twenty white arms and twenty white legs pumping up and down, marched on a distant road, controlled by a short man walking alongside it, yelling, "hup 2,3,4!"

Our driver, I later discovered, was to be our squad sergeant, our drill master and our chief tormenter – a man in khaki shirt, khaki shorts, tight belt and green beret, who leaped down from the high cab and walked stiffly round the back of the truck, like someone with very sore piles. He told us to get off the fucking truck and get into fucking lines, march like the *slapgats* we were to the fucking CQ stores.

*Slapgats?*

As we marched past the squalid prefab barrack rooms (A Company, B Company and C Company), clumps of soldiers in uniforms, polishing boots and belts on the steps or weeding lawns, curled their lips at us and chanted "Fresh-puss, fresh-puss, fresh-puss" in unison.

*Fresh puss?*

INVENTORY:
Bags, duffel; 1
Uniforms, combat; 1
Shirts, drill; 1
Shorts, KD; 1
Boots, combat; 1 pair
Boots, black; 1 pair
Tins, mess; 2
Shorts, PT; 2
Seasick green-manure brown shirt; 1
Cap, combat. Also called cap, cunt.
*Cunt caps?*
Envelope, Pink (hide in new combat shirt)

Civilian clothing (sea-blue shirt, stained by the sweat of fear and rain, the blue faded jeans, the sneakers) to be dumped in the wire-mesh storage room, to be collected on your first weekend pass, in six weeks' time.

Haircuts: Go, go, go, far end of the hangar. See that bad-tempered old man with an electric razor? Thirty seconds each. Move, move, move. Short back and sides, with the bonus of a bleeding neck if you are lucky.

Now divide the three hundred ugly, shorn, uniformed boys into platoons. Worm your way towards Craig Hardy and Gamma, to be with them. 6RR, B Company, Alpha platoon, intake 156, army number 111563N, Rifleman Williams, sir. Remember that. Repeat it after me. March to new barrack room – that long concrete stall with tin roof and rows of bunk beds lining each wall, its central aisle a mass of green metal lockers. Rush in, squeeze between Hardy and Gamma and stuff your duffel bag in the locker next to the bunk bed, on which a sheet, blanket and pillow will be neatly stacked.

"Hi." Hardy jostled me. I had not spoken to him since my announcement that I was a Jesus freak, and he had not spoken to me. Using sleight of hand, I concealed the pink envelope in the crack between the locker and the concrete floor.

Miraculously, according to Bianca, he and I were now soldiers-in-Christ. "I heard that you became a Jesus freak too." I was rewarded with a punch in the gut.

Although it was rumoured that they put blue stone in our tea to curb our sexual urges, our primary functions were sexual. We were called "fuckers", "wankers", and our beds were called "wank-pits". The entire female species was reduced to the generic word "pussy"; and if we showed any feminine traits ourselves, we were called "cunts". The only pursuit worth acknowledging was sexual intercourse, and we had to add the obligatory adjective "fucken" to intensify every sentence ("Get your fucken stick belt straight, you fucken cunt"). Anything bad was verbalised in terms of defecation and urination: "You're in the shit"; "You buggers will be shitting off tonight, if you don't pull your finger from your arse"; "Don't piss off Sarge or he'll crap on you from a dizzy height."

Sergeant Viper was his real name, so he said. He was our instructor, and was well versed in the art of humiliation and dehumanisation, having sent many a boy off to die in the war with unquestioning and grateful obedience.

"Cunt caps off in the barrack room." (To this day, I still have no idea why those camouflage denim caps with peaks and flaps at the back to protect your neck from the sun were called cunt caps and not combat caps, but in the army, like the church, it was not our place to question, but to trust and obey.) We stood to attention in front of our bunk beds, and the lanky, poisonous-looking man with an upturned nose inspected each new recruit. In the next six weeks, he told us – though not in so many words – we were to be terrorised, degraded, humiliated, shamed and psychologically tortured. Apparently that made us better soldiers.

Sergeant Viper's instruction manual had its own rules. Make them feel guilty. They can do nothing right; they are always in danger of punishment. The universe is unjust; they must never feel safe or at rest. Stick belts must shine, the Sergeant must be able to see his own leering face in their boots. They must run until they drop, get so thirsty that they will beg to drink their own piss. All day, all night, punish them for the slightest offence. Guilt and fear must drive them. Rouse them at midnight and force them to run around the airfield, shouting at them, telling them that they have made you mad and you can't sleep because you are ashamed of them. Not fast enough, do it again before Sarge loses his temper. And sing, you buggers:

> *Cause we're all Rhodesians and we'll fight through thick and thin,*
> *We'll keep this land a free land, stop the enemy coming in,*
> *We'll keep him north of the Zambezi 'til that river's running dry,*
> *And this mighty land will prosper 'cause Rhodesians never die.*

Night after night, make them run down endless dirt roads with packs on their backs, their mess tins clanking at their hip-bones, their rifles getting heavier and heavier, helmets pounding into their skulls with every step. Dress them up in full combat uniform, full webbing, with rifle, four pouches of ammunition, heavy steel helmet; run them through trenches of mud, across fields, over fences, up and down hills. And then get them up and ready in time for inspection at five a.m., with everything clean.

Gamma still didn't know that he was a 'fuck-up'. The Illusion Mongers had sewed their seamless reality around him so tightly that even now, in basic training, he thought himself invincible. But he lagged behind on the nightly route marches. He could not box; he could not do star jumps; he was getting us into trouble. Sergeant Viper roared his jeep behind us, pushing, pushing, pushing. Keep in a squad. Don't drag. If one lags you all suffer. Sing you buggers:

> *Sometimes I wish I was a Bluejob up in the sky*
> *I wouldn't have to walk if I could fly*
> *But I'll be a brown job until I die*
> *With ten years to go in the RLI.*

Even though we tried to keep Gamma at the front of the squad to stop him falling behind, he sagged in our neat squadron, dragged us back, and finally dropped onto the road. Sergeant Viper had to swerve to avoid running him over.

"Squad, halt." He stood over the heap of human flesh in the dust.

"Please, sir." Gamma held onto Viper's polished toecaps as the Sergeant kicked him away.

"Squad, by the left, quick march."

That night, while we were 'boning' boots with Kiwi polish and rubbing belt buckles with Brasso (to this day I cannot smell those without wanting to throw up), Hardy took Gamma aside. "Sergeant Viper is very disappointed with us. We're all on a shine parade tomorrow morning because of you."

"Careful, guys, you know who I am," said Gamma, clenching his fists and taking a karate stance. "Remember who you're messing with."

The pause while Gamma stood with bony fists clenched enabled the rest of us to gather round, like in the old days at school, and goad him on. "Come on, Gamma! Show us your muscles." Gamma karate-chopped Hardy's chest. But Hardy was in no mood to play Illusion Mongers. His first blow landed on Gamma's jaw. Next moment Gamma was doubled over in pain, falling to the ground. He looked up in bewilderment at a fragmented universe. He saw the crowd laughing – surely they were not laughing at him? He didn't defend himself; he just dropped into the corner, like a spider in a flame. Hardy kicked him and kicked again, and soon others were kicking at him too.

"Puss-face."

"Girlie."

"Mary, Mary, quite the fairy."

At inspection time, Gamma was still crumpled up, none of his kit ready. Hardy called a hasty conference: we would fail the inspection. But Hardy had a plan. He walked to Gamma's locker, pulled out all its contents, pulled the sheets off his bed and bundled them all into the metal rubbish bin outside the back door. Then with the same vehemence, he propelled the broom against Gamma and pushed him out of the door. Gamma held his hand over his eyes, unresisting. Hardy pulled him up and dumped him into a dustbin, jammed on the lid and wiped his hands as if he were disposing of a sack of smelly manure. "Stay there till after the inspection."

Six-thirty a.m. We stood by our beds. We had laid out everything perfectly squared off and consistent: beds in line, towels in line, mess tins in line, sparkling shiny boots in line with a string along the floor. Knife, fork, spoon, razor, brush, comb and toothbrush had to be a certain distance from each other on the towel on the bed. Clothes had to be ironed and pressed in a square pile; blankets and sheets had to be bitten into a 90-degree fold. All dust specks had to be gone. We had slept on the floor so that our beds were perfectly made; we had not used our eating utensils or razors so they could gleam and shine; our clothes were immaculate; our boots were so shiny we could see ourselves caricatured in them.

"Here he comes."

The platoon stood like Grecian pillars as Viper stamped into the entrance. He was an angry Jehovah, needing placation. And we were all willing to please, eager to show our innocence. No words were spoken for a whole five minutes while he paced slowly up and down the room, frowning, prodding with his stick, running his white glove along the tops of lockers, staring closely into people's faces while they gazed ahead.

"Is this some kind of joke?" Viper paced up to Hardy, wiped his glove on the floor and pressed his finger against the boy's nose. "What do you see here, shitface?"

"Nothing, sir, Sergeant Viper."

"Nothing? Nothing? It's a pile of shit. This is a pigsty. You people live in a shithouse."

Our righteousness was rags in his sight.

"Did you shave this morning, laddie?" Viper was an inch away from my face.

"I… yes, Sergeant."

It was a chargeable offense not to shave. Everything was a chargeable offence. Of course I had shaved, at five in the morning, in cold water, with eight other boys crowding to see in the same mirror, all of us in a smelly ablution block, where lines of other boys were defecating in a row of toilets with no doors or walls to screen them from us, where ten boys showered in a hot mass under three nozzles hung from the roof.

"Did you use a mirror?"

"Yes, Sergeant."

"Next time use a razor – it's sharper."

"Don't you want this button, laddie?" said Viper, pulling the loose thread of another boy's shirt so the button popped off. "You're on a fucken charge for not having a button."

A fucken charge, I discovered, was like a misdemeanour. But punishment was severe. For dust on your locker, or traces of Brasso on your belt, or dried mud on the heel of your boot, you would be doubling away to the 'box' – the Military Police prison where the MPs would make your life hell. By the time he had finished, we were all guilty, quivering wrecks. We were dirty, disgusting, filthy cunts who had let Sergeant Viper down very badly. We were unfit to be soldiers. He wanted to be proud of us, but he couldn't. And if we thought it couldn't get any worse, a grating of metal and a groan from outside the back door interrupted the Sergeant's Grand Disappointment Speech.

"What the hell is that?"

The lid of the dustbin, in view of the barrack room, moved. Even Viper's smug anger vanished for a second. He watched the lid jostle up and down, and listened. We tried very hard to look straight ahead. A shaved head emerged, covered with dust, scrapings of polish and fluff and a tear-stained face stared up at the Sergeant's white gloves and dazzling belt.

"Sir, please…" Gamma crawled out of the bin, crashing it to the ground, dragging with him all the dirt and filth we had concealed and thrown away. Viper turned to see our guilty dismay (we quickly snapped back to attention), then rounded on Gamma, who ran obediently in the direction Sergeant Viper was pointing, to the guard room.

We had all heard stories of the detention barracks. MPs with red peaked caps revved people constantly, day and night. DB meant no sleep, no rest, no food, and solitary confinement. We had seen poor exhausted troops running with cement bags on their backs, with an MP on either side shouting at them until they dropped. I shut my eyes and held my breath, the tight stick belt making me dizzy. Hardy bulged his eyes at everyone in warning. But Viper was smiling.

"What happened?"

"I beat him up, Sergeant."

Viper frowned. "No."

"No?"

"No," insisted Viper. "He slipped in the showers. That's what happened. Clear?"

"Sergeant," said Hardy.

"I want to see the last man in his weapon training gear, lined up on the road outside."

★ ★ ★

*It is distressing to both my staff and myself to learn periodically through anonymous letters to the press, of dissatisfaction amongst a few parents and few trainees. I would like to give you my personal assurance that in basic training your son has been treated with fairness at all times, and I am very certain you will see an improvement in his physique and self-discipline.*

*Lieutenant Colonel, Commanding Officer, Llewellin Barracks.*

★ ★ ★

What are we fighting for? Here's the Rag Magazine from the University of Rhodesia, banned because of the mock advertisement on its back cover. A bikini-clad blonde pouts at the camera. Beside her, a soldier in uniform, crouching in the bush, camouflage warpaint on his face and hands, points a rifle at the hidden enemy: "I know what I'm fighting for: a home, a place for my family to grow up and prosper in a free land. One thing puzzles me, though…" Almost unnoticed at the bottom left of the poster is another inset – of a terrorist, rushing in hate at the white man, high porting an AK, "What's *he* fighting for?"

| DEPOT MAIN KITCHEN BILL OF FARE | | | | | | | |
|---|---|---|---|---|---|---|---|
| **MONDAY** | **TUESDAY** | **WEDNESDAY** | **THURSDAY** | **FRIDAY** | **SATURDAY** | **SUND** |
| Mealie Meal Porridge & Milk Grilled Bacon Scrambled Eggs Baked Beans in Tomato Sauce | Cornflakes & Milk Fried Eggs Grilled Bacon Fried Brinjals | Maltebella Porridge & Milk Savoury Omelette Minute Steak Grilled Bacon | Oatmeal Porridge & Milk Poached Eggs Grilled Bacon Spaghetti in Tomato Sauce | Honey Krunchies & Milk Fried Eggs Baked Beans in Tomato Sauce Grilled Bacon | Mealie Meal Porridge & Milk Scrambled Eggs Grilled Bacon Saute Kidney on Toast | Grilled Broiled Poached Fish Cak Parsley |
| COFFEE | | BREAD | | MARGARINE | | MARMALADE | TOAST |
| Mushroom Soup Beef Olives Cream Potatoes Buttered Gem Squash Spinach in Cheese Sauce Bread and Butter Pudding | Harricot Bean Soup Braised Steak & Onions Grilled Rump Steak Piri Piri Steak Boiled or Creamed Potatoes Cauliflower Au Gratin Sweet Baked Pumpkin Gravy Fresh Fruit Salad & Custard | Cock-a-Leekie Soup Cottage Pie or Meat Pie Chipped Potatoes Buttered Cabbage Creamed Carrots & Parsley Sauce Apple & Plum Turnovers with Custard | Onion & Tomato Soup Assorted Cold Meats Boiled Egg Potato Mayonnaise Tossed Salad Beetroot Salad Baked Beans in Tomato Sauce Swiss Roll & Custard | Oxtail Soup Fried Fillet of Hake Pickled Fish Chip Potatoes Garden Peas Tomato & Onion Salad Strawberry Jam Tart with Custard | Farm Vegetable Soup Steak & Kidney Pie Creamed Parsley Potatoes Baton Carrots Buttered Cabbage Onion Gravy Banana & Pawpaw with cold Custard | Celery S Roast Be Roast Po Roast Po Cauliflo Gratin Boiled H Gravy Assorted Pudding |
| TEA | | BREAD | | MARGARINE | | | |
| Thick Vegetable Soup Meat & Potato Pie French Fried Potatoes Steamed Pumpkin Buttered Cabbage Toasted Cheese & Tomato | Chicken Noodle Soup Grilled Sausage or Braised Oxtail Parsley Potatoes Baton Carrots Buttered Green Beans Fresh Oranges | Minestrone Soup Curried Eggs or Savoury Eggs Lyonnaise Potatoes Gem Squash with Cheese Creamed Spinach Naartjies | Mulligatawny Soup Braised Steak Grilled Rump Steak Boiled Potatoes Vichy Carrots Broccolli in White Sauce Apples | Mushroom Soup Grilled Sausage Grilled Boerewors Creamed Potatoes Grilled Tomato French Beans Cheese Block | Beef Broth Monkey Gland Steak Savoury Potatoes Steamed Pumpkin Minted Peas Oranges | Cream of Soup Braised Boiled I Vichy Ca Savoury Apples |
| COFFEE | | BREAD | | JAM | | MARGARINE | |
| TEA OR COLD FRUIT JUICE AT 10.00 A.M. DAILY | | | | | | | |

★ ★ ★

What are we fighting for? I'll tell you what we're fighting for.

Assimilation: you told us back in 1899 that we blacks would be assimilated into white society once we became 'more civilised'. So when is this going to happen? Now you talk of 'responsible government' and 'separate development', which are merely other words for apartheid.

Land: In 1890 you took our land, and in 1930 you gave us the rocky, barren deserts to live in, keeping 50% of the land for yourselves: 28 million acres to 1 million blacks and 48 million acres to 50,000 whites. Good deal!

Education: Rich European children have free, compulsory school, but our children have to pay if they want to go.

Work: You earn 13.5 times more than we do.

Democracy: We can't vote, unless we can prove we are 'civilised'. And we can dab Ambi on our skins all we like, we'll never make it.

★ ★ ★

Ian Smith: "Our Africans are the happiest Africans in the world. Nobody has yet been able to tell me where there are Africans who are happier – or, for that matter, better off – than in Rhodesia."

★ ★ ★

*Comrade Kill-a-White, how did you come to be a ZANLA guerrilla?*
WAR VETERAN #1 *(Wilfred Mhanda): While I was at the University of Rhodesia, I joined ZANU, which was banned. We had a cell of ten and our main aim was to recruit students for the armed struggle. They would pretend to be going on holiday with the Student Christian Movement but would slip into Botswana and on to Zambia for basic military training. After basic training, we were taken to Tanzania.*

*And in Tanzania you did military training?*
*I became a military instructor, and was promoted to political commissar and then to ZANLA commander. In 1975, I joined the ZANLA high command and was in charge of both political and military training. Our military trainers were Chinese and I was chosen for three months' advanced strategic training in China. The Chinese said that I was far too precious to be sent to the front to fight and I must be kept back as an instructor. Nonetheless I did fight at the front in north-eastern Rhodesia in 1974 and for three months in 1976. I saw plenty of action.*

*How did you like China?*
*The training was very good. I studied under a Chinese lieutenant-general and we studied the Chinese revolution, its guerrilla tactics and battles against Japan and the Kuomintang. But they didn't teach us Marxism-Leninism. They didn't really trust us because we weren't all communists. We had to go out and buy Marxist classics for ourselves. China was a very closed and strange society. The Chinese themselves were essentially racist. Crowds would form and stare at us if we appeared in the street.*

*And what about you? How did you come to be a ZANLA guerrilla?*
WAR VETERAN #2: *They came for us at night and said we had to go with them. Only*

*the boys, the young boys. They marched us through the bush, until we couldn't march any more. We kept stopping every night at another village, where we would demand food and shelter. Then we reached Mozambique. There were thousands of us there. They were very cruel to us, very hard. We trained with wooden AKs and had to chant slogans all night. Then we were sent back into Zimbabwe with real weapons. We were very much afraid of the Rhodesian forces. We would ambush a few vehicles, then run away. We lived in villages, taking food as we had been instructed and making the people support ZANU. We didn't want to do it, to kill, but we did. After a while, we began to like it. It was a nice feeling to play with people, like you do with an insect. We learned to be comfortable, and to live well. Some said that we had abandoned the struggle; no: the struggle abandoned us. We had to fend for ourselves.*

★ ★ ★

And you, white boy? How did you become a Rhodesian soldier? Well, first, I had to learn how not to think for myself. I pretty well managed it. Instead of a conscience, or a voice of reason, I had Viper's voice in my head, nagging at me all day and night. Second, I had to learn how to shoot.

The FN (the Belgian-made Fabrique Nationale) weighed 9 pounds, used standard 7.62 mm rounds, and was semi-automatic and self-loading (which meant that you only had to cock the weapon once, and once you pulled the trigger, the next bullet would be in the chamber). You could fire singly or on automatic, but you had to be careful – a light tap on automatic and the whole magazine of twenty rounds would shoot out in three seconds in a violent arc as the weapon kicked up. It had a grenade attachment, could be fixed with a bayonet for more intimate combat, and its flash eliminator masked most of the tell-tale flash giving away your firing position at night.

We collected these cold, heavy, FN rifles from the armoury and ran onto the rifle range lined with targets. These were cardboard banners on wooden sticks, with pictures of black men staring at us with hating faces, brandishing AK47 assault rifles.

We were told how to operate the rifle, how to load, cock, fire, how to strip the weapon, how to clean the firing rod, the breech-block and the sights with four-by-two. Then we were given twenty penis-shaped gold bullets to insert into the spring-loaded metal magazine.

Patrick Johnson stuck up his hand. "Sir, I can't get…"

"Birdshit, sonny, do you see birdshit…?"

"Sergeant, I can't get my magazine into my gun."

Viper stood over him, his arms folded. "What did you call it?"

"My gun, Sergeant."

To make everyone aware of the enormity of his linguistic crime, Sarge set Johnson on an anthill. "This arsehole has just called this weapon his gun. This…" – he grabbed the rifle from Johnson and pointed it at his private parts – "… is his gun."

"This is my rifle" – holding weapon high in air –

"This is my gun" – pointing to private parts –

"This is for shooting" – waving rifle in air –

"This is for fun" – curling fingers around imaginary penis and masturbating.

"Now back to your firing positions… Not you…" – pointing to Johnson – "You keep repeating that until you learn the difference."

I secretly envied the enemy their AK47, with its banana-curved magazine. Ours were straight; theirs were twisted. We had long butts; they had stocky butts. The rumour was you could bury an AK in mud, let it rust and it would still fire. Not our babies; they misfired at the slightest touch.

Back in our positions, we aimed in unison at the targets. We cocked our weapons in unison, we put the rifle onto 'R', and in unison we pulled the triggers. The kickback hit us all hard in the face, just below the eye, simultaneously. The smell of gunpowder burned in our noses. The spent cartridges (or *doppies,* as Viper called them) shot out the side of the rifles and onto the ground in chinking unison.

"Make safe."

We snapped the safety lever onto 'S', and walked in a long line to the targets.

"This is my rifle, this is my gun…"

We practised until the sun was red on the flat horizon of Matabeleland. After three hours, I was able not only to hit the target but to get a good grouping of shots in a small area of the terrorist's eye, nose, forehead, open mouth and AK trigger finger.

Someone had been swearing in Viper's presence because, for the last half of the afternoon, he had been running around the field screaming, "Oh, my fucking shit, oh, my fucking shit, oh, my fucking shit." Patrick Johnson was still on the mound, wearily lifting his rifle and pointing to his privates. "This is for shooting, this is for fun."

My cheekbone was bruised and my right ear was ringing. I marvelled at how easily we were being destroyed. How easy it is to tear the delicate fibres of one's soul and release the monster, I thought. Sergeant Viper had an easy job. But who would put Humpty Dumpty together again afterwards?

★　★　★

Forget all I said about the war dwindling, soon to be over. 1977 marked the most intense fighting the country had ever seen. By the time I finished my basic training, Security Force Headquarters had divided the country into five operational areas called Joint Operational Commands (JOCS). Operations Thrasher, Repulse, Tangent, Splinter and Grapple sought to stop the torrent of guerrillas coming through the porous borders on three sides.

The new combined guerrilla force, the Patriotic Front, far from being united, spent much of its energy splitting into factions. Fighting in one camp alone in Tanzania resulted in the deaths of over six hundred guerrillas. Yet they were still a force to be reckoned with. The Soviets assisted in the training and management of camps, facilities, supplies of ZIPRA, while the Chinese and North Koreans trained ZANLA deep in Mozambique and Tanzania.

New tactics were developed on both sides. Guerrillas threatened to torture civilians who co-operated with Rhodesian forces. Rhodesian forces threatened to torture civilians who co-operated with guerrillas. The Rhodesians trained Selous Scouts in what was called 'dark phase training', disguising themselves as guerrillas to trick civilians into revealing whether they supported them or not. And in the midst of this, here was I, a lamb being dressed for the slaughter, or, as the politicians called it, 'the ultimate sacrifice'.

★　★　★

I had not touched the pink envelope. It slept safely under the cool green locker in the dark corner of the barrack room. The envelope (I imagined) was creased and dirty, the perfume evaporated, the intensity of whatever sentiments inside muddy brown. I didn't want to open it, having already been hardened into defensive indifference. I preferred to keep her sentiments a mystery, so that I could speculate on all possible futures.

But I had opened my Bible. I carried a Gideons version of the New Testament, which fortunately included Psalms and Proverbs, which I used for my quiet times. The small voice of God had diminished somewhat in the noise of the barrack room, the edgy sarcasm of Viper's shouting and the mocking taunts of my comrades, but I combed my faithful book for words of consolation and encouragement, and recited verses on route marches to keep me going. 'Those that wait upon the Lord will rise up on wings like eagles. Be still and know that I am God. Whosoever that believeth in Him shall not perish but have everlasting life.'

★ ★ ★

*Cramer, John.*
*Killed in action. He died fighting against communism, for the sake of Christianity, for our beloved country Rhodesia. We will keep on praying for you.*

*Garland, Ernest.*
*You paid the ultimate price. Farewell to a brave man. Dearly loved brother of June and Vicky, son to proud parents Steven and Holly.*

*Whittaker, Steve.*
*So sorry we could not have saved him. You died for the country you loved, it will not be in vain, your death will be avenged, deepest sympathy, Aunty Babs.*

★ ★ ★

Gamma returned to the platoon after two weeks. He had missed all the basic weapon training, drill and PT, but he was fitter than all of us. His nose and ears were sunburned to a crisp, his eyes were narrow slits in a leather face, his arms and legs strips of wiry biltong. His posture was no longer rabbit-like. He walked in like a cowboy into a saloon, legs bowed and hands ready to draw an imaginary Colt from his holster. He did not look at anyone, though we all stopped polishing and stared at him in inspection-mode silence. He heaved himself lightly onto his bunk and lay down, stretching his arms around his head, closing his eyes. He didn't speak a word, and no one spoke to him until Hardy returned from the toilet, a toilet roll in his hand. He had missed the grand entrance, but noticed the awed silence.

"Mary, how was it?"

Gamma, eyes still closed, pressed his sunburned lips together. Hardy slouched up to his bunk with an incredulous expression on his face.

"I'm talking to you, Mary."

Gamma opened his eyes and looked at his adversary, as if trying to remember him from his dark past.

"Mary…"

"Craig Hardy." Gamma pushed him with two stick arms so that the platoon bully fell back onto the next bunk. Hardy regained his balance, looked around at all of us, then tightened his lips and clenched his fists.

"Craig Hardy."

Gamma pushed Hardy to the floor. Hardy pulled himself to his full height to look his adversary dead in the eye. But what he saw was inhuman. What Gamma had been through in the guardroom in those two weeks showed in his steel eyes. He pushed Hardy's jelly stomach against the wall. Hardy kicked at his shins, punched his stomach and his face, but Gamma didn't flinch. Then in one practised move (he had been hoisting bags of cement for the last two weeks), he heaved a kicking and punching Hardy onto his shoulders and dropped him in the rubbish bin outside. The lid clanged. Gamma returned, stared around. Ainslie stepped back to let him pass, but he stopped in front of him.

"My name is Peter, Peter Burnett," he announced. Then he was back on his bunk, lying tranquilly with eyes closed. The few of us nearest the door watched Hardy emerge from the bin, shake off the dirt, and without looking back, walk down the path away from the barracks towards the staff quarters.

Viva Mbuya Nehanda! Viva Sekuru Kaguvi! Comrades, comrades, we first took up arms in the First Chimurenga War of 1896–97. But the just struggle to take back our own country was suppressed with unparalleled brutality, torture and cruelty by the white dogs of imperialism. For the following sixty years they thought we were crushed. But following UDI, we launched our Second Chimurenga with the Chinhoyi Battle in 1966. *Pasi Ne Smith!* Against all odds, we fought the racist Rhodesian forces and their Apartheid allies in South Africa, then after 1970, we organised further. We united, and with help from the free African states and our communist allies, began our sustained war. *Pamberi ZANU! Pamberi ZAPU!* You at the back, raise your fist. Sing, damn you. *Pamberi Zambia, Pamberi Mozambique, Pamberi Tanzania, viva China, viva the USSR!*

By 1977, dear comrades, our grassroots organisations had matted all over the fertile red soil of Zimbabwe. Our *hurundwende* infiltrated village, ward, district and mobilised the *povo*, so we had ground support. In return, we provided health, education and self-help schemes for the people who supported us. Our *mujhibas* gave us extra eyes, ears and lips, and our *chimbwidos* kept house for us. We conducted nightly *pungwes* where we re-educated the people, taught them freedom songs. *Pamberi ZANLA! Pamberi ZIPRA! Pasi Ne Smeeth. Pasi Ne General Walls.* Oh, watch out, you rabid Rhodesian ridgebacks, we are coming to get you. We will drive you into the sea. Sing, *povo*, again, again, all night, until the red eye of Zimbabwe dawns on you.

In our fourth week of training, we had to learn how to kill Kaffirs. Oh, so we weren't fighting communists or insurgents or terrorists? No, we were fighting Kaffirs. So if anyone ever tells you it was Communism versus Western Christian Civilisation, or Empire versus Barbarism, or whatever crap history is made of, just remember that day on the field when we had to learn to kill Kaffirs.

Ahead of us was a line of sacks on poles, draped with those terrorist pictures we had been shooting at every day. Johnson was first in line. He took a deep breath, charged with fury, yelled "Kill the Kaffir". He tore the bayonet into the sack and sawdust dribbled out through the terrorist's mouth. Next? Ainslie, Stevenson, Smith, swearing, yelling and thrusting viciously. I edged towards the back of the squad. Gamma ran on hard, thin legs, and stabbed the sack with such fury that the sawdust spilled out and sprayed all over him.

Viper clapped his hands. "That's it, laddie. Don't be afraid of a little blood."

Hardy screamed at the next dummy, ripping it apart. He tore it to shreds, spat out sawdust, tossed it all over the field, shouting, "Kill the black bastard, kill the black bastard." Viper applauded. The remaining few, our hatred cooling, couldn't match this violence. And foolishly, I was the last. I shouted loud and thrust hard, but the dummy swung gently and embraced me.

"It doesn't come from your heart, sonny," shouted Viper. "Do it again."

"Come on, Mary," snickered Hardy.

The others took up the chorus: "Mary, Mary, quite contrary."

I thrust in the bayonet, yelled until I was hoarse, and kicked at the sack.

"Murder the munt," suggested the instructor. "Hammer the hout. Kill the Kaffir." I charged and screamed again and again, improving, definitely, but too late to win the respect of the jeering platoon. I stared around at sneering faces, looking for allies. But they had smelled blood.

"Kaffir *boetie*!"

"We have another Mary in our squad." I made weaker and weaker attempts to stab the dummy, until I crumpled in a heap before the swinging sack, watching the sawdust apologetically dribble out of it.

You may think it valiant of me that I couldn't hate as I was supposed to, but that's not the point. I wanted to conform, to hate and kill, to prove myself. I was not morally superior, I was just weak. And I was feminine in the presence of most of these testosterone-filled boys. In a platoon of only one sex, the lie of black and white polarity is exposed. We are not one sex or the other; we are shades of the two. And in this platoon, I was now seen as feminine.

★ ★ ★

*WOMAN ZANLA EX-COMBATANT I:* "*Whereas you whites were conscripted, and only males fought, we black women joined the ZANU and ZAPU liberation armies in our thousands. Yes, we wanted to liberate our country too, and we demanded that the traditionally male-led nationalist movement provide us with military training. In the training camps, we experienced an equality with men that we had not experienced before. We dispensed with traditional gender roles. In Angola, we lived in the same camps, shared the same facilities, did exactly the same training as the men. Exactly the same. Drilling, handling weapons, topography… everything. We were fighting not only racism, but sexism too.*"

*WOMAN ZANLA EX-COMBATANT II:* "*There were many problems. The men said we were undisciplined and 'bad for the revolution'. We were raped as part of our training, and were forced into 'sex-for-soap' negotiations in order to survive in the camps. No, we didn't fight as equals. We were merely the cooks and carriers of weapons for the men. We had to carry the limpet mines and ammunition between Mozambique and Zimbabwe. It was more burdensome than fighting the war itself. We did not go to fight battles; we only ever went into the liberated zones to stay in villages and serve the fighters.*"

★ ★ ★

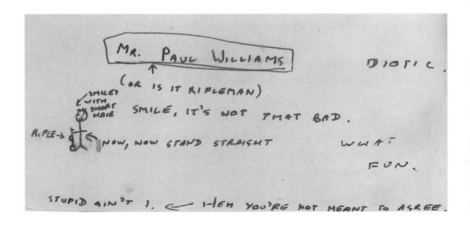

"Look at what I've found." Ainslie brandished my pink letter, flying it above the heads of the others. I leaped up, but he snapped it above me in an arc.

"No, please, come on, Ainslie, not that, it's private."

"Nothing is private in this barrack room, arsehole."

Hardy sneered at me. "Better let me read it, Ainslie."

Ainslie clutched the envelope tightly. "Maybe it's from his boyfriend." He pulled out a slender white card for the whole platoon to see.

"It must be from mommy," said Hardy and snatched the letter from Ainslie.

"Read it out loud, Hardy." Braga and Stevens held me tight, pinning my arms behind my back so I could not escape. Hardy opened the card and mouthed the words written inside.

"Read it aloud, Hardy."

Hardy faltered. His face whitened. Without warning, he lunged at me. "You bastard." The card fluttered to the ground as he hit me full in the face. Then again. My nose cracked. I hit back. I crunched a jaw, an eye, a nose. He boxed my ears, kneed my groin, stomped on my toes.

"Break it up, break it up." Ainslie held me back, and two others held Hardy back by his arms. Ainslie grabbed the letter from the floor and smoothed it open.

"It's from someone called Bianca Pennefather," he said. Hardy struggled and escaped his captors, storming away from the tight circle, banging the door outside as he left.

> *Dear Little Soldier Blue (or should I say Rifleman Smiley?)*
> *What's it like, fighting for the green and white? Do they put blue stone in your tea?*
> *Don't you wish you were a bluejob up in the sky instead of 10 years to go in the RLI?*
> *Are you a shumba drinker? How far is it to Mukumbura anyway?*
> *Bianca (thank goodness girls have name badges) Pennefather*

I had been right not to open the letter before now. It deflated all the wild fantasies I had allowed to grow in my mind. Bianca's letter was an exercise in distant irony, sampled from all the Rhodesian songs I knew she detested. But these troopies didn't know that. A silence billowed over the tight group. It was her name that had a magical effect on them.

"*The* Bianca Pennefather?" offered someone from the back, at last.

"*The* Miss Roosevelt Bianca Pennefather?"

"Miss Roosevelt?" I echoed stupidly.

"Miss Roosevelt of 1974. She renounced the title when she got religion."

"Miss hot chick, big boobs, legs up to heaven Bianca Pennefather?"

Sexuality was not contained in individual desires. It was the air we breathed; it was the cause we lived and died for. It was the motivation for everything we did. It oozed out of the pop songs we listened to while we shone our boots and belts and cleaned the barrack room; it radiated from every single white female within a hundred-mile radius.

Bianca and I were an item, I flattered myself to think, back then. During those two years in the church, my senior years, everyone had evolved the inevitable, natural conclusion that Bianca and I were 'going out'. Everyone saw it – everyone but Bianca.

Of course, I wrote right back. I put all those passionate worlds and universes and desires and mythical beings into pathetic little words that leaked out all their meaning as I wrote them. I wrote sonnets, tore them up, composed long passionate descriptions of my feelings, and finally wrote back a Christian brother's chaste and passionless letter of the Galatians. Dear Sister-in-Christ. But the card had disturbed me. This was no Sister-in-Christ. This was the old Bianca, the ironic, mocking Bianca. I signed the letter 'Your brother-in-Christ, Rifleman Smiley'.

Smiley was a safe enough person. He was the lukewarm joking child, not the lusting, boiling Cavedaschi she had rejected. What would she think of the barrack-room Mary who submitted to masculine terror? But that identity had been obliterated by one wave of her magic wand. To these boys, she was a sex symbol, and therefore I had to be a masculine hero. I had regained my manhood. I had become, as the army recruiting posters went, a man among men.

And of course, in Craig Hardy I thought I had made a mortal enemy. He had been outmanoeuvred by Fate, or God, or the White Goddess, or whoever was now controlling our destinies. I avoided him after the letter, and he avoided me at first. But after a few days, far from shunning me, or spiting me, or bullying me, he was all smiles and light punches of camaraderie. Further, he insisted on renewing our tenuous friendship, tagging along with me as if we were inseparable buddies, jabbing at me with backhanded compliments, calling me Soldier Blue, Blue Job, *Shumba* drinker. And against this double irony, I had no defence.

A soldier, I've been telling you, is a swearing, sex-crazed, abusive, testosterone-filled ball of hate who wants to kill Kaffirs or gooks or coolies, is given licence to rape, pillage, destroy villages and spear women and children. But that's not true, of course. A soldier, as we all know, is the sweet drummer boy on the Quality Street chocolate tin. A soldier is a 'boy in the bush'. He is the plaything of a girl's dreams in the hot night of war, who crawls through the window and hides in her bed until the enemy passes. A soldier (not to be confused with solder, that white fluid sub-

stance that melts under fire) is noble, brave, kind and true.

The soldier I am talking of is best described in the song by Gwynneth Ashley Robin, that fourteen-year-old South African singer who died in a plane crash (may she rest in peace). Wait, I'll play the 45 for you, if you don't mind the scratches. See here, she autographed it right on the MVN label (All my love Gwynneth xxx), when I went to see her in concert on the 'Meet the Stars' tour in 1975. Excuse the Afrikaans accent:

*I will wait for you 'til your fighting days are through*
*When the moon at night is shining bright,*
*I'll dream of you – Soldier Blue.*
*I know you're feeling lonely so I write these lines to you,*
*To let you know I'm longing for my little Soldier Blue.*

*Though you're far away from home, we're all proud of you.*
*You're brave and kind and true.*
*I kneel down by my bedside before I sleep each night*

*And pray my little Soldier Blue soon will hold me tight.*
*Good night little soldier and always remember –*
*and always remember –*
*and always remember –*

★  ★  ★

In the last week of our first-phase training, the townships near Bulawayo became restless, according to reports, heated up, and needed cooling down. Our
platoon was chosen to do the job. Quick, get into your riot gear, bayonets
fixed, take two RLS. Sergeant Viper will drive one, Sergeant Hanson the other,
though he shouldn't drive – he is still hung-over from last night. Take the road
to Gwaai, pass through dusty narrow roads at hell-bending speeds, turn left
when you see the jeering crowds throwing stones, drive them back through the
small streets of the township, kill a few chickens and goats for target practice,
and, as a warning to the locals, aim at the snotty picanins so their mothers
scream in terror, then race away back to Llewellin.

No, don't turn those bends so sharply – oh, it's tipping over, the whole fucken lorry
is tipping over, with half the platoon helplessly strapped to the back. It's slowly
falling, crushing the two MAG gunners on the two corner posts. The rest wriggle
free, but Bennett, the fat guy with glasses, is crushed, ballooning slowly out. My
God, lift the fucken truck, you buggers! We can't, Sarge. Don't stand around,
heave. Call the ambulance. They're like balloons, Sarge. I never thought people could blow out like that. The ambulance takes an hour in the hot dust.
We heave and ho. Sergeant Viper curses his luck. It's happened before. In the
obstacle course he threw thunderflashes and killed two recruits. He can do
nothing but dust his beret and berate fate. Too bloody fast around the corners.
Calling Starlight, we need Starlight ASP. I watch Bennett's eyes, still alive in all
that puffy flesh, blinking at us. The other guy is Nel, the big Afrikaans recruit
no one messed with who was going to join the Selous Scouts after Basic Training. We can't even see him, just his legs. We'll get you out, we tell them, but
slowly these two boys flicker and solidify before our eyes. When the ambulance
arrives (here comes Starlight!), two apologetic skinny medics with two stripes
apiece shake their heads. If we lift the truck, the rush of blood flow will kill

them, give them drips. What are they thinking as they die, do they feel the pain, do they know how disgusting they look?

As we circle the overturned truck, a bus approaches at speed, leaning off the road onto the red dust verge as it passes, respectfully slowing down. But the passengers, Africans leaning out of windows in the heat, on top of the roof rack holding luggage, arms hanging out of the back window, begin hooting, and jeering, and laughing. Die, you Rhodesians, die. Viper starts after them, raises a rifle to the aim position but Hansen pulls his weapon down: "Don't, Ernie." We watch the bus pass as a hard ball of hatred grows in our stomachs.

Recruits of 6 RR Alpha Platoon, I now call you men, who have proved yourselves to be true soldiers and are ready to fight for our country, to obey unquestioningly, without hesitation, the orders of your superiors, to die, if need be, in battle for honour, pride and patriotic duty. Your basic reactions have been honed; your instincts of hunger, fear and pain have been fine-tuned. You are now machines ready to be used in the service of the state. All civilian niceties and the veneer of civilisation have been scrubbed off, peeled off in the sun, and you have become the swearing, sweating troops your country can be proud of, men in the prime of your lives, whose main ambition in life is a beer and a day off. Squad shun. Dismissed.

The party was organised at the Holiday Inn, and nurses were bussed in to be our partners. In the smoke-filled disco room, Manfred Mann's 'Blinded by the Light' played loudly and we recruits drank ourselves sick and silly, danced with the women, and in the blur of our hangovers were back at the barracks without remembering much of what went on. I remember Craig Hardy holding some shadow woman to him, as if he were wiping himself on her. I had no one to hold onto, just the letter in my pocket, the universe spinning in my head with her empty words.

At the end of the six weeks, we signed up for specialist courses. Wrigglesworth applied for signals, Braga for Grey's Scouts, Stevens for the officer's course. Nothing appealed to me, but the threat of not specialising meant I would have another eight weeks' bush training, and then go straight to the war as a rifleman, so I opted for Medics. I thought of the two ballooned dead troops, the laughing picanins, the medics who arrived too late. But what was most appealing to my hermetically sealed linguistic reality was their call sign – 'Starlight'.

I lined up outside the interviewing office, asking people who had been for the interview what to say. Carl Rogers, the red-haired recruit ahead of me in the line, winked and told me it was a piece of old *takkie* if you just bullshitted your way.

"Don't say you're squeamish about killing. Say you want to be in the forefront of battle. Play the game; they get a lot of conscientious objectors, and you don't want them to think you're weak."

When I walked in, I looked calmly intelligent, called the officers Sir, the Sergeants Sergeant, the Corporals Corporal.

"Why are you applying to be a medic?"

"I'd rather save life than destroy it," I said.

"Any medical experience?"

"No, sir, but I'm willing to learn. I feel I could cope with medicine."

"Do you realise a medic is a leader, often at the forefront of battle, who kills as much if not more than the next man? A medic does not have a cushy job. It's not for the faint-hearted."

"I'm not a pacifist. I'm fighting for my country and want to contribute to the war effort."

That settled it. "After your weekend pass, Williams, you're a trainee medic as from Monday, 08h00."

# CHAPTER EIGHT

# DADDY WENT TO FIGHT
# FOR THE GREEN AND WHITE

The army bus drove like hell through the crisp autumn night to get us home for our weekend pass. Thirty deliriously drunken troops chanted 'left-right-left-right-left-right-ley' at the tops of their voices, the closer they got to Salisbury. We hadn't slept all night, and we hadn't slept more than four hours a night for six weeks. But we were going to make every moment count this weekend. Most of my comrades vowed to get pissed, wasted, sozzled, sloshed and motherless; others were going to screw their brains out, get laid, poke, put pipe, hide the little sausage. And me? I was going to make a pilgrimage to the house of the White Goddess.

We were deposited at the Monomatapa Hotel bus stop at six o'clock on Saturday morning as the orange sun dawned on a new world. I stared at the colours, the people on the street, at the flamboyants, at the city clothed in pink morning light. A cheery Pearl Assurance building smiled down at me from a blue sky. I listened to the birds in the trees and hedges (had I never heard them before?). You wouldn't know the country was teetering on the brink of destruction, and that we were all about to be swept off the edge of the world.

Because my mother was Italian, the breakfast she lavished on me spoke loudly of how she had worried, cried and regretted the last six weeks of my life.

"Here, Paul, do you want more eggs, bacon, sausages, fried tomato, brinjal, steak?"

But when I tried to give her the details of basic training, she was suddenly busy in the kitchen with the toast and the tea. My father, on the other hand, was hungry for every detail. He wanted to know what he was in for. He had been called up, too, for Police Reserve duty – and he would also be 'in the shit', so to speak.

After breakfast, I walked the mile to Bianca's house in Greendale – across the railway line, past Roosevelt Girls' High on the left, Churchill Boys' High on the right, across Jameson Avenue and into the circular drive – as if I were marching, though I was only wearing blue and white BATA *takkies*.

After six weeks of black and white, I was not prepared for the civilian world. The trees danced in the wind and bowed their leaves to me; the birds sang in full-throated ecstasy; the grass grew wild beneath my feet. I could walk, turn my head, look people in the eye, untuck my shirt, and no one shouted, called me back into line, or even noticed me. But I no longer belonged to this riotous natural environment. I no longer fitted the flimsy blue jeans, T-shirt and light sneakers. Give me my combat boots again. I am naked without my rifle; my hands don't know what to do.

I hadn't been here for six weeks. All I had to show for our relationship was one miserable letter. I walked slower, trying to pace myself. I was being injected with human fluid again, fatal for the hard, Gamma-like soldier I had become.

Bianca's house always amazed me. It was a *pondokkie*, looking as if it had been built by pioneers as a makeshift lean-to, which had been added on, cemented over and propped up by generations of handymen. Surrounding this patchwork structure was an acre of vlei. The garden was populated by reeds, loud crickets and frogs; the pool looked like the abandoned Grande Hotel pool in Beira; the foot-long elephant grass had never been mowed; banana trees sprouted in inopportune spots in the way of paths, driveways and porches, and a granadilla creeper tangled itself over the front door. The dogs had raced around one spot in the yard near their kennels, leaving a muddy racetrack, and a sagging avocado tree sat in its own excrement of rotting fruit. I picked my way through dog faeces, and nodded to the wary garden boy, who was sitting on an upturned paint can in the shade of the tree, drinking a mug of tea.

So why did I love this place? It was, I suppose, the incongruity of a cleanly washed, shiny-brushed Bianca who emerged from it every morning, and returned to it every afternoon. And as the following heady scenes unfolded in the breathless present tense, I will render them so:

Mrs Pennefather opens the door. Her blonde hair, her eyes are Bianca's: she is an ally. But the rings under her eyes, her hair in those hideous plastic blue roll curlers show that this house is taking its toll on her. Her eyes, though, light up (or do I imagine this?) when she sees me. Who am I to her? What daughter's bedtime confessions does she conceal from me? What advice has she given (Daughter, don't give your love to the first man you see. Just bide your time so your heart will be free...)? But her tired wrinkles reveal nothing.

"Paul, my dear, you're so thin." She gives me a smothering hug. "Bianca is away at camp. They're having a holiday Round-Up. You know where Resthaven is."

"Do you think she would mind?"

"She'd be over the moon." Mrs Pennefather's face sweeps away Sergeant Viper's bitter voice, the crew cuts, male sweat and gun smoke of Llewellin Barracks. The last six weeks wither and shrink. That sweet, small voice is back. Sufficiently sanctioned, I squeeze her hand, thank her and back away. Is it significant that she watches me go?

I drive down the Borrowdale Road, past the horsey suburbs, past the farms, towards Domboshawa, turn left down a rocky dirt road, veer right into the Christian camp grounds and park behind a whitewashed building next to an unoccupied red Mini Cooper. I crunch towards the main quadrangle from where I hear singing. Heads turn and eyes widen as each brother- and sister-in-Christ recognises this sunburned, shorn, emaciated survivor of basic training. Reverend Steve Carter gives me a warm handshake and motions me to sit cross-legged in the circle as the singing – 'Rejoice in the Lord always and again I say rejoice!' – continues. Across from me, 60 degrees to my right, Bianca smiles from behind a shy fringe of hair, waves two fingers, and then looks down. Across from me too, 60 degrees to my left, a shorn, sunburned Craig Hardy sits, in green shorts, 3 COY DRR camouflage T-shirt, smiles greasily at me, and waves two fingers. We remain locked in this position through the songs and through Steve's sermon.

A good sermon, the preacher is saying, is like a mini-skirt. It has to be short enough to maintain interest, but long enough to cover the essentials. But then the frown and the pointed finger of God show us that we are not meant to laugh.

"Our bodies are the temples of the Holy Spirit. We should not engage our bodies in any activity that displeases God. Girls, wear long dresses; wear T-shirts over your swimming costumes. Your bodies must not tempt. Boys, control your desires. Lust is a scaly lizard on your shoulder, and you must not listen to its voice. Kill that lizard, and it will turn into a beautiful, white, flying horse. Love is from God; lust is from the devil. And we are the temples of God."

Basic training has turned Hardy from a podgy mess into a muscle man. His thighs bulge out of his shorts; his arms are tight, glowing muscle. His cropped bullet head makes him look like a Springbok rugby player. His face is full, rosy-cheeked, and his eyes dance with sexuality. He is not tired. I, on the other hand, have been turned into a scarecrow. I am emaciated and gaunt. After six weeks of getting up at 3 a.m. and running all day, I am dispirited and exhausted. Black rings underscore my aching eye sockets. My breath is sour, my ears ring.

After the sermon, the group splinters to play volleyball, soccer, tennis. Craig is in animated conversation with Luke Pennefather, whose Schofield Reference Bible is splayed open on his lap, and he smiles beatifically as I pass. I march past him towards the retreating Bianca, who turns, reddens and backs up against a *msasa* tree as this skeleton of a boy bears down upon her. She is not over the moon. Her foot taps nervously and her pink-painted toes stretch out and wriggle, protesting the rigidity of her posture. She hugs her stomach. She casts nervous frowns over my shoulder at her brother and Hardy. I know how ridiculous I must look. The tips of my ears are peeling red; the prison haircut reveals the pixie shape of my head and my Spock ears; my nose is crackled and red; my lips are thin strips of biltong.

"Did you… do you… did you get my last letter?"

She purses her lips. "What is your last letter? Is it the 'I' in Cavedaschi? Or 'S' in Williams? Or the 'Y' in… never mind. What are you staring at?"

She watches me touch the hairs of her forearm. But she is quick to retreat. She whisks her arm away and scratches it. "That tickles."

We cast furtive glances back at the hall windows. We are in full view of Hardy and her brother, but they are huddling over John 3:16, too busy in a hermeneutic discussion to notice us.

"You were away awfully long. Are you going to be away that long each time?"

"I have a pass every weekend from now on. I'm in medical training."

"So can you make next weekend? My brother (she points to him, but it is Hardy who looks up and grins) leaves for America. We're having a party for him. Can you be there?"

I take her hands and squeeze them. "Bianca."

"I'll take that as a yes. Now let's pray and thank God that you're safe."

She extricates her hands from my grip and hides them behind her back. I close my eyes while she prays: "Thank you, Lord, for bringing Paul back safely to us. Thank you, Lord for this precious…"

It takes a few seconds for me to register that we are not alone. I am suddenly aware that I am in the strong American presence of Steve Carter. Her prayer trails off, and he finishes it for her: "Thank you for the return of Thy servant, Lord, upon whom Thou hast laid Thy hand of protection… Amen." He thumps me on the back in greeting. "They're waiting for you in the hall, Bianca. The women's meeting can't start without you."

She scurries off, for the pastor means to talk to me. He skirts (or should I say mini-skirts) the army issues – he doesn't want to know how I got the sunburned ears or the dark rings under my eyes, or the cracked lips.

"We try to encourage purity and restraint here, Paul. One of the camp rules is not to be alone with a member of the opposite sex. I'm sure you understand that. Even married couples at camp are encouraged to refrain from intimacy this weekend. We're here to purify ourselves."

"I didn't know."

"You're welcome, of course, but we're here to worship the Lord, not to make the Devil's work easier for him. And we have a new convert, so we need to set a good example."

For the rest of the day, I have to be content to sit in large segregated groups of singing, clapping Christians, to sit across from her, listen to sermons about purity and righteousness, to play volleyball – boys versus girls – to eat meals in segregated teams and to throw surreptitious and unacknowledged yearning glances across the room.

Craig Hardy has indeed become a Christian, and is Luke's best friend. They spend all day together, talking, praying, reading the Bible and playing soccer. He pointedly avoids me and I him. We have nothing to say to each other. But at mealtime, when we are lined up to be dished a mysterious concoction of mash and mince on our tin plates, he speaks.

"Leave some for us, Mary."

I feign ignorance, but it is too late. Bianca, in a parallel line across the table, is watching me, and in her guilty face, I know that she knows. And not only she: they all know. Colin Botha, the grinning fourth-former ahead of me in the queue, nudges me. "Mary! Mary! Quite contrary!"

I close my eyes. But I still see the leering, curling lips of Alpha Platoon, 6 RR, Llewellin Barracks, hear their mocking voices as they dance around me: "Mary! Mary! Quite the fairy! How does your garden grow?"

I leave at sunset without speaking to her again. After supper, boys and girls are separated for private talks about how to deal with their sexuality (by denying it), how to relate to the opposite sex (by desexing them), and how to find a marriage partner (by not looking for one). There is to be no contact between boys and girls, no high jinks or nightly pranks; and I drive away without knowing whether she realises I am gone.

But she knows – everyone knows – of my shame. I am no longer Odysseus returning to claim his bride. I am the fool on the hill, the clown, the Mary, Mary, quite contrary. What else has he told them of my humiliation at Llewellin Barracks?

I mean to return the next morning for the Sunday service, but I cannot. It is partly to do with exhaustion. I sleep through the entire Sunday morning, waking up at midday. I am not alone in this. I later discover that most of my fellow recruits, despite their valiant boasting, spend the weekend gonking and pushing zeds. I wake in time for a prearranged lunch at Jameson's with my parents, who chide me for not spending any time with them.

"I haven't slept for six weeks, Mum."

By the time we return from the restaurant, I realise how futile it will be to drive back to Resthaven now. They will be on their way home. And why should I show my sunburned face to them now anyway? I want to phone her house before I leave, but I cannot bring myself to do it. And when I board my train to Bulawayo at six o'clock that evening, there is no Bianca to see me off.

God spends much of the journey with me on the train reassuring me that it's OK. His large hands are cupping me, He has great things in store for me, and all I have to do is wait.

★ ★ ★

*Dear God,*

*Gandhi maintained that men should save their sperm for a healthier life. Refraining from ejaculation would give men more energy, vigour and spiritual clarity, he said. So too the Victorians. If it itches, don't scratch. Temptation is easy to yield to. Your Word, too, confirms this: it is better to marry than to burn with lust, but both are bad. The highest calling is not to do it. Yet I crave the sins of the flesh. I crave them. I'm a nineteen-year-old at my sexual peak with nowhere to run or direct my fervour. We poor Muslims, Jews, Christians are all cursed with a body that desires, that needs, that demands, but must be denied. You gave us a body that craves flesh, but which will pull the soul down to hell if we give in to it. We want to soar, but we plummet.*

*I may be wrong about this, Lord, but I read somewhere (was it in an old Scope magazine?) that sexual restraint is actually unhealthy. The article was entitled 'Are we having too little sex?' Healthy sex, claims the medical fraternity, may reduce cancer risks in males. The more ejaculations the better. Saving your sperm makes you go rotten. And further, there was a correlation with diseases of the sexual organs like prostate, breast and cervical cancer to our attitudes and sexual habits. I wonder if any study has been done where men who refrained from ejaculation became more prostate prone? Monks perhaps? And don't we label a 'healthy' sex life one which involves regular, frequent and unrepressed sexual activity? Breast cancer arises because breasts need to be fondled, loved and exposed, not hidden away and denied. The cervix needs acknowledgement and glorification if it is to gain any healthy self-confidence.*

*I don't know. These are just my smoky ideas through a looking glass darkly, in the solitary confinement of this male prison. Dear God, take me to a world where sex is good, not taboo…*

★ ★ ★

Eight o'clock, Monday morning, DRR Camp Hospital, found a select group of twenty medical recruits lined up outside the low-roofed training room labelled 3 MED COY. My first shock as I joined the squad was that my tenacious buddy,

Craig Hardy, was standing to attention in the back line of medical recruits. He winked at me, and then snapped to attention as the medical officer in command marched up to take the roll-call. I felt the crew-cut hair on the back of my head rise as if he was staring at me, mocking me, gloating in triumph at being here in a space I had thought was my own.

The medic instructor was quick to inform us that, though we were to be treated like human beings (we were now permitted to march around puddles and not through them), the medics' course was intensive, and we would not be allowed any weekend passes until we graduated in three months' time. The army needed medics desperately, and our course was to be condensed so that we could be sent into the field as soon as possible.

So much for the urgent need to get back to Bianca and replace the last ghastly weekend pass with a better one. So much, too, for her brother's farewell party, where we could have made up, kissed and told each other that we were meant for each other. And so much, too, for the many explanations, jokes and anecdotes I had stored up that would obliterate 'Mary' (it's only an anagram of 'army', ha, ha) and re-establish my sentry position as her Little Soldier Blue.

As it turned out, I had little time for self-pity or self-recrimination. The course stuffed our minds with so many facts and charts that I had no chance to ruminate, to brood on my sorrows or even to count the days. My one consolation was that Hardy was here, and not in Salisbury where he could do mischief. Whatever he thought he was gaining by becoming a medic, he had allayed those fears.

On the first day, I chose a bunk bed near the very end of the medical barrack room, hoping to be left alone, but at once, Hardy tagged me and heaved his rucksack onto the bunk on my right. He was all smiles, light punches of camaraderie, as if we were the best of friends. But pointedly, he pinned up a photo of Marilyn Monroe on his locker. I stared at the pouting smile, the intimate, collusive look, the half-asleep eyes, the hint of helpless but seductive embarrassment at her dress fluttering over a windy air vent. Say something, I dare you, Hardy's grin suggested.

On my left was the red-haired boy who had given me the advice that had got me into medical training. He plonked his duffel bag on his bunk and shook my hand.

"Carl Rogers."

"Paul Williams."

The Medics' course was conducted at the DRR Camp Hospital, a low, flat concrete building with one small twenty-bed ward, an MI room, a physiotherapy section, a few doctors' offices, its own kitchen, and an operating theatre. This was where I learned basic first aid: that the human body is a machine and must be treated like one. Charts of the human machine had to be memorised. I learned what to do if the machine lost blood when a bullet caused a leak. Replace the blood, add fuel (plasma), patch up the wound, and don't let germs get in, because like rust, they eat away at the human material. If a leg is broken, *bopa* a straight pole next to it so it grows straight again.

Pain can be easily removed with Propon, morphine, Sosegon, which all numb the electric sensations of the brain and stop the pain messages being sent. For bullet wounds in the head, don't give morphine – it impairs behaviour tests. All bugs, bacteria and mystery ailments can be cured with the wonder drug penicillin, which kills all foreign forms of life in the body, all invaders and aliens. Symptoms of illnesses that need antibiotics are overheating of the body and diarrhoea (bad fuel consumption).

"Five ways to stop bleeding? Quick now wake up, you. Rogers? Hardy?"

"Tourniquet."

"Elevation."

"Cold compress."

"Meditation."

"Tampon."

The power of life and death is in your hands. Soldiers with guns have the power of death; medics with needles have the power of life. You are God. In a contact with the enemy, descend from on high to rescue the wounded, heal the sick, raise the dead. Deliver them up to the higher gods at the hospital bases; then they can live happily ever after. All you have to do is keep the patient alive for the few minutes it takes to casevac (casualty evacuation) them. Keep drips going, attach splints, administer painkillers. You also have to keep all petty ailments at bay while the soldiers are in the bush. For headaches, flu and water poisoning all you need are painkillers, antibiotics and a lot of nerve.

"This is the female reproductive system." The instructor had drawn a large figure on the board and labelled it 'c.u.n.t.'. We were to copy it down and label the parts: labium minora, vagina, labium majora, clitoris, cervix, oviducts.

"Why do we need to learn this, Sergeant?"

"You never know. One day you will be asked to make a baby, or deliver a baby in a remote village somewhere, and we don't want you getting confused."

My discomfort at drawing an open, exposed vagina was due to in part to the feeling that I was committing some unforgivable sin. And I still remembered Actaeon. So every time I opened my notebook, I quickly skimmed past this page. Hardy, however, pinned up his vividly detailed version of the vagina on his locker door. Say something, I dare you, his grin again suggested to me.

The weeks passed. In the hospital ward, we spent our time measuring table-spoons of cough mixture to patients, or changing bed pans, or taking tempera-tures (make sure those *goffles* are not skiving, and heating their mouths before you insert the thermometer). We got to know how the body worked, how to fix it, when it was worth repairing, or when to throw it away and get a new one. I wasn't that good, but neither was anyone else. We didn't know our arses from our elbows. We called the aorta a femur, the labia minora a sphincter, recom-mended laxatives for diarrhoea, diuretics for piles. We pumped air into the bloodstream; we strapped the wrong leg in mock operations.

Hardy was all thumbs. He had no aptitude for medicine, but did not seem to care. His sole purpose in being here, it seemed, was to torment me. This he did in subtle ways that no one noticed, except the silent Carl Rogers, who would pick up the innuendos, flicking his eyes towards me in consternation every time Hardy made some jab at me.

Rogers's approach to medicine was unconventional, to say the least. When faced with a patient with gunshot wounds in the stomach, with sausages and jelly oozing out, he would exasperate his instructors. "The human body is spirit," he would argue. "Ailments are all in the imagination, as is reality. All in the mind. You are causing your own pain and your own reality."

Carl had been to university in South Africa, in Durban, and brought into the dark cardboard box of our barrack room a colourful world from outside and a language spiced with such phrases as "the problem with dialectical material-ism" or "in a post-structural society" or "the inadequacy of rational discourse".

At university, where he took philosophy and psychology, students and profes-
sors alike wore long hair, sandals, bell-bottom jeans and Indian cotton shorts.
Girls went braless and wore no petticoats, sometimes arriving to lectures in
fluorescent bikinis, dripping in brine from the sea. More importantly, he said,
at university you learned the secrets of the universe, that life was more than you
could ever imagine. He had learned to meditate, to astral-travel, to see beyond
material reality to Truth and Wonder and Essence. We were living in a dark
cave, he said, and he would lead us out into the light.

I later discovered that Carl Rogers (or 'Buddha' as we called him) had failed
his first year at the University of Natal, had to leave South Africa on expiration
of his student visa, and on return to Rhodesia had been visited by MPs who had
knocked long and hard at his front door one night and bodily escorted him
into National Service by his long red mane. But for now, he awed us with his
magical powers, and his gestures through the pinprick holes of our cardboard
box to an ideal world outside.

★　★　★

Meanwhile, the government of Rhodesia (so say our medical instructors) is sliding slowly into the hands of communism and compromise. Smith, incredibly, has
agreed to majority rule within five years. What happened to the 'never in a thousand years' promise he made us? How did he capitulate so easily? Well, U.S. Secretary of State Henry Kissinger twisted his arm, made him bend over backwards,
and, squatting on top of him, forced him to say 'nuff!' and concede to the principle
of majority rule. Never in my lifetime, hollers Smith. Knee thrust in groin. Oof!
Not in a thousand years. Arm twisted behind back. Nrrggh. OK, I give up. I
can't hit a man with glasses. Tweak of the nose. All right. I've always believed in
majority rule. Cut off blood flow to neck. Five years? Ha, ha. No problem.

In its policy of appeasement and compromise, the government has foolishly
sprinkled a few race reforms onto the fertile ground of revolt, allowing blacks to
buy white farmland, hotels to become multiracial, and black soldiers to become
officers, magistrates and prison officers. How far will Smith go to appease the
communists before he realises that if you give a black man an inch, he'll take the
whole damn country? Not surprisingly, Parliament is in an uproar. The few sane

MPs walk out of the RF, and promptly form the Rhodesian Action Party, vowing to keep Rhodesia in civilised white hands for all time and rejecting any form of majority rule. Someone has to be holding their finger in the dyke.

★ ★ ★

The other recruits in the barrack room knew Carl from school or from basic training, and were used to his gadfly stings on their thick hides ("If you see the Buddha on the road, please kill him for me, won't you?" or "What's the sound of one hand clapping?"). But I was in awe. I had found a spiritual companion.

"I accept that Jesus was a prophet," said Carl, "but there are many prophets who have insight into truth. Why do you have to get stuck with a Jewish carpenter?"

"But don't you see, Carl, that Jesus was the Son of God? So either he is mistaken, or he is a liar, or he is telling the truth. Take your pick."

"That's called an either/or fallacy," grinned the Buddha. "And if you are forcing me to choose, I will choose all of them. Jesus is a liar, the son of God and a deluded man. Truth lies in contradiction."

"But don't you see, our bodies are temples of the Holy Spirit."

"We are more than our bodies. Our bodies are mere vessels, expressions of our souls. See, Paul, even Christians and Buddhists are in agreement about that. Even the Bible talks of astral travel. Read Solomon, Proverbs. And Christians even believe in reincarnation. But you only get one chance at it. How can you know what to do when you only have one lifetime to try it out?"

"But meditation opens you to evil spirits, to demons…"

"The only demons hovering around us are ourselves, our lower selves, pulling us down, trying to keep us mortal. Our higher selves, however, can be reached by meditation, or if you don't like opening yourself, through self-contradiction. The Zen Buddhists argue that enlightenment can come suddenly, through Koans."

Hardy, as if he sensed that Rogers was my guardian angel, my brighter self, attacked him at once. Maybe now that I was no longer a threat, no longer his enemy, he had to find another one. He thrust a clenched fist into Carl's face.

"That's the sound of one hand clapping. And if you don't shut up with your smart-arse sayings you will find yourself dead on the road outside too." He snatched the book Buddha had been reading, *The Third Eye*, threw it on top of a locker. "Buddha's third eye is his arsehole."

Carl folded bony arms. "You don't believe in reincarnation? Suppose I proved to you that you lived previously?"

"Look, I'm not into this Eastern crap."

"Then you are a dry piece of shit." Buddha turned and retrieved his book.

Hardy looked around nervously. No one, but no one, called him a dry piece of shit. "All right, all right," he said.

"Dead quiet, everyone." Outside clouds scudded past the moon, the lines of eucalyptus trees danced slowly in the breeze, dogs barked in a distant government African compound, and I could hear the earth breathing. Carl produced a gold watch on a chain out of his pocket. In slow motion, he brought the pendant close to Hardy's face, the gold glittering as it caught the light.

"Follow the pendant with your eyes." He swung the watch slowly back and forth. "You are feeling sleepy, drowsy. Your eyelids are drooping." Hardy swayed, his eyes closing as he tried to fight off the heaviness. A few more encouragements in the deep voice of Buddha and he was gone. We all watched closely, trying not to swallow too loudly or breathe too noisily in case we broke the spell.

"Hardy, when I click my fingers, I want you to practise your drill."

Hardy would never do this, we thought, in response to the commands of another recruit. But when Buddha clicked his fingers, the bully of Alpha Platoon leaped to attention and marched stiffly to the end of the room and back, his arms shoulder high, his heels digging into the ground.

"Chin up, chin up," Buddha smiled. "Hardy, halt. Stand easy." Hardy stamped his feet apart and stared at the locker in front of him, oblivious to all around him, only a voice in blackness his pilot. "What would you like him to do?"

Rowan Smith had a suggestion. "Ask him to act as if Marilyn Monroe is in the room."

"Hardy, Marilyn Monroe, the girl of your dreams is here. She is walking in – see, there she is, coming in at the door – she's come to see you."

Hardy pasted his hair down with one hand, adjusted his shirt sleeve with the other, and looked eagerly towards the doorway.

"Aren't you going to say anything to her?"

Hardy smelt the air around him like an animal, and cast furtive glances at this apparition.

"Is she really there?" Hardy looked and nodded. "But she's dead, Hardy. She's been dead for years. She committed suicide in 1960 something, which means you're staring at a fifteen-year-old corpse. And Marilyn Monroe was not even her real name." Hardy stared fearfully at the space ahead of him, and rubbed his hands nervously.

"Don't you think you should lay this poor ghost to rest now? She's been trapped for so long." He pointed to the locker again. Hardy walked to it, and examined the picture of Marilyn Monroe in her frozen pose. He peeled it off the locker, frowned at it and then with shaking hands, tore it up, crumpled up the pieces and threw them into the air. They scattered all over the barrack room, in colourful flutters of arms, lips and legs, until they settled lifeless on the floor around us. Hardy then stood blankly at ease.

"It's all right, she's gone." Rogers turned to us. "This is where we get down to business. We've had our fun. Listen, Hardy, you are now fifteen. What are you doing?"

"I am playing rugger."

"OK, let's go back to when you were seven. You are seven again. Show me what you are doing?"

Hardy fell to his knees. "I'm playing rugger."

"Where are you?"

"Wodesia."

"Now you are five."

Hardy sat on the floor with legs splayed. "I'm playing rugger."

"Now you are three. Think carefully, what do you see?"

We all watched him describe a world without boundaries, with no names, a fresh new world. Carl Rogers was smiling triumphantly. I scrutinised both actors with suspicion, looking for some collusion, some indication of a hoax. "Now listen carefully, Hardy. I want you to tell me what it was like when you were in your mother's womb just before you were born. Can you tell me?"

Hardy twitched and stuttered. "Dark, black," he said. "Want to get out." I shook my head. Rowan mumbled in disbelief. But... Hardy, we knew, couldn't act that well. He was too anxious to communicate the experience and obey the commanding voice in his head.

"Now, Hardy, what was it like before you were born, before you were in your mother's womb, before you became Craig Hardy, before you were alive? Where were you?"

My eighteen-year-old idealistic self watched intently. I wanted something to happen. I wanted Hardy to tell us he was an Egyptian slave who built the pyramids, or a medieval Italian peasant working for a lord, fearful of the Catholic Church. I wanted to peep into the secrets of the universe. And Rogers promised that all would be revealed: glimpses beyond death, outside space and time, outside our narrow life slot. A thin wisp of hope drifted up into our barrack room.

"What do you see?" insisted the voice. Hardy tried to squirm away from it, but it was inside his head. He held his ears; he quivered at the mouth; he began to tremble.

"Blackness. Dark."

"No, before that. What do you see?"

Hardy trembled violently, as if some invisible force was shaking him. His eyes were wide.

"Show me your original face, before you were born."

"What's happening?"

"He must take the leap back into his previous life – or else he has done it and has no words to express what he sees. It must be terrifying to see things without words to describe them. Then you have no defence against the universe."

But he did have words – Buddha's insistent monotone, creating some sort of virtual reality he didn't want to be in, holding him in a space that didn't exist in his own world. Hardy began to dribble at the mouth; his defenceless, shapeless body cringed and collapsed like a spider in a candle flame.

Buddha leaped up. "When I clap my hands you will wake up!"

The sound of his hands clapping jolted all of us back to reality: Alpha Platoon, Intake 156, 1977, a group of eighteen-year-old white Rhodesian males with crew cuts, in a barrack room, about to go and fight a war. Hardy stopped shaking and blinked away the tears from his eyes. He looked wildly around the barrack room.

"Where's she gone?" Still in a daze, he walked over to his locker and stared at the place where the picture of Marilyn had been. Then he spotted the torn butterflies all around the room. We watched in silence as he became aware of us all around him. "And what are you bastards staring at?"

To our surprise, Craig Hardy left Medics training the week after that. There was no connection apparently with the hypnosis episode. He hadn't been doing well, and rather than face a humiliating 'F' grade for the course, he decided to jump ship.

"This is a course for wankers," he announced as he heaved his rucksack onto his shoulders and staggered out of the door. "I've been chosen for Special Ops."

It was a relief of sorts, but then a dark fear began to spider into my nights. No longer under my watchful eye, he could be anywhere, with… anyone…

I also felt mean. He had bullied everyone, yes, but this trick – was it a trick? – was low down and dirty. Buddha said he did it for me and all the defenceless victims of testosterone, but I still felt mean. Hardy was tied to me, I knew, but my other self, this Buddha, was also a tight connection. And if he was going to befriend me, defend me, offer me a space, who was I to refuse it?

Maybe I read too much into friendships – male friendships, that is (I knew I was hopelessly illiterate when it came to female friendships). I have never been able to work out male camaraderie; at school we were merely bonding in the face of adversity, or grouping as a pack of predators to hunt. And with Hardy I was a rival lover, in competition. What relationship was I to Buddha? I soon found out: I was to be his spiritual apprentice. I was a Christian, and his occult powers should have been a direct threat to my world. But I was drawn, fascinated, and now he had bought my allegiance.

The war was being won, slowly and surely, we were told on the Camp Hospital television every night. But the Minister of Defence, P.K. van der Byl (pronounced 'bile') explained that in order to protect the innocent tribesmen in the Tribal Trust Lands from terrorists who came to steal and kill, the government had moved a quarter of a million villagers into those protected areas, fenced and guarded and looked after by the Internal Affairs soldiers. The old huts and villages had been burned to prevent them returning, and in this way, the Rhodesian army was able clearly to distinguish terrorists from curfew-breakers and innocent civilians. Anyone outside the protected village after curfew was a terrorist. Plain and simple. As Van der Byl explained it:

*If villagers harbour terrorists and terrorists
are found running about in villages, naturally they will be bombed and destroyed in
any manner which the commander on the
spot considers to be desirable in the suit-
able prosecution of a successful campaign.
Where the civilian population involves
itself with terrorism, then somebody is
bound to get hurt and one can have little
sympathy for those who are mixed up with
the terrorists when they receive the wrath
of the Security Forces.*

It was a lesson the liberators of Zimbabwe learned very well. After the war was
over, Smith's emergency powers were still
in place, and the so-called socialist gov-
ernment of ZANU (PF) had become black Smiths. Robert Mugabe clarified this
in December 1982:

*We have to deal with this problem quite ruthlessly. Don't cry if your relatives get
killed in the process… where men and women provide food for the dissidents, when
we get there we eradicate them. We do not differentiate who we fight because we can't
tell who is a dissident and who is not.*

★ ★ ★

Because the war was spreading in the country, it had become necessary to call
more men up to serve in the armed forces. Rowan Cronje, the Minister of
Manpower, announced that all men between the ages of 38 and 55 were to be
called up for military service. Up till now it had been only men between 18 and
38 who served in the army. This re-registration exercise made twelve thousand

more men available and spread the manpower load. It was a difficult balance, said Cronje, because Rhodesia's manpower had to be used to the absolute maximum effect, both in the economy and the military. Rhodesia could not survive if the economy collapsed. Nor could it survive if we failed militarily. Black majority rule was not inevitable. Rhodesia was going to fight with all necessary force to keep the country in good hands.

★ ★ ★

*Dear Paul*

*Why haven't you written to your dear mum? In the four weeks you have been in medical training, call-ups have been increased to include men from 38 to 55. Yes, your poor old dad, who has reached the inconceivably old age of forty-five, received his call-up papers yesterday – schoolteachers have to give up their school holidays, and he will train at Cranborne barracks for convoy duty. Even our sixty-year-old neighbour, Mr Willis, has been asked to join a neighbourhood watch patrol, and will serve his country by ambling slowly through Hillside with a Browning automatic at night. Heaven help us if there is an emergency. I don't think he has the strength to pull the trigger, or the hearing to know if there is an emergency.*

*Oh, by the way, a girl is going to stay with me while dad is on call-up – Willow Edmondson. You probably don't remember her – we know the family – her father is high up in Duly's and we met them in Inyanga last Christmas. She's a beautiful girl, just turned eighteen, bright as a ball. She finished her 'A' Levels last year, like you did, and she's at Speciss. She wants to meet you. You know your dear old mother has bragged about you, I'm afraid. She was hoping (as were we all) that you would be home this weekend so you two could meet. Never mind. Take care and see you in two weeks' time.*

*Love, Mum.*

★ ★ ★

Our last week of medical training was spent in shifts of two at the casualty ward of Mpilo Hospital, the black hospital in Bulawayo. It was less glamorous than it sounded. The emergency room was a shabby prefab building swamped with lines of people from the townships – an axe wound here, a knife protruding from a back there, a hacksaw wound on a penis from a jealous wife. We kept a large fish tank of boiling water to sterilise our equipment, reusable metal syringes and a carpenter's array of tools for emergency repairs. All treatment was disappointingly similar: suture. And it was more primitive than I imagined, just a curved needle, with an attached elephant-strength thread. You gave a local anaesthetic by sticking the needle into the open wound until it didn't hurt any more. Then you sewed up the two sides of the wound. Human skin was tough and difficult to pierce, stretching up and out until the needle popped through it. I got the hang of it only by remembering my training. This was not a human being with feeling. This flesh is not soul or spirit but rubber. Numb the pain, then operate: quick repair jobs, patch and go.

Syphilis and gonorrhoea were the most common ailments, and the easiest to fix: 1) examine penis and look for spots and milky discharge; 2) inject 5 c.c. Propen in the buttocks daily for five days; 3) warn the patient to come back every day or his disease will become immune to penicillin (inevitably, he doesn't come back; it is too painful and humiliating, and anyway the sores clear up by themselves, until the second phase of the disease, months, years later, when more sores appear, and the strain is now resistant to penicillin); 4) warn your partner.

"Who did you sleep with?"

"Many girls, doctor, many."

"Tell them all. They all have VD. All of them. It spreads like Royal Washable ink on recycled paper…"

A sea of patients washed through the hospital continuously with VD, headache, hangover, constipation.

"I fell through the window…"

"My left arm is hanging off…"

"I broke my leg in a *panga* duel with a neighbour…"

VD, VD and more VD. No one comes back for a second treatment. How many are out there with VD?

"Accidental discharge of his weapon into my left foot, doctor."

All those sick bodies, these malfunctioning machines. A pill for this, an injection for that.

" Make the pain go away now, please, doctor."

Stitch up this little boy's head, quick, you don't need anaesthetic.

Bubbleyes: quick, a drip to replace fluid loss caused by alcohol (a diuretic, poison), one Propen (severe painkiller), Alka-Seltzer fizz to counteract acidity, vitamin B jab – instant tonic.

"Accidental discharge, doctor, how was I to know she'd get pregnant?"

Troopies with fainting fits, headaches, exhaustion, salt loss. All fixable in seconds. Sterile water injections for the shammers, it fixes them up quick; make it painful, the more painful the medicine, the more effective it is. Chalk tablets for headaches, for insomnia, works like a dream. A body is a malfunctioning machine. I didn't know my rifle from my gun, doctor. Before you mechanically bang two machines together, you have to make sure they are clean or else – VD. Come back tomorrow or you'll become resistant. You have? You have sores all over your body? Why do you have a pus discharge from your rectum as well as your penis? Long, limp, rubber tubes, faulty discharge of urine, it's painful when I piss, Doctor. I can't shoot. This is my rifle, this is my gun. This is for shooting, this is for fun. I have a chick up the spout, she has a bun in the oven, you should have provided rubbers, Doctor…

Three significant stars shone for me in that otherwise dark training. Three bright spots of hope arrived in the form of letters, at low points, to sustain me and to allay my fears. The first was a Valentine's card (even though it was late April), heavily perfumed, which fortunately I was allowed to open in the solitude of my own bunk bed, though Buddha complained about the smell. The card depicted a gaudily dressed cartoon character of a stripper, covering herself with a feather boa.

'For you,' it read, 'I'd drop everything.' The inside of the card depicted the same female figure now naked save for a feather falling opportunely over her breasts and another covering her genitals. And at the bottom of the card, written in Edwardian script, 'Love from a Secret Admirer.'

Two weeks later, I received another card. This one featured a series of dots with numbers which, if connected, depicted a boy kissing a girl. Inside the card, written in different colours, each word in a different script, was her message:

*Do you ever get the feeling that life is just a game, and we don't have all our dots connected? Better you get over here fast so we can connect them up. You probably don't believe this, but I've been thinking of you a lot lately. Your secret admirer.*

I understood. She could not be direct. It was only in humour, irony and distance that she could relate to me. So be it. But her third and last letter before the end of my course was a more direct attempt at communication:

*My Dream: we were on the beach, the golden sands of Durban, and there was no one else around. It was early morning, and we were dancing together in the waves, as they battered us (did you know I was a dancer? No: you know nothing about me; you don't even know who I am, do you?). I was wearing a long blue dress, which I swept around us. The sea battered us as we swayed in its current. Then we were beached onto the sand and ran laughing away from each other.*
*Your dancing queen (only seventeen)*

★ ★ ★

So I needn't have worried. I needn't have dug away at my heart, stringing together long narratives of explanation and apology, rewinding time to re-enact scenarios of that weekend, or how the next weekend should have gone. Abstinence had made the heart grow fonder. Her heart, anyway. I was tying myself in knots trying not to grow any more fond of her. But it had all worked out in the end.

Providence, Fate, God, had taken care of it all. Wait on the Lord. Rest in the Lord. The smiling wife of Steve Carter hovered over me at night, saying, "You're welcome," and the preacher's voice echoed in my dreams: "Delight in the Lord and He will give you the desires of your heart."

After three months, the glorious prize: two white chevrons on the left arm, a certificate and a new self: Corporal Paul Cavedaschi Williams: Medic, MA III. It meant a little more pay; it also meant that I was no longer to be bullied by anyone of my rank or below; instead, I was allowed to bully riflemen and have authority over them. This is how the Great Chain of Being worked.

At the top was Ian Smith, below him the Commander of the Army, General Peter Walls, then all the lesser gods, colonels, majors, captains, lieutenants, sergeants, corporals, lance-corporals, down to riflemen, the lowest of the low. No wait, below them were the civilians, black tribesmen, the masses of people who could be moved like pawns at the whim of others.

The symbol of the medical profession is a snake entwined round a pole. This was the badge on my new beret, on the hospital door, on the letterheads of the camp hospital. It was the symbol of the first Greek doctor, Asclepias, hero, mortal, god, who used a sacred snake to cure people. He even raised the dead, until jealous Hades complained that the natural order was being interfered with, so Zeus struck poor Asclepias dead with a thunderbolt from heaven.

Behold, a modern-day Asclepias: Corporal Paul Williams.

CHAPTER NINE

# THE TERRORIST

*I zik a zumba, zumba, zumba; I zik a zumba, zumba, zay;*
*Hold him down, you Zulu warrior; hold him down, you Zulu chief,*
*Chief! Chief! Chief! Chief! Chief! Chief! Chief! Chief!*

God knows where it came from. To the rhythm of heavy clapping, stamping the two-four beat on the metal floor of the bus, we would sing this song in rounds, on our way to sports fixtures, on our way back, and now all the way back to Salisbury on end-of-medical-training weekend pass.

Shaka's army was run on the premise that Zulu warriors would fight better as single men and would be rewarded for bravery in battle with a wife on return to the *kraal.* This principle still applied, I hoped, in Rhodesian warfare too. She would drop everything for me. We would join our dots. She would be my dancing queen. She loved me, yeah, yeah, yeah. She would wait for me, till my fighting days were through.

This time I was ready for her. The burned ears, nose and lips had healed in the darkness of the medic lecture theatre. I had filled out and was fit, healthy and lean. Hardy would be vanquished, trounced, routed. But of course no action on my part would be necessary. God had done it all. Bianca and I were predestined to be together. Delight in the Lord and He will give thee the desires of thine heart. So, late Saturday morning, I dialled 45063, the number I was to call countless times in that tortured span of my Bianca-drenched life.

"Hello?" Her mother answered evasively. Regrettably, Bianca was 'out'. She was not sure where (waterskiing, she thought, on Lake McIlwaine). Where had I been? I had missed Luke's farewell. I detected a slight hesitation in her voice, as if she knew something I didn't, but these doubts I vanquished as the whispers of the Devil. Have faith. Trust, wait, rest. She would pass on the message. I was not discouraged. I had given no warning I would be home. I couldn't expect her to wait for me, could I, like Gwynneth Ashley Robin did for her Soldier Blue? But what could I do on a wasted Saturday night? The idea had been ingrained in me by Cat Stevens and Elton John and the Bay City Rollers that Saturday night had to be spent in search of love. To spend it alone ("Another Saturday night and I ain't got nobody") was to admit failure as a male predator in his perpetual urge to conquest. All those American TV shows privileged Saturday nights for dating rituals. Yet here I was on my only free Saturday night in two months at home alone.

And home was no longer the house of my childhood. 59 Hillside Road had become a fortress. My liberal parents had bought a pistol for protection, had wired the house for intruders, and had succumbed to the call of duty. My mother baked cakes for the boys in the bush and 'womanned' a post near the barracks for returning troops to nosh at. My father was sitting on his arse on the back of a convoy truck somewhere. He had been gone all school holidays, but before he left, had primed the alarm system so all the windows and doors were wired, and constantly set off by the houseboy every time he moved or cleaned. The 9 mm pistol, locked in a drawer by her bedside, my mother refused to touch.

But what was most different about the house was that it was occupied by a ghostly intruder, a girl called Willow, whose dressing gown hung on the back of the bathroom door and whose scent permeated the house. I had been warned about her in my mother's letter, but had somehow skimmed over the section that announced this new arrival in our lives.

"She's very religious, but not in a bad way," my mother said. "She holds my hand and prays with me at night – for you, for Bernard, for all the boys in the bush, for our country. I hope you don't mind, Paul, she's staying here in the guest room. Why, here she is!"

Willow was all I feared she would be. She was, by prearranged matriarchal consent, my future wife. She was not unattractive ("She has such a good personality"), but what makes people attractive is unattainability. So to have a girl fawning over me, staring at my eyes ("Where did your son get such beautiful eyelashes, Mrs Williams?") made me run a thousand metaphorical miles, and withdraw into my arctic self. Besides, I argued indignantly, I had a girlfriend already.

Willow sat on the old couch, which betrayed me immediately when its cushions gave way and slanted us toward each other until she was pressing on me, her hand lying casually on my lap. She wore her dressing gown with the flamboyance of a stage performer, flicking and smoothing and rearranging it to make the point that she was concealing a very perfumed pink body underneath. She combed wet brown hair in long straight lines while my mother explained why she was here. Her mother had 'passed on', her father was high up in Duly's car sales, but, as he had been called up too, the two women had come up with this mutually supportive arrangement.

We watched Martin Locke's 'Top of the Pops' from seven to eight in the evening. The scratches, splices and bad sync of this new pop video art form in its infancy gave us a youthful Mick Jagger boasting he had Sticky Fingers, Gary Glitter bragging that he was the leader of the gang, and ABBA boasting how much money, money, money they were going to make.

My mother did nothing to prevent the attempted seduction, which proceeded under her very eyes. She retired early that night to leave us two 'love birds' in peace. Willow squashed herself against me, pressed her breasts into my side, tucked her feet under my jeans and slid her hand over my stomach.

"Here," she said, "is a present for you and your mother."

I took the scroll of papyrus on which she had inscribed in looping black ink letters the verses of a poem. "To Paolo and Lina," she had written at the top, and at the bottom she had pasted a small photo of herself, decorated with dried grasses and flowers.

> *Go placidly amid the noise and haste,*
> *and remember what peace there may be in silence.*

"What's this?"
"The Desiderata. Listen. Isn't this beautiful…?"

> *You are a child of the universe,*
> *no less than the trees and the stars;*
> *you have a right to be here.*

*And whether or not it is clear to you,*
*no doubt the universe is unfolding as it should.*

"I knew you'd like it. It's for you. It's what I believe. I don't want to be part
of any institutionalised religion. I am free. As you can be too. Keep it, treasure it.
Think of me."

I held the plaque squarely in front of me, as a buffer against her.

*Therefore be at peace with God,*
*whatever you conceive Him to be…*

"You don't know me," she continued, "but I know you. You have a birthmark
on your left leg. Here." She rubbed her hand up my calf until she located the
brown spot by feel. "You have a scar under your chin from an accident you had
with the Fiat Sei Cento in Italy in 1964. Here… And here is where a lion cub
scratched your nose when you tried to pick it up at Boswell-Wilkie's circus."

I stared fiercely at her handwriting. "I wouldn't call it beautiful. I'd call it
blasphemous… and totally unbiblical. The universe isn't unfolding as it should.
It's unfolding as Satan wants, unless we stop him."

She held my cheeks and kissed me. "Oh, Paul, you're exactly how I imagined,
down to the scowl when you get cross. You had that since you were a little boy.
And the dimple on your chin, that's where God pushed you out of heaven, like this."

Willow had pored over all my photo albums with my mother, and Lina had
told her so much about me, so much that she had cried, and was dying to meet
me. She was to be the sister I never had. But I had no idea who this dripping-
with-desire creature was. She had no distance or irony. She was a gap-toothed,
strange-smelling alien being, too close to my mother for any reciprocal desire to
arise in me. Yet she tried all the tricks in the book – looking for my lifeline, asking
about French kisses, and finally offering to massage my shoulders if I slipped off
my shirt. Or, if I liked, I could massage her shoulders and she would slip off her
dressing gown. She had never been kissed, could you believe it, even though she
was nearly eighteen. Her friends, she said, had been 'felt up', but she didn't even
know what that meant. Shows you what they teach you at Catholic schools.

I yearned for Bianca's aloof perverseness. I resisted this creature, and even invoked Steve Carter's verses to ward her off. "Walk not as other Gentiles walk, having the understanding of their mind darkened, who have given themselves over to lasciviousness," I reminded myself. "Fornication, and all uncleanness, let it not be named among you."

"How can you 'be at peace with God, whatever you conceive him to be'?"

"Paolo…"

"And don't call me Paolo."

"Your mother calls you Paolo. It's such a romantic…"

"You can't conceive of God any way you want. He is God. Man didn't make God: God made Man."

This was my final judgement on her, and thus disentangled, I went to bed smug and prim, and she had to be satisfied with a peck on a sharply turned cheek.

But what did I know about Bianca? Did she have a mole on her left ankle? A smallpox ring on her left arm? I didn't want to know. Details were repugnant to me; I was interested in the form, not the copy. I wanted to look up at the light, not dig deeper into my own darkness. Did I crave to explore Bianca's geography in leisurely detail, instead of in surreptitious peeks? Did I want to know the history of her every scar or blemish, as Willow did mine? No, the fragments, the shards I had collected were enough for me to deal with. They made her more mysterious, gave her more resonance, became symbols, and acquired numinous qualities.

I found the record at last, in its stained white sleeve, with its badly printed MVN label. Artist: Gwynneth Ashley Robin. Song: 'Little Soldier Blue'. The song that made her famous (relatively – I'm sure you haven't even heard of my childhood idol) was her tribute to Jimmy Osmond, 'Little Jimmy'. If she was a twelve-year-old singer and he was a twelve-year-old singer, the song suggested, they should get together.

'Little Soldier Blue' was scratched and worn. I had played it on a Tempest record player which I had bought on NDNI (No Deposit, No Interest) from Radio Ltd, and which played all records slightly too fast – LPs at 35 rpm and singles at about 48 – so she sounded even more chipmunkish. But I loved its cadence, its childish rhyme and rhythm, her South African accent, the generic sound of the Jo'burg studios.

*I'll wait for you till your fighting days are through.*
*When the moon at night is shining bright,*
*I'll think of you – Soldier Blue.*

I have to admit, I had bad, bad taste in music. I liked the most clichéd pop music available – and there was not much else available: Gallo filtered only the most popular songs into this country. My father called my music 'trite', 'superficial' and 'sentimental'. But for me, quality music was not a matter of taste. It was all association. Whatever clung to this music from another world, from emotional contact with ecstasy, made it good. If I had heard Dolly Parton and Conway Twitty sing 'Tomorrow is Forever' at the Salisbury Show at the precise moment I was pining for Bianca, then the song preserved my intense feelings of that moment. If Marie Osmond's 'Paper Woses' could make me cry about all the lost loves in the world, and was a mirror that reflected back to me my own emotional journey, then the song was 'high art'. So what if I was a sucker for ready-made, pre-packaged sentimentality? I kept all those crappy singles and LPs as diaries of the moment, as journals of my own deepest feelings. But it wasn't entirely my fault. The church played a role in my arrested development; Rhodesia had a turn at holding back the march of progress; and Bianca held me in a virginal spell.

Unfortunately, the Gwynneth Ashley Robin single stuck towards the end. No matter how I cleaned it, dusted it and wiped it with spirit, I could not get the needle to jump over the scratch, and I could never play the song to the end.

*Good night, little soldier,*
*And always remember –*
*And always remember –*
*And always remember –*

★ ★ ★

Sunday dawned bright and hopeful, and I prepared for Bianca and church with my best (and only) suit and tie. It had been decreed somewhere that men had to wear suits and ties for church, out of respect for God's presence, and women had to wear high heels, their best dresses, hats, perfume and make-up, although my perverse intellect argued that if God was supposed to be everywhere at all times, surely you couldn't really fool Him by dressing up on Sundays. The sun and sky had to be shut out because Satan apparently had claimed more and more of the world as his and we had to barricade ourselves in dark sanctuaries in order to remain pure.

Although our Hillside church was non-denominational, in the last two months Steve had thought it wise to join financially with the Baptist Union, to call ourselves Hillside Baptist Church, and to hold services at Central Baptist Church in town. North-Eastern Bible College, it turned out, was Baptist, as I suspected Hillside had been from the very beginning too, as all the theories he had promoted and practices he had instituted were no different from those of the Baptist Church on the corner of Fife and Rhodes Avenue. Central Baptist was a huge white building, free of iconoclastic adornments, full of suited rich white people. The Pastor was a white-haired, wise old gentleman who began each service with the quavering injunction to "Seek the Lord while He may yet be found". Today, however, the Youth Pastor, Steve Carter, would conduct the service.

I planned to arrive early, waylay Bianca, and sit next to her, share Bibles, hymn books and whispered conversations. Willow, however, appeared in a blue cotton dress, hair tied back, ready for church. My mother insisted, and so weeping Willow sat demurely in the front seat as I drove with sinking heart.

"God lives in Nature," she announced. "He didn't make churches. So why go to church to find God?"

"Then why would you want to come to church?"

She placed her hand on my knee. "Paolo."

"We're late."

The church was full and the car park overflowing, so we had to park a block away and walk. Now we were really late. Curse you, Willow, I thought, hating her perfume, the knock-kneed way she walked, the fluffy dress she wore, and the way she crabbed me off the pavement. The organ greeted us with what was supposed to be a joyful noise, and two men in dark suits welcomed us into the vestry with handshakes, programmes and hushed admonitions to sit upstairs in the overflow gallery as the hall was full.

My plans for a holy *tête-à-tête* with Bianca in the downstairs pews were dashed already, Willow insisting on a *ménage à trois*, but there was one benefit of sitting in the top balcony: I had the hawk-eye advantage of overseeing the entire congregation. I located Bianca at once in the third row, in a blue dress, gathered white puff sleeves, her hair spread over her back in a fan. On her left, her mother and father huddled over a hymnal, while she leaned to her right, holding a hymnal too, sharing it with a boy in a dark suit. All I could see of him from here was a thick neck, white collar and shorn black head.

Of course, Craig Hardy was a Christian too, I had to remind myself. And he too had a weekend pass. He had insinuated his way into her personal space, and he had had two months to do it. But had he received three love letters from Bianca, declaring her feelings for him? I was still not unduly perturbed.

Steve's sermon focused on God's Plan for Our Life. God was a large giant, cupping the world in His hands. He had made it, loved it and was in complete control of every single event that happened in it.

"God knows your every thought, your every desire, your every wish. He listens to your every prayer and knows your needs. The very hairs of your head are numbered." I watched the bald heads of the congregation below, wondering if God had to continually recount because of hair loss. I stared at Bianca's hair, wondering what it would be like to sift through her strands of sunlight.

"God has a plan for your life. 'All things work together for good to those that love God,' says Paul. All we have to do is trust." Did God's plan for my life include that shining angel in the third row? If God was in complete control of every event that happened in the world, if everything happened for a reason, and there was meaning in the universe, as Steve argued, then surely God was allowing Bianca's distance by design. It was not for me to question, but to yield to His will. It did not matter that Craig Hardy was snuggling up to her before my very eyes. It did not matter that for two months I had been prevented from explaining the situation to her. There was a purpose in this, to make me strong, to test me, to keep me faithful. And, of course, the girl sitting next to me was a temptation which had to be resisted if I were to unite with my better half.

Throughout the service, I fixed a glazed stare on Bianca in the hope that the sheer force of my passion would reach her and make her turn around, but to no avail. My plan was to bump into her at the end of the service, and pry her away from Hardy. After the final hymn, when Willow slipped her hand through my arm to be escorted downstairs, I pushed past the slowly shuffling congregation, only to find myself shaking hands with the Deacon.

"Are you and your girlfriend new to Central?"

"Yes," said Willow.

"No," said her unhappy suitor. "I'm from Hillside. Steve's my pastor. This is my mother's friend." I craned my neck to see if Bianca was ahead or behind me as the rows emptied out. There she was, in the bright sunshine, the gallant Hardy allowing her to sweep past him so he could talk politely to her mother and father. Meanwhile, the Deacon would not let my hand go. "Steve's my brother. I'm Clive Carter."

"Nice to meet you, Clive," said Willow. "Paul's told me a lot about Steve."

Impatiently, I pushed past him, anxious not to miss Bianca as she disappeared round the corner of the main doorway. Willow flitted after me. There was Bianca's parents' car, the yellow Datsun 1200 I had seen so often at her house, and her parents, waiting.

"Who is this, Paul?" asked her mother.

"I'm Willow Edmondson."

"Edmondson of Duly's?" Mr Pennefather shook Willow's hand. Mrs Pennefather tried to inquire about my medic training, but I was too distracted to engage with her. She cast furtive glances at Willow, then back at me.

"Is Bianca…?"

"Bianca…" Mrs Pennefather waved nervously at the red Mini that glinted at us in the parking lot. Through the crowd, I saw Bianca being escorted by Hardy, who opened the car door for her, slammed it shut, then jumped in the driver's seat.

"I need to speak to her, Mrs Pennefather," I said, trying to be heard over the roar of the Mini, which was already driving out of the parking lot and onto Second Street. Willow was in earnest conversation with Mr Pennefather. They were talking cars, of all things. Mr Pennefather knew her father was a big noise in Duly's and he wanted a new car. Sanctions had limited the manufacture of cars to primitive Rhodesian versions of Fords and Datsuns at Willowvale, and the waiting list was long. Could she have a word with her father about the new Ford? "I have to go, Willow." But it was too late. The dying splutters of the Mini Cooper could still be heard, but they were soon lost among the other sounds of a still Sunday noon. You could hear the rumble of the daily Air Rhodesia flight taking off from Salisbury airport, twenty miles away, the twitters of birds, the buzzing of bumble bees, and the ticking of red corrugated roofs as they expanded in the sun.

★ ★ ★

The news that weekend was dominated by the Rhodesian Front's (RF) overwhelming victory in the general election. All 50 seats reserved for whites in the 66-seat parliament went again to Smith. The Rhodesian Action Party (RAP), led by twelve right-wingers who split from the Pry Minister's party (vowing never to allow majority rule) were decisively trounced. The left-of-centre National Unifying Force (NUF) in their call for a swift transition to black majority rule were also defeated, humiliated, shamed and despoiled. "Nobody but a fool would disregard the kind of result we witnessed today," Smith smiled.

Under the current voting system, the country's 85,000 white voters elected 50 white MPs. Eight black MPs were elected to represent the country's six million black people, which was apparently a fair deal, because only 7,000 of them were eligible to vote anyway. ZANU leader Robert Mugabe and ZAPU leader Joshua Nkomo denounced this mandate white Rhodesia had given to racism, pigheadedness and intransigence. They announced that the two main guerrilla groups (ZANLA and ZIPRA) were to ratchet up their assault on Smith's minority government by combining their resources in a formidable alliance under a central command, the Patriotic Front (PF). So eNUF of RAP, we had two fronts buffeting our population, with some gadflies prodding each of them.

★ ★ ★

Lunch was a conversation between my mother and Willow about male intransigence.

"Penny for your thoughts?" Willow nudged me to pass the potatoes to my mother.

"I was thinking about Clive."

"Paolo's so unaffectionate, isn't he?" complained my mother.

"No, Mamma," said Willow. "All that British reserve is just a front. I bet you underneath is a passionate Italian heart."

"So British! He takes after his father."

"Who isn't here to defend himself," I pointed out.

"What about Clive?"

"Didn't he have a Rhodesian accent?"

"So?"

"He had a Rhodesian accent."

"Why shouldn't he have a Rhodesian accent?"

"Men." Willow shook her head at my mother who shook her head at Willow. They both laughed.

All afternoon, Willow sewed, cooked and read magazines with my mother, while I brooded in my bedroom with the door shut, reading my Bible, hunting for a message, a word from God, some explanation of why the earth was spinning in the wrong direction. I wrote and tore up letters to Bianca. I listened to the radio. "Love the one you're with," sang Stephen Stills. "Any love is good love," sang Bachman-Turner Overdrive. I finally called her number, only to wake up a grumpy Mr Pennefather from his nap, and to be informed that she had been invited out for the afternoon, and, yes, he would pass on my message.

I had one last chance to see her before I returned to Llewellin that weekend. Rhodesian tradition deemed it obligatory that all churchgoers of marriageable age go to Gremlin, the American-style drive-in restaurant, every Sunday evening. Those with cars took those without, and half the fun was squeezing into the backs of Beetles or Morris Minors or sitting four abreast on Chevy bench seats. Once there, we spilled out into the cool evening, sat at stone tables and watched the cars drag race down Enterprise Road. It was the one place we were free to be white boys and girls together. We shouted our orders into speakers, and were served by black waiters who brought burgers and fries, chicken-in-a-basket, milk shakes and banana splits.

I sat among the Hillside Church girls, anticipating the moment She would arrive. But Willow, who had insisted on accompanying me, entered into the spirit of the occasion, and acted as if she were to all intents and purposes my girlfriend.

I heard the roar of the souped-up Mini Cooper before I saw it. Bianca sat in the front seat. Hardy drove smoothly into the parking lot, ramped over the pavement in a mock attempt to run us over. Inside the car, Bianca held her hands to her mouth as the girls squawked and scattered from our table. I sat grimly still, though the Mini's chrome bumper nudged my leg and stopped with such force that Bianca lurched forward. Hardy called out through the window – "Sorry. Minnie Mouse has a mind of her own" – then leaned over to undo her seatbelt. To her credit, she leaped out of the car and joined our group, but the smirk on Hardy's face meant that he had won some competition he had invented.

And the look on Bianca's face told me that she was well armoured to distance all suitors who dared to attempt penetration. Every time I tried to disengage from Willow and approach her, Hardy was there to counter-approach. He had a Scofield Bible to share with her; he had Christian music to play over his Superchronic car tape player; he had a gold cross pinned on his tie; and he had given Bianca a gift – a 'Consider Jesus' badge pinned to her lapel. He was a hideous parody of me, just as I was a hideous parody of him.

Whatever Bianca's feelings, her disdain or her indifference to him, he did not give her a chance to make them clear. He made sure that I did not get anywhere near her that evening. But I was determined. No matter that the world was crumbling beneath my feet, I had those letters. So while he was in the 'john', as he called it, I offered her a lift home. She wistfully declined, looking askance at the Mini Cooper as if it would bite her if she refused him.

"I did promise," she said. "He made me promise. And it looks as if you have company, anyway…"

"Bianca, I have to go back tomorrow. But I'm a medic now. I passed my training. I'll be here next weekend."

"That's what you said last time you were on pass."

"I'll be here next weekend, I promise."

She bit her lip, and looked at me. "I know what you're thinking, but it isn't true. Trust me. Believe me. It isn't true."

"Same here," I said, cocking my thumb back at the smiling Willow in the front seat of my car. "It's not what you think."

All this took place against the backdrop of a glorious amber sunset, the heavy blue night pushing us down. At the end, I could not see her face, and the weak yellow streetlights were haloed by flying ants. But that confession from her lips could have launched a thousand soldiers into war. The glow of contentment sustained me for the whole week. She was my secret admirer, and could not, would not, be open about it. Hardy was her smoke screen to hide her love for me. And she understood – I prayed she understood – that Willow was simply a decoy too, that we were star-crossed lovers, Bianca and I, who, like Romeo and Juliet, had to hide it from the world.

★  ★  ★

On our return, my mother, who had been waiting up, learned that I meant to take the late night train back to barracks. "Paul, you should spend more time at home on your pass. Pay more attention to your poor mother."

That's why you have Willow, I wanted to say, but you palmed her off on me. I said nothing and my mother took herself to bed, kissing me on the head. I waited for Willow to do the same, but instead she brought me a cup of hot chocolate to sip with her in my room.

"Your mother's amazing," she said.

"I know."

"No, you don't. You don't give her any credit. You don't open up to her. You're so cold to her."

"I'm not."

"Why don't you tell her what you're going through in the army?" Willow tucked bare legs under her, pulled her short nightie over her hips and sipped her hot chocolate. "She's worried sick. And she was in a war too, you know."

"I know."

"She was a Partisan in World War II. She was nearly killed in that war, Paolo. That's why it's breaking her heart that you're in the war here."

"She never told me that."

"You never asked her."

"So that's what you two talk about behind my back?"

"Her family had a shop in Bardi, a small Italian village, and the Americans bombed it."

"The Americans?"

"The Americans were trying to bomb the bridge on the river Taro and missed. And she was helping the Partisans against Mussolini. They used to hide people in their cellars when the Germans came. The Germans used her and her sisters as human shields on the front of their vehicles to ferret out Partisans. She had to cook meals for the Germans and pretend to be nice to them."

"Why are you telling me this?"

"You don't respect her. You don't even acknowledge she exists. Your mother's a war hero. And I love how she met your father in England when she was sent there as a reward for helping the Allies. It's such a romantic story. I love your mother."

"She told you all this?"

"Paolo." She put her cup down and held my hands. "You look so unhappy. Why?"

I pushed her octopus tentacles away, folded my arms tight, and sat back. "Willow, Willow," I mocked. "Where did you get such a name, anyway?"

I found the answer late that night in a note she smuggled into my pocket. I read it to the rollicking motion of the train, in the weak yellow cabin lights of the carriage, on the way back to Llewellin Barracks.

> *Willow is the name my mother gave to me. She said that I was a tree planted on a river. No matter how rough the waters are, she said, no matter how you are whipped and snapped, no matter how badly people treat you in life, she said, you will bend, bend, bend, but you will never break.*

★  ★  ★

On the eight o'clock news, President Kenneth Kaunda declares a State of War between Zambia and Rhodesia, rolling out his anti-aircraft guns onto Lusaka golf courses with orders to shoot on sight any Rhodesian aircraft that violate his country's airspace. To prove his point, he lobs a few mortar shells over the Zambezi River at the Victoria Falls Hotel. There is some concern, but finally the management decides not to cancel the nightly sundowner cruise for tourists along the Zambezi River.

A fifteen-man security-force patrol tracks a team of guerrillas/terrorists/*makandangas*/freedom fighters/armed insurgents through the Ndanga Tribal Trust Land to Dabwe Kraal and the white soldiers overhear a *pungwe* in progress. The guerrillas escape in the darkness, and the soldiers open fire, leaving seventeen women, twelve children and seven men dead, and thirty-one wounded; the latter have to wait nine hours for medical help to arrive.

A white farming family, their black servant and an eight-year-old child are murdered by terrorists who flee across the border into Botswana.

A Christian farming family is under siege in their farmhouse, surrounded by terrorists who threaten to burn the place down and kill them all. They pray with eyes tight shut, and when they open them, the terrorists have fled. The terrorists later explain that the house was guarded by white angels with wings and flaming torches, one at each corner.

Many young black men are leaving the country to take up the cause of freedom and liberation. They ride buses to the Botswana border, then follow the 'fire': a phantom burning bush guides the would-be liberators to Francistown, where they are received by guerrilla trainers who take them to Zambia, Tanzania and sometimes Russia.

★  ★  ★

My first assignment as a medic began at six o'clock on Monday morning at the DRR Camp Hospital. I was to be a duty medic for a while, to get the hang of things, and was answerable to the hospital Sergeant Major, a large triangular man (pin head, flat stomach, wobbly) called Staff Sergeant Loots who carried a mace around with him. He was fanatic about sepsis and about cleanliness. The enemy was anything dirty. Floors had to shine, walls had to gleam, hands had to be scrubbed, masks had to be worn. Cleanliness was next to godliness, and we had to be vigilant to keep Satan away. Loots would put us on a charge if he found dirt under our fingernails. In every room, MI room and ward sat bubbling tanks of antiseptic, bottles of Jeyes Fluid, and jars of yellow Cetramol to sterilise needles, cotton swabs, bandages, flesh. "Because," he warned us, "everything is deteriorating. Everything turns to shit."

The joke was on Sergeant Major Loots, though. His name backwards was

'Stool', which meant, in medical lingo, a piece of shit.

So my first few days as a medic were spent scrubbing my soul, my heart, my mind, my hands, my boots, my MI room, my patients, my cotton swabs and my needles. I punctured sterile skin and antibioticked hundreds of patients. I wore a starched uniform, with two new chevron stripes. I inspected the troopies with the objective detachment of a mechanic at a garage, including their jokes.

"Doctor, doctor, it's running down my back."

"What is?"

"My spine."

"Doctor, doctor, it's all around me."

"What?"

"Air."

"Doctor, doctor, what's wrong with me? Everything I eat turns to shit."

But at the end of the week, I would be with Bianca. However, on Friday morning, as I was counting the hours until the six o'clock train from Bulawayo to Salisbury – or should I just hitch a ride and get there in five hours? – I was summoned into Loots' office and told to stand to attention while he picked white lint off my lapel.

"We have a big fish coming in today, Corporal Williams, a terrorist. And I want you to look after him this weekend."

"A terrorist?"

"He's the commissar of a large group, and he's been swimming in a hell of a lot of craptus. The treatment card will be given to you by the doctor as soon as he's had a look at the patient. You take it from there. He's all yours."

"But sir, I had a weekend pass…"

"You're not questioning my direct orders, are you, Corporal?"

"No, sir."

★ ★ ★

He was a 'qualified gook', as the Sergeant Major called him, and he knew all the enemy's plans against us, the location of guerrilla base camps and arms caches, the location and layout of the ZIPRA command centres in Zambia. Normally, such evil vermin (again the Sergeant Major's words) were zapped, slotted, scribbled, eliminated, wasted on the spot. It was futile to take such scum prisoner, bring them to court only to sentence them to death, so the State of Emergency gave the soldier in the field the powers to execute justice. But this case was different. It was imperative to keep him alive – orders from high up – so that we could extract all this precious information out of him.

Medics, army patients and staff watched at the hospital entrance as the terrorist was wheeled in on a stretcher. One medic walked by his side, holding up a drip which obscured my view of his face. As he was wheeled into theatre, a limping man in pyjamas bumped the stretcher. "Kill the fucken gook."

This was 'my' terrorist. I lolled outside the theatre, waiting for the doctor to give me instructions. Two men brushed past me with notebooks but were stopped by the Sergeant Major.

"Sorry, gentlemen, you won't be able to begin work on him for a few days. He's being heavily sedated with morphine and needs intensive care for the next twenty-four hours. Once he's in the ward you can return."

The short-cropped blond man with pale eyebrows held up a manicured hand in protest. "Our instructions are not to leave the patient for one minute. He must be handcuffed to the bed at all times."

"Gentlemen, he won't even be able to open his eyes for a day or two. Nevertheless, we'll give you beds in the ward."

"It must be a private ward," butted in the other soft-spoken man who was in his forties. He wore polished brown crocodile-hide shoes which squeaked at his every step.

"Suit yourself," said the Sergeant Major, with arms up in mock surrender. "I'm just in charge of this hospital."

"We would not like to risk anything happening to the patient," said the blond man, with measured emphasis on each word. "He must speak to no one but us, and no one must have contact with him, except the medic treating him. We'll bring in his food, take him to the toilet."

Loots pointed to me – I was still hovering around the corridor, craning my neck to see in the theatre. "Corporal Williams is the man assigned to treat your patient. He's our brightest new medic here. And very good at such menial tasks."

I was the sharp focus of six blue eyes for a moment and received a curt nod from one man, a sweep from head to toe from the other, and a wink from the Sergeant Major. I stood to attention and saluted; it was all I could think of doing.

"All yours, Corporal," grinned the doctor as he handed over the RX1033 treatment form.

"Ward six," barked Loots to me as the theatre door opened and the stretcher poked its way out, banging a naked black foot, which was not covered by the white sheet, against the door. The only other part of the patient showing was the face: shut eyes, wild woolly brown hair, thick, dry, cracked lips, black, black skin and a wiry, stubbly chin. The two security men jumped into action. They walked smartly behind me as I wheeled my charge through the admiring throng of pyjamaed patients. The drip swung from the stand attached to the head of the stretcher, and a tube disappeared under the sheet. My eyes had already located a brown stain, at shin level, which was steadily reddening.

Once I had transferred my new patient from the stretcher, I perused the doctor's instructions. Treatment was to begin immediately and was simple: apply Glick 'n Ick dressing, bathe and clean wounds with Cetramol every day, watch for gangrene and sepsis, administer antibiotic injections QID, give drip for first three days only, decreasing the quantity gradually.

Glisterine and Ichthamnol is a gleaming brown/black sticky substance like molasses, from the swamps of darkest Africa. But medically speaking, Glick 'n Ick has healing properties and when applied to wounds, halts septicaemia, encourages new growth and binds the fibres.

Treatment began immediately. To my consternation, when I walked back into the ward with the large jar of G & I in my hands, my patient was awake, his sharp eyes assessing me. The two men were pacing the room restlessly, waiting for the terrorist to recover his wits sufficiently so they could begin their interrogation. The first act they had performed on him while I was out was to handcuff a limp black hand to the bedpost. I checked the drip, which was strapped and bound to his other arm and suspended on a metal stand, dripping a steady saline solution into his vein.

I pulled the sheet aside. He was dressed in army boxer shorts and a 'C' Company T-shirt, looking just like one of the black RAR soldiers. I noticed at first only surface wounds, with pieces of flesh gouged out here and there, but no internal damage. I judged he had been hit by shrapnel from some sort of mine. I noticed two gunshot wounds where bullets had grazed the skin and tumbled into fleshy areas of the thigh and shoulder. Then I started, not having noticed it until now: the left leg was merely a stump cut off below the knee. Why hadn't this been indicated on the treatment form? I unwound soiled bandages that stuck painfully to bits of flesh, until I had exposed a weeping pink ball. I looked up to see if the man was in pain, but he showed a stoic front, oblivious to the squeamish tingling in my gut.

The leg wasn't gangrenous, but pus-white plasma had grown over the inflamed areas. I scratched the pus off with an abrasive pad and then swabbed it with cotton wool dipped in Cetramol. The leg flinched.

"Did that hurt?"

The man looked uneasily at the two civilian men, gave a twitch of a smile at me and shook his head. The two men peered over my shoulder. "Oh, my God," said one. "I can't take this." The other tapped his shoulder. "Doc, we'll be outside in the tearoom. Don't leave until we get back."

"It doesn't look that bad," I said to the terrorist. His eyes swirled into life, then the milky film of blankness covered them again, and I returned to work. The operation took quite a while. Each wound oozed yellow fluid. I cleaned until the flesh was pink and shiny. I covered everything with Glick 'n Ick, then wrapped the wounds in clean crepe bandages, which immediately became soiled and brown.

When the security officers returned, the terrorist, who had been staring vacantly at my two chevrons, closed his eyes.

"Thanks, Doc," said the blond man.

The treatment was to continue for weeks. Bianca, I told myself sternly, would have to wait. I called her at the first opportunity, and the phone rang and rang. On the fifteenth ring, I lost my nerve and hung up. In 1977, there were no answering machines or email, and mobile phones were far-fetched inventions seen only on Thunderbirds and Star Trek. I wrote her a hasty letter, Army Mail, on official DRR Hospital letterhead I had filched from Loots' desk, to impress upon her the importance of my absence. A life is in my hands, I wrote. I am making the difference between the life and death of an important man.

Every day I found the two men there, one taking notes, the other pacing the room in his crocodile-shoes, asking questions and politely waiting for the patient to reply. I only caught snatches of the conversations, for as soon as I came in, the blond man would sigh, slap his book shut and say, "That's enough for now. Let's take a break." And they would leave me to unravel bandages, swab pus, dab black plasma on plastic pink flesh, give antibiotic injections, check for bedsores.

The terrorist watched me intently, aware of every move I made, every nervous tic in my manner, every shifty glance I stole at him. He showed silent interest in all the proceedings, obliging and assisting me in any way he could, rolling over at appropriate moments, or raising his leg, or nodding for me to go on when I thought it was hurting too much. When the Security Branch people were in the room, he was dull and opaque, sullen and stupid. But as soon as they were gone, he radiated intelligence. It was disconcerting. Medical training had taught me to see the patient as a machine to be jabbed, stitched up, patched. To see him in any other way could be disastrous. How could you suture, cut open or inject if you knew you were doing this to a human being, or if you could imagine how it felt? But here was my first patient stubbornly insisting on being human. Instead of an inert object to work on, I had a being who lived, breathed and exhibited a tunnel of thoughts that brightened and faded, like mine. And what was worse, this man was no ordinary patient but an Enemy of the State.

You three great lions of Zimbabwe, we hear you calling, you who sit under the umbrella tree and call our true names, and slough off the names of dogs given to us by the white man. I see you, Mukwati of the Matabele. I see you Kagubi of the Shona, and Nehanda, the woman, your death wounds still fresh for your part in the first Chimurenga. Your voice is loudest, your finger insistent in its accusation. Mwari declares it. Our suffering is caused by the Makiwa and our deafness to their lies. You said it to our grandfathers, and now you say it again: the whites must be driven from the land. Oh, Nehanda Charwe Nyakasikana, you are the female incarnation of the oracle spirit Nyamhika Nehanda. Mbuya Nehanda, you are the grandmother of present-day Zimbabwe – help us now to finish your task.

★ ★ ★

"I'm sorry."

"No, it doesn't hurt."

This was the first time he had spoken to me directly. His voice was strong. Well, what did I expect – the whining apathy of a *chimbwasunguta*? Here was a real live terrorist, a man who had been trained to kill, had swum across the Zambezi with Claymore anti-personnel mines strapped to his back, who had lived on turtles, and had probably murdered, raped and terrorised people.

"Is it better?" said the patient.

"The sepsis should be gone in a few days."

"You're a good doctor."

"I'm not a doctor." The body, I meant to say, is a miraculous instrument with mechanisms to heal itself. Blood congeals, lymphatic fluid seals the wounds, allowing new fibres to grow, then a scab protects the delicate process of regrowth, until it is as good as new. Well… I looked at the stump of his leg… almost.

"You look too young to be in the army. Too young to be good at medicine."

"I'm just doing my National Service."

A medical officer walked into the room to get some Betadine. I adopted – reflexively – a rough, brusque attitude in bandaging the patient, pulling the bandage tight, treating him as an inert object. But when the officer was gone, the terrorist smiled. "What is your name?"

"Paul." I dabbed a wound with Cetramol, checking the yellowed gauze for sepsis.

"Msipa," he said. "Comrade Msipa."

The days rolled by. I called her three more times. The first time, Mr Pennefather grunted, "Who?" and I hung up. A day later Bianca herself answered. "Craig?" she said, and I replaced the receiver with a trembling hand and rage in my throat. The third time Mrs Pennefather said she would pass on the message that I was busy with a terrorist. We're all praying for you, Paul. You're not in danger, are you? Yes, Mrs Pennefather, I am. I am.

Another week went by. I had checked on my patient's progress daily, and every time I was in the room he seemed relieved to abandon the wooden expression he had to create for the questioning officers. I was surprised at how much information he contained. They spent hours each day coaxing it out of him. All day he would talk, his lips drying, his face expressionless, and all those facts, figures, names, places, code numbers poured into their notebooks. Soon the Air Force would be bombing training camps, arms caches would be located, villages would be visited, terrorist sympathisers arrested.

But something else was growing in me too: guilt at my secret conspiracy with the enemy. I would suddenly switch to slit-eyed efficiency when they looked up at me in surprise, following the patient's benevolent smile. I was in league with the man, even though I had said or done nothing to indicate any disloyalty to my uniform. Whatever it was, I felt guilty whenever they saw me interacting with him, even dressing his wounds. They watched and whispered to each other, pointing at his obliging movement of an arm or the gentle way this medic dabbed his wounds.

"You have a scar in your heart."

The interrogators were out of the room. "Sorry?"

"I can see. You are troubled. Is it girl trouble?"

"There's no trouble."

"It's girl trouble."

The words were out before I knew what they were. "I don't know. She's… I don't know."

"Is she a cock teaser?" He smiled so broadly that I could see all his teeth and his pink gums.

"No."

His laugh was an old lorry starting up. "She's a cock teaser. She's trouble. A woman is always trouble."

"It's not that. I don't understand her. I don't know where I stand with her. I…"

"You expect to understand her?" Here he started up his engine again. "One day, my friend, I must give you some advice about women."

After all these weeks of dressings, interrogations and dabbings, I began to look forward to my daily routine and expurgation. I was proving my worth as a medic. This was my apprenticeship in Llewellin DRR Hospital and the Sergeant Major was happy with the way I had handled my first case. Soon, he promised, I would be ready to be sent out in the field. And the conversation and meeting of eyes with the patient was comforting too. It meant I was good at my job; I was bringing him back to life, healing this man and making him more and more human. But the next day I walked into the ward and found an empty bed: no terrorist, no interrogators, no healing fibres.

He's escaped. Or they've moved him to another ward, now that he's healing. Or they've discovered I was being too familiar with the enemy and have discreetly moved him away. I knocked on the Sergeant Major's door.

"Williams, what can I do for you?"

"Sir, I… the prisoner, the terrorist?"

"Oh," he smiled. "We should have told you…"

"Have you moved him?"

"Williams, you did a very good job on those wounds. I must say, I'm very pleased with your treatment. I'm going to recommend that you qualify as a fully fledged medic."

I nodded my head. "You mean he's been discharged?"

Loots pushed a flat hand into the air and laughed. "Discharged. Yes, you might say that, Williams. You did a fine job. That weekend pass you wanted? Take it. I'm taking you off hospital duties from now on. On Monday, I'm sending you with B Company on their bush trip. It's nothing much, just an exercise. Nothing major will happen, it's just to get you used to being a medic on your own in the bush. Enjoy your weekend." He pulled up some papers in front of his face. I was dismissed.

"Sir." I saluted, stiffly backing out. "Thank you, sir."

It was only much later that I found out what had happened to the terrorist. The two interrogators had found out all they needed to know from him, had closed their notebooks, and squeaked out of the hospital in their crocodile shoes. The terrorist was put in a prison truck and driven to Salisbury where he was tried *in camera*, sentenced to death for crimes of terrorism, and hanged a few days later.

# CHAPTER TEN

# THE HAMMADOOLAS

Literature is overwhelmingly prejudiced in favour of the male as victim and against the female, who is the satanic deceiver, seductress, witch, predatory cock teaser. Robert Graves said it; the Bible said it, Comrade Msipa said it. In ghost stories she often figures as 'The White Lady', and in ancient religions as the 'White Goddess'.

Since puberty, he has suffered from a condition of angst which attacks him incessantly. If he stops his frenetic pursuit of white goddesses and looks down at the spinning world under him, he sees that it all rests on nothing. His condition usually attacks him at mid-afternoon in the heat of the day, in the empty suburbs of his drowsy, cicada-drenched city, or when a sewing machine hums in the distance. He is not sure what to do with such a black hole, or 'ache' as he calls it. It sucks away at his life and the façade of meaning or semblance of happiness he is trying to create.

Christian evangelists are quick to pounce on his weak spot, calling it his 'God-shaped hole'. His peers recommend stuffing it with sexual conquests; the movies tell him he needs to fall in love and to press himself against a partner-shaped other to seal it. Yet to his amazement, no one else around him appears to have such an affliction. His fellow Rhodesians live life simply, as if existence poses no problem beyond foraging for food, housing and a succession of consumer goods. They train to be accountants, engineers, secretaries. His parents, for example, want nothing more, it appears, than a materially comfortable existence. He, on the other hand, is cursed with an inner consciousness and an unsatisfied oversensitivity to his surroundings. At this point, after only three months away from the church, after his descent into hell, he has blasphemous thoughts. He secretly admits that it is a girl-shaped, not a God-shaped hole in his soul. And only one girl will do.

There was no doubt a conspiracy between his mother and Willow. He could see in the hand gestures, eye movements and pregnant words that the empty space of the last two weeks had been stuffed with analysis, with life plans, with programmes for him to follow, and it had been determined that she was the one destined for him. His mother had created in Willow the illusion that she was in charge of his marital destiny, and that the way to a man's heart was through sexual seduction. But he could not bring himself to believe that his mother was encouraging sexual intimacy. She would not call it that. She wanted him to love Willow, to marry her and to live happily ever after, with Willow as the daughter she had never had. "You'll never find a girl like her, Paul."

Neither be cynical about love, said Mr Desiderata, for in the face of all aridity and disenchantment, it is as perennial as the grass that grows.

Willow was omnipresent, omniscient and omnibenevolent all weekend. At inopportune moments, she would appear in the corridor, dripping from a smelling-salts bath, her towel wrapped carelessly around her, more to reveal than to conceal, or sit at his feet in the evening, massaging them, her pyjama shirt open, exposing a white breast for his eyes to worship.

She wasn't a true Christian, of course. He knew that. She believed in all sorts of unbiblical, mystical heresies. She recited The Desiderata as if it were the Lord's Prayer. She prayed with his mother who was a Catholic. She believed that all religions were one, that love was God and God was love, and that if we loved we were in God, and could be God. Yeah, right. But then who was he to talk? He had his own idolatry to contend with.

"Paul, how nice to see you." Mrs Pennefather opened the door to welcome this 'boy from the bush'. I had arrived just as Mr Pennefather was revving the tiny Datsun 1200 in the driveway. Bianca was at home. They were off to Bible study. Could I baby-sit her? She was going to be all alone tonight, but now she had company. She winked as she climbed into the car and Mr Pennefather drowned out her goodbye with the fart of the revving engine.

Bianca presented herself in the frame of the front doorway, through granadilla vines and shafts of dying sunlight. She had changed; I had changed. Too much time had gone by, and we had grown more apart than ever. I had grown closer to adulthood; she was still cocooned in childhood. We touched hands politely. She did not look at me; she watched her daddy and mommy (as she called them) in their blue Rhodesian Datsun diminishing down the road. "Good timing," she said.

We were alone in her house. Fortune should have favoured us. In my back pocket were three letters, which I kept fondling for reassurance. But Bianca sucked in her lips and brooded in a chair in the far corner of the room. She looked desperately unhappy.

"Well?" She rocked on her seat, holding one leg up with her hands and wiggling her bare foot. "You didn't come last weekend. Or the weekend after that. You promised. You didn't come for Luke's farewell. And now you turn up at the wrong time."

"The wrong time?"

"This is not the best time to visit."

But I was not going to waste precious time beating about the bush. I marched over into her space, and sat next to her. "I didn't know you were a dancer."

"A dancer?" She looked alarmed.

"Bianca." I touched her hand, circled her fingers gently with my own, then gripped her hand tightly. "Drop everything for me."

"Drop everything?"

Her mouth hovered close to mine as I held her face so I could kiss her quivering lips. I say 'could', but I mean 'should'. And I see now (in wise retrospect) that she wanted me to. She relaxed, her lips softened and she closed her eyes. "You're my dancing queen," I said. "I'd love to dance with you on the beach."

Her eyes opened and her lips tightened. "Dancing Queen?"

"ABBA. It's no use denying it. I know your secret."

For a second, I had broken through, but only for a second did she look naked. Then those heavy, ironic eyebrows returned. She pushed me away in playful rebuke.

"ABBA? You're too late. ABBA's *Greatest Hits* has been turned into a beautiful flower pot."

Today, I would have known what to do. I would simply have kissed her. I would have spoken a different language. Instead, I did the most foolish thing I had done since I had offered her my Chocolate Pop back in 1972. I hauled out the letters from my pocket and lay them on the table, as if I were showing my winning hand at poker. For you, I'd drop everything. Let's join our dots. My dream.

She swallowed. "And?"

"Now what have you got to say?" I meant, you can't deny your feelings for me. But she stared at me with the quiver of a cornered mouse. Her eyes said, "I've never seen these before in my life." Her lips said, "What are you trying to say to me?"

At this point, I should have left. Or at least realised something was amiss. But so sure was I of my righteousness that I waited and waited, allowing the silence to grow heavier and heavier. And then it was too late. A knock on the door saved me from my stunned stupidity. "Oh, shoot," she said. "I was going to tell you, but my mother as usual interfered."

The door pushed open and in stepped a boy in military uniform, heavy boots, the beret of the Special Ops division, sergeant stripes on his shoulder, and a glint in his eye. We glared at each other; he smiled. "Paul Williams," he said.

"Craig Hardy," I said.

"Paul," she called after me. "Where are you going? Oh, for God's sake, why are you doing this to me?"

Willow was waiting up for me at ten o'clock as I crept in the garage door and creaked my way across the parquet floor. My mother was asleep, and Willow was reading in her room. But she was heavily rouged and her eyelids were painted with parrot-blue eye shadow. She crept into my bedroom and slid into the cool sheets with me, as if she knew what had happened. We held each other, careful to keep our private parts away from each other. No, we didn't 'make love'. We simply pressed our souls together, those aching lonely souls that needed the other half to be whole. We didn't fit, but we pressed our bodies together and held tight. And if she felt a pulsing desire in me, she knew that it was meant for someone else.

"I know it's wicked of me," she said. "But I was staying here, in your room, for all those lonely weeks and months, looking at your photos, and I fell in love with you. Your mother told me so much about you, I already knew you."

"Willow, I love someone else."

"I know. That blonde thing."

"She's not a thing."

"She doesn't love you."

"She does love me. And I can't help it. I love her too. I'm sorry."

"I can't help it either, Paolo. You can't help loving someone."

"Or not loving someone. Willow, I wish it was another way, but I can't. I will love her until I self-destruct. It's a genetic thing."

"Just kiss me," she said, holding my face.

I never saw her again. Willow married someone called Paolo Bellafiori in Bulawayo at her spiritualist church, and after the war they began a settlement on a farm in the Lupane area. It was a Christian Commune based on Desiderata-like sentiments. But in 1982, the *gukurahundi* was in full force, when Mugabe's Fifth Brigade massacred the Matabele. Ndebele dissidents were rampant – all forty of them – and Mugabe's Fifth Brigade punished the whole Ndebele nation for voting ZAPU by killing 20,000 men, women and children.

And in the same year, a group of bandits murdered all twenty members of the Lupane Christian Commune, all except for a seven-year-old boy who hid in the storeroom, witnessed it all, and lived to tell the tale. Willow's six-month-old daughter was killed with a bayonet affixed to an AK, and she was also found dead with bayonet stabs to the abdomen.

I have only one photograph of Willow, which is attached to the hand-written Desiderata framed on my wall. She is sitting on the couch on my mother's lap, smiling bravely at the camera. She is wearing her blue eye shadow, her face is full of hope and love, and I am surprised how beautiful she is, how she looks, to my present-day eye, like the girl I could have loved and married.

★ ★ ★

The train back to Llewellin took all night and arrived at five a.m., taking me back to the world of logic and order, and antisepsis. Because operations in Matabeleland were becoming more intense, more and more companies were deployed in the south of Rhodesia. Medics were in short supply, so I was officially designated to be a 'roving medic' and would be assigned where needed. My first bush assignment was with my old *alma mater*.

As a dog returns to its vomit, or a murderer returns to the scene of the crime, so I returned to B Company. But this time I had two stripes to protect me, and a special status. I was no ordinary soldier. And as our medical instructors had told us, in medical matters we could supersede the chain of command. Even colonels get piles, our instructors had told us. And remember, officers catch VD from toilet seats.

I mooned down B Company lines, past ten oil-dripping Bedford trucks, called 'RLS'. These creatures had been modified especially for our military purposes, with back-to-back metal seats welded down a central aisle facing outwards, painted green and brown, and covered with green netting as camouflage in the bush. Recruits scurried to and from these vehicles, carrying tents, boxes of ammunition and food supplies, while corporals and sergeants roved up and down the convoy, barking instructions. I climbed onto the back of the lead vehicle and sat on the medical pannier, a black metal box with a red cross on it, containing – I assumed – antibiotics, morphine, painkillers, suture needles and antiseptic, bandages, and emergency packs for the soldiers in the bush. I sat forlorn in the winter sunshine, prominently displaying my two stripes. And, yes, soldiers scurrying past braced up to me in respect. Power fills a vacuum, and power felt good to me that day. It was my only consolation.

Out of the small prefab building labelled 'Quartermaster' emerged my old tormentor, Sergeant Viper. I wanted to stand to attention and stiffen up, but checked myself. I was now a corporal, and all NCOs (non-commissioned officers) were equals.

"Morning, Sergeant."

The lanky instructor squinted up at the bright red, yellow and green medics' belt and the black beret I was wearing, and showed his teeth. "Ah, the doc's here."

I had not seen Sergeant Viper smile before. "Remember me from Intake 156, B Company, Alpha Platoon?"

"Your face is familiar." Viper's gaze was unrecognising. The trauma and humiliation of six weeks that would probably scar me for life had left him untouched. He jerked his thumb in the direction of the building. "We're leaving as soon as the Major is ready. Are you all set?"

"Yes…"

Turning his grimace into a scowl, he spun on his heel to address the hundreds of troops lying in the shade of the *msasa* trees. "On the trucks, you bunch of wankers. The Major doesn't like to be kept waiting."

While the soldiers already on the trucks were white, the clumps of men who emerged from the shade were black. Each soldier wore the shield and *knobkerrie* emblem of the RAR – Rhodesian African Rifles – on his beret. Viper aimed his chin at them. "A new experiment, Doc, in our modern nonracial society. Did you know that our white Rhodesian army which is constituted to preserve white civilisation is comprised mostly of blacks?"

No, I didn't know. I lifted my eyebrows in polite surprise.

"90 percent. Regulars. And they volunteer, for God's sake." He climbed into the driver's seat of my RL.

I leaned back, trying to relax into my new position of power and status. I was now one of them. It was my only defence against the weekend, against the destruction of my self. I took on the uniform, the solid starch, the rank, the snaky pole image, and baked it into my skin in the sun.

It was a short-lived reign.

"Get the fuck off that truck." The voice was a primal expression of command. All I saw from my position on the top of the truck was a blue beret. I stared stupidly, trying to interpret what he meant, because I first thought the word "fuck" was a noun.

"Medic-puss. Jump down and help me with this trunk. Don't just gawk at me." The voice belonged to a major, with one gold crown on each shoulder lapel, in blue SAS colours, cream beret, blue belt. "And salute, you pile of dried pig shit."

I saluted, jumped down and stood to attention. The Major thrust his chin up (I was taller) to fix blue eyes on me. He was a shrunken version of Roger Moore, I thought, a retired James Bond. "Well?" His fury was a spring about to uncoil. I bent down to pick up the trunk but couldn't move it. The Major impatiently wheeled around, marched to the front of the cab and hoisted himself up onto the roof like an arthritic monkey. "Start up engines."

This was my first *connaître* with my new nemesis, a man who would haunt me well into my future, who would pull me further down the path of non-existence for twenty-five years. In that moment, I could see the essence of all that was to occur, as if I already knew what was fated for me, what our dangerous relationship would bring. He dismissed me as if I didn't exist, and the fault line of my weakness ripped open. Because I was unable to respond, all the rage, all the helplessness, all the injustice was swallowed in a gaping black hole in my soul. Bianca had spewed me out of her mouth, and here was further confirmation that I did not exist.

I was still struggling to get the trunk up onto the truck when a soldier ran to my assistance. His strong arms pushed from below and I pulled from the top. Just in time: the truck pulled off, with the Major still standing on top of the cab, a rifle in his hand. I hoisted up the soldier who had helped me with the trunk.

"Buddha!" My heart flooded with relief. "What are you doing here?"

The red-haired boy grinned back at me and showed his stripes. "My housemanship. Same as you." He reached out to shake hands. He looked well. His face tanned, red hair cropped short, he looked comfortable in his faded uniform, and held his rifle affectionately.

"They're sending two medics? What for?"

"This is our big test, to see how we do in the real world. But if one of us screws up, there's the other."

The Major had climbed into the cab and the back of his shaved head showed through the back window. I could not stop staring, compelled by the ugliness of the badly cut blonde hair. Buddha cast wary eyes at the Major's head. "So you've met Moggy Madox?"

"Moggy Madox?"

"He spends his weekends marching around the barracks in uniform, looking for duties. They say he never takes leave. Can't handle being out of uniform."

"You must have a screw loose to sign up regular with the army."

"I'm counting the days," said Buddha. "I've got to get back to university to finish my degree in psychology. But you can't wish away the present. You have to live into it."

All this as the convoy wended its merry way through the Bulawayo suburbs, the chain of noisy, smelly RLs in camo green and brown out of place in this sleepy, flat town of acre-wide plots and wide ox-wagon streets. We were on display. We were the 'boys' going off to war. A white father and son stood on a porch and waved. Houseboys and nannies watched us pass and stood motionless as the African troops yelled in Ndebele and waved blue dollar bills at them.

In less than half an hour, our convoy was grinding its gears up into the barren hills and bald granite rock *kopjes* of the Matopos (Rhodesians spelled it Matopas, for some reason, but the original name was *Matobo*). The grass was dead yellow, the trees skeletal. In Rhodesia, winter was a dry three months of blue skies, dust and no rain.

The Matopos Hills are a world of huge, heaped granite boulders that look as if they are the playthings of giants. As soon as you enter this National Park, another Africa descends upon you. This vista enchanted Ndebele kings and colonial settlers alike. The tomb of Cecil John Rhodes is carved in these rocks, which are more accurately described as mountains, they are so gigantic. They are around 3,000 million years old and have emerged as balancing monuments because of millions of years of soil erosion and weathering. You can find caves in this area where the San people lived 100,000 years ago. The area has a deep spiritual significance for the Rozwi people who believe that the Matopos Hills are the resting place of their ancient ancestors.

"The Major loves these trips," said Buddha. "They're holidays to him. A whole company to order around. Watch him extend this one to two weeks."

"Two weeks? I thought we were going to be back by the weekend. I have to get up to Salisbury."

"Fat chance. Try to see it as a holiday. Haven't you always wanted a holiday in the Matopas?"

I suppose I did. Besides, there was no reason to go back to Salisbury for the weekend.

The trucks turned off the main road onto an insignificant dirt road near Maleme Dam. Fortunately, ours was the leading vehicle – fortunately because the dust covered the nine other trucks in brown clouds behind us. The road squeezed us between two enormous boulders. I stared up at the pock-marked lunar rock face above me. Orange lichen grew on many of the rocks, but otherwise they were elephant grey. Trees grew in cracks, splitting some in two. Others had ghosts of waterfalls cascading or dribbling down their sides, and still others were bald. In the distance, on top of one, I noticed movement. Stick figures danced to the beat of a mournful drum that echoed across the valley and returned the sound out of time to the dancers. I pointed up in alarm.

Buddha shook his head. "Religious ceremony – *Vapostori*. How the hell they get up the rock I don't know. Maybe they can levitate."

I watched the bodies circling a central cross, silhouetted against the blue sky. They were the size of ants. Our trucks, from this perspective, shrank too, as if we had entered the Land of the Giants. We were not the centre of the world any more but little insects in this ancient, volcanic world. Once these rocks were molten lava, I thought, flowing blobs that had cooled over millions of years. We were trackers on an alien planet. Buddha, too, was staring out at the vastness of the Matopas. It reassured me, because it made the army a little smaller and the real world of Africa outside a little bigger.

And the sky was so blue. It was as if some special effects artist had imposed it onto the set of a bad science fiction movie. How could you ever hope to compete with it? But compete with it we did. The trucks jerked to a halt round a corner and the dust had hardly settled when Major Madox leapt onto the cab of the truck, pointed his rifle up and shot off a series of excessively loud bursts into the sky. The figures around the cross, still visible in the far distance, scattered in panic, disappearing into the folds of the elephant-grey stone. Bam, bam, bam, bam. It was the Major's reaction to this bigness, his display of mastery over the environment.

"Debus."

In a single sweeping move, as they had been trained to do, the soldiers leapt off the sides of the trucks and into the bush, rolling, taking cover, pointing their rifles outwards into the dry brown scrub and acacia trees. I started towards to the side of the truck too, but Buddha pulled me back. "Lie low."

It was a pre-rehearsed exercise. He described it to me in whispers while Major Madox shot commands over us with a loud-hailer. "Sweep through the killing ground." The troops crashed through the bush, firing outwards, skirmishing past each other. "Now back. Cover the vehicles."

I didn't see any pattern. Figures crawled in and out of cover, shooting haphazardly at the sky and the enormous granite boulders. The Major bellowed commands and waved his hands and rifle in the air. Finally, he fired an arc of tracers at the sky in a long burst of automatic fire. Hot cartridge cases tinkled onto the back of the truck and on the medical pannier.

"OK. Regroup. Set up for the night." The soldiers emerged from their hiding places and lined up at each truck to collect their supplies.

"Is this it?" I asked.

Buddha nodded. "Same old haunt. Just don't take the Matopas for granite." I looked around. There was nothing to differentiate these giant mountains and dry low scrub from any other part of the Matopas. Buddha indicated a clump of trees to the left. "An old farmhouse we use for base camp."

The Major's voice cut in. "Stores. CQ. We want rats for three days. Stick commanders will collect from truck three. Eye-Sergeant will give out the maps." He pointed his rifle at us. "One from each stick will collect a medical pack from the medics here."

Buddha and I hauled the pannier to the side of the truck so that we could dispense the medical packs that had been prepared: aspirin, drips, morphine, patches for bullet wounds, bandages, all neatly folded in small satchels with a bright red cross on each. The Major scrutinised us from above.

A 'stick' consisted of a small group of five or six soldiers, the commander and second-in-command white, the rest black. Each stick, armed with radio, stores, medical pack and map, took off in a different direction into the scrub. Remaining on the trucks were the drivers, the signallers, cooks and medics. The cooks were black; the rest of us were white. Major Madox gave another command, and the trucks edged off the dirt road into what looked like a riverbed, but which led through dense acacia trees – one snagging my sleeve by its thorns as if to say, don't go in there – and opened out into a clearing. A farmhouse in need of urgent repair and paintwork greeted us. It had once been someone's beautiful home, I could tell by the way the flower beds surrounded the verandas and the driveway curved around to a portico entrance to a long porch, but Africa had done its work. Grass grew three feet high through what had once been a paved road, the roof was caved in where a large tree had fallen, and the once-white walls of the concrete building were muddy brown with various tide marks from what must have been the nearby flooded river. As we drove nearer, I saw that every window was broken and bullet-holes had shattered the plaster on every wall. Sand bunkers had been dug in the four corners of the garden, and mouldy sandbags had been piled up against them.

"Welcome to paradise," whispered Buddha.

The trucks parked in *laager* fashion around the main house. Once the Major had jumped off our truck and walked through onto the porch, Carl and I unloaded the medical pannier and jostled it around the back of the house. At his direction, I struggled onto the back veranda, which skirted the whole farmhouse, supported by Greek-style pillars. "Best place for the M.I. room is well out of the Major's way."

"You've done this all before?"

"Last two weeks while you were skiving off at the camp hospital, I was assigned on a bush exercise with His Truly."

I peered in through a window to see the Major and Sergeant Viper stamping through echoing hallways, designating ops rooms, storerooms, the officers' mess and bedrooms for themselves. Two African soldiers carried the officers' belongings through behind them.

We swept away broken glass and lay down sleeping bags in the sheltered corner, against the brick wall of the kitchen.

"Doc!"

I jumped at the voice, which I was beginning to recognise as One-Which-Must-Be-Obeyed. We tramped through the house, through the kitchen, a bar, and into what must have been the lounge, where the Major was sitting on a canvas stool surrounded by his belongings. Sergeant Viper was setting up his maps and pinning them to a wall.

"Sir?"

Major Madox's eyes bulged. "Did you come through the house?"

"You called us, sir." I waved my hand in the direction of the back veranda.

"Don't ever do that again. This house is for officers only."

Buddha stood in front of me and smartened to attention. "We're sorry, sir."

"I want you two to stop malingering and find some wood for a fire tonight. And make a guard list of all who are at base camp. We don't want terrs attacking us here." He sat down again and waved us away. I saluted smartly and wheeled around, marching out of the open French doors.

"Who does he think he is?" I whispered, when we were out in the bush collecting wood.

"Anyone below the rank of major, as far as he is concerned, is his skivvie," said Carl. "Don't take it so personally. He's just sussing you out. He'll leave you alone if you just humour him. And whatever you do, don't answer back."

We collected piles of dry *msasa* kindling, found some logs behind the farmhouse, ready sawn and stacked, and set the fire in the middle of the front lawn for the braai. Carl made a guard list on a scrap of newspaper he found in the kitchen, putting both of us on first watch so we could get a good night's sleep afterwards.

Although the flames were crackling high at last light, and soldiers had gathered around it in a circle, watching the cooks lay out spirals of *boerewors* and slabs of steak on a blackened grill, the food was not ready by the time I had to go on guard. I circled the farmhouse, around the perimeter where fences had once demarcated its boundaries, and cut a path through the trees, my rifle pointing into the dark. I watched the mountains turn into dark giant shapes; I watched the sky turn from blue to black; and I watched the Major by the firelight. He raised a bottle to his lips with his left hand, which in silhouette looked deformed. He was a short man who strutted as if he were about to explode. I could not stop watching him. His movements were as exaggerated as if he were playing charades, strutting like Mick Jagger on stage, pushing people's shoulders like Superman does, or pointing a threatening finger like Vorster, the South African Prime Minister. And when the wind changed, I could also hear him laughing like an old RL engine.

# CHAPTER ELEVEN

# HOW TO BE A TERRORIST

*Dear Bianca,*

*Picture me, on guard, walking through the smells and sounds and scrapes of a wild African night. The granite hills block out the stars in oval Dr Seuss shapes. The tall grass brushes my face as I patrol, and the trees' figures slowly dance in the wind, watching me. At first, I saw a terrorist in every shadow, until Carl told me that this is a safe area, surrounded by our troops, so if we see any shadows, they're likely to be our own. Now when I think of a 'terrorist', I no longer think of those target images of hate-filled charging monsters; I think of the patient in the hospital – the one who offered to give me advice about women. I won't tell you what he said about you.*

*Guard duty is mindless. All I do is count the minutes. The only way I can get through it is to play an album in my head. I've chosen The Moody Blues' Seventh Sojourn. Remember we melted all the other Moody Blues albums because of their pagan content? This one I spared because of side two, track one: 'We look around in wonder at the work that has been done, by the vision of our father, touched by his loving son.' I start with 'Lost in a Lost World' and sing it all the way through to the final cut, 'I'm Just a Singer in a Rock 'n Roll Band', at which point I know that I've spent exactly thirty-nine minutes and thirty seconds walking around the camp. Then I do it again with ABBA's Greatest Hits. I skip 'Dancing Queen'.*

*And Bianca, I am still carrying these letters around with me, I'm ashamed to say. I'll hold onto them and read every word until I wear them all out. But don't worry, I won't press you any more about them, or write to you any more. From now on, you will be a ghost in my mind, a Virgin Mary to whom I pray without ceasing. It sounds silly, but allow me this one indulgence, as you will allow no other.*

★ ★ ★

"Paul, Paul!"

I nearly dived under the nearest rock when I heard this voice from the darkness close behind me. "Carl?"

"You gave me the heeby-jeebies, mumbling to yourself like that. Here's some supper." Buddha had brought with him a plate of cold, burnt steaks and two warm Cokes in chipped glass bottles.

"I'm on guard. I'm not supposed to be eating."

"The only terrs around here live in the Major's head. This is an army training area." We sat on a fallen tree and ate. The steaks tasted like carbon and gristle, and the Coke frothed hot in my mouth. We watched the cold, black mountains around us, keeping a wary eye on the farmhouse so we wouldn't get caught. The *braai* fire had died down to a red glow. Every so often a twig would snap and a flurry of fireworks would burst into the sky above it.

"What's on your mind, Paul? A cent for your thoughts."

Heavy sigh; time for confession. He grinned in the dark and his teeth glinted as he listened to my story. The stars pulsed back at us. "*Maya.*"

"What?"

"It's all illusion. You think it's real, all these feelings you have, this self you have constructed to inhabit, this need to be, to want, to have, to define, but it's all *maya*. Desire is a corrosive. It destroys you." The stars gleamed in the sky, the weak red Mars in the west, the bright blue evening star in the east. Soon, the moon would rise and wash the night white with its brightness. "Let her go. If you love something, set it free. If it comes back to you, it's yours. If it doesn't, hunt it down and kill it."

"Carl?"

"Joking, only joking. But seriously, she's eating you up inside. That's not healthy. That's not love. That's stupidity. That's masochism. She doesn't love you. Let her go. It's that simple." It was dark now and I couldn't see Buddha next to me, just hear his voice, low, slow and deliberate, as if he were trying to hypnotise me.

I threw the gristle of my steak into the bush and some small animal scuttled away into the dry grass. "That's easy for you to say. It's not something I can help. I didn't have any choice in the first place."

"Why does Miss Rhodesia use Lux soap?"

"Why?"

"Because she has no choice." It was an old joke. 'Choice' was the only other soap on the market.

"But Carl, you don't have the power to change your circumstances. Else you wouldn't be in the army, would you? You'd be at university in Durban."

He sighed. "In the same way that a military instructor destroys the ego and self-identity of a recruit, the Zen master slowly erodes the novice's confidence in his own logical powers."

I shook my head.

"It's a Koan, Doc, remember a Koan?"

★  ★  ★

During this time, ZANU and ZAPU had been extremely busy. In the early seventies, these noble cadres put into practice all they had learned in their training camps in China and Russia by exposing the true nature of the People's suffering, demystifying the superstructures on which the illusions of the country were based, building a culture of resistance. The struggle was a multifaceted *impi* of oppressed workers, toiling peasants, enlightened intellectuals and energised students who marched forward to inevitable, historical victory under the banner of the Patriotic Front. Their underground cells proliferated in rural areas, in urban areas, in factories, in farming communities, mobilising the toiling masses sweating under the burdening yoke of colonialism.

*Interview with Edward Ndhlovu, ZAPU Deputy National Secretary (Dec. 1974): "Our revolution demands patience... We give recruits basic knowledge of explosives and training in the use of light weapons. However, we don't have adequate arms and ammunition for most of those who want to join us inside. Most of our guerrillas, therefore, are still trained outside in socialist or independent African countries... All our militants also receive political training. They study Marxism, Leninism, Maoism, the history of Zimbabwe and writings on either revolutions, such as in Vietnam, Algeria, Cuba, or the Mau Mau in Kenya. Whenever we can, we spend time on political education, since it is crucial in building and maintaining the morale and good comportment among our guerrillas.*

*It is no secret that we base our work on the principles of Marxism-Leninism and that our ideological position is rooted in the masses. The struggle to create a new society such as we are striving for must be based on the principles of scientific socialism.*

*We are committed to a programme of establishing a socialist state and society in Zimbabwe, and this we will do. We will need the support of everyone who has something to contribute, irrespective of race, colour or creed. In the short term there will be land reform and the establishment of peoples' control over all large companies, including the multinationals operating in our country. Later we will go further, but it is difficult to be more specific at this stage. Nevertheless, I am convinced that a free and socialist Zimbabwe will be a better place to live in for all Zimbabweans."*

★ ★ ★

*Here are the rules for conduct of the freedom fighter:*

*1) Pay for whatever you take.*

*2) Be courteous.*

*3) Explain gently to those who do not understand.*

*4) Make it clear what the penalty is for treachery, how it is vital that we remain undiscovered, that the wrath of the Rhodesian Security Forces will fall on them if we are discovered.*

★ ★ ★

*Interview with George Nyandoro, General Secretary of* ZAPU *(1974): "During the liberation struggle our main objective is to seize power – then we can begin the social revolution, begin to put our social principles into practice. When we liberate an area, then we will begin our social revolution from that base – in practical terms. Until that time, until we have power in a liberated area, considerations of socialist programmes and policies are necessarily confined to the realm of pure theory."*

★ ★ ★

Well, if the terrorists were going to swim like fish among the people – our poor innocent tribesmen – and disseminate their murky, algae-sodden propaganda, then we would remove the people so the fish could no longer swim with them.

It was that easy. Rhodesians had fought in Burma, Egypt and Malaya (*It was there that we fought and won*, the RAR song went), and learnt there and in Kenya how to deal with these Maoist tactics of terror. The plan was to move the rural people into what came to be known as PVs, or Protected Villages. This would cut the CTs off from their supplies of food and comfort, and it would also encourage the loyalty of the rural people by protecting them from attacks and providing them with new services.

Unfortunately, these villages would never be adequately policed or protected and the people would not be involved in their management or persuaded of their necessity. They would even begin calling them concentration camps, a ludicrous analogy that was disseminated, no doubt, by the ubiquitous, iniquitous, so-called Zimbabwe People's Radio broadcasts. People would be forcibly removed from their traditional ancestral homelands, but for their own protection. They wanted to be protected; they needed to be protected. True, a financial shortage would preclude proper development of the villages, and they would build them too far from the peasants' fields and away from the burial sites of their ancestors, but they would effectively protect them from infiltration by terrorist indoctrination. They would have water, food and housing. It would be no use their complaining that their fields would be neglected; we would implement a policy of food control, including the use of defoliants on crops in areas from which the peasants had been removed, in order to starve out the terrorists. Thus, we would remove not only the fish but the water as well, leaving our Maoist terrorist high and dry.

★  ★  ★

"Doc!"

It was early morning. My breath streamed white. Sunrise was close, signalled by the myriad birdcalls in the trees, the smell of the African dawn and the luminous pink glow behind the low bushes. Buddha was asleep.

"Doc!"

I wrapped myself around with a combat jacket, slotted on laceless black *takkies*, and picked my way around the veranda to the room where the Major was cocooned in his sleeping bag in a hammock. His blond hair was coxcombed to one side, and his eyes were puffy.

"Sir?"

"Bring me some tea, please, won't you?"

"Yes, sir." I skirted his sleeping area, passed the Sergeant's room, after reassuring myself that he was still entombed in his body bag, and found my way into the kitchen. I lit the gas stove and boiled a saucepan of water. I found Tanganda teabags, Gold Star sugar, Nestlé powdered milk and a chipped mug with a fat elephant on the side carrying a Rhodesian flag, saying 'Rhodesia is Super'.

"Here you are, sir."

"Ah, that's the way, Doc." I turned to go. "Oh, and Doc… Later on today, I want you to look at my corns – they're playing up. How would you treat them?"

"I'd have to see them, sir. I don't know…" We hadn't learned about corns in the medic's course, just gunshot wounds and suturing and VD.

"Oh, and Doc… You must come immediately when I call you, because it may be an emergency. You must run, not slouch here as if you're on a Sunday stroll."

"Yes, sir."

On the agenda for that morning was an activity the Major insisted we medics attend. So after breakfast at seven o'clock sharp, we scrambled onto the back of the Major's jeep, and he bounced us through ravines, *dongas*, over tree roots and down what had once been a dirt road. At a dry river bed, he hooted his horn three times. Out of the bushes, sleepy and dishevelled, soldiers emerged.

"You lazy sods. Assemble for live skirmishing."

Skirmishing: half the line of troops advances while the other half gives them covering fire. The enemy has to duck, which gives our troops a chance to advance on the enemy position. They had been practising this 'dry', without ammunition, but today they were to try it live. While one troopie crawled forward, his partner would shoot from behind, aiming as close to him as possible.

"That's why the Docs are here," explained the Major. "You'd better pray to God your partner has good aim." To start the exercise, he fired into the ground slightly ahead of the line. "There's the enemy," he pointed. "Crawl." And the exercise began.

So this was hell. Bullets whizzed past ears, above heads, tore up the dry ground as if it were cardboard. From where we sat on the jeep, all we saw was smoke, muzzle flashes and dust. "Keep down," the Major kept warning people. "Keep your arse down if you don't want it blown off. McArthur, you'd be dead by now if they were firing back. Your partner's not giving you covering fire." He pushed aside McArthur's partner. "Let me show you."

He clicked the switch onto automatic and ripped the ground to the left and right of the crawling soldier. Dust flew up around him and we were soon all spitting dirt out of our mouths. A bullet twanged against a piece of protruding granite in the ground and whizzed off to the side. "A ricochet!" The Major laughed as if this was an accomplishment in itself. "That's how you do it, Gladys." McArthur wriggled forward, trying to burrow into the earth.

When the soldiers had skirmished the length of the terrain, across the riverbed to the line of trees, the Major gave the signal to stop. The troops stood up and walked back in a long ragged line, panting heavily.

"Watch this, Doc," whispered the Major to me. He lifted his rifle, aimed it between two soldiers and fired. "Ambush," he screamed. "Back again. Enemy to the rear." The soldiers fell to the ground. "Skirmish, damn you." The Major shot again at the trees from where they had just come. So the whole exercise began again. The Major was having fun, firing where he thought troopies were slacking, shooting above their heads to keep them flattened on the ground, shooting into the sky to simulate enemy advancement. Once the troops had reached the trees, he shot into the air on automatic to signal the end of the exercise. Again, the troops stood warily.

"Jungle lane! I want to see the last man under cover. If I see anyone, I shoot."

The soldiers ducked into the woods. The black soldiers disappeared immediately, while the whites were easier to spot as unbroken white patches. But in a few seconds they had all melted into the bush.

"Come." The Major jumped off the jeep and signalled for us to follow. We walked through the riverbed and into the woods. He held his rifle at port, his finger on the trigger. "Docs, shoot if you hear any movement or see anything."

I threw a glance back to Buddha who shrugged his shoulders and pointed his weapon at the bush. But his tapping finger indicated that his safety catch was on. I nodded. But the Major's weapon was on automatic. Without warning, he danced to the left and shook off a dozen rounds into a tree until the wood splintered and bled white. "See, Johnson, you'd be a dead duck if I was a gook." A rustle in the nearby bush was Johnson scurrying to hide deeper in the leaves.

By the end of the morning, the soldiers had been thoroughly shot at, harassed, "scared shitless" (to use the Major's phrase), and deserved a noisy drink from their canteens.

"This is a serious war," the Major told them while they panted in the shade like drooping leopards. "We are not just playing soldiers. You have to risk your lives for your fellow comrades if anyone is to survive. You will soon enjoy the thrill of the 'crack' over your heads when bullets fly. You will feel more alive, alert and even grow addicted to the taste of enemy fire, the more you fight."

He smiled. He had enjoyed himself that morning, and we soon realised how important it was that the Major enjoyed himself.

One small, unimportant incident I remember from that day. In the middle of the skirmish an old, black civilian man walked around the back of the jeep and signalled to us with a white handkerchief. Viper was sent to speak to him, and returned with the message: could we please shoot in another direction, because his village (he was the chief) was in the direct line of fire, and they were afraid of getting hit. They had had to herd all their animals into the *kraal*, and were hiding behind rocks.

The Major raised his eyebrows, stared back at the man who held his handkerchief in both hands, and bowed his head. "OK, time to go anyway."

He was silent all the way back to camp, but when we arrived, the Eye-Sergeant, Viper, hadn't laid out the maps ready for the next exercise. An instant tornado of rage, the Major stamped his feet and balled his fist at Viper's face. "That's just not bloody well good enough, is it? What if we were in an emergency, if we needed them now?"

"We're not in an emergency," said the Sergeant. "You forget, Ian, that this is a training exercise. We're not in the operational area."

Major Madox sizzled in what looked like excruciating pain. His face burned scarlet, his upper torso trembled, and like a bull, he stamped his right foot on the ground. "Nobody, but nobody, calls me by my first name," he called up to the sky. "Especially not a bloody non-commissioned officer. To you, Viper, I am Sir. I am Major. I am your superior officer, and you'd better remember that."

Viper, to his credit, stared coolly at his superior officer, maintaining eye contact, his Adam's apple bobbing in his taut neck. Then he turned 180 degrees as if he was on a drill parade and marched neatly away, leaving the Major to poke his stubby finger into fresh air.

And just as suddenly, the thunderstorm was over. Major Madox blinked once, turned to the stunned circle of medics, signallers and cooks who were watching him in awed terror, smiled and fingered my shoulder lapel. "Cards tonight, Doc, after supper?" And he walked stiffly away to his room.

Supper was the usual braaied steaks and *boerewors*, blackened in the fire on the front lawn. The Major had set up a table in front of it with a gas lamp swinging from the tree above, so that Buddha and I could join him for his game of cards. Sergeant Viper didn't appear for supper, but stood staring at us in silhouette from his room on the front veranda, smoking a cigarette. He had asked the cook, Joseph, to bring his meal to him in his room, but when the Major noticed the black man hastily filching meat from the fire and piling it on a plate, he asked who it was for.

"The Baas, Baas Wiper, suh." The servant spoke in the clumsy language of subservience that had been taught to him, the English that suited the act he had to perform of the stupid Kaffir who had no language of his own.

"So we are not good enough company for him tonight?" said the Major, standing and raising his pistol. Buddha nudged me and raised his eyes to the starry sky. The cook stammered at the approaching figure. "No, sir." He had his orders and so began walking to Sergeant Viper's room, where the Sergeant stood in the shadows of the veranda.

"Didn't you hear me, Joseph? Perhaps you'll listen to this." Madox shot one round into the grass at the cook's feet. Joseph dropped the tray and dived onto the ground, covering his head. Sausages snaked into the air and landed in gritty brown dirt. The Major laughed, staring at Sergeant Viper, waiting for his reaction. To everyone's surprise, Sergeant Viper smiled, stepped out of the shadows and pulled out a Browning pistol of his own. Surely he wasn't going to shoot at the Major? No, of course not. He took cool aim at the cringing servant's forehead.

"Joseph," he called. "Bring me my food." The servant began picking up steaks and boerewors from the ground, picking off the grass and dusting off the earth at great speed. And now Sergeant Viper shot into the dust at the servant's feet, coolly, two close shots that made him dance and leap into the air. Major

Madox, laughing, shot again, a wild burst in an arc around the sausages.

"Leave the food alone, Joseph. Do as I say."

Both men were now shooting in turn, skilfully aiming as close to the cringing servant as possible, so that echoes of the shots mingled with his cries in the Matopas mountains: "No, Baas, please, I bring later, no, Baas."

The shooting match ended in a truce. The Major called Viper over to join him at his table for supper, the servant scuttled off into the darkness, and I was sent to get meat from the *braai*. The Major, in high spirits now, his eyes glinting with mischievous excitement in the gaslight, clapped Viper on the back. "He's all right, you know, he's all right."

After supper, Viper slapped a pack of cards on the table, and Buddha whispered a warning to me. "Don't win too often. The Major's not very good at cards." We bet cent pieces. After each game, the Major and Viper opened another 'dumpie' each, a short brown bottle of Lion Lager. I played as dumb as I could but still managed to win the first game.

"Beginner's luck," muttered the Major. But I soon got the knack of it, and he won the next three games, and humoured up considerably. "You bunch of muttonheads," he roared. "I want some competition."

So I won the next game and the one after that until Buddha gave me a kick under the table. "I can't help it, Carl. I had a full flush."

"Well, cheat, can't you?" So in the next game I got rid of a good pair of aces and lost hopelessly to the Major.

"You're weakening, Doc, you're weakening."

It was nearly nine o'clock and time for my guard duty. The night was moonless and silent. The silhouetted *kopje* above me was Bianca's shape, the wind whispering through the trees was her voice, those sweet-smelling night blossoms were her breath, and the darkness was the texture of her absence.

I sang songs to myself to pass the time. David Bowie's 'Space Oddity', five minutes. Cat Stevens' 'Moonshadow', another three minutes gone. The stars were a milky eerie light and bushes gleamed in a ghostly way. I wasn't looking out for enemies, or even thinking of the vastness outside the camp perimeter.

I was watching the square of light in the Major's room.

I was beginning to despise myself. At Hillside Baptist Fellowship, we had been taught that submission – yielding to God, turning the other cheek to your enemy – was a good thing. But here it felt distasteful. Or was this really submission? Wasn't I simply humouring the Major but acting subservient? What was the difference? When you humoured someone, you kept yourself separate from your behaviour, but as a doormat you *were* that behaviour. You were bigger than the Major if you humoured him and smaller than him if you acted as a doormat. I was doing both. In the Major's presence I was small and shrunken. I made tea for him; I smiled in spite of myself; I took on his outlook, became what he wanted me to be. I couldn't help this eagerness to please, and it wasn't just because the Major was in charge. I was doing it willingly. I was trying to please him to win his approval. But above this, behind it, hovered a self who was not there: the humourer, who could remain intact and inviolate.

★ ★ ★

At the time it was amusing; now it seems bizarre. Sergeant Jones and I were driving in our open jeep through a township (Harari, Rufaro, it didn't matter, they were all the bloody same to us whiteys) and we were vigilant, rifles cocked, looking for the address of a fellow RAR soldier to pick up for his duty at the hospital. We weren't in combat mode, and we were lost. So we did the untypical male thing: we stopped and asked for directions at a corner where a black man in rags was selling Cokes.

Smiling, eager to please, he directed us – you go thea, hea – and when we thanked him and drove on, he shouted after us, "I hope you get those Kaffirs and fuck them up."

★ ★ ★

Once I was waiting at the Bulawayo Sun Hotel for the army bus to take me back to Salisbury for my weekend pass, and I loitered on the street corner, kicking my shoes against the curb. An old man wheeling a Greatermans trolley full of raggedy clothes stopped and smiled at me, asked me for money. I shook my head.

"How old are you?" he said.

"Nineteen."

"You are so young. Smith sends his young girls to fight a man's war."

I didn't know how to react. I smiled at him, and he went on his way.

★  ★  ★

On a weekend pass through Bulawayo, McKechnie (a fellow medic) and I strolled around town on a Saturday morning. We fell in line behind two giggling women who had noticed us and were passing comments about 'handsome uniforms'. We followed them up and down the streets, and they led us on, escorting us through Haddon & Sly, Woolworth's, in and out of the lingerie section of Greatermans, and finally to a Wimpy restaurant in Grey Avenue. We were meant to follow them in, sit down and order them a drink of coffee, and begin chatting, flirting and 'scoring'. But McKechnie said he had to be back at barracks, and I marched fiercely past the restaurant, willing myself to walk in, but unable to.

★  ★  ★

When I tired of walking around and around the farmhouse, I crouched by a rock in the trees for a while and listened to the crickets and cicadas. I felt for the letters that I had transferred from my Bible to my combat jacket pocket and pulled them out, but it was too dark to read them. I identified each by its shape. This is your Valentine card; this is your first letter which saved your skin in basic training; this is your dream letter.

I had not been there more than a few minutes when a silhouette appeared in the door of the living room, framed against the light. Sergeant Viper, tall, lean in his jungle green, stood staring out at the sky. He lit a cigarette, flicked the match away, and then crunched on the dirt towards me. He stopped ten metres away. But instead of greeting me, or scolding me for not patrolling, he walked straight past my rock. I crouched lower, listening to his legs brush through the tall grass. He was heading towards the nearest mountain-*kopje*, 'for a piss', I presumed. But after five minutes, he hadn't returned. I stood and strained my eyes, but he had melted into the darkness. He had his rifle with him, but it was slung over his back. He obviously did not think there was any danger out here. I intended to resume my patrol of the farmhouse, but curiosity got the better of me, and I decided instead to follow him, to see where he had gone. I held onto my rifle for comfort and to push the long strands of grass away from my face as I struggled through them. Ahead, a twig snapped, and I stopped to listen. Yes, I could hear Viper wading through the undergrowth. When he had gone far enough ahead, I followed. He was skirting the *kopje*, but I climbed a large granite boulder and hid in the shadows. Now he was visible below me, as I crouched at the edge of the undergrowth, watching him swish through the grass. He stopped to catch his breath once and to get his bearings – yes, he knew where he was going; this was not a night meander – and then disappeared over the ridge. I waited for a few minutes, my heart pounding, my mind tumbling over the questions it generated.

Feeling exposed and naked without the cover of the trees, I crouched and crawled across the rock, stopping every now and then to listen for sounds. I heard nothing. As I reached the top of the rock, I peered over. I could see shadows, trees, but no Sergeant Viper. I had lost him. I didn't even know in which direction he had gone. I stared ahead into a hollow valley of darkness. If he was in there, there would be no point following him. I crept down and picked my way back to the farmhouse.

Buddha was waiting to take over guard. It was past eleven o'clock. "Where the hell were you?"

"Just patrolling, a little 360."

"You take this thing far too seriously, pal," he said. "It's only a training exercise."

"I'm off to bed. Have to be up at five thirty-six to make the Major tea."

"I'm sure I'm coming down with flu or something. I feel terrible."

"What's wrong?"

"Just terrible headache, body pains, you know, sore throat."

"Have you taken anything for it? Beserol?"

"Naw, I'll be OK. I'll see tomorrow."

"Oh, Carl, if anyone comes crawling back to camp, don't shoot or anything. It's just Sergeant Viper."

"Viper?"

"He went for a walk. If he returns, don't shoot him."

"I wouldn't even notice him unless he walked over me."

The next morning I made the Major his tea. He also wanted a few Valium, as he had run out. "Not much to do today, I'm afraid, Doc. The sticks are all out, preparing for their final exercise. There hasn't been much action for you."

"That's fine, sir."

"Oh, Doc, have a look at my corns while you're here."

I dabbed the crusty yellow corns with cotton wool and Cetramol until his feet were soaking. "Hey, Doc, don't overdo it. You're supposed to clean the corns, not wash my feet."

"B... Carl Rogers, the other medic, is sick today, sir. I think he has water poisoning. I'm giving him Tetracycline and a rest for the day."

"Indeed," said the Major. "And what makes you so sure he's sick?"

"I'm sure he can't help it, sir, being sick."

"He's a little girl. He's malingering, Doc, and you know that too."

I stammered an assent.

"What has he been doing all camp? Sweet fuck all, your friend, except hibernate on the back veranda, pretending to be a medic. Eh? What do you think?"

I moved my head in a non-committal way, dabbing the Major's corns with a special cream I found in the pack that stung like crazy. I hadn't a clue how to treat corns so I used my great skill, acting as if I knew what I was doing and supplying as much pain as possible to give myself credibility.

The Major winced. "You'd better go and see how he is doing. Report back to me."

Buddha was feverish, with a temperature of 104 degrees, his body trembling, and with D&V (diarrhoea and vomiting). These were the classic symptoms of a virus from water poisoning, tick-bite fever or gastric flu. Whatever it was, the cure was the same: antibiotics, in this case Tetracycline. But he would have none of it.

"I don't believe in those drugs, Paul, you know that. They only lower your resistance. The cause of illness lies much deeper."

"Yeah," I replied. "Water poisoning. Drinking polluted water. Tick-bite fever, an infected tick bites you. That's deep enough for me."

"No, Paul, we shouldn't be here at all. That's the cause. What the hell are we doing in Africa in the bush like this? That's the cause."

"You're delirious, Carl. Anyway, if you won't take antibiotics, at least stay in bed all day and rest and drink plenty of fluids."

"I'm a medic too, you know."

I was surprised to see Sergeant Viper at breakfast. He greeted the Major brightly as the cook brought them a generous helping of bacon and eggs. Afterwards, the three of us played Rummy. I let the Major win enough times to keep him happy.

"So, Doc, what are you going to do after your National Service?"

I threw away a good ace which he picked up. "University, sir, Durban, to do a BA."

"A BA? What for?"

"I'm interested in literature, sir, and art, mythology and history. Those sorts of things."

The Major pursed his lips. "A Bugger All? You won't get anywhere with a BA. Do a B Comm. if you want to achieve anything. That's what I would have done. But I had another calling." I gave him the required earnest, son-to-father look. He put down three aces and held onto two cards. I was still trying to get rid of two queens, but I somehow managed to attract all the right cards.

"Up there," he pointed, "you'll find Rhodes's grave. He was a man with a destiny. Conquered the whole rugged country, fought the Matabele, Shona, occupied Mashonaland, civilised it. Rhodesia was once just a dream in his head. Cape to Cairo, one long railway line. He achieved it by hard work. He never rested. Always at it, Rhodes."

I gave him the seven I knew he was waiting for, and he fanned his run on the table. "Rummy. See, Doc, winning is an attitude."

The crime, I thought, is to take yourself too seriously. Paul Williams, you need to lighten up. You need to stop obliterating yourself.

"Doc, this land needs another Rhodes. Someone to stand up again and say, I have a dream. But... he never achieved it. Africa began its decay long before we came along." He stared out at the granite mountains. I looked out too, trying visually to trace the path I had walked last night. I recognised the granite *kopje* I had climbed. Beyond it, I saw a wisp of blue smoke. Perhaps a stick of our troops was camped there and this was what Sergeant Viper had gone to investigate.

"Go and attend to your duties, Doc, and tell me how the malingerer is, won't you? Sergeant Viper and I have some business to discuss."

"Sir." I walked off smartly.

★  ★  ★

Even at the time, it bothered me that Major Madox was such a cliché of the Old Empire. Like Rhodesia, he was a dinosaur. The Ice Age, or the giant meteorite that should have made him extinct, had somehow missed our continent. But history is a hyena that keeps burying and unearthing its prey. "In the long history of the Dark Continent," historian Andrew Roberts wrote in 2005, "the brief period when ordinary Africans were most content, most secure, most justly governed, and least likely to be oppressed by their tribal enemies was when they were administered by the British Empire."

Colonialism, you see, was one big love affair. White interference in this continent was not the root of all evils, after all; it was its salvation. We whites (here you must thumb your white chest if you want to join in) like to think of ourselves as the nexus of history. Africa was at its heyday under the British, and after independence, all African countries declined into a torpor of terror and corruption. So go ahead, Major Madox, if you are still alive. Join again in the hymn of Albion: one long railway to Cairo, can't be too far now.

# CHAPTER TWELVE

# A TRUE WAR STORY

*A true war story is never about war. It's about sunlight. It's about the special way that dawn spreads out on a river when you know you must cross that river and march into the mountains and do things you are afraid to do. It's about love and memory. It's about sorrow. It's about sisters who never write back and people who never listen.*
(Tim O'Brien, *The Things They Carried*)

When the Europeans carved up Africa in 1888, and when the colonisers arrived to exploit the mineral wealth of this country, they were not interested in its indigenous culture, even while making those grandiose claims to be civilising Africa. What they were here for was to loot its treasures. Perhaps they were blinded to its beauty by the tsetse fly and malaria and blackwater fever that struck them, but whatever their reason for disregarding the awe and majesty of this land, they systematically uglified it. They made red gashes in the earth wherever they smelted copper or asbestos, tin or aluminium. Hwange was bayoneted open and its treasures ripped from its mother's black womb, Manghura was a bleeding red wound, Zvishavane gashed open and left exposed to the elements.

It did not seem that they were really interested in Africa's natural beauty, which to me was its primary attribute. I knew this land. I knew the power of its rain clouds with their thousand faces, the volcanic hills, the precariously balanced granite rocks, pitted and textured and lichened, the green grass too emerald to be real, shimmering in the spring and summer, studded with wild animals.

If I am rapturous, it's because this is what made the camp bearable. The rest was hell. But nature was my ally and my friend. The wind whispered at night; the dawns and evenings were major events. I never want to live without seeing another African sunset, I would say to myself. I was an animist, though I didn't realise it. I only had to look within to see the gods squirming in each molecule and cell of life and motion of the grass stalk. The flame lilies I came across were blessings, surprises, reassurance that God, or beauty, or truth was alive and well.

I didn't see many of the boasted four hundred bird species that soared through this area. I saw the occasional eagle fingering the blue sky, and a few bouncing buzzards attacking the carcasses of dead animals, but mostly the animal life here was hidden from me, except at dawn, when a myriad birds flooded the air just as the red sun dusted the horizon. At sunset, too, they sang in cacophony to signal the glory of the event. But I felt excluded. I was not quite a Wordsworthian Romantic; I did not think birds held the key to a happiness that was denied me, but there was a life, a riotously ecstatic life, outside my reach, and we dumb humans were blind to its rhythms and patterns.

There was the usual queue of patients at the veranda, and colds, flu, foot wounds and VD to attend to. Buddha was asleep still, feverish, but stable. After I had treated everyone, I decided to sit quietly and read my Bible, more out of despair now than for consolation. For a secluded spot, I chose the rock I had crouched behind the night before.

After reading the Psalm of the day and applying it to my life, as you do a horoscope reading, I reached for Bianca's letters in my coat pocket. They were not there. The night before, on guard duty, I had smoothed them between my fingers in a rosary-like chant, recalling every word in each letter, to pass the time and to obliterate my last meeting with her. When Viper had approached me, I had hastily stuffed them back into my combat jacket pocket, but I saw now that they must have tumbled out somewhere on my night walk.

Making sure the Major was not watching, I climbed through the *msasa* forest which led up the *kopje*. I could track my path by the trampled grass and broken twigs. Ahead of me, a wisp of blue smoke twirled into the sky, and I used this to keep my bearings. I beat the bush, swished the grass, prayed, but to no avail. The letters were nowhere to be seen. I clambered up the small *kopje*, stood on the granite mound I had climbed last night, and surveyed the area. The farmhouse behind me sat snugly in the clearing. The jeep's mirror gleamed at me in the sunlight. The cook was washing and peeling potatoes. Major Madox was inside, I presumed, reading or examining maps and plans of his troops for their final exercise. But on the other side of the *kopje*, I traced the wisp of smoke to a clump of trees at the base of the next hill. Then I saw – or thought I saw – a fluttering pink piece of paper at the bottom of the hill. As I climbed down, I held my rifle in front of me, expecting danger.

Yes, here it was, a pink envelope with Bianca's spidery handwriting – Little Soldier Blue (or should that be Rifleman Smiley?). It had fluttered down the hill in the night and ensnared itself on a *wag 'n bietjie* bush. Now where were the others? I saw another flicker below me as the terrain levelled out. The wind last night had been a cool south-westerly, and it had scattered my soul over the harsh, dry Matopas. I waded through the grass, caution thrown to the wind as I reached for the letters. I took possession of the Valentine Card, but saw that the rest of them were strewn on a hard patch of trodden earth in a clearing ahead. I saw thatched huts, mud walls, small fires burning. I stood behind a clump of trees, staring into an African village.

The only concept I had of an African village was the tourist model set up at the Salisbury Show every year. I held in me the worst stereotypes of Africa that the West had perpetrated on its people. I lived in Africa, but I knew nothing about it. To me, Africans were a homogenous mass, devoid of culture, history or intelligence. I saw no intricate fibres of protocol, custom or tradition.

So what did I see now? Women carrying wood to and fro, babies on their backs, tightly knotted with blankets. One woman stirred a huge pot of *sadza* on a crackling fire in the centre of the compound. Other women talked softly in Ndebele. Three men sat around the fire on small wooden stools. Another man slept on the ground, propped up against the side of a hut. Chickens squawked as they scratched the swept ground for food. I crouched down, puzzling over how I was to retrieve my letters without being seen.

My dilemma was solved for me. A scampering behind me alerted me; someone had been following me. Major Madox, I thought in terror. Or Sergeant Viper, about to grab me by the scruff of the neck, asking, why were you following me? Or terrorists? I instinctively pulled the rifle around and aimed it at the whispering grass. A woman's arms reached for the sky, and she stepped out from behind a tree. "Don't shoot, Master." I saw an old woman in a tattered pink floral dress, with a myriad wrinkles and folds on her black skin.

"It's OK, Mama," I soothed in my medic's voice. She scrambled backwards, trying to edge away. I smiled, pointed the weapon away, and opened my hand. "It's OK," I said. But she fled back into the compound.

Of course, I had forgotten who I was. I was a soldier in uniform, with a rifle. How could I counteract such a monstrous image? I walked into the compound, giving as many gestures of goodwill as I could think of. I held my hands outwards, my rifle in one, but pointing it to the sky. The woman had fled to the safety of a walled-in mud enclosure, but two of the men stood as soon as they saw me.

"It's OK," I said. "I just came to get these." Like a fool, I pointed at the letters with my rifle, then quickly switched hands to point with my finger. I edged towards the two envelopes, picked them up and stuffed them in my pocket. "My letters." No one moved. "From an… *umfazi*." This was one of the only African words I knew. Was it the crude Fanigalo, or was it real Shona or Ndebele? "*Umfazi*. Girlfriend." For all I knew it was a derogatory word like 'puss' or 'piece of ass' or 'squaw'; I had no idea. I had heard it in the context of a conversation my father had had with our houseboy. Wonderson had come to work with a hangover after a session at the Rufaro Beerhall on Sunday night. "Too much Chibuku; too many *umfazis*," my father had chided, and he had grinned foolishly. "Yes, Baas, too many plenty *umfazis*."

Four people were now staring at me. A few children peeped their heads around grass fences at me, and the men stood before me, as if I had summoned them to roll call. The woman continued to stir her large black pot of *sadza*.

"Does anyone here speak English?" I asked loudly. "I'm a medic, a doctor, madoctor." I pointed to the medic's belt, to the Asclepias sign, the snake up a pole. What did this Greek symbol mean to them? All were staring at me in dull terror, or mute respect, I was not sure which.

There is always a point of revelation that you can look back to, or a sudden realisation, and this was one of those moments. At this point in time, at seven o'clock on a winter Matopas morning in 1977, I realised that I had never actually seen a black person before. These were not garden boys, or houseboys or maids or nannies, or Kaffirs or houts. They were simply people. An old man sat on a wooden stool drinking tea, and bless him if he wasn't drinking Tanganda Tea-time Tips, out of a china cup. The kettle was chipped black under its blue metal, and was simmering on a friendly blue flame, supported on a black tripod. On the stool next to him lay a tattered magazine – *Drum* – and on the cover, a woman's face smiled at me. But what hammered home the point was the granite boulder which served as a table next to his hut. A brightly coloured tablecloth had been laid, and a family was in the middle of eating breakfast. A child sat with an enormous slice of bread in her mouth, and an older woman was ladling *sadza* into bowls. But it was the graffiti written in white paint on the rock that did it for me: 'Denzil Dex shot JR.'

Emerging from the hut was a man with a white peppercorn beard, who reached out his hand to shake mine. Inside the hut, I could see a carpet, a lounge suite, a TV and an aerial poking out of the straw roof. Children peeked around the doorway to look at me.

"Tea?"

The man – I was sure he was the man who had complained about our shooting the day before – gestured to the kettle and I shook my head. Nevertheless, a china cup appeared and tea was poured. Milk? Sugar? I smiled and reached for the cup. "Thank you," I said, nodding to the woman who was holding the cup out to me as if I had a contagious disease.

The man raised white eyebrows at me. "See where the bullets hit?"

"I'm sorry we didn't know… we were training… a training exercise…"

He showed me the grouping of bullets on the rock, the chipped granite, the white chips, and I lifted the cup to my lips and drank the sweet, powder-milk taste of strong Tanganda. I slung my rifle over my shoulder, and sat where they indicated.

"I came to fetch these letters…"

I was aware I was speaking as if to a garden boy, and that my language was condescending. They understood me perfectly well. I tried to speak normally. "Thank you. It's very good, thank you."

★ ★ ★

"Doc, Doc, where the hell have you been? I've been doing your work for you."

The Major was calling from the front lawn, standing over someone lying prostrate on the grass. His legs and arms were splayed out, and his face was covered
with a cap. The medical pannier was open on the grass, and the Major held a
Normal Saline drip high in the air so that the fluid would flow down the plastic
tube into the patient's arm.

I rushed to the patient, taking the drip from the Major, and knelt. "Buddha?"
I recognised Carl Rogers only by his bony arms and legs, which were nailed
through his clothing to the ground with tent pegs. "What happened?"

The Major stood and wiped his brow. "I came to check on your patient.
Found him extremely pale. So I suggested a little sun to regain the vitamin E
that he lost." I opened my mouth to object. You don't put a high temperature
patient in the blazing midday sun. But the Major held a fat, cautionary finger
to my lips. "But then Doc, after an hour's sun treatment, I realised he was dehy-
drated. So I practised a little needlework on him. What do you think?"

I crouched to see the canula thrust into Buddha's vein in his elbow joint. A
little bruised, but the drip was working. I pulled the cap from his face. Buddha's
eyes were closed, and he did not acknowledge me.

"Physician, heal thyself," called the Major. "What kind of a medic is he,
anyway?"

"You OK, Carl?"

Buddha blinked at me and then closed his eyes again. "Those who know do
not speak."

The Major shoved the cap over Buddha's mouth and frowned at me with
mock horror. "He needs help, Doc, he's delirious. After all I've done for him,
the ungrateful bugger."

"Sir?"

"He's not only a bad medic, he's a very bad patient too. Listen, Doc, you look
after him now. Make sure he gets lots of rest."

When I was sure the Major was safely out of range, I pulled the drip out.
"What the hell?" I whispered, rubbing Buddha's bruised arm and applying
pressure so the bleeding would stop. He sat up slowly, and I supported him as
we walked back to the veranda.

"Where were you, Paul? As soon as you were gone, the Major told me to get up and sort out the fire. I told him I was really sick, so then he began all that nonsense."

The anger that erupted out of me took me by surprise. "He can't do that to you! He can't just rummage in our medical pannier. You know that we actually have authority over him as medics. He is not allowed to mess with our medicine. Or with people's health!"

"I'm not going to confront him on his terms."

"What other terms are there? We must face up to him."

Strong words for a coward. I could not conceive of facing up to the Major, or crossing him in any way. I had admired Viper for doing so, but also thought him foolish.

"I put myself in a state of extreme concentration and was unassailable," said Buddha. "The Major couldn't get to me. If you want to initiate a conflict with a volcano, you do so. But I'm in survival mode." He walked over to his sleeping bag, climbed into it and closed his eyes.

"Carl, we have to stand up for ourselves."

"You're a Christian, aren't you?"

"Yes."

"I thought Christians were supposed to be pacifists."

"No."

"Yes, they are. Turn the other cheek. If your enemy asks you to walk a mile, you walk two miles. You know."

★ ★ ★

The confrontation came sooner than I expected. I cursed myself for bringing it on. All afternoon, our little house on the prairie was subjected to the bombardment of the Major's taunting voice. I didn't want to think about what was going on; I had watched it all the day before. Various black soldiers had been sent back for punishment – accidental discharge, sleeping on guard, insubordination – and the Major had willingly taken on the task of punishing them. He had found an empty water tank and made them run round and round inside its perimeter with heavy sandbags on their backs until they dropped from exhaustion.

Today he had taken them on a different route. Glistening with sweat, each detainee had been running around the farmhouse and climbing up and over each of the ten trucks, with the sandbag tucked around his neck. They had already been at it all morning. Behind them swaggered the Major. "Left right, left right, keep those knees up. No staggering, Moyo, you won't get any sympathy from me. Get those knees up!"

A true medic would intervene and object to this treatment on health grounds. But I could not imagine myself even having a loud enough voice to break the Major's trajectory of violence. As one soldier faltered on the truck and collapsed onto the ground, the sandbag making a 'doof' sound as it landed on him, I leaped up and ran over onto the lawn. The Major put out a hand. "Don't give him attention. He just wants attention." Then to the still body lying there: "Is this a prank to get some rest, eh, Mpofu?" And he prodded the prostrate man's buttocks with his boot. I stood, angry enough to let my real self show. Now was the time. Buddha watched me, smiling, his arms folded.

"Let me look at him, sir." I strode to the prostrate man, trying to carry myself with the authority of a medic who took precedence over a Major in matters of medicine. I crouched on my haunches and tried to lift the sandbag. It was much too heavy. My impulse – the empowering adrenaline that had overridden my common sense – drained swiftly. The Major prodded my backside with his foot, trying to overbalance me.

"I'll decide when you can look at him, Doc. He's doing a punishment. Punishment is not supposed to be pleasant – it's supposed to be rough and painful."

I stood and turned, mustering all the courage I could in the face of the dizzy red fear that blinded me. I was supposed to look the Major in the eye, and I almost managed it by squinting (the sun was mercifully behind him), but my voice was faltering and rapidly found its familiar cringing tone of humility. "But… he might have heat-stroke, he might have hurt himself…"

The Major called to God in the sky. "Medics! It's supposed to be painful. I suppose you want him to run around in the shade, or better still to sit in an easy chair while I bring him cold beers?"

"No, sir, I mean…"

"It's time you fucking learned about what the fucking army is really about, Doc. We're not here for our comfort. We're fighting a fucking war, unpleasant though it may be. That means killing people. I don't know why the fuck we need medics when we're trying to kill people."

"Sorry, sir, OK, sir."

The Major wagged a finger at my nose. "Only when I call you, you understand?"

"Yes, sir."

★　★　★

"I tried, Carl. You saw me."

Carl nodded. "The man of wood sings, the woman of stone dances. This cannot be done by passion or learning. It cannot be done by reasoning."

"Who are they going to point fingers at, eh, Carl? The Major? No, they'll say it was our responsibility. We should have said, on medical grounds, that it was no go. You and me. Let's try working together." I marched around the farmhouse, trying to diffuse my fury. I hated Carl now, as I hated myself, as I hated the Major. This was not healthy. I would soon be hating the whole world and pulling it all over me in an apocalyptic rage with a grimace of satisfaction.

If black people in this country had a problem with self-obliteration, I was a prize chameleon. I merged so seamlessly with my environment, into what people wanted me to be, that there was no way of telling if I was really there. Why didn't I have a backbone? A spine? A centre? A core? Who the hell was I anyway?

★　★　★

*In an act of barbarism worthy of another age, terrorists this week forced an African to cook and eat his own ears. Another gang of terrorists also slashed away part of the upper lip of a black woman. These acts of savagery, committed by men whom some call 'freedom fighters', herald the future in store for the people of Rhodesia if the terrorists were ever to gain control. Men who can commit crimes such as these, and still sleep soundly at night, are in reality animals in human guise. The communist nations arm and train terrorists and use them as willing tools to gain political ends which have nothing to do with freedom. It is doubtful whether the terrorist or his leader has any political objectives worthy of the name, outside the exercise of raw, naked power. They want power and they will do anything to win power. These men are armed thugs, criminals bent on taking Africa back to another age, when it was known as the Dark Continent. To dignify them as 'freedom fighters' and 'guerrillas' is to afford them a status they do not and will never deserve.*

★  ★  ★

I remember the cool, pseudo-BBC accent of the radio announcer who read this diatribe against the Patriotic Front, and the way he pronounced 'power' as 'pah' in that smug way that showed how civilised we were. Nevertheless, I was suitably outraged. I was a puppet nodding when the media pulled my strings. Later, at university, I scorned my own gullibility. It was obvious propaganda. Who would force anyone to eat their own ears, except maybe a Selous Scout acting on behalf of a brutal fascist regime propping itself up by any means necessary? These were the very tactics of the Rhodesian regime itself. And such propaganda was an attempt to deny the very existence of a Black Nationalist movement or cause. I scorned the naiveté of Rhodesian whites to fall for such naked, blatant drivel.

Later still, twenty years after ZANU (PF) had taken power, I changed my mind again. If the Mugabe thugs were now forcing farm workers to eat their own ears, cutting off lips of schoolteachers who were opposition supporters, torturing people who did not carry ZANU party cards, then it was likely that this had been their very *modus operandi* back in 1977. So the Rhodesian propaganda machine had been right after all, and I marvelled at how accurate their predictions were. The armed thugs would be so-called 'war veterans', and the 'criminals' were the *chefs* in power, bent on dragging Zimbabwe back to the dark ages of fear, terror and tribalism.

After independence, I took care to purge any Rhodesianness from my being. I became 'Zimbabwean'. I was pardoned for my sins, I became a comrade, and I obliterated my past. You may have even heard me on Zimbabwe Broadcasting Corporation – Radio Three, deejaying to the tune of Cde. Grey and Cde. Kadungure. Like me, Rhodesia was no more. It was an illegal entity whose years 1965–1980 had ceased to exist. The Rhodesian history books had been filled with white heroes and colonisation. After independence, Zimbabwean history books neatly obliterated the entire ninety years of colonialism.

After Mugabe's triumphant destruction of Rhodesia, I explored Nyanga and found multiple layers of civilisation at the Van Niekerk ruins. First, I discovered the ruins of the Rozwi people: terraced hills, 'slave pits' (fortified hill structures) and millet traces. Second, I excavated the ruins of a white empire, the charred, overgrown remains of a Rhodesian civilisation and its vain attempt to leave a mark on this continent: picnic tables, *braai* pits, toilets, a sign directing people to 'The Falls', the ruins of a refreshment kiosk. As in Shelley's poem, all that remained of this civilisation was the artist's handiwork, the writing on stone, the arrows pointing into the wilderness. Look on my works, ye Mighty, and despair!

But I found a third layer of ruined civilisations sleeping in those hills. First the Rozwi, then Rhodesia and now Zimbabwe too. The dream of independence, of sovereignty, of freedom was also gone. Zimbabwe, the people chant, is dead, dead, dead.

★  ★  ★

When I returned from my walkabout, I found the entire camp personnel, all nine of them, in the ops room on the front veranda. "Doc, you need to be here too," barked the Major. A stick of soldiers had trooped in to report that a gang of terrorists had been sighted.

"Villagers have confessed to harbouring and feeding them. A typical terrorist pattern – they come in the night, terrorise a *kraal*, demand food, rape the women. Then they are gone."

Sergeant Viper drew red lines on maps spread out on the table. "We surround them and then close in here. A two-kilometre radius and we ambush them."

The Major tapped a spot on the map with his finger. "My bet is that they're harbouring with the locals, blending in with the villagers."

Once we had all gathered in the front yard, Major Madox and Sergeant Viper faced their assembled audience. Sergeant Viper spoke. "All sticks are deployed already in the field, so we need them to hold their positions. We need every available man here for the plan." I looked around at the camp soldiers – two black cooks, a sick medic, four black soldiers on punishment, and me.

The Major swept his gaze around, but he saw soldiers, machines, tools to be deployed in the cause of justice. "We spread a hundred yards from the huts and wait for them. We'll spring an ambush. Three a.m. tomorrow."

"How many villages are in the area?" asked a soldier. "And which village are we speaking of?"

The Major: "One village, in Chiweshe Communal lands, half a kilometre south of the farmhouse. Used to be the labourers' compound for this farm. Now in the service of thuggery and banditry in the name of freedom and liberation."

★ ★ ★

I was roused by one of the cooks, who whispered "Half past two" in my ear. I jumped up and we grinned at each other, both shaking our heads at this madness. I let Buddha sleep; he was in no state to go with us.

The Major was fully dressed and waiting on the road with his pack on his back and radio slung over his shoulder.

"Come on, Doc, where's your bum chum?"

"Sick, sir."

"He'll be sicker if we lose the war. Get his arse over here now."

"He'll be a liability, sir."

The other soldiers were assembling and Sergeant Viper arrived to distract the Major and save me from a torrent of abuse.

"Very well, leave him to die."

So that was it. The Major was in a Vietnam war movie.

The group of soldiers huddled together to keep warm, wishing they were still sleeping. Major Madox took the lead, turning off the road to the right of the *kopje* I had climbed the previous day. We trampled loudly through the bush, the cooks puffing for breath, the Major cursing and shushing them even more loudly, his voice cutting through the night air. I trembled with the cold but also with the realisation that we were acting, however badly, in a movie the Major believed to be real. As we sighted the village in the starlight, we halted and crouched down while he whispered instructions to us. We were to surround it at a distance of one hundred feet and lie in wait for any activity.

"Expect to see, just before first light, the gooks leaving the village. Shoot to kill." Nine of us spread thinly around the village. I kept twenty feet between me and the Major, finding myself a hollow ditch by a tree to lie in. I pointed my rifle towards the village and promptly fell asleep.

## CHAPTER THIRTEEN

# FRIENDLY FIRE

*Hokoyo*! Aid and abet a terrorist and you get a hefty fine. Report a terrorist, on the other hand, and we'll pay you $8,000. *Hokoyo*! Journalists must not disseminate information which prejudices the security of the state or is harmful to Rhodesia. *Hokoyo*! We have increased National Service for white heterosexual males from nine months to one year to eighteen months. *Hokoyo*! The state of emergency has been renewed for another ten years, and we have put in place further measures in the interests of law and order. *Hokoyo*! The mandatory death penalty has been extended to include training of, failure to report the presence of, harbouring of, and false information about, terrorists (except for pregnant women and children under 16). *Hokoyo*! The country is obese with war. Rhodesian military units have geared themselves up to combat the war on all fronts. Fire Force will hunt you down; the Intelligence Corps will smell you out; the Psychological Warfare Unit will win your hearts and minds (when we have you by the balls, your hearts and minds will follow); Guard Force will keep the Protected Villages free of terrorist vermin; Grey Scouts, Selous Scouts, SAS, RLI, RAR have you in their net, so tremble with fear, you *makandangas, mujhibas, chimbwidos.*

★ ★ ★

The high-pitched screech of baboons woke me up. I was numb with cold, and my rifle had tumbled to the ground. I flexed my fingers before picking it up. The golden dawn of early spring streamed across the hiding place I had chosen; it must have been about six-thirty. I craned my neck to discover that the others had all advanced on the village, and left me behind. Through the grass, between grass roofs, I caught sight of a blue beret: the Major was standing in the centre of the compound. I rose to my feet and crept to where my comrades had formed a catchment circle around the village and were milling around miserably, searching huts, poking their rifles into bushes. Clearly no terrorists had been found. As I stepped into the clearing, hoping no one would notice, the Major swung around, lifted his stocky Uzi and aimed it at my head.

"Doc. Good morning. Nice of you to join us."

"I was investigating…"

"Arsehole." The Major lowered his weapon. "What kind of a war is this when you think you can sleep on guard? We all could have been killed because of you. Doc, you're on a charge. As soon as we get back to Llewellin, it's straight to the box for you." He turned away in contemptuous dismissal.

The baboon screamed again, coming like mocking laughter through the thin walls of a grass hut. And I realised that it was not a baboon. "Are they–? Did you–?" I asked. Moyo, the black soldier who was at base-camp for insubordination, the one I had tried to save from the Major's wrath the day before, stumbled out of the hut, dragging a sack-like object behind him. I stared at the withered mass of wrinkles, tears and blood. I expected a woman, not this man crumpled in pain and defeat. Moyo released his cargo to brace up to the Major, and the man knelt in supplication to the soldiers in front of him. "Nothing, *sair*," reported Moyo, saluting the Major. "He knows nothing about *makandangas*." And without warning, Moyo struck the man in the face with his rifle butt so that he collapsed to the ground.

This was the old man who had offered me tea. My impulse was to rush forward, to shout "No", but the Major had trained me well. I was rooted to the spot, my teeth clenched, my fists tight. I stared wildly around, trying to recall these people from my visit yesterday, knowing they recognised me.

The performance was a tired parody of something seen many times before. This was a show that had been staged so many times that people were now going through the perfunctory sleepwalking motions, they knew their parts so well. This village had enacted the same scene in the First Chimurenga, the Second Chimurenga, the Gukurahundi, the persecution of the opposition MDC. People suffered, died, were buried. But for me it was the first time. My eyes were opened to something of the nature of the white man in Africa, and the nature of the black man too.

The Major, his foot on a stump, ordered all the villagers in a circle around him. Moyo kicked and prodded each villager into position. From inside a hut, another scream cut through the air. "Shut her up, Moyo," the Major called. Immediately, Moyo bounded into the hut and after a dull thud, there was silence.

Meanwhile, Sergeant Viper emerged from a hut on the perimeter. He held a young man by the scruff of his cast-off servant's uniform, and pushed him into the centre of the compound, where he fell like a sack of manure at the Major's feet. Viper kicked his back for good measure. "Major, this one is ready to talk."

The young man wriggled in the dust like a disturbed earthworm, trying to bury himself in the hard red earth for protection against the Major's glaring eyes and steel Uzi barrel. "No, master, please, no hurt, sir, no."

"You harbour terrorists?" said the Major, twisting the boy's ear so that he coiled on the ground like a corkscrew. The villagers watched without expression. The Major was putting on a show for them, but only the soldiers were appreciating the performance. I am not sure if their smiling and laughing was obligatory, but it came on cue as the Major looked up at them for their response.

"No, sir."

"Were there soldiers here, gooks, men with guns, terrorists?"

"Yes, my master, he come, in the night, for women, my master. He take food, drink, want women."

The Major let go of the man's ear and stood back, squinting around the circle. Viper looked uneasy, but hardened his lips into a grim smile. Moyo ducked his head as he emerged from the dark hut, grinning and shrugging his shoulders.

"Moyo," said the Major. "This is how you do it, you stupid bastard. This guy's talking." He thrust the barrel of his Uzi into the boy's privates.

"Master, that's all, we have no choice. We have to do it, otherwise, kaboom, shoot." The man made the sound of a rifle shot, the sound we made as kids when we played cops and robbers, cowboys and Indians. Pu! Pu! Pu!

"Why didn't you report to us?" said the Major. "You stupid *houts*. We can protect you. We can stop them terrorising you." He pulled his Uzi away and slung it around his back. Then he smiled – actually smiled – at the terrified boy, and crouched down to look into his eyes. He spoke with the confidential familiarity of a friend.

"When were they here?"

"The other day, sir, my great lord. Two nights and yesterday. They come one, one, for food, for women, for tea. We give them, we afraid, the soldiers."

Sergeant Viper, pacing from foot to foot, turned his back on the show and stared out at the green *kopje*, now haloed by the rising sun. The Major stood again, caressed his chin, and strolled around the circle, watching each bowed head. "I think what we have here is a case for hearts and minds. Moyo, here, I need you to interpret." The Major leaped up onto a granite rock and opened his arms.

"We have come here to help you. We are the Rhodesian Army and our job is to protect you from the terrorists, from the evil men who come to you in the middle of the night, who rape and terrorise and steal from you."

Moyo listened, translating it all into Ndebele. He gesticulated wildly, threatened with fists and rifle, contorted his face in terrible expressions, in charade form acted out rape, terrorism, stealing. The black cooks laughed at his obscene antics, but the villagers stared blankly at the Major, ignoring this clown.

"These bad men, these terrorists, are communists and socialists. They want to take away your land, possessions, and control it all, and they will kill anyone who does not agree with them." He paused for Moyo to interpret. "Do you all understand? If you see these men again, you come to me, you report and you will have a reward. You will live in peace if you co-operate with us, but *hokoyo*! If you feed the terrorists, if you harbour them, they will only kill and murder and rape and steal more. They want the whole country."

Moyo interpreted, dragging out the rape scene a little too long, so that the Major cut impatiently into his speech. The villagers nodded violently at him, murmuring "Yebo" in unison.

My eyes flicked from one villager to the other, hunting, searching, trying to correlate the image in my mind to the reality. They were acting, these people, as stupid, ignorant villagers. They were wearing masks of humility. Where was the man I saw yesterday? There! He was looking down, but when he looked up, his yellow eyes accused me. Our interlocking stares froze, and he immediately looked down again so as to avoid recognition. But I had made eye contact. I'm sorry, I said with my eyes. Another woman stole a look at me, then lowered her face to stare at the hard, packed earth. Did she understand what I was telling her? I was on show now, and others were watching me too. I mustn't upstage the Major, who was making his point by opening his hands in a gesture of honest communication.

"Capitalism means you can own your own land, cattle, wives. The tragedy about communism, the diabolical thing about communism, ladies and gentlemen, is that they want to take away your land, your huts, your cattle, goats, pigs, chickens. And worse, your children. They want your children too, my friends. Take a child from the age of five and indoctrinate him and he'll kill his own parents for the Party."

Moyo translated. He ran from hut to hut, chased after a squawking hen and kicked it, then singled out a small naked pot-bellied child, pulled her up to stand and held her head until she squealed with pain. The cooks laughed loudly at the show, and the black soldiers clapped. Sergeant Viper had turned around to watch these antics too. "What a character, a real stooge."

The man who had crawled in the dirt was sitting with his head between his knees. The only communication that was taking place, I flattered myself in thinking, was between the villagers and me. I shook my head, darted a disapproving glance at the Major and Moyo, then back to them. We're all *penga*, I was trying to say, but I dared not raise my finger to my head and circle my ears in the classic sign for madness.

"Where did they go, the terrorists?" the Major asked. The crouching man, thus addressed, pointed feebly in the direction of the *kopje* which hid our farmhouse.

"Damn. They gave us the slip. Take this man for questioning further at base camp and let's go." Moyo heaved the surprised man to his feet. He had thought it was all over. "No see," he said frantically.

"Oh, Doc, Moyo overdid it with the one gook. Just take a look at him, will you?"

"Sir?"

"In the hut," said the Major, pointing to the dark entrance of the hut where the screams had come from. "Samson will guard you." He marched off with the others, leaving me to peer timidly into the darkness. The villagers sat still on the ground.

I had been left in charge. "It's OK," I told them. But they did not move or give any indication of hearing me. Samson, an RAR soldier who smiled

incessantly, guarded me by crouching outside the perimeter of the village with
his rifle pointed at the hot, ticking bush around us.

In the hut, a dark shadow lay on the floor, stiffening in terror as this white
man with a rifle loomed in the doorway. I waited for my eyes to adjust to the
gloom. I took off my medic pack and dumped it on the ground. I clattered my
rifle down too. The man began to breathe slower. As he became more visible,
I saw that he was bleeding from the nose and mouth. I first cleaned him with
swabs of Cetramol, and pressed hard to stop the nose bleed. Two teeth were
loose, one knocked out. His lip was cut open by a blow from a heavy metal
object or rifle butt. I wiped away as much blood as I could to see the wound
clearly. I worked with distaste, but in the manner I had learned at Mpilo hospital.
The mouth needed suturing.

"You'll be OK," I soothed. "It will all be all right."

The man was not looking at me; he was staring at the doorway. My testicles
tightened in fear. I turned. A black fist gripped the mud pole of the door frame,
and a shadow slid across the block of sunlight, leaving me in the dark again.

"Yes?" I cried stupidly, to mask my fear. "Samson, is that you?"

The silhouette of a young woman – why hadn't I noticed that the hand was
female? – darted back, in fear too, and then the head of a young woman peered
in. I did my best to smile. "He's going to be OK." She disappeared at my voice,
then came back, a hand over her mouth. "Come in. Sit. Help me." I beckoned
her into the cool darkness of the hut, and she crouched down, peering at my
medical pack. I made sure that my rifle was well to one side – in my paranoia I
thought she might grab it and shoot me dead. I opened the pack, and showed
her the needles, the bandages, the *muti*. My pride at my efficiency and ability
to help was mixed with shame at being part of the group that had caused the
injury, and a desperate anxiety to prove I was not like the rest of them.

"What is your name?" I asked her as I pressed the wound, waiting for the
anaesthetic to take effect. The wounded man had his eyes closed, his face surrendered in trust when he saw this white man speaking and smiling at the girl.
She shook her head. I pointed to myself. "Paul." I pointed to her. "You?"

"Nomsa."

"Nomsa?"

I saw only the whites of her eyes and the glint of her teeth. "It won't hurt," I explained, pinching the man's skin near the wound. "He's numb from the anaesthetic." She stared at me in what must have been horror at my callous man-handling of the wounded area.

"Finished." I stood. "He'll be OK now. In two weeks, he must have the stitches removed, OK?" I collected my pack and rifle and moved towards the door. She shrank from me. "I'm so sorry. I'm really sorry. He's *penga*, he's crazy, that man." She curtseyed, clapped her hands and just as I turned to go, spoke, "Please sir, Doctor."

"I'm not a doctor."

"Please."

"Tell us. Before."

I knew what she wanted to say. "Warn you? I will try. But I can't control him – he's *penga*. You understand?" Now I could make the gesture freely, and she smiled, imitating my movements, circling her ear with a finger. "*Penga*." I tried to shake hands, but instead she withdrew and curtsied, bowing her head.

I walked out into the brightness of a new morning and a sunny sky. The villagers stood aside to let me pass and I smiled as best as I could at them, collected my sentry, and tramped out into the bushes over to the *kopje*. The ground began to go soggy under my feet.

★ ★ ★

"What's up, Doc?" Carl stretched.

"How about you? Feeling better?"

"Yup. Just a hangover, it feels like."

"You missed all the action at the village."

"Don't tell me the Major's been at it again?"

"Again?"

"Every camp, he concocts some story about enemies and sends us all around scouting for imaginary terrorists all night."

"Well, he… yes," I said. "He did it again."

"Any prisoners this time?"

"One for interrogation."

"Paul, this happens every time. How can this man be let loose on the world? We'll have to let the poor bugger out."

"We?"

"Last camp, I let out three prisoners, from the village. The Major thought their comrades had come in the night to free them or they escaped on their own. No one suspected it was me."

"I don't believe it. You weren't caught?"

"They wouldn't have known what to do with him anyway. They would have had to let him go, and that would have seemed weak for the Major. I did him a favour."

"OK. How do we do it?"

"Come. But get cleaned up first. You look like a bloody ghoul risen from the dead."

"Well, you're the one who believes in reincarnation."

Buddha and I slunk around the farmhouse, keeping out of sight of the main living room area. Behind the RLS, fifty or so yards down a footpath, we found the old servants' quarters. Carl picked one whitewashed, square concrete structure and sidled up to it. A high window was still paned with glass, and the green metal door was newly padlocked. We put our ears to the door, and I heard the restless shuffling of someone on a pile of hay.

"I can get the key easily," whispered Carl.

"How?"

He winked. "Ops room. Where all the truck keys are."

I shook my head. "Carl, are you sure we're not asking for trouble?"

"Yes, we are asking for trouble. We're confronting trouble. Instead of lying on our backs and taking it. I'll do it tonight, when you're on guard. Otherwise you'll never know what they'll do to the poor bugger. He has to invent imaginary terrs for the Major."

So that night, while I was patrolling the perimeter, humming Neil Diamond's 'Walk on Water' to myself, I watched Carl Rogers pace boldly into the ops room, which was deserted, disappear round the back of the trucks, then return with a jangling key on a huge metal ring. He tinkled it at me.

"Sssh."

"No problem," he whispered. "He's safe back in the village. I told him to *hamba.* And I left the door open and the lock, as if he forced his way out."

★ ★ ★

*Dear Bianca*

*I'm stuck in the Matopas for ever, it seems. The Major loves it here and won't go back to base. He's extended our tour of duty for another two weeks. Every time I have a chance to come home, the army whisks me away. But what is the use of coming home anyway?*

*I can't pursue you any more. I can't write to you, phone you, or visit. So I have decided to do the only sensible thing, on advice from my friend here, and from the various Quiet Times I have had here. Let go and let God have His wonderful way. I can't force fate, or you, or predestiny. I was trying to possess you, but I will not pursue you any more. If you love someone, Buddha said, set her free.*

*I have not heard from you. Nothing but silence, a large universe of silence. To be honest, there are moments when I don't even think of you. I'm busy with struggles here of my own. But I always think of telling you about every detail when I return. I always think of things in the light of your approval, as if you are my moral barometer. In CS Lewis's* The Great Divorce, *heaven was Platonic reality; hell was a bad copy. An angel tried to persuade a man whose lust was a lizard on his shoulder to give it up, and when he did, it turned into a beautiful white winged horse on which he rode off into the sky. That's me. I have given you up (not that you are a lizard). Watch for me in the sky. Think of the* MOBIL *petrol garages with those winged horse signs. I have loved them since I was a little boy. Maybe this is a sign for us. Let's be winged horses and fly together into the blue sky.*

*Your brother-in-Christ,*

*Smiley*

★ ★ ★

*Dear Paul*

*Your Dad here. Who'd have thought it? I'm dressed up in denim camo like you, hunched over an* FN, *and patrolling the road from Salisbury to Fort Victoria. We're based at ------------. What we do is organise the convoys — you can't travel on your own on the main roads any more, it's not safe — so we give the public some reassurance that it's under control. It ---- of course...-----. But we give it our best. Most of us don't know the barrel from the butt. All we have to do is clear the road ahead and then drive ahead and behind the cars.*

*Sorry I missed you last holiday – seems like you were up to a lot of hi-jinx with a certain female visitor staying at our house???! (Mum told me.)*

*Terrs zapped our convoy twice already. They ----------------------------------------- ------------------------------. I was nearly a goner. But it's OK. Thirsty work. If you hear the news reports that a headmaster from Hillside has been killed, don't worry, it wasn't me. Poor old ------------- copped it on our last run. He ----------------.*

*Basic training – how did you cope with that red-faced idiot belly-aching at you all day? After a few minutes of our drill instructor's abuse, we couldn't take it, so we formed a committee (typical Headmasters) and requested that he talk normally – we weren't deaf – and that he refrain from using four-letter expletives. He was so taken aback, he didn't know how to react. He wanted to yell at us some more, I'm sure, but he wasn't used to teachers and headmasters as his recruits instead of the usual cannon-fodder. I mean, really. Anyway, after that he was a lot more civil, but there were many holes in his sentences where the swear words were supposed to go, and he didn't have much to say, actually, once the swear words were gone.*

*Take care. I hear you're in the ------------- enjoying the-------. Wonderful place. See if you can visit ------- grave while you're there. It's spectacular.*
*Lotsa, Dad*

★ ★ ★

*Dear Nomsa*
*It will be all right. He'll be OK. You see, I'm a medic, a madoctor, who is trained to heal, to protect and serve, to clean up the mess after the Major has gutted and spilt blood. But he's* penga, *that man.* Penga, *you understand. Look at the distance I am demar-cating: him... me... you. You want me to warn you next time? Next time is tonight, tomorrow, every day. Major Madoxes and white soldier ants are crawling all over the soft, black skin of this country.*

★ ★ ★

I was roused by the signaller violently shaking my bag. The sun shone red through the zig-zag *msasa* tree branches.

"Doc, come quick, someone's been shot. Down in the gully." I looked for Buddha but his sleeping bag was flat and empty – he was on early guard duty. "The Major's radioed through."

"The Major?" I shouldered the emergency medical bag and trotted down the road towards the dry river bed where the signaller was pointing. I was wary of trickery; the Major had often done this to me.

In the river gully, I found Sergeant Viper sitting on the back of the Major's jeep, talking urgently on the radio. When he saw me, he jumped down to run with me. "Round the corner." We both ran now, round a clump of bushes towards an open field, where two white corporals were pointing their rifles at a group of African troops. In the centre of this knot of people crouched the Major who looked up at me with weak blue eyes. "You're too late, Doc." I had caught him in the act of covering a body with a blanket.

I unshouldered the emergency medic pack. "Let me look at him, sir." I knelt over the blanket, prised the Major's fingers from the body he had been trying to conceal. Face down was a RAR soldier in uniform, now drenched with blood, a white viscous substance around his neck. The back of his head was missing. Blood gushed slowly from a wound the size of a clenched fist.

"Cover him, Doc," the Major ordered.

"Let me just… do my job." I felt for and found a bullet entry wound in the man's forehead, just above his eyes. The man was still alive. His pulse was beating slowly, and he was bubbling blood out of his mouth. The black soldiers who were watching had fallen into silence and crowded over me, pressing against my back and head to get a better look.

"Cover him, Doc," ordered the Major.

"He's still alive, sir."

Viper stepped between me and the black soldiers. "Everybody back. Give the man some air. Give the Doc some room to work." The soldiers pushed harder, jolting my arm, and calling out in Ndebele. One man wailed into my ear. I didn't look up, but I felt the collective anger of a dozen men over me.

"Throw down your weapons." Viper pushed the soldiers back and away from the circle. "Now!" I heard him cocking his rifle and, looking up in fear, saw him circle slowly around us, gesticulating with his weapon at each soldier in turn, until each had backed away and had placed his G3 assault rifle on the ground. The white corporals on the outside of the circle picked up each weapon. But this did not stop the black soldiers shouting. One man pointed at the Major and let a string of what had to be Ndebele swear words fly at him. The corporals now cocked their weapons and guided the RAR soldiers back, herding them away from the wounded man, the Major and me.

I didn't feel in any danger. I was too busy with my own panic, trying to follow procedure I had rehearsed dozens of times in training. Set up a drip. Remove the man's tongue from his throat. Easy in theory, in the cool lecture room of 3 Medical Company, Llewellin Barracks. But in the prickly heat of Matopas, with a dozen sweating soldiers cursing me, the Major trying to pull my hand away and cover the patient with a grassy blanket, with my hands clammy with hot blood, and the rich thick smell making my stomach churn, I could not think straight. His tongue was slippery, covered in white bile and blood, the veins had collapsed or receded, and before I could find one, the arm had swelled up in a dome where I had pumped in the fluid. The Major hovered over me, stammered something I could not hear, and placed a combat jacket as a cushion under the man's head. Viper announced that he had already organised casevac operations on the radio and had also brought a stretcher. Two African troops helped me lift the man onto the green canvas and heaved him onto the waiting Crocodile truck, and I motioned them to stay with me for the ride so they could help. One looked guiltily back at his comrades who had been rounded up in a tight group, guarded by the white corporals.

"We expect to see thumbs up when you return," called the Major, and I nodded from the top of the truck. Viper jumped in the driver's seat, started it, and ramped it up the gully onto the road. He drove recklessly, deliberately trying to catapult us out of the back of the truck, it seemed to me, aiming for the potholes and rocks and corrugations in the dirt road. I tried to stand over the wounded man and hold the drip steady but couldn't, so I squatted over him, trying to balance by holding his body tight with my knees. I had my last glimpse of the Major as we swung around at the edge of the field. He was trotting towards us, his hand up, his thumb cocked and waggling, as if he were trying to hitch a ride.

The trip was a nightmare. I feared that the drip would stop or pull out of the vein at every bump (I had managed to get it in eventually, after four failed attempts), and my hands were shaking even more violently than the truck. When we finally reached the Bulawayo–Beitbridge tar road, the wounded man stopped breathing. I tried to remember my medical training. When you don't have an artificial airway to stop your patient swallowing his tongue, I recalled, you have to keep his tongue out manually, and resuscitate him. "Can anyone do mouth-to-mouth?" The two men crouching on either side of the wounded man stared blankly at me. "OK." I cleaned the man's mouth of white frothy porridge, pulled out the dry pink tongue, took a deep breath and blew. I had to keep cleaning his airway and mouth of blood and the viscous white substance with every breath I took. I pushed the chest down; I blew into the mouth. It made me sick: the blood was as pungent as warthog shit. I rhythmically pushed, blew, pushed, until I was dizzy for lack of breath myself. But the man wouldn't breathe. Even with a heart massage, he had no life of his own. I wiped the blood from my own mouth and looked up.

We were now in Bulawayo, speeding through red lights with the horn blowing full blast. But there was nothing to be saved in this man. The two stunned RAR soldiers stared at me as if I was responsible, as if I, who had been pummelling the man's chest, blowing into his mouth, had caused his death.

"The hospital," Viper yelled out of the cab. He veered off to the left and turned into the entrance of Bulawayo Central, while I tried for the last time to blow into the man's mouth. Was I doing this for show, now that the emergency unit was clambering onto the truck to take over? I wiped my bloody hands on my longs.

Then I was off the hook. Three scrambling hospital workers carried the stretcher, one took the drip, and all four disappeared through the open glass doors of a white oblong building. I flopped down on the grass verge. Viper leaped out of the cab and ran off into the nearby restroom. The two troops stood uneasily by my side, eventually helping me up and guiding me into the building. We followed the passage of our patient through wide corridors, brushing past patients and hospital staff in clean white uniforms. They gawped as we passed. Only when I saw myself in a passing mirror did I see what they were staring at – a week of dirt from the bush, blood on my hands up to my elbows, around my mouth and forehead, clothes soaked in dark dripping patches of red and white and grey matter. Outside the operating theatre, we were told to wait. Here I caught up with myself, got my breath back, and was able to ask what had happened.

"It was the Major, sir. Showing us how to shoot and take cover. John lies down in the grass and we all watch him leopard crawl." One soldier acted out the scene, crouched down in the hospital hallway, while the other trained an imaginary rifle on him.

"He wants to show us how hard it is to shoot a man lying down and crawling forward like this. But John, he was impatient. He asks the Major a question. Why do we have to do this all day? Same, same, all day. The Major is angry. Shouts, pushes him. He says it will save our lives if the enemy shoots at us. Then we will thank him for training us. So John lies down, crawls. The Major shoots, one, one. John lies still."

"Then," interrupted the other soldier, "he thinks John is playing games with him, John is pretending. Get up, Mpofu! Get up, Mpofu! he says. He shouts at him, but John just lies there. Get up, Mpofu. The Major, he shoots again, very angry, but now we know what is wrong."

An elderly white man in a lab coat stepped out of the door and beckoned to me. The two RAR soldiers tripped close behind me. "No chance," he announced. "We couldn't get his heart going. His whole system collapsed."

The two soldiers began wailing simultaneously. The doctor waved at them, trying to quieten them down. "A brain injury like that is almost certain to be fatal. There's nothing you could have done to save him."

Another doctor emerged from the room, peeling off bloodstained gloves. "Did you get the terrs who drilled him?" I stared blankly at him. "Let's hope so."

I pulled the two wailing black soldiers with me outside. Their distress was irritating me. "Come on, we'd better go back. Where's the Sergeant?"

Viper was sitting on the grass in front of the truck with gecko-white skin and pressed lips. He raised his eyebrows at me, and I shook my head. "There's no way he could have lived with a wound like that."

Viper whistled. "We are in shit-street now."

★  ★  ★

★  ★  ★

*****, *****, Private, Second Battalion, Rhodesia Regiment, killed on active service in an accidental contact with another Army unit, 19 October 1977.

*****, *****, Rifleman, Fifth Battalion, Rhodesia Regiment, killed on active service in friendly fire, 20 October 1977.

*****, *****, F., Rifleman, Second Squadron, Rhodesia Regiment, killed on active service in an accidental contact with another Army unit, 22 October 1977.

*****, *****, Private, Ninth Division, Rhodesia Regiment, killed on active service in accidental fire fight, 24 October 1977.

*****, *****, District Commissioner, killed on active service, mistaken for the enemy by an Army unit, 25 October 1977.

Repeat *ad nauseam* until the Honour Roll is full, then scrub out the first names and start again.

★  ★  ★

Even before we reached the farmhouse, the anxious eyes of white soldiers were upon us, as they waved us down to pre-empt our arrival at the farmhouse. The African troops, we were told, had been hustled individually to their separate bivvies, away from the Major, who was standing as we arrived, back to us, on the veranda. He didn't turn as we approached. Only when Viper touched him on the shoulder in a gesture of sympathy, did he look around in surprise, as if he hadn't heard the roaring and juddering of our Crocodile truck for the last twenty minutes through the vast Matopas silence. He still didn't look up at us, but at the grass in front of him, as if he were searching for a small object he had lost. The lines on his face had increased since we had been away, and his face was ashen. A foolish triumph hit me, but I pushed it firmly away.

The white instructors banded together; we were the only people free to move about the campsite with our weapons. The corporals patrolled the bivvies to make sure the African troops stayed where they were. I joined two men, who took the truck down to the river to wash the floor. I was astonished to see that it was drenched with thick purple blood. It looked as if I had been playing in it, splashing it all over my face and hands and clothes, for I was scabbed with it all over. I washed in the river too, scratching and picking away at the stubborn streaks.

I had brought no other denims or long-sleeved T-shirt (we had been wearing full uniform all this time), so I had no choice (or Lux) but to huddle in my PT khaki shorts and green T-shirt. I laid the blooded clothes on a hot granite rock to dry, where they looked like a parodied, flattened, dead Doc.

Buddha pelted me with questions as soon as he saw me. I filled him in as best I could. He whistled softly. "I guess that's the end of that. We'll be home soon, Paul. That's the good news."

I sat down for the first time in hours.

"One thing, they won't even think about the prisoner escaping now," said Buddha. "Everything has been packed away. We're going home."

In the soft late afternoon, a small vehicle whined its way from the main road to our campsite. By the time I had emerged from my afternoon stupor and depression, the Land Rover had parked on the front lawn, and I had missed the grand entrance of two military officers in full regalia, brass pips, red sashes, shining belts, embossed peak caps and shit-green uniforms. That's the Commanding Officer of Llewellin and his Second in Command, whispered a corporal as we watched from the cover of a veranda pillar. I had never seen such high-ranking officers before.

In the next hour, orders were given to assemble (including the African troops) in the large clearing in front of the main veranda. The unofficial army motto, as it is in all armies, I suspect, is Hurry Up and Wait. We waited an hour. I felt as if I were a journalist at a White House press conference, waiting in the hot sun for the bigwigs to emerge from their cool, dark quarters. But Major Madox must have been sweating too. The African troops were weaponless, and the white corporals skirted our gathering, swinging their weapons. No longer did anyone believe that the enemy was outside our camp.

Finally, Viper emerged to stand us to attention, and with all the pomp and ceremony that could be mustered in a dry, stinking hot Matopas afternoon, three officers in full uniform marched onto the front veranda. The commander, I presumed it was he because of the ostrich plume in his helmet, cleared his throat.

"I am asking you all to not be emotional about this, to try to act like men, like soldiers, to see this as it really is, an unfortunate accident. We must all remember that mistakes do happen. The Major here" – he turned slightly to the left to acknowledge a shadow standing behind him – "the Major is a man whom I regard as a dedicated soldier doing his best for you all, and he has made it his job to save your lives by making sure you are equipped to survive out in the bush amidst a treacherous and barbarous enemy. And he has done his best."

The black troops were not impressed. Most of them looked sulky, surly even, with eyes twitching in secret conspiracy.

"Quiet." A corporal nudged one soldier with his rifle.

"Let him speak, if he wants to speak," said the officer.

The soldier who had been selected took a smart step forward and saluted, then came to attention again, driving his foot onto the dusty earth. "It was no mistake, sir. He often said he would shoot us if we weren't good enough and now he has done that. He aimed his pistol and shot our brother John who is dead."

It was a courageous enough speech, but I was surprised that this soldier then began to sob loudly. Soon those around him were wailing too, and were shouting in Ndebele, raising hands to the sky.

"Silence!" The corporals were edgy, trying to herd these emotions with their rifle butts. Another soldier stood forward. "We want Major Madox himself to apologise, to tell us why he did this thing."

"Yes, we want Major Madox."

"Major Madox!" The chant was taken up by all the black troops in unison, and they clapped and stomped their feet to the rhythm. I was trying to edge around the side of the veranda when I saw one of the white troops cock his weapon and indicate that the others must do the same. Surely they were not going to shoot?

"Easy. Easy." This was Viper, talking to his corporals as if they were dogs.

The Commanding Officer, however, held his ground, hid his obvious fear and instead stood forward and screamed above the noise. "What, are you a bunch of women, wailing like this?"

The soldiers stopped chanting.

"I thought you were men, soldiers, tough RAR *makonia* fighters. Are you?"

"We are." The reply was automatic.

"You've got to expect this sort of thing in a war. What will happen when your best friend gets killed by terrorists in a contact? Will you give up and wail and cry like little girls? Or will you fight back?"

"We will fight back!" shouted the black soldiers. They responded instinctively to the rough red voice of the Commanding Officer. Now he could afford a long silence, in which he marched up and down the ranks of the RAR troops, as if he were inspecting them at a drill parade. Each soldier braced up as he passed.

"Sergeant, I want you to strike camp in one hour. We are returning to Llewellin." He shook his head. "We've had to cancel this trip, not because of the Major, but because of your weak minds. You've failed as soldiers. You show no strength to let an incident like this hinder you from your duty to the country. Wouldn't you rather stay and fight as soldiers?"

My heart sank. No, no, I thought, don't let him talk you into staying. But the first soldier who had spoken stepped forward and stamped his feet to attention. "No, we don't want to stay to be murdered by this man. We will return to Llewellin."

Major Madox's eyes were on each soldier, his expression also one of disappointment at their betrayal of him. His loyal troops had all turned against him. He had failed to turn them into soldiers.

"Let's go, Major." The Commander led Madox away to the Land Rover, after first letting him collect his bag, which he hauled by himself this time. He was flanked by the Second in Command and the Commander. The corporals and white soldiers still held their rifles pointed at the black troops. I stood helplessly watching.

No one moved. We listened to the whine of the engine until we heard nothing but the cicadas and the wind through the trees, then Sergeant Viper motioned the corporals' rifles down. "Unload. Company, stand easy. Company, dismissed."

The black troops now broke ranks and knotted themselves in small groups, talking loudly.

"Right, let's behave like soldiers. I want you all on the trucks in half an hour," shouted Viper. "It's all over now. Let's just go home and forget all about it."

The troops dispersed to their bivvies to pack. Viper turned to the remaining white soldiers. "Fucking close. If old Wing-Nut hadn't done his thing, this precious cock-up of an experiment would have failed."

What made these black soldiers tick? This "precious cock-up of an experiment" was to get them to fight against other black people. Did they share the same motivation to fight as whites did? Was it a matter of preserving Western Christian Civilisation to them? And these were regular troops, signed up for ten years at little pay, hardships and no rank. What were they fighting for?

The molasses in my brain only unclogged as we lurched forward onto the dirt road, leaving the farmhouse behind forever. By the time we had packed and driven off, the Matopos was lion-tawny with dusk. The *kopjes* turned golden, then grey, and by the time we turned onto the main Bulawayo road, they were black molten blobs. These silent hills watched as the trucks noisily ploughed through their sanctuary. I looked for the mythical figures on the hill where we had left them, but it was too dark. I imagined these Vapostori dancing slowly around a huge cross, trying to come to terms with this large spiritual world engulfing their small human lives. How would I deal with this huge feeling inside me? The mountains, the blood, the ache, the pain, the blackness. And that cold emptiness of Bianca's absence and silence.

We drove through grids of white Bulawayo suburbs. I stared into cosy little houses with their twinkling lights in lounges and bedrooms; I watched the blue flickering lights of televisions (was it *Bewitched* tonight or was it *I Dream of Jeannie*?); I followed mothers bringing steaming dishes into dining rooms (was it roast beef and potatoes tonight, or chicken?). These families may have heard our trucks, but they could not see us, and they could not see the great dark black night outside. They could ward it off with their outside lights, they could huddle in their whiteness, but did they know that they were surrounded by volcanoes, black rocks, a huge night sky and the blood of Africa?

But a few white families out for sundowners on their verandas did see us. Boys rushed from their suppers to watch – Look, a convoy! – pointing and identifying the trucks (Crocodile! 2.5, RL! Puma!); and the daughters waved at the heroes of their land, defending their honour and peace so they could live pretty lives in pretty houses and pretty families. I waved back at them, concealing my bleeding wound as well as I could.

★ ★ ★

Paul: "Will I see you again?"

Carl: "I hope not. I've got sixty days to go. Then I'm out of here, off to Durbs. Meet you there, on the other side."

Paul: "You bet."

Carl: "On the other side, where the sun will shine, where everything is fine…"

Paul: "Where the grass is green, and the air is clean…"

I never did see him again. Carl Rogers was shot and killed on his way to casevac some wounded troops in a contact. Perhaps as he was dying, he tried to give advice to whoever was treating him, telling them that the body is spirit, all is *maya*, and not to worry. This body, this life, was all a clay construction fabricated by desire, and now he could let it go. Perhaps, as he died, his spirit flew up and perched above the scene on a crooked *msasa* tree branch, and smiled down at the vain attempts to resuscitate his lifeless body, free at last from its confines, free to escape the hot history and time of war, suffering, pain and desire.

# CHAPTER FOURTEEN

# THE TRIAL

There is no racism in Rhodesia, so said the new advertising campaign. We can solve all our political problems by being nice to each other. Street relations with blacks have always been good. And to prove it, a Black American singer (the South African Neville Nash) was now promoting harmony in our country.

> *Harmony, Harmony,*
> *Let's all live in harmony*
> *And peace will come to earth again.*

Not only was it irrelevant to my life, but it rang so false that I don't know who was buying it. The politicians? Certainly not the 'boys in the bush', or the restless black majority, who didn't even listen to Radio Rhodesia, and instead tuned their dials to the urgent, poisonous Voice of Zimbabwe, broadcast from Mozambique on AM.

But the age lines and crow's feet of the war were already showing on me. I had hoped to escape unscathed, to glide through this phase of my life untouched, and then to resume my life from where I had left off in January 1977. Ten months of training had changed me for the worse. I had counted the days, as every army recruit did, and had calculated how many days to go: only fifty-one and three-quarters now until 'real life' – whatever that was – began. But my soul had already been snagged and ripped.

Here I was, stepping off the train at six a.m., Saturday morning, on a glorious weekend pass, with all its promises of happy endings. Yet Salisbury looked grey this time. Civvy street had lost its lustre. My four weeks in Matopas had been the colourful world, and this looked like a faded copy. I did not look forward to wearing my Wrangler blue jeans imported from South Africa, my Snoopy T-shirt (the one I had bought in Lord Kitchener's fashion store in town depicting Snoopy lying on his kennel thinking, "Someday I must give up this mad, carefree existence"), my red, blue and white Bata *takkies*. I liked my rifle, my coarse denim camo tucked into my heavy boots, my webbing (water bottle on my left, bayonet on my right), and my beret weighted on the left side of my head. I marched into the civilian world of Salisbury's bottom end (Railway Avenue, Manica Road, into First Street), head up, chin up, spirits well up. I had been blooded.

The capital's main street had been closed off to traffic, and on Saturday mornings was an orgy of girl-coloured pedestrian foot traffic. But I was too early. The shops only opened at eight o'clock. Even the Wimpy and the Golden Arch restaurant (McDonald's had been kept out of the country by sanctions) were still shut. The only people in the street were a few delivery 'boys' on their bicycles, a crew of black men off-loading crates into a side entrance of Barbour's, and a Chinese woman sweeping the doorway of her 'Kaffir store' with a straw broom. I waited on the sunny side of the street for a bus to take me to Hillside, and when none was forthcoming, walked the three miles home.

Seven a.m. My mother and father welcomed me with all the affection and fervour they had saved up for a hero back from a brave war, rather than a prisoner of war who had been tortured and released. It was school time, so my father was here too, and he wanted to hear about my adventures, about the war firsthand, because the news he received on TV was censored by the Security Force Headquarters. Was it really as bad as it looked?

Bernard: "Any contacts?" (A contact meant an encounter with a terrorist.)

Paul: "No."

Lina: "Dad's been playing army too while you were away. Soldiers versus terrorists. That's all he can talk about."

Bernard: "We're losing control. There are huge areas we don't dare even drive through, no-go areas. Did you find that, Paul?"

Paul: "Well…"

Lina: "What did you eat out there? Was it warm enough at night? Where did you sleep?"

Bernard: "They send us as sheep to the slaughter. Paul, did you get my letters?"

Paul: "I got one."

Lina: "I got two. But why did you put all those black lines through it?"

Bernard: "Black…? It was censored. The cheek. They read our mail now?"

Lina: "Black lines all through it."

Bernard: "See what I'm saying – they don't want us to know. If we knew what was really going on, we'd high-tail it out of here like everyone else."

Lina: "What's this country coming to, when all we talk about is terrorists and war and politics?"

Bernard: "We don't always talk about terrorists. We talk about…"

Lina: "Have you heard anything from Willow, Paul?"

Bernard: "You know, her father moved to South Africa. They knew it was time to leave. They're not fools."

Lina: "You haven't heard from her, Paul? You were such good friends. Did you ever write back to her?"

Bernard: "You know when a country has had it, when your neighbours up and leave. The Glees… the McLoughlins. We'll be the only ones left."

Lina: "Where are you going, Paul? You haven't finished your breakfast. So crusty. Even Willow said so. And she was like my own daughter."

It's always easy to blame your parents for all your psychological traumas. I blamed mine for obliterating my self, my voice, my impulse. But they weren't the only ones at fault. I blamed the church for making me submissive. I blamed Rhodesia for making me a white male pariah. Oh, I blamed everybody: Bianca for her illusive, elusive games; God for not giving me brothers and sisters on whom to sharpen my social skills; the cruel fates for reinforcing my paralysis. But today would be the end of that old, hesitant, unsure, obliterated self. I would stop blaming other people for my passivity.

Forget her. That had been Buddha's advice. Detach yourself, he had said. Desire is what is making you unhappy, so stop desiring, stop wanting, stop torturing yourself. But all this damming up of my passions in the last few weeks had made me ache even more. So I was in a tremble to get to Bianca's house as soon as possible. I had so much to tell her, so much to prove to her. I would return to the moment where she had confessed that things were not as they seemed, that contrary to appearance, she was in love with me. Didn't her letters prove it? Didn't her denial prove it? Didn't my fervent, faithful, constant, burning desire for her prove it?

I didn't want to be a whiny voice on the phone. I wanted the element of surprise. I marched down Moon Crescent, shoved open the gate, braced myself for the dogs (they didn't show), swept the overgrown creeper out of my eyes, and knocked on the door. A radio was playing next door, and the Lyons Maid Hits of the Week was about to begin. But the announcer (Don Burdett? Sally Donaldson? Colin Botha?) was playing one last 'square' song by Nat King Cole. I heard it through the hedge, in strains that ebbed and flowed with the slight breeze.

> *Are you warm, are you real, Mona Lisa*
> *Or just a cold and lonely, lovely work of art?*

I knocked again. I'm not the Paw-Paw Cavedaschi you used to know, Bianca. I'm not Smiley, either. I'm not backwards any more. I'm not submissive. I have become what you want me to be, a Rhodesian soldier. No, not your sentimental Soldier Blue, but the real thing. The one who inchers people. The one who gets his girl. And I'm not taking no for an answer.

The dogs barked from inside the house somewhere. I knocked again and then peeped in the front window. The lounge was empty of people, the saggy furniture hunching in one corner, the television in the other, and the dogs barking at me from the couch. Through the kitchen window, I spied a heap of dirty washing piled up next to a sad washing machine, half the washing spilling out of its oval window. Two dog dishes stood in the centre of a muddy red floor, with Kibbles Treats sprayed all over the linoleum. The dogs scuttled into the kitchen to bark at my intruding image in the window.

I patrolled a quick 360 around the house and, balancing on a convenient concrete brick in the flower bed, peeked into what I guessed to be her bedroom. The bed was a ragged mess of sheets. Tumbled blankets and clothes were strewn over chairs, dressers and floor space. The dogs barked at me from behind the closed bedroom door.

"Hello?"

I toppled off the brick I was standing on, composed myself and tried to look as if peering into a girl's bedroom was a completely normal thing to do on a Saturday morning. The sun was behind him, so I had to squint to see who was talking. A boy – nine or ten years old – had been watching me over the fence. I pointed back at the house in self-defence.

"I was looking for Bianca Pennefather."

"Are you her boyfriend?" The boy climbed onto the fence and balanced on the fence post. To a nine-year-old, to be someone's boyfriend was not a compliment.

"No." I turned, began walking up the drive, away from the house. And in one instant, I saw the futility of my desire. It may have been the words of my new prophet, Carl Rogers, or it may have been the shame of being exposed as a Craig Hardy-like peeping Tom, or it may simply have been the glimpse I had had of myself through the eyes of the nine-year-old boy. But it was in this moment of time that I decided to give her up.

"Are you in the army?" the boy called after me.

I turned back, stiffened up. "Why?"

"Harmony *houts* did you cull?"

"What?"

"Harmony, you know the Harmony campaign," said the boy. "On TV."

"I haven't been watching TV," I said. "I've been in the bush."

A crocodile skin had grown over me during all those guard duties, in all those humiliations by Major Madox, and in my failed attempt to save that RAR soldier's life. These events had converged and conspired inside me. I had been mini-skirting around Bianca for so long, that now I was determined to be strong. I would not fawn, grovel, stammer, placate or humiliate myself over her any more. I would not phone her, visit her or even think about her ever again. I was not in love with her. I was not obsessed by her. Her breath was not the wind; her eyes were not the sky.

Salisbury the Sunshine City had a deserted air, like the ruins of Pompeii. My Saturday was spent in a dizzy emptiness, stepping through the rubble and smouldering ruins of what was once civilisation. Sure, there were colours, a bustling First Street mall, and all the shops were open now. I sat at a wrought iron table eating a Wimpy burger, watching the world go by, then I pottered around the Treasure Trove, Kemsley and Dawes, Kingston's, Meikles, Barbour's, Saunders, Consolidated Motors (get with CM, there's a part of us everywhere), Radio City, Radio Ltd. But I was not really here, or rather, this place was not here for me. The war had not reached Salisbury yet, and the city lagged behind in some romantic idea of the past. It was in denial. But as I crossed Cecil Square to catch the bus, I realised that it was I who was in denial.

The town was flourishing. Miraculously, in spite of sanctions, in spite of the war, Salisbury was a working monument to Rhodesian propaganda. Here was a functioning city. The plumbing worked, the electricity worked, the cars had petrol (blended from sugar cane), and all essential goods were available at sanctions-busting prices. There was zero inflation, no national debt and the shops were full, not of plastic junk imported from China, but of indigenous material. Local clothes were made of David Whitehead cotton, and everything used was recycled. I watched black people walk smartly by in suits, pacing next to white businessmen in safari suits, shaking hands with each other, eating with white men in restaurants. At least that's how it looked to me. Stupidly, I kept seeing Bianca: there she was, rounding that corner, her flash of blonde hair swung into a pony tail. Here she was, at Lord Kitchener's, browsing through T-shirts. At Martin Locke's Spin-a-Long, she sat in a listening booth, with oversize headphones, grooving to some new LP. I had to keep doubling back on myself, skip around corners, duck behind pillars, so as to avoid the many Biancas I saw that day.

★ ★ ★

Saturday night, 8 p.m. The media hysterically insist that we are still winning the war. Look how many terrorists we are killing, compared to how few of us are getting killed. Nevertheless, Security Force Headquarters regrets to inform us of the deaths of more and more soldiers killed in action against terrorists. Seven Rhodesian soldiers have been killed in action at Vila Salazar which had been subjected to heavy mortar fire again on Tuesday. However, we have a TV special after the news that is of national importance. Viewer discretion is advised.

I could not pull my eyes away. It was vitally important, the announcer's voice told me, that I watch this. So we sat passively, like a hundred thousand other white Rhodesian families, and let the images do their work.

"Security Force Headquarters announced today that a cross-border raid was made into Zambia on information given that there was a terrorist base there at Lomba. The Air Force, led by a code-named Green Leader, kept the whole of the Zambian Air Force at bay, with orders to shoot down any plane taking off, while the other planes destroyed and bombed the terrorist camp. Approximately 1,200 terrorists have been killed and this is a major victory for Rhodesia and her forces."

The Rhodesia Broadcasting Corporation had gone along for the ride and displayed film coverage of the event. They had filmed, from a bumpy cockpit window, clouds of smoke in bushy areas, then running ants, machine-gunned ants, dying ants, in a wasteland of savannah. After the attack, when it was safe, the plane had flown lower so that we sweep through the debris and death. A thousand women's and children's rubber torsos lay in scattered positions. Terrorists, the announcer said with awe and fervour. I could not take my eyes off the pictures, these gory messes of what were once human beings, and I could not stop my ears to the RBC's nasal insistence that these monsters deserved to die for all their terrible crimes and would-be crimes, and that I shouldn't feel sorry, but quell any tender feelings. Put up a glass pane in front of your heart; you have to watch this. It looked like Pompeii, with the people frozen into running, or sleeping, or sitting, or playing positions. But instead of a volcanic eruption, it had been the bombs and bullets of the Rhodesian army. My feelings were supposed to alternate between revulsion and exultation, and if the RBC had been successful in meshing them together in me, I would have become the good Rhodesian I was meant to be.

★ ★ ★

*Navigator/bomber:* "Steady: I'm going to get them. Steady."
*Green Leader:* "Yes. Fucking beautiful."
*Navigator/bomber:* "Steady, steady. Now. Bombs gone. They're running. Beautiful. Jeez. You want to see all those bastards. The fucking bombs are beautiful."
*Green Leader:* "Roger, just let me get onto the fucking tower and give them our bloody message. Where's this fucking piece of shit?"
*Navigator/bomber:* "That was lovely. Fucking hundreds of the bastards. It worked out better than we could have… They ran straight into the bombs."

*Green Leader:* *"Those fucking bastards."*

I knew something terrible was happening to me, to the country, to the people, to its soldiers, civilians, and to its psyche. The stench of death was all around me. Hatred was squeezing and strangling our beloved country and wouldn't let it go.

★ ★ ★

Hillside Non-Denominational Baptist Church Fellowship headquarters had swollen with worshippers. The more the war intensified, the more religious people became, and even after we had lost the war, whites joined the church in droves. Hillside Non-Denominational Baptist Church Fellowship now met in the cold barn of Eastridge School Hall on Sunday mornings. I walked down Braeside Road, dressed in my Sunday best (polished black shoes, suit, even a tie, for God's sake), and was warmly greeted at the door by a toothy Deacon who handed me a badly printed programme on recycled paper.

The seats were huddled in a central square facing a small lectern covered with a purple cloth. Sunlight attacked me in rectangles from high windows and plunged the rest of the hall in darkness. There were very few people I knew. Widows and widowers sat in isolation; families with daughters sat in tight rows in the front. All young and middle-aged men were on active service, fighting for God and their country. I sat on a cold, empty pew, took up the hymn book and sang to the out-of-tune piano, the hymn we had sung in assembly every week at Churchill School.

> *The Church's one founda SHUN is Jesus Christ the Lord*
> *She is His new Crea SHUN of WORTA and the word*
> *From heaven He camen SORTA to be His holy bride;*
> *With His own bloody BORTA, and for her life He died.*

In the closing verse, a blonde sliver of sunlight slid across my pew and into the place next to me. "Can I sit here?" She swept her hair away from her face, smiled at me, and held onto my arm to balance herself as she shared the hymn book. I pointed to the trembling words we were singing (*Like them, the ME CAN LOW LEE, on high may dwell with thee*).

"Hi."

"B… Bianca?"

I had expunged her so thoroughly that I found it difficult to conceive of her existence. We sat for the sermon, me with legs crossed, she rustling and rearranging her dress around her. She was dead and gone, but nevertheless, to make sure there were no leaks in my soul, I built a brick and mortar wall between us, slowly, one brick at a time. I did not listen to her rhythmic breathing, or touch the blue cotton dress against my side, or feel her radiating body heat. Instead I concentrated on the sermon, on Steve's passionate appeal to be dead to the desires of the flesh.

I didn't know it then, but Steve Carter was already planning to leave Rhodesia. He had grown up here, but he had fooled us all, and himself, into thinking he was American. Soon he would be jetting off to north-east USA with his green card, his American family and his American accent and be gone forever.

But today he was still as large as life. And his message was simple. Everyone else had got it all wrong. Jehovah's Nitwits refused to serve in the army; Morons (sorry, Mormons) made up their own religion; so-called quote unquote liberation theologists believed that Christ had told them to take up arms against so-called unjust governments, like the Reverend Cane and Banana, Bishop Unable Muzzle Era, and the Irreverend Nab a Dingy Sit Holy. They called themselves men of God, when it plainly said in the Bible that we must submit ourselves to the governing authorities who have been put there by the Lord. The Much Deformed Church had been led astray by Satan, too. Yes, Satan, the Deceiver, was all around, ready to devour and confuse. Whereas Our God – he smiled and opened his arms to the huddled congregation in the dark – is a Righteous God.

My mind was, of course, fully focused on the sermon. I was certainly not bathing in the perfumed aroma from my left. But I had to say something to show that she was dead to me, that I was no longer dancing to her tune. And I was proud of the cutting irony I used to measure the distance I had travelled from her.

"Where's your friend Craig Hardy?"

"Who?"

"Hardy."

"I don't know." She shrugged the boy off as if he were a fly on her forehead.

I rubbed the goose pimples on my left arm. Go now; get away, walk out, my guardian angel whispered. But she tugged at my shirt in the final hymn, and her fingers curled over mine as we steadied the hymn book in front of our faces. "Don't leave yet, Paul. I have to talk to you."

> *Mid toil and tribulation, and tumult of her war,*
> *She waits the consummation of peace for evermore;*
> *Till, with the vision glorious, her longing eyes are blest,*
> *And the great church victorious shall be the church at rest.*

Outside, in the cool of the trees, she twirled a ring around her finger, bit her lip. "I'm so glad you are here. I have something to tell you."

"I'm all ears."

"I want your advice." I stared at her left eyelid which was fluttering. "Promise you'll still be my friend. Promise you'll be my brother-in-Christ?"

"Cross my heart and hope to die."

"I also want you to be the first to know."

The birds in the tree above us were squawking so loudly and she was speaking so softly that I had to incline my head towards her and lip-read.

"I'm engaged."

A poem we had learned by heart in English the year before suddenly played in my head: a poem about the dead in hell listening to the smooth, silvery, sweet voice of an angel.

"Didn't you notice the ring?" She displayed the sparkling diamond set in the centre of blue amethysts as a sword, a sparkling knife whose shafts of reflected light glittered at me in mockery. How did it go, that poem?

> *So smooth, so sweet, so silv'ry is thy voice*
> *As, could they hear, the damn'd would make no noise,*
> *But listen to thee, walking in thy chamber,*
> *Melting melodious words…*

"Please say something, Paul. Aren't you happy for me?"

"Congratulations." I meant to say it sincerely, but it came out sharp and skew and mean. Next minute she was crying, and dabbing her face with a blue handkerchief.

"Please tell me how you really feel."

"I thought you said you didn't like him."

She blinked away the tears, wiped her nose on her shirt sleeve. "Not him, you silly goof. Not Craig Hardy. Did you think...?" She punched me. "You idiot."

"Who, then?"

"You don't know him. He's an old friend. We have been going out for yonks."

"And you love this... him?"

"Of course I love him. Would I get engaged to someone I don't love?"

She buried her face in my shoulder and wiped her nose, this time on my shirt. I waited for the world to stop spinning and settle down before I spoke again.

"I do have one question for you."

"What is it?" I tried to hold her at arms' length, but she insinuated herself deeper into my arms, so that I had to cradle her head on its cushion of apple shampoo-scented hair, and wipe away her mascara-laden tears with a forefinger.

"Ask me, Paul."

"Y... you... you didn't write those letters, did you?"

"What letters?"

"The ones I showed you. The Valentine's card..."

"I wrote you a letter."

"One letter?"

"I'll write you more letters if you want. I was going to if I didn't see you today. I was going to write to you in the army and tell you about my engagement. Corporal P. Williams. Corporal Punishment Williams, DRR Hospital, Llewellin Barracks. See? I know your address. I was going to write to you."

"You didn't write about dancing on the beach in Durban? About dropping everything?"

She shook her head. "Should I have written that?"

"No." I stroked her head with the comforting hand of a brother-in-Christ. "No, you shouldn't have."

★ ★ ★

Thus the glass plate slid permanently over my heart, thick, three-inch blue glass, shatterproof, soundproof so you could not hear the screams of the damned. Even so, her words replayed themselves over and over. Whenever I closed my eyes, I was in the centre of a black Glisterine and Ichthamnol swamp of primeval matter. There was a black hole beneath me, a swirling void into which I was being sucked.

But she did see me off at the airport that evening. I had procured a military discount seat in Air Rhodesia flight RH 354 to Bulawayo for $18 one way. She stood in the drafty hangar which served as the domestic terminal and hopped from one foot to the other, turning the engagement ring round and round her finger until it was red and swollen. A lump in my throat prevented me from saying anything, and an invisible six-foot barrier prevented me from hugging her tight.

She pressed a letter in my hand. "Read it on the plane, Paul. Not now."

It was good to get back to the army. I busied myself in the hospital, performed my duties with bitter zealousness. You have the shits? Take sulphaguanadine. Tick-bite fever? Take tetracycline. VD? Penicillin. Broken heart? Take these – they'll numb the pain. And lots of self pity will help. It's all *maya*, all illusion.

And at this point I was accosted by Major Madox. I was injecting 5cc Propen into the buttocks of an ailing basic training recruit when he stamped into the MI room, jumped the queue and stood before me, scrutinising my medical performance. Here was the stuff from my nightmares: blue eyes, blue belt, blue beret. The patients (those who were soldiers) stood to attention and saluted him, squashing against the wall in respect to let him pass.

"Doc?"

"Major Madox?"

"The trial is next week. Tuesday 08h00 at Brady Barracks. They want you to testify."

"Me?" I wiped the buttock with a swab, and threw the syringe into the steriliser tank to join the other recycled glass and metal syringes. The patient pulled up his trousers, and winked at me as he sidled out of the room. I spoke to the steriliser tank. "What for?"

The Major took off his beret and wiped the tight red band where it had left a mark. "Doc, you don't think it was my fault, do you?"

I found a pile of bandages on the counter top, and wound a washed, recycled bandage tightly around my hand. At first, I had no idea what he was talking about. But I had no difficulty crumpling into my familiar old spineless self.

"What do you think, Doc?"

"Well, sir… I…"

The Major squeezed my shoulder in friendship, in camaraderie. We had been in the bush together. "Doc, I'm sure it was a ricochet, you see. A freak accident of nature." His eyes were too intense; I couldn't look back at him. I fiddled with the bandage, unwound and rewound it, then clipped it with a safety pin. But Major Madox was not looking at me. He was staring into the past, at the scene on the field, reliving the moment he shot John Mpofu in the head, and he was positioning his body as he had done that day. He acted out the shot, recoiling at the kickback, and squinting through imaginary sights. "The bullet must have bounced off a rock and hit the man. I know what I'm doing. I wouldn't shoot a man like that. I've got good aim, I'm a marksman. I aimed in front of him."

A ricochet? A clean wound like that? Now I too was in the field, examining the wound with my finger and holding the mush of the back of the head. The bullet went in neatly, a small hole in the front forehead, and came out messy. Or did it? I tried to evoke the picture I had been trying so hard to obliterate. A ricochet would tumble the bullet, surely, and go in messy. I didn't know. He wanted me to remember it his way so badly that I couldn't see my picture of the past, only his.

"So you see, Doc, it had to be a ricochet. A deflection. You've seen ricochets in targets."

"It could have been, sir. It might have been. There's little way of telling, I suppose."

He gripped my shoulder again. "Attaboy, Doc, we can't be sure. Thanks, Doc." He rubbed the dark rings under his eyes. "It worried me, Doc. Day in, day out. A ricochet? A direct shot? But if you say so, too… See you next Tuesday – the Military Council Chambers…"

★ ★ ★

*Dear Paul*

*I know all about you. I really do. I know you helped an innocent prisoner escape in the Matopas. I know you stood up to some horrible Major who was mistreating soldiers. I also know you saved a fellow soldier from the Major. He had food poisoning, and you helped him. How do I know these things? Why didn't you tell me? I had to hear it from my friend, Suzanne Rogers.*

*I also know that you didn't get stuffed into a bin to avoid inspection in basic training, in spite of what Hardy has said. Your nickname wasn't really Mary, was it? Smiley Cavedaschi, you certainly have a lot of nicknames. Who are you, really?*

*The point is: I need to know what you think. It's very important to me. Please write and tell me honestly. Dave Cobbler is an old friend. Well, he's not that old. He's twenty-two, South African, and he and I have been going out for ages, off and on. I tried to tell you. Yes, I know I'm too young, but he's prepared to wait until I'm eighteen. He's in Cape Town finishing his engineering degree. He wants me to join him when I finish school. You don't know Dave – he's a wonderful guy, but that's not the point. The point is… I don't know what the point is. I have to be very clear about all this. And to be clear, I need to know what you feel. You tell me what the point is, please? Seriously, I really need to know what you think, what you feel about this.*

*Paul, Paul, Paul. I want you to come to the wedding. If Luke is not back from Bible school by then, I want you to be best man. Pleeease! Write back. I'll be waiting.*
*Your friend, Bianca XXX*

*H.O.F.L.A.N.D.*

★  ★  ★

Corporal Paul Williams was called to give evidence. Dressed in his best army clothes, newly starched and with all traces of bloodstains gone (that was a mistake), when called he marched smartly into the room. He was told to sit in front of a desk. Facing him were the smiling Major, the stern Commander of Llewellin Barracks and two other officers, one tapping a pen against his teeth, the other chewing something bitter. They were in civilian clothes, and looked suspiciously like the two CID men he had encountered in the camp hospital. The Major's blue eyes were on him all the time. He could still feel the man's grip on his shoulder. And he was trying to deal with the destruction of a whole Pompeiian city inside himself.

"Corporal, you were present at the shooting of Private Mpofu on the 20th of October, 1977. Is that correct?"

"Well, no, sir. I was at the base camp and was summoned by radio to the place where he was shot."

"What were you doing at the base camp, Corporal, when you know you were supposed to be with the troops when there was live firing?" This was Major Madox.

I gave him a look of reproachful innocence. He had ordered us around. He had made all the decisions; how could he now pretend I had any free will? He nodded to the plain-clothed civilian who wrote something down in a large notebook.

"When you examined the wound, Corporal, would you suggest that it could have been a ricochet?" asked the officer, whom I dubbed Churchill, because he resembled the portrait at my high school of the Prime Minister of England.

"Where exactly was the wound, entry and exit, and what size was it?" asked the tapping pencil man.

"Um, it was about here." I indicated with a finger on my head, "and came out about here, I think," making the hole about the size of a clenched fist at the back of my head.

"Wouldn't you say the wound was here, Corporal, more towards the top of the head?" Major Madox demurred. "That's how I remember it."

"I can't remember exactly where, sir," I offered. "I didn't look that closely."

"You didn't look closely, Corporal, even though you were the medic examining the body?"

"Come on, Doc, you must remember."

"Is it true, Corporal," quizzed Churchill, "that Sergeant Viper was the one who attended the deceased, made all the necessary casevac arrangements, while you looked on?"

"No, sir. Yes, sir. He made the arrangements, but I… I gave the patient drugs and a drip and mouth-to-mouth all the way back to the hospital. There was blood everywhere. I even swallowed…"

"Spare us the gory details, Doc."

I smeared away imaginary slime with my hands.

"We've read reports, Corporal, that your competence as a medic is questionable. Is it true that your grades in the medic course…?"

"Is it true that you sympathised with the enemy at the DRR hospital, getting in the way of lawful interrogation and procedure?"

"Isn't it true, Doc, that I had to kick your arse to get you going at the Matopas, doing your job with the other sick medic while you were goofing off?"

"Could it be that this patient died because of your incompetence as a medic?"

I couldn't speak. My lips were dry pieces of biltong. "I had blood all over my clothes, sir. There was blood in my mouth."

"Major Madox, you were there. How would you assess this medic's performance at the scene? Your statement –" he peered down at a sheet of paper – "suggests that this medic neglected his duty."

I looked up at the Major, startled, and he stared hard at me while he spoke.

"Corporal Williams did his best. But that best of his wasn't good enough. Just simply wasn't good enough when it comes to matters of life and death."

The officer leaned over to the Major. "Let's move on. Now, Corporal, in your opinion, could the bullet have been a ricochet?"

I tried to get a picture of the wound, but somehow I could only find a close-up of Bianca's face. "I'm engaged! Didn't you notice the ring?"

"Come on, Doc, think," said the Major.

"Well," I began, shaking my head but only succeeding in shaking her face from side to side. "I suppose it might have been, but…"

"Just one more thing, Corporal. What was your impression of the Major before the accident? Was he subject to uncontrollable fits?" He was reading from the sheet of paper, obviously from another witness. "Would he shoot wildly at people at random? Did he ever act irresponsibly?"

I sat in silence as the words sank in. How could I not reply to this obvious truth?

"In other words, Corporal," helped Churchill, exasperated at my blank face, "we are trying to ascertain whether this act was just an unfortunate occurrence or if it was an irresponsible misuse of power on the Major's part?"

The sky-blue eyes burnt into me. My throat was restricted and my body contorted. The words were there somewhere, lodged in my throat. He's *penga*. We all know it. Moggy Madox, they call him. But all I could hear was the Major's prompting. Was I simply a puppet, a ventriloquist's dummy? I wanted to do this man's bidding, to say what he wanted me to say. I had to soothe him; he was upset, insulted by these accusations. You know what happens to the Major if he gets mad. I had to humour him, pacify him, quickly. What was the difference between being a doormat and humouring? One is a joke at the expense of the other. I wanted to say, "He pointed his gun at our dear brother John who is now dead." But the words wouldn't come out. They were waiting for an answer.

"I… er… think that Major… er… Major Madox… It was just an unfortunate accident, nothing…" My voice trailed off. The shootings near the troops, the terrified eyes of the cook, the laugh of the Major: how could I describe all this? It was all *maya*, all subjective, wordless, not hard evidence. Corporal Williams was the accused, the dithering incompetent, and the Major was the strong, clear-minded, upright, civilised man. Corporal Williams was not to be trusted.

"That will be all, Corporal." I stood while they walked slowly out of the room, the Major pausing to shake my hand. I had said the right thing. I had obliterated myself. But there was a price. The world was crashing onto my head, and lava, black molasses flowing out of me. It was then that I threw up, vomited hot white grainy porridge all over the officer's desk, ran out, my throat burning, my body reeling, my spirit nauseated, and my thoughts spiralling into the dead world outside.

*The Department of Manpower announces that call-ups have been extended for university-goers. Due to the increased need of already trained manpower in the field, Security Force headquarters has decided that university-goers who were to demobilise at the end of this year after one year's training, would now be required to do the full eighteen months in keeping with fairness to our other recruits who have been recruited for this time. The Commanding Officer Recruiting has your best interests at heart. The University of Rhodesia and all universities in South Africa begin their academic year in January, so we wish to assure you that no time will be lost in preparations for your respective careers. After eighteen months' service, university-goers*

*will be allowed to leave the country to attend university, providing they return every December for yearly camps.*

★   ★   ★

I am now amazed at my blindness, my poverty of perception, my insensitivity. Bianca's actions were a cry for help. Yet I stubbornly, blindly, perversely sealed her fate and mine by taking her at face value, and by cutting her out of my life.

I volunteered for duty in the hospital every weekend, and twice a week for night duty. I slept in the Night Room so as to be on call, and to buffer myself with the comforting hum of machines, the bustle of patients, the smell of medicines. I was a good soldier for once, with no rebellious life forces rising in me. I cut them out in a merciless surgical act, using the anaesthetic of action. I remained numb for as long as I could. But the wound would gape open, and the pain would wake me at three in the morning. Bianca, forgive me, I can't write back. Don't expect me to be your friend. I don't want to see you again, ever. Cross my heart and hope to die.

★   ★   ★

I was meant to demobilise at the end of December, but with the new edict, I would be in for another six months. So, as consolation, I had been granted a whole week-long pass. It was the longest I had ever been away from the army since the beginning. I didn't want it. It was a gaping hole to fall through. I took the night train from Bulawayo to Salisbury on purpose. Although the journey was only four hundred kilometres, the train stopped at every siding and took the whole night before it crawled into Salisbury Station. I chose an empty sleeper carriage to myself at Bulawayo Station and closed the door to discourage company (Whites-only carriages were always empty, while the Third Class black carriages were jammed with squawking families and suitcases). I was still in army uniform, but had not brought any civilian clothes to change into. I did not have a pressing need to wear jeans and floral shirts, or red, white and blue Bata *takkies* any more. The Garratt moved slowly out of Bulawayo, through all the ugly sidings, past the smoking factories, past Cement, a factory town which submerged its surroundings in white powder, and into the flatlands of Matabeleland. The sun set fat and red. I closed my eyes.

"Paul! Hey, man, what are you doing here?" I woke to see another resurrected nightmare in my carriage. Sergeant Craig Hardy, Special Ops, of all people, sitting opposite me so that our knees banged together. He was, however, sporting no Sergeant stripes, and no Special Ops uniform, just the normal rifleman camo of the Rhodesian army. I made no comment, but I knew he was no Sergeant.

The train had stopped at its first station. It was already dark. "Where are we? How did you get on?"

"Heany Junction," he said. "I just caught the train. Going to Salisbury for a pass. And you?"

"Yes." I folded my arms.

"What are you doing for your pass?"

"Nothing."

All Aboard; the sad whistle signalled the driver to jerk the train as hard as he could forward, and to slowly build up speed until it rattled my teeth.

"I'm going to a nightclub on Saturday, to pick up some chicks."

I closed my eyes again, trying to make him disappear. He sat in silence for a while, but I could feel him wriggling, and blowing out his mouth. I opened my eyes and spread my hands in a helpless gesture. "What?"

"Listen, Paul, I've made arrangements this weekend to meet these chicks in Archipelago, you know, the discotheque in Baker Avenue. Why don't you come along?"

"Well, I…"

"Come along, china. I need some help with these chicks."

"I may be busy, but I'll see. Thanks."

# CHAPTER FIFTEEN

# SLEEPING BEAUTY

*And as I go through my life, I will wish for her, his wife,*
*All the sweet things she can find;*
*All the sweet things they can find.*

Christmas Eve, 1977. The nightclub was a black-walled, smoke-filled underground basement in Linquenda House on Baker Avenue. I winced as I followed Craig Hardy in, paid what was then an exorbitant fee to a doorman who looked me up and down to make sure I was over eighteen and not wearing jeans and *takkies* or T-shirt. I sat at a padded, beer-sticky table while Hardy ordered four cane and Cokes from the bar, the drink of choice in Rhodesia because our wine was pure vinegar, our brandy tasted like cat's piss, and the only good spirits were distilled (as was our petrol) from our very own Lowveld sugar cane.

"So where are your dates?"

"Patience. They'll be here soon." He slid into the black leather seat and squinted at his watch. "We'll take them around the Christmas lights when they've had enough of the disco."

I sank back into the couch and closed my eyes. In a disco, the five senses are replaced by artificial ones: sight – flashing lights; touch – greasy tables; taste – alcohol; smell – smoke, sweat and perfume; hearing – the throbbing beat of Budgie's 'Baby, Please Don't Go' from *Never Turn Your Back on a Friend*.

I watched each woman with cold interest. After all, Hardy had promised me a date tonight. But in the light, it was difficult to distinguish age and delicacy. They were either sitting with grey-haired, hard-faced elderly men, or propped against the bar, drawing in cigarette smoke instead of air. I watched tight couples dancing in the four-foot-square dance floor where heavy speakers beamed a barrage of non-music onto them from the ceiling, and flashing lights distorted their faces and bodies. This was not a place for me. The ache throbbed louder than ever. Here I was, shut off from anything green.

"They'll be here soon." Hardy grinned in the ghoul-light of the strobe. He tapped his fingers. He had finished his drink already, so I downed mine to burn away any hesitation. The two other drinks glinted at us on the table, mocking our pretensions of meeting any women here. The alcohol made me spin, but God's voice was still a stern masculine rebuke in an American accent. The wicked, whose feet run to evil, spend the night drinking, pursuing women. Yes, I thought. I want to do it. Let me have at least one chance to see what it's like. Let me fill that void.

Hardy nudged me and pointed at the cleared dance floor. The bouncer adjusted the spotlights so that they now leered at a set of faded purple curtains at the back of an impromptu stage.

Three girls pounced onto the stage and jerked their bodies to an excessively loud version of 'Jingle Bell Rock'. I say 'girls' because that is what the MC called them, and what Hardy called them, too, but each of them was old enough to be my mother. I thought them ugly, but then what did I know about beauty? I was obsessed with a frozen-in-time image of a fourteen-year-old, and anyone without that snub nose, that silky blonde hair, the ironic smirk on a bright-eyed face, was a graub, gruk or growler. These 'girls' tried their hardest to look the part – anti-wrinkle make-up, schoolgirl dresses, ponytails, fingers in coy mouths – but they didn't fool me. Every so often, the light played tricks, though. In a gesture of the hand, or a flick of the hair, I saw a glimpse of an old free state, but for the most part, they were comical parodies of beauty. And to make it even more ridiculous, each wore reindeer horns on her head.

In slow, provocative movements, the three girls shed their schoolgirl uniforms to reveal glittering red and green bikinis underneath. Each wiggled her fluffy reindeer tail, butted her partner in playful rivalry, and finally danced off stage to return on all fours, dragging a sled. A blonde, female Santa Claus perched on the seat and waved to her audience as she was pulled across the stage. She wore a huge fluffy red overcoat with a white fur collar, and sported an incongruous white beard and red hat. To the tune of Grand Funk Railroad's 'Flight of the

Phoenix', she shed her coat, then hat, then beard, then oozed out of one red body suit after another, thinning herself down until she in was red tights. She played her long, blonde hair over her body, fanning it against the light, over her face, over her breasts. Her make-up was garish, but somehow the red-apple cheeks, parrot-blue eyeshadow, fierce red lips and green fingernails worked.

The males in the audience cheered and shouted lewd suggestions while the girl threw herself from one dancer to the other, fixing her eyes at a point in space far beyond this room, and pursing her lips with beckoning, inviting looks. She couldn't see anyone in the audience, I was sure, because of the blinding spot-lights, but I was convinced she was staring straight at me.

The blonde hair, of course, was what did it – this was Bianca's hair. I imagined a Bianca who opened herself to me as this dancer was doing, instead of closing off, who smiled, stripped, cooed and flirted. I couldn't take my eyes off her. It was amazing what I could do now that I had vacated my five senses. Bianca was a fading copy; here was the original. But the more I ogled this dancer, the more familiar she looked. It's just déjà vu, I told myself, until a lightning bolt of memory struck me. I was not simply projecting Bianca onto her. I was not just on the rebound, looking to fill a vacuum with a similar shape. This was someone I had met before in my life.

Then, as I combed my memory for encounters I had had with white god-desses, I remembered. This was Penny Woods, the girl from Alfred Beit School, my first love, Sleeping Beauty. And here she was, all grown up. Her features were accented by make-up, with rosy cheeks, bright blue eyes, fierce red lips which pouted and parted, and she was dressed like a doll. But she was still the same Sleeping Beauty.

Now I hoped with all hope that Hardy's dates would not come.

"I can't understand it," he muttered, interpreting my bulging stare as boredom. "They're normally very punctual." We gulped down the two extra drinks and he wisely ordered no more "until they get here," but I could not draw my eyes away from this dancer. The memories danced in me whenever she moved her mouth or her hands. She snaked out of the red suit to show a glitter-painted body, naked save for two green nipple caps and a red tanga tied with long red bowties. She turned to the curtains, pulled off the green dots, and, still with her back turned, flung them into the audience for some lucky male to catch. For her finale, just as the lights went out and the music screeched to a halt, she turned around, hugged her breasts, and pulled the long bowties slowly so her red triangle sagged, slipped and fell. When the garish lights snapped back on, the dancers dipped behind a curtain, leaving behind the layers of clothing for the MC to pick up – the schoolgirl dresses, Santa outfits and the red tanga.

Hardy stood and pushed past me, shouting to be heard over the hot applause. "Maybe the bouncer didn't let them in. I can't understand it. Listen, I'll see if they're waiting outside the club."

I did not take my eyes off the curtain where the blonde Santa Claus had disappeared. Through a chink, I saw scurrying shadows as the girls changed, or rather, put on their clothes, and sure enough, once the music had started again ('We Wish you a Wombling Merry Christmas') and the dance floor was again packed with bobbing bodies, I spied the four girls file out in evening dresses through the curtains. Three aimed for tables, but she – the Santa Claus dancer – headed for the bar, and wiggled herself onto a high bar stool. She scanned the dark club with narrowed eyes.

With the acidic courage of two cane and Cokes, I bee-lined for the bar. I walked up to her, lost courage and walked past, walked past again. On my third attempt, I stopped, sat on the vacant stool next to her and stared at the crowd as she was doing, screwing up my eyes as if I were looking for someone.

"Hello, Sweetie." She ran a finger down my leg. I was too terrified to look at her. "Want to buy me a drink?"

"Sure." I pasted a nonchalant smile on my face and ventured a look. The devil was in the details: flabby cheeks, bags under sparkless eyes, a tightness around the mouth, a pock-marked pasta flesh.

Of course I am being unfair. In those days, I equated beauty with moral goodness, as they do in fairy tales. I had projected onto her another person, an ideal, non-aging teenage goddess. I tried to hide my repugnance, and fortunately, she misread me: I was shy. The blurry image on the old TV ad, with the rush of feeling that I had imposed on those blurs, was now close up, grainy, too real.

"Are you Penny?"

"That's me. Short for Penelope. What were my parents thinking?"

"I used to go to school with you. Alfred Beit. You remember the pantomime. Do you remember me? Tickey? The Honeybeat, the leaves?"

One eyebrow arched in cynical rumination.

"Shillings," I prompted.

Yes, I could see Sleeping Beauty in her but it was in the remote distance, in twinges and eye muscles; only a few pure movements remained of the mouth from the schoolgirl from 1965. A barman clunked two drinks down in front of us and I hastily pulled out a brown twenty-dollar bill to pay for them. Sleeping Beauty picked up her glass and sipped thoughtfully.

"You're the girl in the pool. The Rhodesian Front advert. On TV. I'm Paul. Remember me?"

"What the hell are you talking about?"

"You gave me a tickey and said to call you when I was older, remember?"

"No shit?" She nodded her head vigorously, looking at me with a bewilderment that told me she didn't remember.

"You used to call me Tickey."

"Well, the price has gone up since then."

"What do I call you now?" I joked. "Ten cents?"

"Fifty bloody dollars, chap. I do, I do remember now. You were that seven-year-old kid who followed me around."

"I loved you then," I said. "That was me."

"Fuck." This was an expression of amazement and good fortune, apparently. She was moved, and I watched a transformation in her, an old life form return to her tired shell of a body. Her eyes sparkled. She stared hard through the smoke, through the noise, through the black wall, and by the red glow on her face and the dazzle in her eyes, I knew she was seeing those bright, sunny days of our childhood.

"Shit. Those were the days, hey? Hell. I was so... naïve. Well, I was a bloody child. You know – what was your name again? – Paul, I used to think that pantomime was the beginning of something big. I was going to be somebody. I knew it. I felt it. And" – here she gripped my leg to steady me so she could confess her secret – "I believed it. I was Sleeping Beauty. When I sang, I really believed it."

"I believed it too."

What had she done since then? Oh, it had been the start of showbiz for her, that damn play. "Chin, chin! Down the hatch."

I drank in her familiar tone, her confident hardness. She sucked at her glass, and I imitated her, bracing myself for another stomach-eating deluge of pure acid.

"My parents sent me to the Convent. The bloody Convent. What were they thinking? I'd grow up a nice Catholic girl?"

"You're Catholic?"

"Finish your drink, Paul. I need to get out of this place. I don't like mixing business with pleasure."

"I don't know Salisbury all that well," I said. "Where are we going?"

"My place. It's just up the road, in the Avenues."

We pushed through the crowd at the bar and past the stage where people were dancing. Hardy was back at the table, date-less and now mate-less too. He was drumming his fingers on the table, whistling, as we walked swiftly to the entrance. At the last minute, he looked up, to see his friend Paul Williams being hauled out of the door by the stripper. He stood. "Paul! Paul!" But we were gone.

★ ★ ★

I was in for an adventure, down an unknown path in a labyrinth. The streets looked like buildings from Pompeii, scattered, broken, covered over with volcanic ash. The cool night air rushed past us as we walked, and her heels clicked sharply down the road away from the thumping bass of the disco into the quiet tree-swishing suburbs called the Avenues. I opened the Cortina car door for her and she slid in.

"As soon as I have enough money to get out of this shit-house," she said, "I'm going to South Africa. No damn future here for dancers."

Her flat was old and derelict, the upper eastern quadrant of one of those double-storey houses in the Avenues built in the early years of Rhodesia. The apartment block was surrounded by huge palm trees (a sure sign of colonialists; they planted those damn things everywhere they went), which swayed Hawaiian-style as we climbed a red stone stairway. Greasy yellow lights guided us down a grimy corridor. The door she stopped at was once green, but the paint had peeled off in long stripes, leaving a forlorn red, and the door creaked as she proudly showed me into her humble home.

I looked around in reverent silence at Sleeping Beauty's fairy-tale cottage. By the dim light she switched on in the corner, I saw gnome-like, old-fashioned chairs; a puffy, stuffing-filled, bulged-out settee; exotic pictures on the walls (Picasso-ish puzzles of reality); ornaments and letters and junk scattered all over; a bikini top stretched out nonchalantly on a table; a fluttering costume hanging from the key in the door of a half-open cupboard; a Tempest stereo player yawning open with a record for a tongue and a grinning set of silver dials for teeth. Record covers were scattered far and wide: Deep Purple's *Machine Head* on the speaker, half covered by a flimsy outfit of some sort; ABBA's *Greatest Hits* with the bewitching blonde on the cover sitting up on a park bench; Linda Ronstadt's *Simple Dreams*.

She made me sit on the dusty couch, apologised for the mess, and went to make coffee in the kitchenette. Through the bar that separated it from the lounge, I saw her top half humming around between cups and coffee, kettle and sink.

"Sugar?" She tinkled the cups as if they were bells heralding the next act.

"It's Irish coffee," she explained as I spluttered a first sip. She turned to the hi-fi, fed in a record. "Rodriguez," she said. 'Cold Fact.' I hadn't heard of it before and didn't want to listen to the harsh acoustic guitar clipping out a rhythmic chord to a sarcastic, metallic voice. It didn't go with the decor, with my vision of Sleeping Beauty; it was ugly, cold fact poured onto my beautiful, hot fiction. But Penny seemed to like it. She mouthed the words, twisting her beautiful mouth into jeering, sneering contortions. "It's banned in this country – that's why you've never heard it."

In spite of the rasping record, I caught her bird-strains clearly as if we were back on that playground when I pursued her with a Honeybeat. "Remember all those songs you sang in the pantomime – do you still sing?"

Her hand touched my shoulder as she dregged her coffee. "Tell you the truth, while I was at school, I believed it. That whole shit story of Sleeping Beauty. You wait a hundred bloody years for Prince Charming to come along – and he stamps all over you with his bloody horse. Whammo!"

"I've always thought of you as Sleeping Beauty, since that play."

"I'm not anyone's bloody Sleeping Beauty." She walked over to the bar to put down her coffee cup, and to find the bottle of whisky. She pointed the bottle at me, but I shook my head. "You don't wait for life to happen to you. That's what they like telling little girls. A man has to rescue you. Crap. It's all crap." She included the contents of her flat, me and the world outside her window in the sweep of her arms. "But you're a nice boy." She adjusted the volume of the stereo. "Listen, here's the part…" I listened to the nasal voice of Rodriguez and the raw treble guitar.

> *Cos Papa don't allow no new ideas here*
> *And the music makes it all so clear*

"No, sorry, that's not it," she said. "They all sound the same. Sure you won't have some?" She thrust the bottle in my face but I indicated my coffee, so she took a swig, then slammed the bottle back on the counter. She was drunk, I reassured myself, that's why she was behaving so strangely. She laughed abruptly and took off her high heels, precariously balancing against my shoulder. Then she flung them with hatred into a corner. "Bloody Sleeping Beauty," she said to herself.

The gap between the Sleeping Beauty she had been at school, and what had happened to her since gaped open. I wanted to close it. "It's a sore point?"

She sat down against me on the settee, put her feet on the table and examined her stockinged toes. "Smoke?" she asked, and pulled out a packet from her dress. I shook my head. "They're Paul Revere," she said. "No, Peter Stuyvesant. My brother brings up whole cartons. Smuggles them through the border. No local rubbish for me. International passport to smoking pleasure." She drew in sharply and exhaled smoke in a hard gesture that made her cheeks look ugly. But I looked back as far as I could into the past to summon her true self.

"You know they grow the bloody stuff here, they do it all here then export it and we aren't allowed to buy it here," she said, "Rothmans. Pall Mall. Embassy Bonus, gives you a reason to switch. All that shit, but all for export. All we get is Madison."

Her blonde hair swept against my hand. I rubbed strands between my fingers, as tobacco buyers do when they assess the quality of their product on the BAT floors. The blonde was a fluorescent, transparent absence of colour and substance. I marvelled at how this hair partook of an otherworldly light, of the sun outside the dark cave. Here then was an alien creature, and I was holding an unworldly substance between my fingers: Bianca's hair.

"Your hair is… so blonde," I said stupidly.

She laughed. "It's dyed. See?" This gave me the opportunity to really examine it. "It used to be blonde, but by the time I was sixteen, it was mousy. I started dyeing it when I left school."

She began discarding her clothes with gleeful violence, the bra into the corner, the dress onto the bar counter. I imitated her gay abandonment, casting off clothing wherever I could, trying not to be self-conscious. When we were both naked, she climbed onto me, held me around the neck, our limbs tangled together. Her breasts wobbled into my face, and her nipples leered at me. All that was in focus was the Picasso on the wall behind her. The painter at his easel dabbed a fat brush onto the canvas, painting a strangely constructed girl. As usual for Picasso, she was fragmented – pieces of a girl put together to form a work of art. The pieces did not quite fit, giving the impression that she was a mirror that had been shattered. The girl was nude, with one arm stretched up. Her breasts were white and she had green spots for nipples.

So, with Picasso's painter and model watching them, Paul and Penny euphemistically made love. I tried to recapture the original picture of her, but in vain. The real Sleeping Beauty had evaporated, had fled, and I was left with a heavy, sodden, drunken girl called Penelope Woods who demanded fifty bloody dollars for services rendered on Christmas Eve 1977, in the void of my life.

# CHAPTER SIXTEEN

# WE'RE BACK IN THE STICKS AGAIN

1978 was the 'Beginning of the End' for the white minority government of Rhodesia. We didn't know this, of course; it was bad for morale. But Military Intelligence and the Central Intelligence Organisation began to realise that we were losing the war, or in their terms, that the 'kill' ratio was not as high as the number of infiltrators into the country. Africans who wanted their basic human rights were pouring in through the cracks and we couldn't kill them fast enough. So the Rhodesian government decided to keep control of certain areas – the most productive agricultural lands, the industrial centres and the lines of communication with South Africa. The rest of the country, where law and order had broken down, could go to hell – I mean, was 'ceded to the insurgents'.

Most of these 'liberated areas', as the Patriotic Front called them, were controlled by Mugabe's ZANLA forces. So where was ZIPRA? Nkomo, it was rumoured, was holding them back deliberately, letting ZANLA take the brunt of the casualties, so that he could prepare for what he envisioned as a glorious conventional war against the white Rhodesians, who would take flight, after which ZIPRA would march down the streets of Bulawayo.

★ ★ ★

3 January 1978; 08h00. I have been in the army for one whole year. By now I should be cruising the campus of Durban, barefoot, long-haired, carrying my clipboard from lecture to lecture, accompanying petticoat-free girls who come to class dripping in brine. But because the war is still intensifying (because we are, scatologically speaking, still in the shit), call-ups have been extended for all national service intakes to eighteen months.

And look at what has happened. Have I been 'fucked up' for life? Has it made a man of me? Have I furthered the cause of democracy and spread white Christian civilisation in Africa? One thing is for sure. Bianca was in my grasp last year at this time; now this bird had flown. Another thing too: I was now a *makonia* medic. I was welcomed back to DRR Hospital with the affection of a seasoned soldier. My denims were faded; I wore my stripes with irony; and I didn't brace up to anyone any more. I watched the 'fresh puss' in their new stiff combat clothing, drilling, marching, shining, and was almost tempted to sneer at them. Instead I smiled, waved them down with a 'don't-let's-be-silly-now' hand as they braced up or saluted me. But in the entrance of the hospital, Sergeant-Major Loots greeted me with his cheery self. "Williams! Get your arse over here. The doctor wants to see you in his office – now."

"Sir, I haven't even unpacked yet."

"Corporal, now means last week as far as the doctor is concerned, you know that."

I followed him down the passage leading to the doctor's office. Major Brink was the doctor in charge of DRR Medical Company. The Sergeant-Major knocked, pushed the door gingerly open, and motioned me to wait outside, where I caught the tail-end of their conversation.

"So what do you think?"

"Look… two bloody good medics. Two."

"It's suicide to put a medic within fifty miles of the bloody place."

"Williams."

I was told to sit in the comfortable armchair while two pairs of doctors' eyes scrutinised me from head to foot. This must be Brink. That must be Brandon. The Sergeant-Major turned from studying a map on the wall. Brink spoke first. "Have you rested and recuperated enough, Corporal?"

"Yes, sir."

Brink was neat, smart, crisp and military. He fitted his uniform, and he displayed his crowns proudly, one on each shoulder. He stared at me for a long time, and I went hot, as if he were inspecting my dress, my belt buckle, the shine of my boots. But I knew he wasn't really looking at me at all.

"Corporal, I'm sending you on a mission, to the frontline, to the bush." He picked up a pointer, wheeled round, and indicated a place on the Rhodesian border with Mozambique. "Here." He placed his pointer directly on the artificial straight line drawn at the bottom right of the teapot. "Vila Salazar. There is no medic in the area."

"The troops don't want one." This was Brandon, a quiet, unassuming man who had found his way into the army by bad luck, it appeared, and had resigned himself to wearing a sagging, creased uniform.

"They think they're a bunch of Supermen," added the Sergeant-Major.

"Corporal, your services will be required there immediately, and will probably demand all your skill and experience as a medic. These men at Vila Salazar are right in the thick of danger and scarcely a day goes by without some attack on them."

"I know, sir."

We had all heard of Vila Salazar. It featured almost every news time on the Security Force communiqué: Vila Salazar has been subjected to heavy mortar fire; Vila Salazar was the site of fierce clashes between FRELIMO and the Rhodesian Security Forces; three trucks were blown up by land mine in the Vila Salazar area.

It was legendary. Because of its exotic Portuguese name, people believed it was in the heart of Mozambique, and that the Rhodesians had penetrated and established a base in the centre of enemy territory. But its previous name had been Malvernia and in a period of goodwill way in the past, the Portuguese colony Mozambique and the British colony Rhodesia had exchanged names for the towns bordering their two countries. Salazar was the then Prime Minister of Portugal, the colonising power behind Mozambique. Hence the railway station border post called Vila Salazar, now the frontline against Marxist aggression. Vila Salazar: a stronghold for Rhodesian forces, continually attacked by guerrillas and their FRELIMO allies.

Major Brink swung on his chair. "Captain Breytenbach is the doctor in the Operation Repulse area and is stationed at Chiredzi. You will report to him when you arrive, and when at Vila Salazar, all casevacs go to him, OK?"

"Yes, sir."

Brink seemed relieved that I didn't put up a fight or protest. He leaned over his desk and emphasised each word with his pointer. "Corporal Williams, you are not to breathe a word of this to anybody. Your safety depends upon keeping it zipped. Understood?"

"Walls has big ears," mumbled Brandon.

"Think about national security, don't talk about it."

The Sergeant-Major winked. "Don't even think about it too much."

"How soon can you mobilise?"

"I have all my things packed from the pass."

"The plane, Williams, is waiting for you on the runway. Sergeant-Major Loots will take you in the Land Rover."

"A plane? Oh, yes. Thank you, sir."

I slung the duffel bag over my shoulder and sat in silence as the Sergeant-Major drove me in an open jeep down the back of the barracks to the concrete apron which served as the runway. "Buffalo Range?" he yelled at the guard who nodded and pointed to an old green-and-brown camouflaged Dakota whose propellers were beginning to spin. It sat on its haunches, its tail on a short wheel on the ground, its nose pointed up into the air. Loots shook hands with me without getting out or turning off the engine. "Jump in the doorway. He's waiting for you."

"Who?" I walked to the plane, in a *déjà vu*. I had seen this movie before. Biggles? Daktari? The Flying Doctor? Clarence the Cross-Eyed Lion? I threw in my duffel bag and climbed the metal rungs through an open circular door which was surrounded by metal studs. As soon as I was inside the dark hold, the engines began to throb loudly, and the aircraft taxied unsteadily across the tarmac. There were no seats, only boxes, straps and benches along either side. There was no door and the gaping circular entrance, like an old-fashioned television screen, showed me the ground and bushes whizzing past and dropping away below as we took off. I tried to sit on the bench, but kept getting lurched off onto the floor. Eventually I managed to worm my way forward to the pilot's cockpit. The pilot patted the empty seat next to him and I gratefully strapped myself in. We were the only two on board.

"Hey, Doc, you made it. Have to get these supplies to Buffalo Range, chop-chop. Flown before?"

"Yes, I mean, not actually flown. I've been in…"

"These Dakotas are marvellous," he yelled. "Still going strong. We'll keep them up in the air as long as we need to. Like the Viscounts. We recycle everything in Rhodesia, even our planes."

Now that I was seated, I could enjoy the flight a little more. The plane seemed slow and lethargic but dependable. How do you describe the personality of a plane? It was large, friendly, smiling, old-fashioned and broad-shouldered. Or perhaps I was projecting the pilot's easygoing demeanour onto this lifeless machine. He flew dangerously low over tops of trees and took delight in swinging the craft around and chasing wild animals he spotted: lumbering elephants, graceful giraffe and white-ring-arsed antelope. He veered towards a village of mud huts and roared at it so the inhabitants scattered into the forest while others lay flat on the ground, staring up at this huge prehistoric pterodactyl gliding slowly over them. He laughed good-naturedly at his own antics, swooping up to avoid an escarpment, so that I spun, feeling dizzy and disorientated. But I also felt the inklings of a new sensation, the carefree, god-like taste of limitless power.

"Hold the yoke." The pilot told me which was up and down and and let me fly for a while. I pulled the lever back to make the plane go up, but he urged me to stay low. "Helicopters fly high to be safe, Dakotas fly low. We're a sitting duck for a brave enemy." So I settled down to nestle on the tree tops again, flying through a forest fire, up into the swirling smoke, skimming the surface of the world. To see every living thing run at my terrifying dinosauric appearance cheered me up.

"I take over now, Doc. We're near Buffalo Range." He pointed to the right at a clearing of army tents, trucks, a grass runway, with a camouflaged helicopter sitting at one end. Ant-like soldiers bustled around. We circled slowly and lurched down, but as we approached the runway, the pilot suddenly throttled up into the sky again.

"What's wrong?"

The pilot pointed to two choppers, circling a nearby hill, out of which soldiers were firing with tracers, like mad mosquitoes zeroing in on a lump of tender flesh. "A contact!" he murmured fervently and pulled the microphone towards him. "Need assistance?" The radio crackled and a nasal voice curtly informed us that it was only a routine exercise. We were close enough to see the huts huddled on the hill, some alight. "Target practice," grinned the pilot and he swung the craft round to land, bumping and straining on the rough runway. A cloud of dust followed us and soon enveloped the whole camp. I crept back to collect my duffel bag and jumped out of the TV door. The pilot pointed to a green square and I nodded and walked off the runway in that direction. I rubbed my eyes and spat dust from my mouth as a tent emerged out of the brown haze. Was this what happened every time a plane landed or took off?

I used to love this part of the country when I was a child because of the names: Triangle, Cashel Valley, Buffalo Range. The tropical, sticky-sweet lowveld of Rhodesia, it was now Joint Operation Command (JOC) Repulse, and the Vietnam of the conflict. The areas of the war, as it had intensified, had been divided into different operations – Operation Thresher, Hurricane and Repulse. But JOC Repulse was not like its name at all. It was casual, friendly and humid, like (I imagined) a Durban beach day.

Captain Breytenbach was waiting to meet me in the medics' tent with a pannier packed ready at the entrance. He was stern and nervously meticulous, making sure I ate a good army breakfast (greasy eggs and bacon, weak coffee and cold, hard toast) before escorting me to three trucks lined up outside the mess hall.

"Whatever you do, don't let them give you any cheek. They've refused a medic up to now. Anything you need, just radio through and we'll send it, OK? But you won't need anything. Vilas has supplies for Africa, I'm sure. They've requested every drug, bandage and drip we could spare."

"OK, sir." I smiled bravely, a small child on his first day of school.

"You're on the ration run to Nyala and there the Vilas crowd will sort you out. I haven't radioed to them in case you get ambushed. And have a piss before you go. If you hit a land mine, a ruptured bladder is not the most pleasant thing in the world."

He waved a stiff farewell at me and indicated the trucks on the dirt road.

I found a seat next to the black medical pannier on the lead vehicle and strapped myself in. Sitting up there already were two soldiers from the JOC, with CQ lapels, whose job, I took it, was to distribute the rations at the various bases along the way. One, a whiskery, shrunken man, was complaining nervously. "Two ambushes yesterday on that road and I don't want to be in the third. You know what happened to the last ration run?"

"What happened to the last ration run?" I asked quickly.

"Now he's fu... fu... fucking asking," said the other CQ storesman, a burly man with a woolly black balaclava over his head and face. "It was blown sky high by a boosted bloody la... land mine. Killed all the blokes, all fu... four fuckers, and rats were scattered all over the countryside for the terrs to pick up. When Fire Force got there, everything was ga... ga... gone."

The first man smoothed his moustache. "We're sitting ducks. The gooks have overrun this whole area, and we're passing through it. We've lost control here."

"Shut your fucking mouth, Tu... Tu... Taffy. The Rhodesian Army has not fucking la... la... la... lost control."

I fixed a polite smile on my face to hide my terror, and clutched the medical pannier for consolation as the truck started up and wheeled down a dusty road. "Cock weapons!" called the driver from the cab, as he cocked his, cradled it in his lap so he could drive, the barrel propped out of the window.

"They could tar the bloody road, you know." Taffy waved a hand at the contoured red dirt track ahead, which snaked and narrowed between waving long grass. The CQ storesman's point was reinforced when, after only fifteen minutes along the road, we had to veer around scattered, twisted metal – what I took to be chunks of lorry. A huge hole had been blasted in the middle of the road, but without even slowing down, our truck detoured on a new makeshift track flattened into the grass. Bullet holes riddled every road sign we saw. But we didn't see much. The dust on the road was so thick, in spite of *guti*, that I could not keep my eyes open. My rifle, cocked and ready, was clogging up with dust too. I was afraid it would jam if I had to fire it.

"Keep your shooting eye closed, Doc, so if we're ambushed, you're all right." Taffy showed me how to cover the *doppie* cover of my rifle. His finger was on the trigger, and he waved his rifle as if aiming at passing enemies, but clouds of brown, choking dust billowed up around us, making it impossible to see past the edge of the truck. We travelled for an hour in this way, along the debris-littered track, stopping once at a base camp to off-load crates, then continuing on the narrow road, getting more and more into dangerous territory, apparently, if I was to judge by the increasing skittishness of my comrades. I was dry-throated, sweating, and burning in the sun; my arms were red and the back of my neck burnt already. How the man wore a balaclava, I didn't know.

Suddenly the truck screeched to a halt and the dust overtook us.

"What's the matter?" I blurted out.

"We're here, sonny." I saw nothing but bush, dusty green, with shimmering heat phantoms. "We choose a different rendezvous point every time so the ta… ta… terrs don't get wind of it."

"Where are the bastards?" said Taffy. "We can't park here for hours like sitting ducks." We waited five minutes, a long time when all you hear is the screeching of cicadas and are watching every flick of the grass for crouching enemies. After ten minutes, the driver radioed through to base. "Tell the Vilas bastards to get their arses into gear."

We waited another ten minutes. "I don't like this at all, not at all," the balaclava man muttered, sweat running down the sides of his face.

"Why don't we go on to Vila Salazar ourselves and drop the rations?" My naïve suggestion brought on a bout of laughter from the whiskered man, though it sounded more like a cough.

"You must be out of your fucking tree."

I pictured hot earth shelters, mortars pelting down on us, dust, dust and more dust, and no running water. I would rather be with the Major in the Matopas any day. I was going to be stationed in a hell-hole these soldiers would never dream of visiting even for a ration drop-off. Now I prayed the 'Vilas bastards' would not arrive. Maybe they would have an accident, or a truck breakdown, so we would have to turn back and I could stay at the JOC. And I prayed that whichever way we went – back or forwards – we wouldn't hit a land mine.

★ ★ ★

The Rhodesian Army Corps of Engineers, zealous buggers, had laid a mine fence along the border of Mozambique twenty-five metres wide and fourteen hundred kilometres long – the second longest military barrier in the whole god-damn world. No gook would get through that, they told us. When all was said and done, eight thousand ZANLA border-hoppers were killed or maimed by the minefield. Good job, boys! Now that is something to be proud of.

ZANLA were not to be outdone in the land-mine war. In their efforts to maim and kill, they planted Soviet anti-tank land mines in the roads all over Rhodesia. They managed to blow up over two and a half thousand vehicles, kill over six hundred people, and maim – oh, at least four or five thousand. Well done, ZANLA!

★ ★ ★

"Here they come!" I listened to the drone of a vehicle approaching from the east. We saw nothing until a 4.5 skidded around the dirt road at high speed, wheelied when it came within ten dangerous feet of us and broadsided our truck so that we were showered with stones and dirt from the road.

When I saw them, I wanted to laugh from pure relief. They were straight out of a Sergeant Rock comic. MAGs were mounted on each corner of the vehicle, and the dozen or so soldiers on the back benches were burned brown, bare-chested, and wore tin helmets decorated with leaves, twigs and tree branches. I had the impression that they had especially dressed up for the occasion. One enormous soldier on the roof of the cab, his MAG trained on us, smoked a cigar. The other soldiers were smoking cigarettes, and one was sucking beer from a dark brown Castle bottle. Each gunner had wound gleaming gold coils of ammo round and round his shorts and bare shoulders, and wore them like medals. All had beards. The lead soldier on top of the cab stamped his foot and the driver turned off the engine.

"Hey!" He leaped from the cab onto our truck. "The lizards are here already. What have you got for us today?"

"You're almost an hour late," complained Taffy.

The man lunged past me to get at the boxes. His gold bullet medallions swung over me as he reached to open a box and stare at the can labels. "Have you got the mail?"

"Yup, here you are, and you've got a medic, too."

The huge man frowned at me. "We didn't order a medic. Oh, what the fuck," he said when he saw my frightened face. "Jump on, Doc, with all your gear. The lizards will give you a hand. Get those nipple-wrenches to work, Shorty."

Taffy nervously helped with the trunk, while the 'Vilas bastards' boarded our vehicle and hauled off their booty. "Wait," said balaclava man, sweating as he tried to hold back some of the cargo. "Not all of this is for yo… yo… you."

"It is now." I was helped onto the 4.5, a helmet was thrust onto my head and the truck started up. "Cheers!" The truck roared into a three-point turn, skilfully showering the HQ truck in dirt again, as the soldiers cat-called their goodbyes. The 4.5 pulled off at a speed that pushed me back into a seat. I fastened the seat belt, fumbling to tie my helmet strap with one hand and keep hold of my rifle with the other. The others weren't wearing seat belts; they weren't even sitting on the seats provided, but on the edge of the truck, pointing their weapons at the heat haze. One soldier was pretending to shoot at bushes, making childish shooting noises with his mouth (pew! pew!). I wondered why the large man on top of the cab – he was obviously in charge – didn't order them to behave, especially in such a dangerous area. But he was preoccupied with scouting ahead, staring at the sides of the road as they blurred by.

"Here. Here." He stamped his foot on the cab roof and the driver screamed the vehicle to a halt. Before the dust had caught up with us, he had leaped over the front of the cab and engine and onto the road. I clutched my rifle tightly and held my trigger finger rigid. All I could think of was an attack, or a land mine. But no: we had stopped to examine a BSA Police 2.5 truck lying on its side in the ditch. The leader ran up to it, wrenched off the beautiful long whip aerial from its bonnet and threw it up on the truck for others to catch. Soon all of them – except me and the driver – vaulted off the side of the truck and began pulling off all the loose pieces they could find – spotlights, mirrors, radio, battery, wiper blades.

"If we don't take it, the gooks will." The leader grinned at me as he climbed back on, his arms cradling a long black army-issue torch. He tossed me an emergency medic pack he had found in the vehicle too. "Even something for the Doc." Then we were on our way again, the driver revving the engine far too high, skidding around corners far too fast, and jolting the fixed grimace on my face far too often. "That's our Captain," said the soldier near me.

Then I saw the craters. I couldn't figure out what they were at first – smooth, sandy patches of scorched earth where the grass and trees and scrub had been burned as if by meteorites. There was one on my right, then more to my left, then one plumb in the middle of the road. The truck veered smoothly around it. The soldier next to me consoled me with a 'don't-worry-it's-nothing' gesture of the shoulders. "Mortars and rockets that overshot."

Five minutes later we arrived. Out of the flat, green haze of the countryside protruded a thin Eiffel-tower scaffold. The truck aimed for this tower, and soon we were driving pell-mell straight down a fenced-in corridor of high barbed wire and aiming directly for a large black and white sign so full of bullet holes I could hardly read it: BSA POLICE VILA SALAZAR. The truck showered it with dust as it skidded into a gateway enclosed in huge rolls of barbed wire and double fences, with signs every ten metres showing the ominous red skull and crossbones: DANGER MINEFIELD AREA. Another sign on the gate barring our way warned NO THROUGH ROAD: CUSTOMS AHEAD. But as we hurtled towards it, the nine-foot-high gate swung open miraculously to let us through into an enclosed perimeter, closing behind us once we were inside.

Before the vehicle could park, we were surrounded by dozens of white soldiers – I say 'white', but these people were tanned so dark as to be brown, and wore no clothes to speak of, just khaki shorts or underpants. They swarmed after the vehicle, calling out and demanding their mail and rations. We parked underneath the huge mast, fifty feet tall at least, which looked like some kind of transmitter.

We were in a compound that had once been an old farmhouse, or a customs post, or both. There was a main building ahead of me, various outhouses, long oblong blocks of smaller rooms, a rusty water tank on stilts, and underground bunkers at intervals, humped with sandbags. But this was not what I was looking at. Each building was chipped with thousands of little round holes. Some had gashes in them as if someone had attacked them with an axe, and there were gaping holes the size of elephants in some roofs. One outhouse had completely collapsed into itself. I couldn't see a clear spot more than a few inches square that was not chipped by... bullets. Yes, they were bullet holes. I estimated there were thousands – perhaps hundreds of thousands – of them.

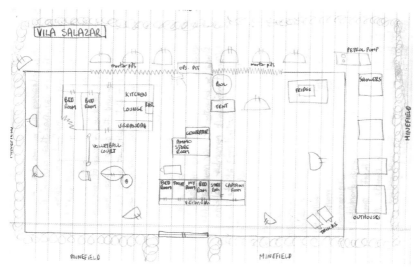

In spite of the doctor's words, they were pleased to see a medic: "Hope the new Doc is good at shrapnel wounds." I climbed off the truck while three near-naked men carried my pannier behind me. The Captain, even taller and bigger than I thought now that he was walking by my side, put his hand on my shoulder and guided me to the long building closest to the water tower, and along the veranda to what he announced as 'the Doc's room'.

"I get a room? Thanks, sir."

"Watch who you're calling 'sir'. The name's John. John Kirby." He winked.

"Corporal Williams – Paul, Paul."

"No formalities here, Paul-Paul, or it's the box for you." The three behind laughed.

I ran my fingers lightly over the wall. The bullets had chipped off plaster in three-inch circles, but had not penetrated much into the solid brick.

"We've had very little action here lately," said the Captain. "Just a quick rev every now and then. The boys are getting restless."

"Every now and then?" I was left alone to unpack in a small room that had once been a storeroom, but now had "H-O-S-P-I-T-A-L" scratched on the wooden door. The room was piled high with field dressings, but little else. The window was broken; in fact there was no pane in it, nor was there any bed or furniture. I sat on the trunk and thanked them as they trooped out, leaving me to unpack. But I didn't even have time to let my heart sink before a whiskered soldier knocked on the open door.

"Doc? Have you got any mozzy spray? I've been bitten to death." I didn't, but had a repellent cream in the pannier which he eagerly squeezed onto his sun-browned hand and rubbed all over his wiry shoulders. "Can I keep this?"

"Listen, what can I do for a bed?" I asked.

"We'll find a door lying around somewhere. Just prop it up on bricks and you're as comfy as if you were in a five-star hotel. Keeps away the rats. By the way, I'm Gypsy. Follow me."

"Paul." He led me outside into the relentless sun. The gate we had just driven through was now not only shut but *boppered* with barbed wire. If this was the only entrance, and it looked like it, the camp was now completely sealed in. Gypsy guided me to a mound of sandbags, which surrounded a wood-framed burrow into the ground. We crouched into it and felt our way down rough steps into an underground pit. It was damp and cold, a relief after the searing sun outside. Gypsy clicked a switch, and a weak, naked light bulb showed us where we were.

"The generator," he replied to a silent question and I recalled the hum I had heard continuously since my arrival. The shelter was a square hewn out of cool brown earth, reinforced with stout beams which looked like old railway sleepers. The roof was supported with I-beams of steel from an actual railway line. A slit of four inches all around the ceiling afforded us a ground-level view of the camp. On the floor was a door on bricks.

"You can take this bed if you want, but bear in mind you might have to spend a few nights down here." He shook my hand again, and crawled out of the bunker, leaving behind an after-image of a toothy grin.

I must have been still in shock. Now that I was alone, for the first time since this ordeal had started, I sat on the 'bed' and cried. Vila Salazar was so different from the picture in my mind. It seemed suspiciously too casual, too relaxed, too informal. No one wore shoes or long trousers or shirts, and no one carried rifles. What about the bullet holes in every wall, in these bunkers? Perhaps the hostilities had died down, and the bullet holes were from a long time ago? Perhaps I was too uptight, listening to too many war stories from HQ? Perhaps it had all been war spin?

I lifted the door and with a struggle shoved it sideways up through the passageway and out of the bunker. I positioned the four bricks in my 'Hospital' room and set up the bed neatly in the corner, wondering how high rats could jump or climb. I spread out my sleeping bag and stuffed a combat jacket with wound dressings for a pillow. Then I took off my army boots and massaged my toes. They had been crushed for a year in these hot boots and were the worse for wear. It would be a relief to let them grow fallow for a few weeks. I pulled off the starchy shirt and denim longs that now stank of sweat. Luckily, I had brought my army issue khaki boxer shorts, green army T-shirt (with Operation Repulse written on it, and a picture of a leopard pouncing). I found, at the end of the passage, a full bathroom with sink, toilet, shower. I splashed my face with cold water, stared at the *Playboy* centrefolds pinned up above the mirror.

Now I was ready to report for duty. I grabbed my rifle and walked outside, feeling oddly under-dressed and vulnerable, but overdressed compared to the soldiers I passed, who were wearing white shorts or underpants. The central house in the middle of the courtyard was obviously the headquarters, and I marched towards the lounge where I saw a group of soldiers talking together. Over the hum of the generator, music blared from a speaker fixed up on the corner of the roof, facing towards the courtyard. The South African Radio 5 jingle boomed out, 'Here's the place we say, have a happy day,' and John Berks's voice announced the next song. Around the corner of the courtyard, a group of soldiers (it seemed odd to call them soldiers) were playing volleyball on the front lawn; others were lying in the sun on a concrete patio, while still others were splashing in a blue, sparkling swimming pool.

In the centre of this base camp, the dipole (as they called it) towered into the sky, leaving a thin shadow across the pool and house. Two flags flew on the tower, one the green and white Rhodesian flag, the other a plain platinum blue. 2 RR Mortar Platoon, it read.

OK, I thought, this must be a lunch-break, or it's a public holiday today. Or perhaps they take a break when the ration run arrives (one or two were frowning and mouthing words over letters in the shade of a tree). The only work going on, as far as I could see, was at the RL, where four men were unloading boxes and crates of foodstuffs. A black cook (I presumed because of the khaki 'houseboy' suit he wore) directed them where to take each box as he read the labels. But the rest of the whites were lounging out in the sun. I was white-legged compared to these soldiers because even in the Matopas we had had to wear full combat uniform all day at the Major's insistence. As I climbed the steps of the red veranda, I had to step over a soldier who was lying on his towel, naked, reeking of coconut oil. "My dick needs a tan," he explained.

I walked across a cool stone floor to the group who were sitting at the bar on the veranda. It was a proper bar: stools, fridge, spirit cabinet. A man with rat whiskers and weasel features was playing a guitar, competing with Radio Five, singing and strumming frenetically Mike Westcott's parody of 'Tipperary'.

> It's a long way to Mukumbura.
> And we're going up there to stir… stir… stir.

No, the record was not stuck. This is how the end of the song faded out on vinyl, but these lusty troops continued singing the word with great gusto, while I stood at the back of the circle watching them. *Stir! Stir! Stir!*

Stir (v. intrans.): to cause trouble. Schoolboys often stirred by provoking fights, or teasing. Sir, I hit him because he was stirring with me. But now overgrown schoolboys in army uniforms had stirred so much in this country that they had killed over 6,000 troublemakers in the last five years. They had bullied, burned, tortured, raided, degraded and raped. We were all Rhodesians and we fought through thick and thin to keep this land a free land, stop the enemy coming in. We stirred.

"We'd like to welcome the new Doc to Vilas with a free frosty," said the rat-like singer to the barman, who handed me an ice-cold Lion Lager.

"What are you doing with your *gat*, Doc, don't carry it around like a *fresh-puss*, man." Here the barman clicked his fingers and Gypsy stood and saluted. "Take the Doc's *gat* to his room. He thinks there's a war on."

"*Ja, baas*," grinned Gypsy, weighing my rifle gingerly as if he had never seen or touched one before, and trotting off with it.

"So, Doc, drink up, tell us who you are."

"Paul," I said, downing as much as I could in one gulp. This was the measure of manhood – how fast you could down a beer.

"Not so fast, Doc. Only the first one's free."

"I hope you'll do better than the last Doc."

"What happened to him?"

This precipitated a volley of laughter. "He got sick. Real sick. Full of holes. We had to patch him up and casevac him home to his mama."

These men were in their thirties and forties, even fifties. I couldn't place them. I couldn't imagine them in army uniforms, marching and saluting, but nor could I imagine them wearing suits in offices in town. And they were smiling at me, without malice, sneers or hidden secrets. I tried to identify the leaders, those with rank – the corporals, sergeants and NCOs – but I couldn't.

"Are you all regular soldiers?" I asked.

The guitarist, who introduced himself as Slinky, spat out a mouthful of beer. The barman grinned and patted him on the back. "He didn't mean it, Slinky. Don't swear, Doc. Slinky is allergic to the army." Slinky waved his hands in mock terror and feigned an epileptic fit. "We're on call-up camps. We do two-month stints here once a year. We're 2 RR Mortar Platoon."

"Come to Vilas and get bombed," grinned Gypsy, who had just returned. They clinked bottles and Slinky struck up the next song.

> *We're back in the sticks, we're back in the sticks*
> *We're back in the sticks again.*
> *It's the fifth time we've been to the flipping chateen*
> *We're back in the sticks again.*

I had only been in platoons with eighteen-year-old National Servicemen, controlled by regular officers. But now the Rhodesian Government was calling up every man up to 65 years old. My father was out patrolling lonely highways; businessmen were taking two months' work off a year to do camps. These were men with regular jobs, families and lives.

"Trouble is we've been here a month already and I haven't got a tan," said Gypsy. "Too much time in the shelters."

"Gypsy, you were born with a tan," called the burly man from the back. Slinky chimed in his two cents' worth: "Why do Africans smear Ambi on their face to look as white as they can, and Europeans try to make themselves as dark as they can?"

The Captain, the large man in charge, walked through the entrance, and I tensed up immediately, as I expected everyone else to. Now we would be put to work. "Come on, you buggers, I told you to unload the ammo into the front shelter."

I stood nervously, ready to obey orders, but instead, everyone booed him. "Ah, Captain, get off our backs," said the barman. "We don't want to waste our beers. And we were just chatting to the Doc."

He frowned at me, screwed up his face. "OK. But if you're not down there by the time I finish my beer, you'll all be doubling away to the box."

"Me, me, I want to double away to the box," said Gypsy.

I only found out later that the 'box' was a large cold room at the end of the perimeter where all the beers and provisions were kept. As punishment, people would be sent to carry crates back to the bar, and get a free one for their efforts.

The Captain caught a Lion Lager bottle which the barman neatly slid along the counter to him, and sat on a stool next to me to drink it. "Paul, I want to show you around so you feel at home. You've met the fellas, now you need a tour, a what-do-you-call-it, a renaissance."

"A reconnaissance," corrected Slinky.

★ ★ ★

"The kitchen…"

Two large gas stoves squatted in the middle of the room, a huge fridge and freezer occupied two corners, and a long wooden bench running along the entire wall sagged with piles of tins and vegetable boxes that had just arrived. I grinned at the cook who was defrosting steaks the size of Africa in the large sink. Today must be some special occasion. Through the back, we stopped to inspect the people swimming naked in the clear pool, which reeked of chlorine. Beyond the pool was a mound of earth running the length of the perimeter, punctured with a black and white sign: WARNING: YOU ARE NOW ENTERING MOZAMBIQUE!

The Captain, or John, as I had to get used to calling him, waved it away. "Just a souvenir. Mozambique is two hundred metres *lapa*." He pointed ahead to a cleared, raked field which abutted a line of double barbed-wire fences. "Minefield. We're safely mined in on all sides, for two kilometres, except the Gaza

Strip, which is the entry and exit point you came though this morning. Safe as houses here." I looked at the crumbling buildings around us, roofs falling in, walls collapsing. "In a manner of speaking."

Over the mound were eight mortar pits, with long mortar tubes trained outward into the haze that was Mozambique. We climbed down into the main bunker and I was shown the ops room: an elaborate control panel, a wall of dials and radios, and a television scanner and screen. On the wall of the pit was a Cuban rocket launcher captured by the platoon earlier that month. I greeted a grinning operator on duty who was eating a UFO-shaped toasted ham sandwich which he called a jaffle. Through showers of crumbs and jaffle breath, he showed me how the controls were wired to the dipole, on top of which was a scanning video camera with telephoto lens. This could sweep the whole length and breadth of Malvernia, the border town in Mozambique. I peered at the screen and the operator panned slowly so I could get a good view of the town: a church, an occasional isolated building shrouded in bush and trees, and a few houses. The picture was black and white, but well defined. I could see every detail when the operator zoomed in, even the steeple on the church.

"Not much to see, but there's enough FRELIMO hiding there with moving mortar positions to keep us on our toes."

We crawled out of the bunker into the bright sunlight.

"Any questions?"

"Are we safe here?"

John roared with laughter. "Paul, bullets don't penetrate. The only way is from the top, and we're dug in. When you hear a mortar, you dive into a pit. But FRELIMO haven't figured that out. They haven't got the hang of twentieth-century warfare yet. When they fire a mortar, it overshoots by miles, and it's usually a fluke if they hit anywhere near."

I nodded; that explained the craters kilometres away from the camp.

"You must come up when we have a rev, so you can see what happens, but for now… take it easy. I make no promises, but tonight I'm organising some entertainment." He winked, and left me at the pool in case I wanted to swim, or play volleyball, or catch a tan. My name was added to the list of guards in the bar.

"Sorry, Doc, it's the one thing we have to do," said Slinky, "even the Big Chief does guard."

"Sounds fair enough."

"All's fair in love and war."

Supper was a *braai* on the lawn outside the veranda. I counted twenty soldiers – men I should perhaps call them, or perhaps hippies; one man had cut his combat jeans in flares, sewn pink stars on the bottoms and painted psychedelic twirls on the patch pockets. "I know bell-bottoms are out of fashion," he said. "But I'm waiting for the return of the Sixties."

Each person was issued with a large steak, a ring of *boerewors*, salad, a baked potato and a dollop of wine sauce prepared by the black chef, who I noticed sat down to eat an equal portion and drank beer with us too. I say this because, in our land of harmony and our army of equal opportunity, even RAR soldiers with the same rank as Europeans had not been permitted to eat with us in the Matopas.

I sat near the fire, mellowed by the beer, full of meat and potatoes, at peace with the world, reflecting on my good fortune. This was a haven, a paradise in the heat of a terrible war, of which I had seen very little and hoped to see still less, a hippie commune at the centre of a fascist regime of discipline and boots and uniforms.

As soon as the sun set, we were plunged into a hot darkness, until stars the size of crumpled aluminium foil bathed us in an eerie light. Slinky sang love songs from Jim Croce and Bread, and the hard army self that I had cultivated as a defence against the world began to peel off. First to go was the guilt. I noticed how conditioned I was to justify my every action to win approval from my superiors. Here I could flop down and let the guilt ebb out of me. And with it went the anger, the fear and the resentment that had kept me in a tight knot for a whole year.

"If you've all finished your food," announced John, "I have something for dessert." And he pulled out a one-metre-long metal tube. "No, you filthy buggers, it's not what you think it is. It's an Icarus rocket launcher."

Icarus rockets were long, green flares sent up by lost persons to alert aircraft and give positions for search parties. With whoops of excitement, the men followed John to the perimeter fence to press against the blackness of Mozambique ahead. He loaded the tube with an Icarus rocket, aimed it in the air at 80 degrees and pulled the trigger. The tube jolted the big man's shoulder as the rocket shot into the sky. It whizzed a green path into the dark, and then exploded high above Malvernia, spraying fireworks over the whole town. "A modified Icarus," he admitted bashfully.

"Another one, Chief. Pretty, pretty." But almost immediately I heard two dull thuds and ten or fifteen seconds later two explosions on our side of the fence. I knew what this was; I didn't have to be told. I scrambled in fright to the bunker below, but when no one followed, I peeped my head out.

"Learn to recognise that, Doc," said the Captain. "Oh, but I see you already have. It's the 60 mm mortar, of Russian origin, fired wildly by panicking, roving mortar positions of FRELIMO, who do not bother to calculate height, trajectory, distance, nothing. Judging by the time gap between thump and explosion, I would say they missed us by three kilometres. Not bad when you're only three hundred metres away."

I climbed out of the pit. Gypsy and Slinky were laughing, or coughing, I was not sure which, but I stared suspiciously at them (not that I could see anything but shadows). "Don't worry, Doc, you'll get used to it. When we first heard a mortar over us, we all shat in our pants."

"Speak for yourself, Slinky," said the Captain. "No more tonight, fellas. Perhaps tomorrow."

The first night in the medic's room on a door was a restless one. I was used to sleeping on the ground, so the door was not the problem. Nor were the rats, with their scuffling forays across the room on tapping claws. It was the explosions that kept me awake. The first time, I leaped up and grabbed my rifle, thinking that we were being attacked by mortars. I was ready to rush down to my bunker – I had carefully traced my steps to get there in the dark earlier that day – but no one else stirred. I listened, heard nothing but cicadas and the wind in the trees, so I lay down again and fell asleep. But after half an hour, I was rattled awake by small arms fire in the distance. I sat up again. Boom! went an antipersonnel mine, far away, and then a series of machine gun bursts in the distance, like an echo of a past war. I looked out of my window at the star-drenched house and yard. Still no one had stirred. This was lunacy.

Here we were in the middle of a full-scale war and no one was awake. Then the icy thought struck me: what if they were all dead, murdered in their beds by FRELIMO or ZANLA and I was the only survivor? But as I crept out of the room and down the corridor, I could hear the snores of the Captain and see three bodies curled in sleeping bags in the next room. I stepped off the veranda and onto the sandy yard. I breathed in deeply, tried to relax, even as I heard more explosions echoing against the main building, but coming now from the west.

Then suddenly the night sky hit me like the voice of God that knocked Saul off his horse. There were so many stars that the whole area was lit up like a Christmas parade. The buildings were milky white, and the shadows had colour. I didn't know starlight could be so bright. The Milky Way stretched across the huge expanse above my head, taking up half of the sky. I could pick out Venus, Mars, Jupiter. A veil lifted from my eyes and a rising swell of emotion overwhelmed me. I am on the top of the world, I said to myself.

Then from close by came a noise, the crackle of a twig, someone sneaking in the yard. My heart beat hard; my hands tingled cold. "Who…? How did you get in?" I had been right about FRELIMO. The camp was overrun. I gripped my rifle and pulled it up into firing position.

"Hey, Doc, can't you sleep?"

The guard stepped out of the shadow of a tree. I let my rifle go limp, as if I had been merely stretching my arms. He wasn't even carrying a weapon.

"What are all the explosions?"

"Hey, relax, Doc. Those are just mines in the fields going off. Animals stray into them and set them off. Damn nuisance – we have to go and replace them every few weeks or so – the mines, not the animals." He stepped out into the starlight, and I recognised the barman.

"And the rifle fire?"

"FRELIMO." He pointed across the perimeter at the twinkling lights of Malvernia. The enemy was that close. "They want to keep us on our toes, I expect, or more likely they think the antipersonnel mines are mortars directed at them. They're bloody jittery. Or else they're the guards trying to keep awake. I wish we could do that. I need some target practice."

"Doesn't anyone ever get hurt?"

"FRELIMO couldn't hit a barn door," said the guard, repeating the slogan I was to hear *ad nauseam* for the next few weeks.

The next morning I was woken up at five with the roar of the generator motor. I was still wearing my PT shorts and T-shirt; my uniform was all packed in the trunk. The night had been cool, but already the sun on the horizon was warming us up. My first priority today would be a suntan, I decided.

Slinky and Gypsy were already sizzling bacon and eggs in a huge pan in the kitchen. Radio 5 blared from the lounge speakers. "Greetings and salutations, Doc. Help yourself." I was wading through a plate of eggs, bacon and fire-singed bread (or toast, as they called it), when the Captain ambled up from the ops bunker.

"Please can we give them a bit of a rev today, Boss?" said Gypsy.

"Look, Gypsy, I've got something I want you to do after breakfast. The antenna on the dipole has jammed. Can't you climb up and unstick it? We can't get a tilt out of our remote control."

"Sure thing, boss," grinned Gypsy.

So after breakfast, we gathered around the dipole and watched Gypsy shin up the ladder. He was halfway up when I heard popping sounds directly above my head. I made a motion for the veranda, but as Slinky and the Captain did not budge, I stood my ground as bravely as I could. Gypsy stopped climbing, but made no effort to come down. Instead he peered out into the morning haze. "The bastards are firing at me," he yelled down at us.

"They can see him climbing the dipole?" I whispered to Slinky.

The commotion brought more of the soldiers out onto the front lawn.

"Can you see anyone, Gypsy?" called someone behind me. As if in reply, another shot whizzed past us, popped, and then thumped in Malvernia. Gypsy slithered down as fast as he could. That one was close, it seemed.

"You didn't fix the antenna," said John sternly. "What's wrong with you, man?"

Gypsy scowled. "You go up there, then."

"Don't worry, Gypsy. Go after dark, then they can't see you."

"You coward, Gypsy, they'll never hit you up there," called a red-faced man from the veranda. A burst of automatic fire interrupted Gypsy's reply and even the Captain ducked instinctively. I heard the bullets thud into the wall at the front of the farmhouse.

"Looks like you started something now, Gypsy," called Slinky. But no one moved until a mortar burst close by and the ground shuddered.

"They mean business today," said John. "Let's go, men." The men scattered to collect their rifles, and to dive into their designated mortar shelters. I realised, as I was skidding down into mine at the back of the compound, that they were all mortar men, and would be in mortar pits at the front. I trembled alone in the dark, listening to the others let rip with automatic weapons. In return, as if they were politely waiting their turn, FRELIMO replied with the echo of automatic fire. Most rounds cracked high in the air, but I heard a few thudding into buildings around me. One whizzed and skimmed the ground above my shelter. Another thudded into the railway sleeper above me, dislodging crumbling sods of earth. I spat dirt out of my mouth and wiped dust out of my eyes. I learned to anticipate every explosion by the dull thud as it was fired from the FRELIMO side, then the whiz overhead, followed by the explosion. Most whizzes went over and exploded miles away, but a few landed close by – how close I couldn't tell, until I was sure one had hit the shelter itself. The whole shelter rocked and I smelled gunpowder and smoke. I flattened myself against the darkest corner, my rifle pointed at the entrance. I expected FRELIMO to charge through at any moment with fixed bayonets. But five minutes later, it was all over. Both sides, as if by agreement, stopped shooting at almost the same time.

"OK, all clear."

I peeped out to see the men ambling slowly to the main farmhouse, again with no weapons. I crept out and joined a cheery, excited group who explained that after each 'schtonk', or 'rev', we had to report to the lounge to show ourselves and assess damage and casualties.

"All present and accounted for," declared the Captain. "Now for damage assessment." Slinky held up his towel, which had been on the line to dry, and was now torn with bullet holes. "Fuck those bastards," he muttered. "They did it on purpose. They knew it was my towel."

"Bad news, guys," said the red-faced guy. "They hit our pool." Everyone swarmed outside to see. Sure enough there was a crater on one side of it and water was already seeping out of the crack the mortar had caused.

"War is hell," said Gypsy. "How would they like it if we *donnered* their pool?"

"They don't have one," said the red-faced man. "But if they did, we'd sure as fuck schtonk it too."

The mortar-men went off to clean their mortars and the rest of the men lay in the sun again. I was still shaking, stunned. John patted me on the back. "First time for you? Have a drink, it'll help." I took the beer he was offering and opened it with the open end of an empty FN cartridge.

"Next time, come up to the front line with us, Doc," he said. "We'll show you a good time."

Gypsy immediately set to work on a dummy. He stuffed his full combat uniform, boots and cap with rags and cushions, fastened the boots to the end of the trousers, attached a stick to the flapping hands, and tied the dummy onto the flagpole rope. Only when he hoisted the rope up the dipole did I realise what he was up to. The dummy was meant to look like him.

Sure enough, as he jerked the body up the dipole, FRELIMO spotted it and twanged a shot at it high in the air. The crowd cheered. Gypsy began jiggling the dummy up and down the pole as if it were climbing up and down at top speed. More shots were fired wild, and then – a direct hit. A bullet thudded and tore through the stuffing of Gypsy's combat jacket.

"That would have been me," shouted Gypsy.

"That must be the marksman with telescopic sights."

"Or else a lucky shot."

John nodded. "Let them get excited about it." So Gypsy jigged the dummy up and down the pole. It looked bizarre; what must the enemy think? That a man was shot, but was still climbing up and down the pole?

"They'll think we're a bunch of Supermen."

After half an hour of jiggling the dummy and watching it get shot, Gypsy tired of the game. FRELIMO kept it up, shooting furiously, taking turns, it seemed, until the dummy was full of holes and its stuffing drooped out. When FRELIMO grew tired of shooting, Gypsy was free to climb up and fix the camera at the top of the dipole without interference.

★ ★ ★

I'm ashamed to say that I soon settled into the atmosphere and grew to acquire the taste of this new drug. I grew used to the excitement of a 'rush', as they called an attack. I very quickly warmed to a golden tan. I listened to Radio 5 all day long, which gave me an exotic taste of the glorious life to be had in South Africa. Adverts boasted of products I had never heard of before, and the latest British and American music played all day. "All we need is a beach," I said to Gypsy as we lay on the grass at the pool.

"Doc, it's not always like this, you know. It's Murphy's Law that when we have a medic, nothing happens."

"So what does happen around here?" I asked.

"They killed seven of us on our last stint here in October – a mortar landed right in the middle of one of our pits."

Back in my room I packed shrapnel kits, re-checked the entry under 'Shrapnel wounds' in my medical book and had the packs ready.

My favourite time was night duty. I didn't mind getting up in the middle of the night; I could sleep all day anyway. The nights were humid and tropical, and the stars bathed the compound in such a magical light that I was on a different world, somewhere far, far away from earth, watching its petty affairs with de-tached amusement. Earth was that little twinkle over there, or the solar system was that flickering dot in the dark part of the sky. I strolled silently barefoot down a star-illuminated path around the farmhouse, a Coke in one hand, en-joying the time and space I had for reflection, in which to expand and grow, to see myself in perspective. I felt special, as if I were a guardian of the whole world, watching from its rooftop.

If I was on duty with someone else, I would sit by the glowing embers of the fire and chat with him about good times in 'civvy' street, about girls we knew, or wanted to know, about parties we had been to, or wanted to go to, or pretended that we had been to. We talked about what we would do, once the war was over. Slinky, for example, was going to live on the beach in South Africa and beach-comb all his life; he planned to sleep in the sand, laze around, stay tanned at all costs. But mostly we wouldn't talk. We would warm ourselves by the fire and listen to the vast si-lence around us, interrupted occasionally by the echoes of voices over in Malvernia.

We could hear faint ghost-like sounds, as if the people there were not real.

One night on guard I heard gunfire break out in the west. It was returned by troops within the country. "Odd," said Slinky. "There are no Rhodesian troops around here at all. Perhaps FRELIMO are firing at their own troops, or ZANLA is having it out with ZIPRA?" The battle went on for several minutes. We heard shouts, screams, strange echoes and dream-like voices distorted in the clear pool of the sky. Slinky was convinced they were ghosts re-enacting a war scene in the spirit world.

"Any woman back home waiting for you, Doc?"

I shook my head.

"I know there's someone. You can tell Slinky, marriage guidance counsellor *par excellence*. Other people's marriages, that is. Mine's a pile of shit."

"She's engaged to someone else."

"When is she getting married?"

"Sometime next year. But…"

"So? Go get her, you idiot. Where are your predator instincts?"

"I'm not much of a predator."

"Do you love her? You still love her?"

"No. No, I don't."

"Have you told her how you feel about her?"

"I don't feel anything for her."

"Sure, Doc. Sure, you don't."

★ ★ ★

It was near Vila Salazar in Gonakudzingwa Camp (now Gona-re-zhou Game Reserve) that the BSAP held Joshua Nkomo and his ZAPU leaders for ten years in a prison camp. He was arrested on 16 April 1964 and spent the next ten and a half years in detention. "If you hold a lizard in your hand, he will scratch to get out," Nkomo had said. "If Smith holds us back from what every man deserves, we will resist the oppressor by all means available. Even a lizard wants to be free."

During his time in detention, he studied political science, negotiated secretly with Rhodesian political officials, and was finally allowed to go into exile in Zambia, after promising to renounce violence. Apparently he was looked after quite well in the camp. Rhodesians complained that it was more of a holiday camp, that he was even being groomed for leadership, that he spent weekends strolling around Bulawayo with a nervous bodyguard, that he had it so good here that he grew fat and lazy. His colleagues, however, complained that Nkomo was deliberately overfed so that he would become grossly overweight and incapacitated.

At the same time, Robert Mugabe was also in detention in Mashonaland, where he studied for three degrees in economics, political science and government (didn't he boast later that he had degrees in violence?). In detention, he strengthened his control over ZANU and ousted Sithole as leader. But there were also rumours that it was in his ten-year detention that he was emasculated (the story goes that he contracted a syphilitic disease and had his testicles removed, making him forever bitter against whites). He was also released into exile after renouncing violence. It was then that the armed struggle began in earnest, and both Nkomo and Mugabe united as the Patriotic Front to inflict the most violent assault on the country ever waged.

★ ★ ★

"Doc, come and see what we're rigging up at the frontline." I could hear the loud squawking of feedback, and the Captain's solemn voice: "Testing 1-2-3-4".

"It's a new loudspeaker system," said Slinky. "We've had it for weeks but haven't had time to set it up."

"What's it for?" I asked, as I followed him through to the humped perimeter. Two naked men were tying trumpet speakers onto trees on either side of the bunker. The others were watching, arms folded, pointing, giving advice as to the direction of the 16-inch speakers.

"Propaganda. New idea from HQ. That's why we have Gypsy on the trip. He's not a mortar man. He's here because he can speak Pork and Beans." I still didn't understand until we ducked down into the bunker and saw the Captain speaking into a microphone. The amplified voice boomed above us from the outside speakers.

"Too bloody loud, Jones."

The Captain explained his new toy. "This way we can talk to them instead of shooting, Doc. The new policy of reconciliation and negotiation. The Rhodesian government is trying to negotiate some sort of settlement and the new phase is psychological warfare."

"Settlemunt my arse, let's slot *floppies*," quipped Gypsy.

But John was insistent. "No, listen, guys, there's a new unit called PSYAC or something – Psychological Operations Unit. Set up by an ex-combatant from Vietnam. They seek to win the enemy's hearts and minds."

"If you have them by the balls, their hearts and minds will follow," said Gypsy.

"Shut up, man, where do you get your material?"

"The Rhodesian Ministry of Propaganda," shrugged Gypsy, offended that no one laughed.

"So what do we say over the microphone?" said Slinky. "I could play some soothing guitar music for them, calm them down."

"That's actually a good idea, Slinky, for once," said John. "Not your guitar, I mean, that would really be cruel. I mean playing music." He grabbed the radio cassette. "Let's test it with this. Then we don't have to bellow. We can surprise them with speeches later." He flicked the tape button and pressed PLAY, placing the speaker next to the microphone.

"Hey, that's my Rhodesian tape," said Slinky. "I left it here while I was on radio duty to work out some songs on the guitar."

"Terrific," said the Captain. "Let's go outside and listen."

Sure enough, with its bass thumping and its tinny treble, the hissing Dolby tape was amplified and beamed across into the grey-green vegetation of Mozambique.

> We are the shumba drinkers, we drinks a dozen a day
> We are the shumba drinkers, why work when we can play?
> Ek sê, ek sê, ek sê, ek sê.

"Great music," said Gypsy. "Isn't that Mike Westcott?" The men on the mound who had mounted the speakers began dancing, singing the words and doing the actions in mock imitation of a party.

"But what are we supposed to broadcast over the Mozambique flatlands?"

The Captain frowned. "In Portuguese, a set of documents to be read out, to break down the morale of the enemy, to convince him that he is losing the war, false information about the war to misdirect and confuse him. Oh, all sorts of dirty tricks. Devised by an expert from Vietnam who is now working for our government."

★  ★  ★

Vila Salazar had always been a problem for FRELIMO. It was the entry point from where many raids had taken place into Mozambique by the white Rhodesians. Mapai, a ZANLA base, had been attacked dozens of times, and Selous Scouts and other infiltrators had stolen FRELIMO uniforms, vehicles and had taken their role.

Mugabe's HQ was in Mozambique, and ZANLA was a pain in the arse for FRELIMO. A state of war existed between the two countries, and acts of aggression had continually been perpetrated on Mozambique: blowing up bridges, supply lines, destroying infrastructure, funding and fuelling a resistance movement (RENAMO) to destabilise and overthrow the FRELIMO government, all by the bloody Rhodesians. They were troublemakers, real shit stirrers. But ZANLA was, of course, the root problem. FRELIMO had at first insisted that they be kept contained in camps, and their weapons held by FRELIMO until they were to leave the country and cross into Rhodesia, but an increasingly arrogant leadership had arisen. Mozambique, meanwhile, was overrun with Rhodesians in hot pursuit, or engaged in what they called External Operations.

A typical raid would consist of a small clandestine force (white and black Rhodesians dressed as FRELIMO soldiers, in FRELIMO vehicles, speaking Portuguese) crossing the border at Gona-re-zhou, and following the rail line to Jorge Do Limpopo, destroying all ZANLA camps and installations along the route, then turning west to Mapai to destroy ZANLA camps in the area. The Rhodesian Air Force would be used only in the event of an emergency. They would sometimes be backed up by heliborne assault, or a Hawker Hunter airstrike, but often the raid would occur with only a few men, called a 'Flying Column'. Once a 'Flying Column' of 110 men was supported by the 81 mm mortar platoon from Vila Salazar. Mozambique complained that the raids were often focused less on ZANLA kills than, for example, on the destruction of the entire Mozambique railway in the Gaza Province, because (it was claimed by the Rhodesians) ZANLA had been transporting their equipment and stores to the Rhodesian border, and the destruction or capture of a large number of FRELIMO military vehicles (again claimed by the Rhodesians to have been used to ferry ZANLA troops to the border).

# CHAPTER SEVENTEEN

# IT'S A LONG WAY TO MUKUMBURA

After the war, in its first assessment of war damage, the Zimbabwe government estimated that there were over a million antipersonnel mines still buried somewhere in its soil. In the Sango area (Vila Salazar), in an area of only 50 square kilometres, there were more than 100,000. Rhodesia wanted to make sure that its borders were secure. Vila Salazar wanted to make sure that we were not attacked in our beds, or while we were swimming in our pool, or eating *boerewors* around the campfire singing 'Home on the *Kopje*'.

And I was steadily growing lax. I was becoming one of these invincible, flippant superheroes. Every night, starlight drenched me with its magical potion and began the chemical change in my personality. No longer was I a yes-boy, or a meek Christian sheep. I bathed in the laid-back superiority of 2 RR Mortar Platoon, grateful to them for making me visible. Here no one 'pulled rank'. We were all in the same boat. My duties as a medic were minimal, because no one did anything to get hurt. The only major complaint was a hangover, called 'bubble-eyes', which I cured with Panadol, saline drip and a shot of vitamin B complex. I began to feel as invulnerable as they did, and my rifle lay where I had left it after the first 'rev'.

And what of Bianca? Was she in the stars at night, her breath on the warm wind blowing through Mozambique, her motion in the leaves of the trees? No. The wound in my heart was healing. I was growing stronger, more real, more independent. From my comrades I was learning a wry distance, a way of seeing myself as separate from her and the world. My pain, I reasoned, was sexual deprivation. And what was sex, after all, but a banging of two sweaty bodies together? If I had slept with her early on, I would have freed myself from a long, courtly love convention that had almost destroyed me. 'Free me!' Uriah Heep sang on the radio every day (Radio 5 was as repetitive as US top forty stations). 'Won't you free me? Free me from your spell.'

My other main responsibility was radio duty, where I had to sit in the ops room, watch Malvernia on the TV screen, and listen to the army radio one hour a day. I listened to the war activity around me with awe. Although we ourselves had little to report, Vila Salazar was respected and always had priority over the airwaves. Our call sign was 74, but we never had anything to say: NTR, nothing to report. But what happened around us was frightening.

"Contact, contact," a stick radioed into base. "5 ZANLA CTs engaged fire."

"Confirm 5 CTs, Sunray?"

"Affirmative, request fire fighters."

"Unavailable, shoot it out, do not pursue. Do you copy?"

"Copied, but hot pursuit requested. We are already in enemy territory."

"Shit! OK. But you're on your own. Good luck. Over and out."

"Nyala, come in. Do you read?"

"Roger."

"Zapped them. Two dead, others fled."

"Any friendly casualties?"

"Negative, over. Curfew breakers, *maningi*."

"Roger, out."

CTs, I had to remind myself, were Communist Terrorists. Friendly casualties were Rhodesian troops killed, and curfew breakers were civilians caught in crossfire. To neutralise, of course, meant to kill; to apprehend meant to torture and then kill. Hot pursuit was the term used to justify crossing international borders, when the enemy engaged in contacts in Rhodesia, then fled back into Mozambique. The Rhodesians allowed themselves the right to chase the insurgents back into neighbouring states, violating international law.

Contact, contact, we have contact. To me, it sounded mystical, science-fictional. I would listen in awe to this engagement with the invisible enemy all around us, while we sat safe and secure, our egos inflating and growing fat with heroism, watching the country deteriorate around us.

A week, two weeks, three weeks, a month in this paradise and I was brown, healthy, bearded and looking like a surfer. I was content to stay at the farmhouse day after day, learning to play Slinky's tricky guitar techniques. ("It's the only way I can get women," he told me. "I'm so bloody ugly.") With only four short months to go, I would be out of the army in July. And I knew what I would do. Comb the Natal beaches. Play in a rock band. Meet up with Buddha at university and study for a Bugger All degree. But after six weeks, the radio crackled into life with our call-sign and announced that a medic would be sent with the next ration run to replace me. I had done my time. I went straight to the Captain.

"No, Paul, sorry. We don't control the medics. That's all done from Bulawayo. Your boss wants you back." I packed bitterly, pulling on my hated denims, shirt and boots. I didn't even fit the pants any more – the belt was too tight. Why couldn't I spend my last few months here?

The driver of the 4.5 revved impatiently for me at the open gate. On it were Gypsy, Slinky and the Captain, who had come to escort me and to collect rations. Gypsy had wound ammunition round his naked chest and stood with the MAG on top of the cab, a bandanna round his head. The other MAGs pointed outward.

"You're all coming to see me off?" I asked, hoisting up the pannier.

"Make sure we get our correct rations," said Gypsy.

John snorted. "If we did, we'd starve. And we've got to approve of the new medic. If we don't like him, we send him back."

"I wish you would," I said. "I'd give anything to stay here."

"Doc, you're crazy. We've had a quiet few weeks, but if you had been here just before…"

"We like him crazy," said Gypsy.

I squinted up at the dipole as we drove outside the perimeter. The dummy was still tied to the flagpole, and spun leisurely in the breeze, the stuffing in its head spilled out onto the metal frame. I stared out at the hostile terrain the road followed, snaking through demarcated and ploughed land-mine fields, then sidling along the railway line as far as I could see. The Captain pointed at the toothless railway line and the holes and mounds of earth beside it.

"As you can see, the railway's not used any more. This used to be a thriving little border post with a direct rail link to Lorenço Marques – what do they call it now?"

"Maputo," said Gypsy. "The great whore."

"That was in the good old days. When FRELIMO took over, they kept our rolling stock, attacked the border post, and the Customs guards scarpered. There were train ambushes, so we figured, what the hell…"

"It was a hell-hole when we set up base here, Doc," said Gypsy.

"You guys did it?"

"Cock your weapon, Doc. You're getting slack, we're not in Vilas now."

"Sorry." I cocked it and pointed it out into the bushes that whizzed past uncomfortably fast.

"We set it up in stages over the years. The engineers came and laid the minefield first, but we were the ones who schlepped all the railway sleepers to the compound. We dug all those shell-scrapes and bunkers. We set up the possie like it is now. It's home."

"Pity when the war's over. I feel sorry for the poor buggers trying to straighten this whole thing out. Don't think the railway will ever run again…"

I stared back at the dipole, now an almost indistinguishable arrow above the trees. The truck had veered west, then turned sharply east again, and was now heading in the direction of Nyala, our nearest rendezvous point. When the war's over, I echoed in my mind. I couldn't imagine it being over; it had been waging for most of my life. "So why," I asked, "do they keep firing mortars all the time, if we're so dug in? What does it achieve?"

The Captain laughed. "War, Doc, what does it achieve? Fuck all."

Gypsy objected. "Bullshit. We're here to fight for our country, to stand up for what we believe in. You don't just let life happen to you. If some murderer comes in to attack you in your house, you fight back. You assert yourself, you don't throw your hands up in the air and say 'what does it achieve?'"

The yellow dirt road branched into two, and the truck veered at full speed down a smaller, overgrown lane, then spun around and stopped dead in its tracks. The dust caught up with us and covered us.

"What's wrong? Are we here already?"

"Just a quick detour, Doc. The pump…" He pointed with his rifle towards a muddy pond. "The water supply generator is buggered."

Slinky and I stayed on the truck on guard while the others leaped off to fix the generator. The 'lake', as they called this ten-acre-square muddy swamp, had been a dam, an old farm water supply, I guessed, used to supply the Vila Salazar reservoir. Two orange pipes led out of a small concrete block on the water's edge up to the railway track.

We watched them sweat in the midday heat for ten long minutes until, with a shout of triumph from the Captain, the motor chugged into life again. Slinky pulled on my arm, and whispered so close to my face that his moustache tickled my cheek. "How would you like fish for supper, Doc?"

"I'm leaving, remember?"

"Oh, yeah. Well, watch this anyway." He shot furtive glances at the others while their backs were turned and pulled a grenade from his pack. "Want to throw it, Doc?" I shook my head at the grey pineapple. He pulled the pin with his teeth, stood up and flung it hard into the centre of the lake. The explosion was muffled by the water but was nevertheless astounding. The sound cracked and grumbled in the bushes like a thunderclap. The lake rippled and buckled.

"What the fuck?" shouted the Captain, swivelling round to reach for his rifle.

"It's OK, boss, just a little fishing." He turned to me. "Dead fish will pop up to the surface and we just have to pick them up."

The others ran back to the truck. "Warn us, Slinky, you little runt," said the Captain. "We thought we were being attacked."

Slinky laughed loudly, and Gypsy grinned too, showing his rotten teeth. "I like giving you guys a *skrik*." But no fish rose to the surface. Debris, weeds, yes, but no fish. "Shit," said Slinky, "I think I must have got them all last time."

"Target practice," yelled the Captain suddenly, pointing to a little cottage at the other side of the lake, probably where the keeper who maintained the pump once stayed. The three men aimed and fired. A window shattered.

"Come on, Doc."

I lifted my rifle and aimed at the chimney, but the bullet went whizzing high in the trees. I had to remember that my rifle pulled upwards and a little to the left. I tried again. This time, I hit the wall, but I wasn't sure as they were all firing at once. It was like golf: I had to correct my slice. After carefully shooting twenty rounds, I was hitting the door with accuracy. But when Slinky rattled the MAG on automatic over the surface of the lake, tripping bullets across the water, the Captain ordered us to stop. "Enough, guys, we'd better go meet the lizard brigade. They'll be shitting themselves, waiting at Nyala for us."

So with renewed gusto, we reloaded our weapons and drove back onto the main dirt road at the reckless, helter-skelter speed I was finding exhilarating. Whatever it was that had grown in me in Vila Salazar, I had to carry it back with me.

But at the rendezvous point there was no truck waiting for us.

"The buggers are late."

"Correction. We are late. Maybe they gave up on us?"

"Naah."

We waited in the sun, listening to the silence of the bush around us. "Something's wrong, Boss. They radioed their departure hours ago."

"OK," yelled the Captain. "Let's go." He waved the truck forward. We were going to find them.

★ ★ ★

"Stop the truck. Get down. Debus." The truck slid to the left, because we were going way too fast. Before it stopped, John leaped off the side into the bushes, holding his rifle high in the air as he tumbled and rolled. Slinky, the driver, skidded the truck skilfully to a halt, leaped out of the cab and dived under the chassis.

Gypsy and I looked at each other in a split second of puzzlement before we were also on the ground, crawling for cover in the low thorn bushes.

I burrowed my way into an acacia bush and poked my rifle through at the road, as I saw the others doing. The heat pressed down on me; my heart beat loudly. Then I saw why we had stopped. A 4.5 had overturned on the side of the road facing us, its front wheels gone, its axle sitting in a blackened crater, which was still smoking. I didn't have to think too long to figure it out. The supply truck had hit a land mine. As it was the usual practice of the guerrillas to lie in wait, then pick off the victims of land-mine attack and steal the provisions, they could be still here. We could not simply investigate; we had to clear the area first. It looked as if it had happened within the hour, so it was very likely that if any insurgents had been waiting for this event, they would still be in the area, watching like us from the cover of the acacia scrub. The Captain, with vigorous arm motions that would have attracted the attention of anyone within a five-kilometre radius, signalled for us do a '360'. We crawled through the bush in a complete circle around the truck, looking for a convenient place the guerrillas could be hiding. I leopard-crawled noisily in the dust. The bush was scrub with thorn trees and small *msasa* trees. It was sparse enough to see that no one could hide here.

"OK. All clear." Slinky kept guard on the truck and Gypsy crouched in the bushes, while John and I investigated. Provisions were scattered all over the road and in the bushes. The boxes must have been flung high in the air to land so far away. But I was more interested in the live cargo. One HQ soldier had been thrown clear off the back of the truck with the boxes and limped to us gratefully.

"Just sprained a foot, I think," he said.

"How many are there of you?"

"Four. One driver, one medic, two storesmen."

"See why you don't wear a safety belt in a land-mine area?" said the Captain. He pointed to a groaning soldier stuck under the truck's side, trapped in his safety belt. He was bloated and swollen, his circulation cut off. "Damn, Doc, get busy. Let us know what to do."

"First, I want to check the others." I opened the cab door to find the driver unconscious at the wheel, knocked out on the shattered windscreen. But his pulse was fine and he was breathing normally. I checked for broken bones, then pulled him out. Gypsy stepped out of the bush and helped me lay him on the road. The CQ who had been thrown clear took off his boot and dressed his own wounds with a kit I threw him so that I could attend to the most serious – the man under the side of the truck.

"He's trapped tight. We can't pull him out, eh, Doc?"

"No." The man was still alive, blinking in terror and pain. His arms were puffy white balloons, his face distended, and he was becoming less human every moment. What could I do? If I lifted the truck, he might survive, but the chances were minimal. The shock would kill him when his circulation returned. But what else could we do? We heaved and rocked the truck and lifted it an inch, then it dropped again. Its full weight was on him.

"Slinky, Gypsy, we need you, quick." The CQ guy came too, and we all pulled and tugged and panted. But it was no use. The soldier was turning blue before our eyes, and was being slowly chopped in two. Mercifully, he was now unconscious. His mouth dribbled, his eyes slowly closed and the gurgle I had been told to recognise as the death rattle issued from the depths of his being.

"OK, OK, he's gone. It's OK," I said before I knew what I was saying.

"Where's the other soldier?" said John to the CQ guy. "You said there were four."

"Storesman!" called the CQ guy. We searched under each wheel, then looked in the bushes to see if he had been flung far, injured and unconscious, but there was no sign of him.

"Is he the medic?"

The CQ pointed solemnly to the blue, ballooned arms and head of the dead man. "He's the medic." So much for my replacement. I threw a blanket from the cab over him.

"Storesman, where the hell are you?" screamed the CQ soldier.

"Shut up," cautioned the Captain. "This is a terr area, a what-you-call-it, liberated area. They live here – they're probably watching us now, waiting to attack."

"But where could he be?" Then the thought dawned on me. Abducted by terrorists? Was that possible? Had they beaten us to it?

"He probably ran in a panic as soon as the land mine hit," soothed the Captain. "His rifle's not here. That's what I would have done, knowing that the terrs might be lying in wait for me. I would run for cover, to get as much distance between me and them."

"He can't be on the main road – not east at least – we've just come that way."

"Then maybe he tried to walk back west to Nyala. We must spread out further and search. He can't have gone far."

Slinky didn't like being stationary for such a long time in the silence of the bush. He lit a cigarette and took long hard drags from it, passing it to Gypsy. "Why didn't we bring the *zol*?" he said. We moved the unconscious driver onto the back of the truck and the HQ soldier hoisted himself into the cab. "We can't leave these two here. I'm for going back, getting a search party, dropping them off…"

"We won't be long, just a quick 360 again…"

In the split second that it takes for the brain to register external stimuli, I knew we were being attacked. Hot bullets cracked over us, others thundered into the ground, dusting us, and others twanged into the truck. We were unprepared. Gypsy was still crouched over the unconscious driver, the rest of us exposed against the sky on the truck, discussing what to do. I pushed myself over the edge of the truck and dived onto the ground. But as I didn't know where the bullets were coming from, I didn't know which side to hide behind. By the time John was pointing wildly into the thicket on a short rise ahead of the truck, I was already firing back. Blind anger rose in my throat as bullets whizzed past, popping over my head, thudding, snapping, crackling – bullets that I realised (with full consciousness for the first time) could kill me in seconds. The MAG began to fire from the truck and I looked up to see Gypsy bravely (or stupidly) standing to reach its mounting on the cab. He fired wildly, around and around, covering the whole countryside with tracers.

"The copse," yelled the Captain, jerking his rifle onto automatic. I was firing one round at a time, fearing that I would run out. Slinky was under the truck, letting rip with all the four-letter words he knew, and taking pot shots. I saw running figures, flashes from AK muzzles, shadows which kept running as I pumped bullets into them. They were moving in all directions. Ghosts are unkillable, I thought wildly. Is that why they don't stop when I shoot at them?

"They're running," I yelled.

"They've stopped firing." I saw figures scattering. I counted three, four, five, one split into two…

"There are dozens of them," yelled Slinky, firing on automatic and expending a whole magazine in seconds. But the MAG halted its chugging fire. Did Gypsy have a stoppage? If so, we were done for.

"Hold your fire." Gypsy stood high on the cab and craned his neck. I stood cautiously, staring and trying to hear beyond the ringing in my ears. I shook off hot casings from the Captain's rifle all over my jacket. The figures were now dancing around the woods in shadow, spinning around. I blinked my eyes.

"They're still there. Down!" But the Captain motioned me to stand. "Doc, there's nothing there." I looked again and saw nothing. The ghosts were a product of my dizzy, adrenalin-drenched mind.

"Careful, guys, I don't know if we got them or they're just bluffing, or have retreated to a better vantage point."

I blinked to get rid of the dancing ghosts in my retina.

"I got one – I saw him go down," squeaked Gypsy.

"Gypsy, Doc, give us covering fire. Slinky and I will skirmish round to the killing ground and check it out. Doc, cover me on the right, Gypsy to the left. Doc, stay here and guard the wounded."

"Is everyone OK?" I yelled, putting in my bit as a medic.

"Sharp, china." Even the HQ man was OK. He had lain low in the truck, snuggling up to the unconscious driver.

"Go!" John and Slinky ran, dived, leopard-crawled round in a pincer movement, while Gypsy and I fired sporadic bursts to the left and right as they approached the copse.

"Oh, my God," yelled John. "Cease your fire, you blokes, come and look." We walked cautiously towards him, expecting to see a thousand dead guerrillas, AKs scattered in the woods, and wounded enemy combatants ready to roll over and set off grenades as we approached. I was still wary of an ambush from the left and right, and kept looking for the illusive figures out of the corner of my eyes, trying to distinguish them from the ghosts that were playing tricks, darting into bushes and up into the sky. But they were vanquished when we saw the Captain standing over a dead body.

It was not a guerrilla, a terrorist, an insurgent, an enemy combatant, a freedom fighter, a gook, a terr or a floppy. It was a white, eighteen-year-old Rhodesian soldier, in uniform, in the HQ colours of Operation Repulse, lying prostrate, a rifle in his hand. He was a bloody mess of bone, blood and flesh. He had been shot up so much that I couldn't see his face. Bullets had hacked his legs and arms, ripped apart his stomach so that the intestines and other shapeless organs were exposed, gutted his chest and shattered his right shoulder. His mouth was a blood sack, one eye was gone, and stuffing burst out everywhere. Blood gushed quietly from an artery in his right leg.

Gypsy swore. "Bloody terrs. They shot him up bad. And we didn't even get one of them." I tried to picture it. They had taken him as a hostage, fired at us, retreated, killed him. But the Captain shook his head.

"There were no terrs here."

The shadows fled. All those fleeing figures, running and diving and leaping? I had seen them. Honest, I had seen them.

"Why did he shoot at us?" said Slinky, as he walked up to us. "Why did he bloody well shoot at us? How were we to know?"

I crouched by the face. The soldier was dead, beyond any help. But there was a familiarity about him, the buck teeth, the rabbit posture. A scream shot up from my queasy stomach. "Gamma," I yelled. "It's Gamma."

"We don't know who he is... was," squeaked the HQ who had hobbled across with Slinky. "He was jittery all the way, kept stuttering about attacks and terrs. A strange guy. Full of bravado, but very scared."

I was sure it was Gamma. The face was contorted in death and so bloody that I would need to wipe his face and stitch the slack jaw together before I could tell. But the spinning dread in my stomach convinced me. "I think I knew this guy. He was at school with me, he was... in training with me, he... what the hell did we do?" The sky was asking the question, pressing it down on me. We all pleaded our excuses, loudly.

"He was firing at us," said Gypsy indignantly. "I thought he was a dozen terrs."

"We panicked," I said. "We just fired back..."

"He was pumping our truck full of lead," said Gypsy, appealing to us all as witnesses. "The little bugger, was he mad? Did he think we were terrs?"

The HQ guy nodded. "We kept talking all the way about land mines, about how the terrs come back and kill off the survivors."

I could see him when the land mine hit, panic-stricken, with a poor view of reality, blinded by fear, hardened with a new bravado that pushed beyond reason and humanity. When he was flung off the back of the truck, his confused impulses, his poor perception and his misconstrued bravado took over. He was running for cover, hearing the groans of the dying medic. Then he saw a group of men – brown men in shorts and bandannas, not Rhodesian soldiers – carrying prisoners away. He fired blindly in panic.

"Chalk up another successful contact," muttered the Captain. Gypsy laughed, trying to ignore the heavy blue sky that was pushing us down. "How are we going to report this?"

The Captain laughed too. "Just tell the truth, Gypsy. Land mine kills one, injures two. We casevac the wounded, retreat under enemy fire, we retaliate, enemy kills one HQ personnel in firefight. Is that clear?"

We all nodded. I stood and tried to push the image of the dead body out of my mind. Gamma. Peter Burnett. That frail human being we had laughed at all through school and who had skirted the outer frame of our vision, haunting us with the thought that perhaps we were like him, but making us grateful that he could become the decoy for our fears and insecurities.

"We all put a bullet in that guy. No use trying to explain to HQ," said Gypsy. "Board of enquiry we don't need."

"We can't blame ourselves," said Slinky kindly to me, seeing my distress. "We can't feel guilty about it." The four men began to walk down the knoll back to the truck. I stared back at the corpse. "What about his body? Aren't we going to…?"

"We retreated under enemy fire, Doc. How could we pick up the body? If anyone else wants to come and pick him up and the dead medic, he's welcome."

I walked slowly back with them, unable to think clearly. I felt like they did. We didn't want to touch this body; we didn't want to claim him as our own. And if we wanted to stick by our story, we would have to leave the dead behind.

The Captain was warming to his new version of the truth. "And of course we lifted the supplies before the attack. No, no, better still, the terrs took the rations. We'll requisition more." Gypsy was already hoisting boxes of provisions onto the truck. I heaved a medical pannier onto the truck too, and placed it next to mine.

We sped back to Vila Salazar at full speed, trailing behind clouds of thick dust over the nightmare scene until it was a wisp that dissipated in the air and we could shake it off. The sight of the dipole and the dummy was a consolation. I was returning to my sanctuary. I hadn't thought I would see this place again. But my heart couldn't soar; it dragged heavily behind me in the dirt.

"Hey, Doc's back. How did you wangle it?" I was cheered as the hero as I handed down the provisions. Gypsy told The Story, an heroic tale of bravado. The Captain reported the incident on the radio.

"That'll teach them a lesson to try to replace our Doc," said the red-faced man. "Let's see what they do now."

I laid the unconscious driver in a back bedroom of the house to recover and placed the bewildered HQ newcomer in charge of him. He was terrified that he had been brought to Vila Salazar, of all places. I had a closer look at the sprained ankle, bandaged it tightly, smiled weakly as the man looked in terror at all the bullet holes and craters within the perimeter. "Don't worry, it's safe as houses." I asked him to watch over the driver and call if he woke up, then trotted off to join the celebrations that accompanied every ration run.

"Double rations. Long Life milk from South Africa. How did we get all this?"

"We didn't," said the Captain sadly. "The terrs got all of it, so we have to do without. We'll have to order more." 2 RR Mortar Platoon cheered and formed a line to pass the crates of beer, food cans, potatoes, meat and vegetables to the kitchen, where the black cook was smiling and directing operations.

"I think we can have a *braai* tonight," announced John, "if you buggers go and collect wood outside the perimeter. And we'll make our two guests welcome."

Our dark secret was safe. But if you looked closely enough, you could see Gypsy nodding at Slinky too often, or John clapping me on the back with too much gusto, and the three of us throwing furtive glances at the dark night outside the perimeter. I tried hard not to think of the cold, mutilated body of a schoolmate, abandoned in the acacia scrub for the jackals and hyenas to sniff and paw and tear apart.

Meanwhile, a letter had arrived for me, from Beitbridge. I didn't know anyone in Beitbridge, but then I recognised my father's steady handwriting. He was patrolling the roads to the border. How was I? He hadn't told mum about Vila Salazar – she would go berserk if she knew – so he told her I was merely on a bush exercise in the Matopas and couldn't write for a few weeks. But he was not doing too well. Two of his colleagues had been *donnered* right next to him. Without a medic, they had not been able to save the men. Couldn't I request a transfer? He was thirsty all day, and now drank beers like a sailor. It was a hopeless cause, he added (between the censored lines), but he was enjoying it. The best time of his life. But what they were doing there, he didn't know. How was I? Safe? If he had known that his only son's life was at risk, he would have sent him away. Nothing is worth dying for. He'd come to realise that. He didn't want to bury his son in this soil. And if we ever got out of this bloody war, we would do things differently.

I wanted to return to the invincible mood of the last few weeks, but for the next few days I developed a terrible case of D&V, or what was commonly called 'the shits'.

The cause was food poisoning, or tick-bite, or stomach bug, or stress (it had happened to many during basic training), or whatever. I took Lomotil, sulphaguanadine, Kaolin and morphine, but nothing worked. My bravado had been seriously damaged. My exhilaration had turned to a clenched fist in my stomach, the aggression had whimpered off into a corner of my being. Whatever had rubbed off on me was now gone.

Gamma, may you rest in peace. I certainly was not able to. I changed magazines and cleaned my rifle, because the firing rod was caked with carbon. It was no longer an inert piece of metal, but a weapon that had shot at a human being, and had possibly killed him. Even worse, it was not just any human being, but a friend, a school classmate. Perhaps Gamma had seen ghosts too, AKS, terr targets. They had run at him, and being well trained not to think but to act on impulse, he had fired at them. What were we all doing, thousands of us Gammas, all with tailor-made realities which enabled us to see the enemy? I began to see the shape of my Rhodesianness, of my power and stupidity. I thought of the fleeing terr figures in the forests, my enthusiastic shooting, the festivity of the bullets. I trembled at my poor perception of reality.

As it turned out, the joke was on me. The soldier we had shot in the woods was not Gamma. Three years after the war, I went to see a British farce at REPS theatre in Harare, Zimbabwe. During the intermission, a gawky twenty-two-year-old tapped me on the shoulder and shook my hand vigorously. "Paul?"

"Ga... Peter?"

I stared at this ghost for several minutes before I could believe the truth, and then, to his bewildered embarrassment, embraced this Christ figure. Gamma had survived the war. He had come through unscathed, or at least less damaged than the rest of us, or maybe only as damaged as he had gone into it. But he was alive.

★ ★ ★

That evening, as if it wanted to prove itself to me, Vila Salazar began to live up to its reputation and return to its former status as the legendary centre of the war.

The *braai* took place at the cracked pool, which was now almost empty. We used the crater next to it to stockpile wood and at sunset a crackling bonfire was blazing. We sat in a circle around it, warming ourselves, drinking beers.

The driver had regained consciousness, so our two guests were given a warm welcome. Huge steaks and *boerewors* sizzled on an enormous grid on the fire and Slinky brought out his guitar, urging us all to sing to the tune of Tipperary, the Rhodesian adaptation:

> *It's a long way to Mukumbura, it's a long way to jol*
> *It's a long way from your home town*
> *But you can have yourselves a ball, with your muckers...*

"Rhodesia is our only home," yelled John, with drunken, glazed eyes. "We married here and our parents are here." For a wife, he held a *Playboy* centrefold to himself and grinned at an imaginary audience. He pointed to the derelict farmhouse. "We're buying our own home and bringing up a young family. Why should we give this all up?" He pointed to all of us.

"We're here to stay," said Gypsy in a high-pitched voice. "That's why we're going to have a party that can safeguard our future." John thrust his stomach forward and pointed at his protruding beer-*boep*. "Safeguard your future, vote for the Rhodesian Front."

The party was well under way in the dark night, when a mortar exploded outside the back perimeter. Only two people this time ran for cover: the two newcomers. "Trust FRELIMO," groaned Slinky, "just when we're starting to enjoy ourselves. What do they think this is, a bloody war or something?"

"Come to Vilas and get bombed," slurred the red-faced man, saluting the night with his beer bottle. Another mortar hit. "They can hear the singing." I looked up in alarm, knowing how much sound carried. Our smoke and fire-light was also a beacon in the dark night. "Can smell the food too, poor starved communist buggers," said Gypsy. "Hey, come on, guys, my steak's not done yet, where're you going?"

The men had ditched their food and were running eagerly to the ops room, following the Captain. When we were all tightly packed inside the shelter, he pounced on the microphone. We heard the speakers click loudly. Everyone was a little drunk, and our Captain, my Captain, was laughing recklessly as he switched on Slinky's tape at full volume. The song boomed out into the darkness.

Not bothering to duck for cover, the Captain led us outside again to listen.

*They can send their men to murder*
*They can shout their words of hate*
*But the cost of keeping this land free*
*Will never be too great*
*We will stand tall in the sunshine*
*The truth upon our side*
*And if we have to go alone*
*We'll go alone with pride.*

*'Cause we're all Rhodesians*
*And we'll fight through thick and thin*
*We'll keep our land a free land*
*Stop the enemy coming in*
*We'll keep them north of the Zambezi*
*Till that river's running dry*
*And this mighty land will prosper*
*For Rhodesians never die.*

More mortars and small arms fire answered our provocation. They had heard us. "A real rev," yelled Slinky, delighted. "Man your stations."

I ran for cover. Bullets zinged into buildings, sang through the grass, clanked into the water tower and roofs. I ran low, following the mortar men into their front bunker. This time I didn't want to sit alone. But I guided the two frightened HQ guys to my bunker behind the farmhouse and they gratefully dived into it.

"FRELIMO, *seus cambroes, oicao musica que e fasista e capitalista*," shouted Gypsy into the microphone.

"Unprovoked attack," reported the Captain, sitting comfortably in the control seat of the ops room. "Request permission to retaliate, over?"

Immediate response. "74, copied, go ahead, Sunray Major gives go ahead."

"Roger, copied, over and out," said the Captain with unrestrained glee.

The bullets and mortars were coming thick and fast. I listened to the noises and explosions and the muffled music playing through it. Bullets ricocheted off the speakers, through the trees.

"Hope everyone is underground. We're going for it. Mortar Pit One, OK?" First, the captain ordered a smoke bomb so that he could see where he was shooting. On the TV screen I watched it land. "OK, One, lower 20 degrees. Number Two, you're accurate. Three, adjust left…"

The idea of the TV was clear now. We could see exactly where we hit and identify the firing positions of FRELIMO by the tell-tale puff of smoke in the bushes. But as soon as we fixed their position and trained the mortar tube on the spot, they would move. Smoke bombs soon covered the whole town of Malvernia in a hot, white mist. A bush fire had started behind the town, one of our first wild shots.

"Now high explosive," announced John. I heard the bombs land, and saw the explosions, but did not know if they were on target.

"They're in the bloody customs house," yelled Gypsy, pulling on John's shoulder. I craned to see as the red-faced man zoomed in the camera.

"Customs house, 30 degrees left," announced the Captain. I saw a flag fluttering as they homed in close to the front entrance. FRELIMO troops were scurrying in and out with boxes. It looked to me as if shovels were flying up and down at double speed.

"Too late for that," grinned Gypsy. The first mortars went wide of the house, but then one hit. The TV screen was clouded and when it cleared, the building was a wreck, a pile of rubble, with no FRELIMO in sight.

I was supposed to feel exultant, but I kept seeing the image of Gamma's mutilated corpse in front of me. FRELIMO soldiers must be lying on the ground like that by now. Technological warfare triumphs when we can no longer see our enemy face to face, so he does not have blood, guts, a family back home. We can play video games and watch their deaths on a TV monitor, feeling triumphant, the satisfaction of a good kill, all the things American movies have bred into us.

"We gottem," screamed John. "Well done, guys. Where else?" He scanned the ground with the video.

"What's the idea?" I asked, trying to sound merely inquisitive about war strategy. "They can't run over here, we can't gain any ground, so what's the point of attacking, shooting all these mortars?"

Slinky nodded. "These mortars cost a hundred dollars apiece, at least. We're just burning money here, Doc, for the hell of it. It makes us feel good."

Gypsy shook his head. "We can't think of money where sovereignty is at stake. That's what this is all about. National sovereignty. And it's simple, Doc. They attack us, we retaliate. It's a matter of honour."

"We want Mozambique," said John. "If we occupy LM we could have beaches, tropical paradise, prawns…"

A flash lit up the church and through a puff of smoke, I could see the steeple on top. As we zoomed in, we saw dark figures scurrying into the building. Were they real? The Captain focused, gave the co-ordinates of the church.

"Bull's eye, Rowan, right on the steeple." The cross had fallen off, but the church was somehow still standing, until one wall slid down and the roof followed in slow motion. I closed my eyes. My first impulse was to cheer, smile and clap the TV bombers on the back, as John and Gypsy were doing; my second impulse was to shout "No!" and to pull out all the plugs I could find.

"Shit."

I opened my eyes. The TV screen had gone blank.

"They've hit the video camera."

"No way, how could they do that?"

"Fluke," growled the Captain. "Now we're firing blind, like they are."

The firing at us continued unabated – mortars, RPGs, machine-gun fire. FRE-LIMO were giving it all they could give. Why? It seemed like a rage, a resentment against the Rhodesians rather than a planned attack. They knew this 2 RR Mortar Platoon was safe. Perhaps that was why. It was a battering of fists against an iron door.

"Gypsy, want to go and fix the monitor?"

"Not on your life."

"Any other volunteers?"

Four men walked into the bunker, from Mortar Pit Number Three.

Their faces were covered with brown, green and black camouflage cream. Their grinning white teeth and eyes made them look ghoulish. "Hey, why no more shoot-shoot, boss?"

"We've got a plan, boss."

"Spit it out."

"We sneak round the town in radio contact, tell you where to fire."

"No way, too dangerous. Remember last time that happened?"

"Come on, boss."

He shook his head. "Last time the radio wiped out. We didn't know where you guys were, we could have been firing at you. And you got up to a lot of mischief too."

"Come on, boss, we'll be back here around midnight. We'll be safe."

"No way. We stop the attack. We can't waste bombs. You guys stay put." The four camouflaged soldiers trooped out of the bunker, grumbling. "Bloody idiots," said John. "Last time they were caught in Malvernia between FRELIMO and friendly fire. Didn't know where they were. They think they're Scouts, acting like that. They're mortar men."

The TV screen was silent, grey, the mortars had ceased firing and the FRELIMO fire was dwindling too. "No fun shooting unless someone shoots back at you," explained Slinky. "Perhaps they think it's a supper break?"

"Perhaps we should play some Portuguese music, to calm them down. They didn't seem to like 'Rhodesians Never Die'."

The Captain yawned. "OK, guys, back to the beers."

We waited for the small arms fire to cease, and sat around the campfire. The embers were still glowing red, and some blackened steaks were still smoking. Gypsy rescued his, and offered a new round of drinks. We had settled into the silence when the red-faced man came scampering up to us with a portable radio, which he handed to the Captain.

"74, this is Lemon Scouts, come in, over."

"Shit, they've gone into Malvernia," shouted the Captain. "The war's over, you guys, come back." But there was no reply.

Only the next morning could we survey the damage. The other end of the house had been hit with a mortar, and the roof had caved in on one of the bedrooms. Fresh bullet holes were everywhere, and the water tank had sprung new leaks. And, as we suspected, the video camera at the top of the dipole had been smashed by a bullet and lay shattered on the ground below.

"No more revs until we get that fixed."

We requested supplies on the radio and this was when we got the bad news. The plan from base was that the entire platoon, me included, would be replaced at the end of the week, when new equipment would arrive. There was a law, apparently, that you couldn't spend more than two months at a time at Vila Salazar. Still, leaving didn't feel as bad as the first time; the entire platoon was leaving too. The two HQ personnel would return with us to JOC Repulse. Base also informed us that the dead soldiers had been picked up at the ambush site, identified and buried, and we were congratulated on our handling of the affair.

The Lemon Scouts returned from Mozambique in the late morning. John didn't speak to them as they walked in single file, dirty, with streaking black paint sweating down their faces and legs, each of them looking cheerful and rebellious, and each itching to tell of their adventures. "Come on, boss, we brought you something."

John didn't look up from the *Playboy* he was reading on the veranda. They threw a brown leather bag at his feet, and trooped off to shower in the office block. Soon everyone was crowding around the Captain, who still refused to look up. We wanted to see what cargo they had brought back from the badlands. Once he was sure the four were out of sight and in the showers, he pounced on the bag and poured the contents on the red stone veranda. "Buggers." But his eyes lit up as he sifted through the papers. I saw lists of names, maps, notes and official letterhead correspondence typed in uneven typescript.

"What is all this? Must have sneaked right into FRELIMO Command to get this. And these?" He picked up a wad of unopened envelopes, with names and addresses on them. "The cunts have stolen their mail," he roared. "Gypsy, get your Portuguese arse over here, we need a translator."

The four 'scouts' trooped up to the veranda, shiny clean and beaming with triumph. The Captain eyed them coldly. "You're on a charge, Waddington. You and your stick are in charge of the bar. Free beers all round." And he threw up the letters in the air, laughing. "Well done, guys. This is what I call a psychological war."

"The central Command was blasted, boss, completely. We just walked in, took the mail and what was on the desks and ran."

"What's so great about getting their mail?" asked Slinky.

John summoned Gypsy to the front. "Morale, information, and Gypsy here is going to find out the soldiers' names, read up on their family life, and demoralise them a little."

"Far out." Gypsy clapped and whistled. "This is what I call a war." He ripped open the first envelope, addressed to FRELIMO Command, Malvernia, and began tracing his finger over the words, moving his lips silently.

"What do they say, Gypsy?" called out Slinky. "Read them to us."

"What they are *going* to say is more to the point, fellas," he said. "I'll have them ready to read out in about an hour."

We stood on the mound, listening to Gypsy's voice in Portuguese. No one could understand what he was saying so he translated it as well for our benefit.

"Forces Requests, this is Sally Donaldson, your forces sweetheart, and this is the voice of Radio Mozambique." His voice boomed out in the hot morning sky. "Comrade Themba, here is a letter from your wife. She has been sleeping with your best friend, Miguel, who is also at the frontline in Malvernia."

"Let's hope Comrade Themba is listening, not dead. He's the commander of the mortar unit," said Gypsy aside to us. "I've doctored the letter..."

A shot pinged over our heads. "Themba," yelled Gypsy, delighted to get a response. "Comrade Themba, you hear me, you are a *cornuto*." Three more angry shots skewered the air. Was this a direct response to the words Gypsy was reading, or just a jittery reaction to the noise?

"Here's a message to Aluardo. Your wife is safe here at Vila Salazar, and so is your daughter, having a good time with the Rhodesian white soldiers. The girl goes for a dollar a time, but the wife is so ugly, she has to pay us."

A machine gun ripped a burst of automatic fire, followed by two rifle shots and then a mortar pounded the ground, overshooting our base by a mile or two.

"See if you can hit the speaker, FRELIMO. Themba, you first. First one to hit the speaker gets a night with Aluardo's wife."

"Better tell the men to get into their possies, Doc," ordered the Captain. "They're probably standing around gawking at the show."

Sure enough, as I crept out, they were standing on the mound, laughing, watching, pointing. Two cracks overhead and a thud into the adjacent building made me duck low as I passed on the message. But I was too late. The mound I was crouching behind shook, dust sprayed up into my face, and Slinky slid down the bank next to me, clutching his leg.

"Are you hit?" But he ignored me, and scrambled up onto the bank, still clutching his leg. "Are you OK?" I called to him.

"You FRELIMO bastards!" Slinky yelled, shaking his fist at the border post. Then he raised his rifle and aimed, coolly, deliberately, looking for a target.

"Down, Slinky." I tugged at his boots as bullets cracked over us and thumped in front of us. Crack and thump gives you the location of the shooter – you hear the bullet crack over you before you hear the thump, which is when it was being fired. The time between the two revealed how far the gunner was. This is what he was listening for.

"Communist pigs."

I examined his leg, fearing he had been shot, but the bullet had luckily just nicked the skin. It wasn't even bleeding.

"Aluardo!" taunted Gypsy in Portuguese, "you can do better than that!" The sound of Slinky's tape player clicking on heralded a musical interlude. "Defections to the West are now being processed. Come across and you too can listen to Western decadent music like this. *Ciao.*" Gipsy signed off, leaving the music playing. Bullets whipped past us now thick and fast.

I knew the feeling. Late at night, when you are trying to sleep and a neighbour is playing loud music, all you want to do is go out and shoot the hi-fi to death – especially if the music is John Edmond's 'Troopie Songs'.

> You may call us rebels and you may call us rogues
> We were founded by an Englishman by the name of Cecil Rhodes
> We fought for this dear land of ours and many men did die
> And we might have to fight again for this is UDI.

This song always made me think of Allan Wilson and the Shangani Patrol, those rebellious, roguish Rhodesians who tried to defend their stolen paradise, but found themselves surrounded by Matabele warriors in the 1890 rebellion, fighting to the last man as the enemy cornered and advanced on them. In a *laager* made from dead horses, they sang 'God Save the Queen' and said the Lord's Prayer, until all twelve of them were killed. So the story goes. I could imagine this community of anarchic, long-haired, bearded, music- and drug-lovers in this Vila Salazar *laager* fighting recklessly to the last man in the spirit of adventure and rebellion, drinking Lions and chanting 'Rhodesia is Our Home'. I saw my own reflection in these people, my own confines of illusion.

★ ★ ★

2 RR Mortar Platoon's two months' stint was over. It was only fitting that I left with them: I was one of them now. Each man packed his bags in slow motion, walked low to the ground, hoisted up the cargo onto the truck. They had lots of booty. Gypsy took the smashed video camera for a souvenir, but left the rags of the dummy to flap in the morning breeze. On the border fence section of the perimeter I 'found' a triangular CHENJERA: CHIMBAMBAIRA (DANGER: MINES) sign full of bullet holes from both sides. Slinky took the *Playboy* pin-ups on the living room wall. Once we were loaded up, we waited for our replacement platoon, due to arrive any minute. The general mood was that we had been cheated. We hadn't had enough of a holiday, we hadn't had enough excitement, there had been no climax or resolution.

Slinky wanted to show me around the old customs house, and Gypsy wanted to do more with the broadcasting system. John had promised more fun with the Icarus. Instead, they had to become ordinary citizens again and go back to suburbs in the city, put on suits and ties, cut their hair and beards, go to eight-to-five jobs and behave within the confines of civilisation, in families, with wives and kids. The golden hue would fade. Mine, too. But I had seen a glimpse of the future here. In a few weeks I would be out of the army and find a Vila Salazar of my own, somewhere on the coast of Natal perhaps, somewhere free and golden. The replacement platoon arrived in all its white-faced glory, full

kit and fear. These soldiers had never been here before, so 2 RR relished in its role as tour guide, pointing out the mortar craters in the ground, the latest bullet holes, the dummy up the dipole. The new Captain had proudly brought with him a new video camera. "How do we get it up there," he asked, "if, as you say, they snipe at us?"

"That's your problem," said our Captain. "We used a dummy, you try something else."

I recognised the medic by his belt and sweaty black beret with gleaming gold snake. We shook hands and I showed him his underground shelter, the MI room and the medical panniers (I had amalgamated the pirated pannier and now was proud of my well-equipped bush hospital). John called our last muster parade (we were still barefoot and in shorts). The new platoon looked on in disbelief as our Captain inspected us, looking for traces of cleanliness and short hair. "Corporal, your tan is not as even as it could be. Have you been slacking enough?"

"No, sir."

"Medic, your hair is still not touching your ears. You didn't get a haircut, did you? I hope not."

"No, sir."

Then we threw ourselves onto the back of the trucks, which screeched through the gates, the drivers trying to leave as much dust in the faces of our replacement platoon as possible.

"Hadn't we better dress in uniform for our return?" I asked John.

"Hold your head up high, Paul. You've been to Vila Salazar."

I wore my black *takkies* in case of ambush (I didn't want to run through scrub and thorn bush barefoot). In the truck rearview mirror I caught a reflection of a person I didn't recognise. Was this me, this long-haired, brown-faced, golden-tanned hippy? We sang heartily as we left, until we were out of earshot of the compound. Then the driver 'put foot flat' as commanded by the Captain, and we flew at reckless speed down the dirt road to Nyala and JOC Repulse.

"See, Doc," said Gypsy, "the faster you go, the less likely you are to hit a land mine. By the time it goes off you are a hundred metres down the drag."

"Bullshit," said Slinky. "When are you ever going to stop speaking bullshit?"

The heat of the bush hit us in waves from the dirt road, and the dust in our eyes soon choked our song and spirits. I looked back at the dipole and the dummy which the new mortar platoon had already discovered and were jiggling around to see how it worked. It looked as if it were saying goodbye.

Vila Salazar today is a ghost town. Its name has been changed to Sango, yet it remains much the way it was when I left it in 1978. The last picture I saw of it was in *The Herald* sometime after independence. It was an aerial view clearly showing the west wing of the house demolished, the pool gone, the dipole still up, but the storeroom where I lived in ruins. I have always meant to go back there, to trace the steps of my nineteen-year-old self, but the land mines, the new war, and now the infrastructure of the country prevented access. I would have to go as a colonial explorer, if I wanted to return, with all my supplies, a carry troop and a topographical map, as all the roads are potholed and grown over. My urge to return is urgent, though; fragments of Vila Salazar are still lodged in me, and I have left behind shards of myself in its perimeter. Its mystery remains: whatever was left behind there, I have to go and get it back.

"Goodbye, Vila Salazar." An old fear crept into me, despite the carefree company around me – fear of attack, and fear of going back to Llewellin. But as we arrived safely at JOC Repulse, Chiredzi, I saw that my world had changed.

As our truck roared into camp, soldiers in uniforms stopped to stare at us. "Salute, you arsehole," shouted Slinky at an HQ clerk who was watching. He hastily braced up. "Morning, sir."

Gypsy howled. And for the first time, I was in on the joke. Rank did not matter. We had crossed the river of death to hell and returned, golden, reborn, immortal. Troops pointed to us. "Vilas," I heard from a voice of hushed respect. "They've been to Vilas." And others said, with equal respect, "They're bananas."

I reported to the medical room, anxious to try out my new super-powers. A Captain was sitting at the desk, bent over some file. My instinctive reaction was to tense up, to salute and call this man 'sir'. But I consciously expanded myself into my Vila Salazar self. "Excuse me, I'm Williams," I said in a bright voice, "back from Vila Salazar."

The Captain stood, pushing over his chair in his haste to stand up, and gave me a many-toothed smile. "Are you the Corporal Williams I was expecting?" He stared at my brown legs, my *takkies*. This was a new army recruit, a doctor,

I presumed, who had been sent on call-up. All doctors immediately became Captains in the army. He was in a stiff uniform, newly starched and pressed. He was what they called a fresh-puss. I smiled. "You are…?" I reached out my hand and he shook it vigorously. "Hardwick, Captain Hardwick." He stumbled on the rank, a little ashamed of it, not knowing how to use it.

"How long have you been here, Captain?" I asked, sitting down.

"I've been stationed here since last week. The war is really getting out of hand, Corporal. Everyone is being called up, now, even essential services. It's been terrible. Two medics have died since I've been here. I was wondering if you were going to make it. We were worried about you, after what happened to Corporal Chambers."

"I wish I was still there. Who gave the orders to send me back?" The Captain worried his stiffly uniformed body in a gesture of apology and helplessness, indicating an imaginary load of bureaucracy weighing on his head.

"Sorry, Corporal, it's regulations. And I'm a doctor trying to do a medical administrator's job. Your Major Brink at Llewellin requested that you rejoin B Company for their final manoeuvre, where you should have been posted at the beginning."

"B Company!?" I exploded. "I don't want to go back to…"

The doctor hunched his shoulders. "You can't stay longer than two months in Vila Salazar at a time. Major Brink explicitly said he wanted you back. He has another assignment for you."

"I don't even get a weekend pass? In fact, if you're talking law, I should get a week off."

He waved his hands in the air, smearing my words as if trying to erase them. "I know. I know. It's disgraceful. But we've just lost two medics…"

"Where is B Company stationed?"

"Near Gwanda, in the Matopas, at their old training base."

"I don't want to get stuck out in the *hammadullas* somewhere."

"Corporal, I must be frank. The war has taken on a new turn. It's open on all fronts now, not just at the border areas. Matopas is in the thick of it. They're short of medics, and call-ups have been extended for everyone. They even called me up!"

"When do they want me?"

"As soon as possible."

As a parting gift, he handed me a letter that had arrived for me from Salisbury, a slim blue envelope with spidery drawings and writing on both sides. It was addressed to Cpl P (for punishment) Williams, and forwarded from DRR Hospital, Llewellin Barracks. Postage 4c: Roebuck head, blue background.

> *Private keep out.*
> *Only PAW can break the seal.*
> *Shortened version of Paul ? Williams*
> *Sorry for the decorations. Couldn't stop myself.*

I contemplated not opening it, but before I knew what my fingers were doing, it was torn open and the letter unfolded.

*To my dearest Paul*

*I suppose your silence means that you disapprove. Or perhaps it means you don't care less. I don't know. I don't even know if you'll get this letter. Did you get any of my others?*

*I'm not naïve. I know what is going on. You have a girlfriend, some dancer, some model. Older than you. I should have known you go for older women. So it looks like we're drifting further away, instead of closer together. So I want to leave you with a true picture of me.*

*How much do you know about me? What picture do you have of me? I'm not just blonde hair. That's all people see of me, some blonde dummy. Is that how you see me?*

*This is who I am. You probably won't get this letter, or reply to it, but here goes. I'm a confused seventeen-year-old Roosevelt girl, a Rhodesian girl who is very insecure. Fear, doubt and self-hatred are my closest friends. You wouldn't think so, would you? I use words as a big screen to hide behind. Big, brave, icy words. But inside?*

*Why am I getting married? Why am I leaving the country and starting a new life with Dave in Cape Town? Because I am a ghost here. I'm invisible. No one sees me or relates to me as a person. I'm Miss Roosevelt, or Blondie, or Little Miss Muffet.*

*I'm leaving for South Africa at the end of the term. Yes, I decided to quit school after M Levels and go down and join him. My parents have got me into a secretarial college in Cape Town. Actually it's my parents who are moving. They want to get out of the war. They've had enough. So what reason is there for me to stay? Dave is Rhodesian, but he left the country before he was called up.*

*I hope you're happy with your model, dancer or whatever. I thought you would have gone out with that Willow girl, she had the hots for you. Someone else had the hots for you, but she was too messed up in the head to ever admit it.*
*Love*
*Bianca*

# CHAPTER EIGHTEEN

# IT'S FUN TO BE THIRSTY

Bentley, George. We will never forget and we can never forgive those terrorists who cut your life short. May your death serve as an example of true bravery and courage. You fought to the end. Long live Rhodesia! Your dad, mum, sister and relatives.

Rogers, Carl. A true hero, he died for a cause not his own. Your faith in life beyond death is our constant consolation. Suzanne, Peter, and your Mother and Father.

Wrigglesworth, Peter. Died in action, the way you wanted to in the cause of freedom. Your courage and sacrifice will be remembered. Dad, Mum, Eric and Celia.

Chambers, Lionel. Victim of a land-mine attack. Only three months to go, and your life was taken. May the Good Lord hold you in His everlasting arms until we meet again. Your fiancée, Barbara.

Paul Williams's hair. His golden brown locks turned white some time in the two months he was at Vila Salazar. He didn't notice, because there were no mirrors there, but when he looked at his reflection in a truck rearview mirror at JOC Repulse, he was amazed to find his fingers sifting through foreign grey strands of dead hair. Or perhaps it had happened instantly on return to the JOC, after reading Bianca's letter. Paul, your youth will always be remembered. You sacrificed your colour for Rhodesia. Now you are as white as the rest of them.

★ ★ ★

I had hoped for an airplane escort, but had to settle for an army Land Rover ride to the Matopos. I was escorted by two RAR soldiers, both armed with machine guns, and a nervous white driver. The *guti* stung my face as we whined along the main Chiredzi–Bulawayo road at fifty miles an hour through miles and miles of dessicated lowveld bush. We passed nothing except a derailed Garratt engine, where a land mine had blown up the track. But as the road began to squeeze between giant outcrops of rock and balancing granite boulders the size of houses, my spirits soared. I was entering holy ground.

For the Ndebele, the Matopos was a sacred place. Even Rhodes, the wily conqueror, felt the awe of this land. In the 1896 anticolonial rebellion by the Ndebele people, Rhodes set the famous *indaba* in these granite hills. The Matopos also moved Lord Baden-Powell to found the Boy Scout movement. And Rhodes was buried in its granite monoliths. I knew that for the rest of the troops, these hills were a mere picturesque backdrop, but for me they were the locus of spiritual power. *King Solomon's Mines* was inspired by this site, and the bastard son of Haggard, Wilbur Smith, located the mythical treasures of Lobengula here in *The Leopard Hunts in Darkness*. From this land, I could draw courage.

At a bridge over a wide river, the Land Rover veered down a dirt road to the left of the bridge to an army encampment in grey tents.

"This is where you get off, Doc. Good luck," called the driver, who did not even turn his engine off. I leaped over the side, and he spun off up the road. The bridge was heavily guarded by RAR soldiers who peered over at me and then stiffened up and saluted when they saw my medic belt and beret, with the snake gleaming in the sun. They directed me down the dirt road to some camouflaged tents in the undergrowth, and I walked through the cloud of dust down to the campsite.

It was a glorious site, perched high on the flat top of a *gomo*. For hundreds of miles around, blue outcrops of granite erupted, crumbled and prostrated themselves, opening for the flow of the mighty river. I say this ironically, because at the moment it was a mere trickle, pooled in drying-out gobs in a half-mile-wide sandy expanse. You could walk across it and not get wet. Where were the pods of hippos which sported in its waters, the crocodiles that prowled its banks?

I walked in a shimmering heat haze that rose up from the ground. I headed for the tent with a white cross painted on it, peered inside its hot, musty canvas. "Howzit, Doc." A soldier stepped out into the bright sunshine and thrust his hand out. I stood back, stumbled over a root in the ground. He was as surprised as I was. "Paul? We were waiting for a medic but I didn't know it was you."

It was Craig Hardy – the same cheeky face, the sly squint eyes. I kept a wary distance, but he was genuinely pleased to see me. He was wearing a full army uniform and was sweating heavily, so I could smell the mingled Brut and sweat, and see the damp patches under his arms and between his legs.

"B Company, Paul." He shook his head.

"So what really happened to Special Services?"

He waved the accusation away. "Just can't escape B Company. But nor can you, it seems. But not for long. We only have one month until we get out of here."

"Thirty-one days to be precise."

He invited me to sit on his medical pannier. In the centre of the large tent stood a forlorn gas lamp, and on either side were camp beds stacked with blankets and pillows in a tight row. A door on bricks served as a table, and the medical trunk we were sitting on was obviously the chair. Magazines were strewn around, *Reader's Digest* mostly, but also copies of *Scope* and a well-worn *Playboy*.

"Boy, am I glad to see you," said Hardy. "They figured I was in medic's course at Llewellin so they volunteered me to be one till you arrived. I know fuck all about medicine." He grinned and pointed to the pannier. "Haven't a bloody clue. I just guess by rummaging through."

"Have you had any serious cases?"

He shrugged his shoulders. "The serious cases are easy. They're dead when they arrive here or they die before I know what to do. No, the trouble is the silly cases, like corns and gout and stomach aches. I'm clueless."

I was seeing two people: the old Craig Hardy, full of bravado and machismo, but also a small Hardy attempting to win approval. Something had happened to him since I had last seen him. He hunched his shoulders and spoke loudly. "The Major says I make his blood boil so I don't hang out much at the main tent," he said, indicating a large clearing, the ops tent in the centre of it. "Medic suits me fine, but now you're here…"

"What are you going to do now?"

"If you don't mind, Paul, I'll hang around here with you. That's what I was planning to do." He was treating me as an old pal. How did he reconstruct the past, I wondered, to see me as a trusted friend? But I detected uneasiness, too, in the way he sweated and stole cautious, fearful glances at me. "You must meet the other guys here, they really know how to party."

"Where are they?"

"At the moment they're out in the pub. The barman is a guy called Rigor Mortis. He's set up a real *lekker* pub, made it out of hessian and tree trunks." He pointed to a tent and an area demarcated by four-foot-high sheets of brown gauze material. I nodded. He was waiting for reciprocal friendship but was given none, so he continued talking, to fill up the silence. "There's not many whites here. We're with an RAR bunch as all the whites are instructors and the blacks are the troops. Quite a good arrangement. Less of us get killed that way."

Back to the old system. Trying to fight off the gloom, I wondered how I would live above all this. My newly acquired self-confidence would work, I was sure. But for how long? I unpacked my camo T-shirt, the one I had worn at Vila Salazar with the logo Vila Salazar 2 RR Mortar Platoon kokied on the front. If anyone had any doubts where I was from, this would put them in their place. I imagined I would be the only one wearing shorts and T-shirt, but I stuck to my guns. Hardy squinted sceptically at the shirt. "I don't think you'll be allowed to wear that around camp."

"I'll do as I damn well please," I said, in the loud, mocking voice I had picked up from Vila Salazar, the parody of an officer's arrogance, learned from Captain Kirby. But here I kept a straight face. "Is this place hot?"

"Boiling," he said, wiping the sweat off his brow. "But we still have to wear full camo and boots. The Major insists…"

"No, I mean, lots of action, terrs."

"Oh, ja," he laughed. "Every day we have a contact and some terrs get zapped. But they mostly get us in land mines, the cowards."

I nodded, trying to keep control of my proud front. But now I was on the other side, unprotected by fences and minefields. We seemed vulnerable here, surrounded by these granite rocks.

"You should have been here the other day," continued Hardy, warming to a subject that helped him reclaim a little of his authority. "The guys were playing soccer with a terr's head. The Major joined in too as a referee. We had goals and everything." But I didn't want to hear about terrs' heads.

"What am I supposed to do here all day?"

"Better see the Major first, let him know you've arrived. Sure you don't want to change?"

Hardy took me down a dusty pathway to the main ops tent between two huge *msasa* trees. He made me wait outside while he stood politely at the door, knocked on the metal pole, and announced me. I stepped inside. At first, all I saw were a myriad particles of dust floating in the shaft of sunlight that bisected the room, but when I had adjusted my eyes, a nightmare resurrected itself. A man stood before me, in all his proud and stocky glory, wearing blue SAS colours and white beret.

"Major Madox?"

"Doc."

I hoped it was an illusion, but no: Major Madox stared at me, seemingly unsurprised by my appearance, rolling his tongue in his cheek. The other man in the tent turned from his desk to scrutinise me, and I found Sergeant Viper looking contemptuously at me. But I wasn't prepared to cringe before these men any more. I knew how much I had grown. A new emotion of self-worth had replaced submission. I was brown, long-haired, dusty, in shorts and a Vila Salazar T-shirt. Viper turned back to his map, but Major Madox continued to size me up.

I didn't need to ask about the trial. He had got off on a technicality, perhaps even because of my dithering, because a ricochet meant that his intentions were noble and because they needed aggressive men like him in the field. How could they punish him when there was a war on? How stupid of me to think they would find him guilty. He had been found innocent, let off with a warning, or had even been promoted. He had come blustering back as commander, more cocksure than ever. But here was a reminder of his past come to haunt him (or so I flattered myself into thinking). I had to say something. "So you... the trial went all right?"

His face turned ash white and he pressed his lips together. This was a taboo subject. Well, if he wanted me to keep a secret, I could, but only in return for respect. "Corporal, you're here to do your job, to save people's lives. Not like before eh? No more botching up casevacs…" Then, with a twisted smile, he dismissed me.

So he didn't want to keep the past a secret? No unspoken gentleman's pact? I stood my ground, as he turned his back. "Not like before? I hope not. Perhaps I had better keep an eye on *you*, sir, this time, to make sure you do *your* job properly." And I wheeled round and was out the tent before he could turn on me.

"Wonderful man," whispered Hardy to me as we walked back to the medic's tent. "The Major, a true soldier, seen some action in his time. What was that all about, last time…?"

I shook my head. I would not use the ammunition unless I had to.

★  ★  ★

The mess tent was called 'The Gook's Arms' because of two dried lengths of biltong dangling from the centre pole, a souvenir from some encounter with the enemy. It had been built under the shade of huge evergreen kigelia and jackalberry trees which bowed over the water, shading it from the thirsty sun. The small *kopjes* that rose up from the valley gorge were covered in dense mopane woodland – a low, grey-green cover for as many insurgents as wanted to hide there.

The view was magnificent, a hunter's viewing spot in days gone by. Apparently, the area offered exceptional kudu, leopard, bushbuck and eland in large numbers, and bushpig, crocodile, duiker, giraffe, hippo, impala, klipspringer, sable, steenbuck, warthog, waterbuck, wildebeest, zebra, monkeys, baboons and a large variety of nocturnal cats. Needless to say, I didn't see any of these guys. All I saw with my European eyes was a bleached dust bowl of a campground, and all I heard were cicadas screeching. Granted, it was the beginning of winter, and in the Rhodesian winter, nature receded into a brown, droughtlike hibernation.

A rusty sign, filched from some tourist resort that had been in operation here before the war, was affixed to the bar pole:

*There have been sightings of Crocodiles and Hippos:*
*Please take care by the riverside.*
*EXTREME CAUTION ADVISED.*
*A little care can prevent a ruined holiday!*

"This is the Doc," announced Hardy. They all cheered in greeting, though I recognised very few people. "Hey, Rigor Mortis, a beer for the Doc, he's an old B Company man." The barman was a white-haired, white-eyebrowed, white-skinned man wearing a large hat and a holster, but otherwise in normal combat uniform. He pulled out the pistol, twirled it round then thrust it back into the holster. "Go ahead, Hardy, make my day." He leaped around the bar (tree stumps covered in khaki bivouac material) to shake hands with me.

"Welcome, man. You've got rank." Most of them were still riflemen, and had been moved around from camp to camp since our initial basic training. Hardy, I had thought, was a sergeant, remembering those three white stripes on his arm, but now he was a rifleman.

"Phineas. Here's the Doc to cure your VD," called Rigor Mortis and a grinning African RAR soldier came out from a tent flap behind the bar. "Hello, suh," he said. "You give me 'jections, no?"

"He's got VD?" I asked.

"Ja," said Rigor Mortis, "so chronic he can't go on patrols."

"Too many *umfazis*," said Phineas, grinning so his white teeth glinted in the red dusk.

"He's Rigor Mortis's pet," said Hardy.

"A classic *boog*," said Rigor Mortis, clapping Phineas on the back. Instead of taking offence, the black soldier saluted in a clownish way and marched out in an exaggerated quick march, arms and legs flying. "Ah, he's a good bugger," said Rigor Mortis. "Phineas helps me with the bar."

On the bar was an old radiogram that had seen better days. Rigor Mortis had tuned this to Radio 5. With the help of a long wire thrown up into the high trees, we got pretty good reception at times, civilisation fading in and out with the music and the ads for South African goods.

"Took it out of a hut on one of our raids, Doc," said Rigor Mortis, adjusting the old Grundig bakelite controls. "You think these gooks are poor? They have nothing, but inside each hut there's a TV, I'm not kidding – you can see the aerials. And radios! The guy didn't say a word. He must have stolen it from somewhere."

★ ★ ★

I sat through the rest of the meal in silence. I knew Hardy wanted to bring up the subject of the disco on Christmas Eve, by the way he was bragging about me and our exploits together, how we were B Company men from the beginning, that Viper had been our drill instructor. I thought of excuses, but was unprepared for his announcement when it came.

"Fellas, Doc here screwed a *Scope* centrefold."

It was a conversation stopper. All eyes were on me, beer drinking suspended. My beer frothed up my nose. "What are you talking about?"

"Don't try to deny it, Paul. I saw you after the show. Guys, at Archipelago, at Christmas, we went hunting pussy and Doc here won the main prize – the stripper."

I was greeted with a round of applause, whistles and claps on my back. I tried to protest. "I didn't, we just… we're old school friends…"

"You dog," said Rigor Mortis. "Your sister's best friend?"

"Penny Panties," howled Hardy.

"Give him another beer so he can tell us about it."

"Penny? You know her?"

Rigor Mortis pulled down a poster that was pinned on a pole behind the bar, and passed it to me. It was a two-page colour spread of Miss Scope, the latest issue.

*Scope* was the only magazine in Southern Africa at the time that could be deemed erotic or pornographic, though it did not show naked women, pictures of men and women having sex, or lesbian lovers. South Africa, under its Calvinist mandate, had decreed that not only were blacks to be hewers of wood and drawers of water, but that sex was an evil consequence of the fall in the Garden of Eden, and had to be obliterated from sight. *Scope* was ostensibly a man's magazine featuring stories on war, bikes, cars and women. The women (or 'girls' as they were called) stood or sat in frigid poses in a sterile studio, in bikinis or panties. The laws were strict: no pubic hair, no nipples, no nothing. The odd

*Playboy* made its way from the USA into Rhodesia, and could be found buried under stacks of old newspapers at the Treasure Trove in Second Street, worn and at least ten years out of date, but pornography was banned in Rhodesia, too. So *Scope* was what most men settled for. And here she was: a near-naked girl in a bikini, pouting, thrusting her breasts out and cupping them with her hands. Penny in the flesh – my Sleeping Beauty.

"Penny Panties," yelled the platoon.

"She must be some screw, eh, Doc?"

"Introduce me to her…"

"Is she here in Rhodesia?"

I shook my head. "Not any more." So she had gone to South Africa to become a model after all. And she had made it. So quickly? I scrutinised the picture. It was Penny all right, but not the Penny I had visited in her Avenues flat. This was a painted Penny, a retouched photo, disguising hairiness, the cold mean lines of her mouth, spots and blemishes and moles. "This is not her," I tried to explain. "Not the real Penny. This is just a picture… retouched… the real Penny is…"

Rigor Mortis whooped, lassoing an imaginary bikinied girl. "The real Penny must be orgasmic." Hardy clinked his brown bottle to mine. "Cheers!" They all raised their Lion Lagers at me, "To the Doc!"

So once again, I was a hero, this time one who had earned his stripes by sleeping with the pinnacle of male fantasy. I was the necrophiliac who had had sex with a dead image. And, I reminded myself, because of Hardy, Bianca too held me in this regard.

After the meal, I was still hungry, used to the excessive feasting of the last few months. I was looking forward to some dessert, but none was forthcoming. Before we dispersed to our tents, Major Madox poked his head over the hessian screen and stared at the *Scope* centrefold, which was spread on the table. At once, everyone stiffened to attention. Rigor Mortis slipped the photo under the table.

"The returning patrol's RL is stuck in a ditch," the Major announced. "The driver's hurt, and we need volunteers to help pull it out with a 2.5. Hardy? Rigor Mortis?"

"Yes, sir."

He turned to go, but then stopped, gave me a cold stare. "Doc will go with you to tend to the injured driver."

★  ★  ★

Like good little boys, Hardy jumped up and Rigor Mortis leaped into the 2.5. "I need my medical kit."

"There's one in the back of the 2.5." Hardy pulled me up onto the back of the truck. We were riding shotgun. Rigor Mortis revved the engine high, thrust it into first, and lunged the truck onto a dirt track out into the gulley.

"Foot flat," yelled Hardy.

"I bet you it's Gamma," called Rigor Mortis through the cab roof, which was slid back. "Wait till you meet this guy, Doc." He was driving fanatically fast, bumping over stones and roots in the dirt road, dust billowing out behind us. I peered into the cab to watch his right foot pumping the accelerator and clutch in turn.

"What did you say?" I yelled. "Did you say Gamma?"

At this moment, the red tin roof of a store came into view. Rigor Mortis veered off the dirt track and bumped over a footpath, scattering a few grazing goats, to screech to a halt in front of a store. It was a concrete, one-roomed remnant of the farm store in Doris Lessing's *The Grass is Singing*, selling what whites called 'Kaffir truck'. In the rafters of the eaves outside, I spied bicycle tyres and paraffin lamps. A rusty sign advertised Ambi skin-lightening cream with a smiling light-tanned African face; another, from the sixties, in bright cartoon letters read: FANTA ORANGE TASTES SO GOOD, IT'S FUN TO BE THIRSTY.

Rigor Mortis jumped down, his boots crunching on the gravel entrance. "Anyone got any money? I need some smokes…" As we approached, an old man sitting on the front *stoep* scrambled away, chickens clucked off into the dust, and three picanins hid behind the large water drums against the wall. Hardy and I followed Rigor Mortis inside. On the thin shelves, I spied Willard's crisps and Anadin tablets. A fridge hummed, clinking with Cokes, in the dark corner. A young Ndebele woman at the counter showed her white teeth and waited for our orders. Rigor Mortis merely had to point at the Cokes and Madison cigarette cartons and raise three fingers, and she dutifully piled them on the counter. "And some of those pink peanuts."

"Rigor Mortis loves his pink nuts," gibed Hardy.

As Rigor Mortis reached for his pocket, the woman instinctively ducked behind the counter. "Do you give credit?" he asked.

"Credit," she mimicked slowly, smiling hard.

"How much do we owe you?"

She added up the items, with a trembling finger. "One dollar, fifty-eight cents." A voice behind a bottletop-bead curtain cut in with a low Ndebele sentence. She replied in a hushed monosyllable, then turned to this albino soldier and brushed the goods on the counter towards him.

"No, it's for you. No credit. You can have."

"Hey, thanks." Rigor Mortis tossed the Coke and peanuts to us, and stuffed the packet of toasted Madison in his top pocket. "Next time we pay!"

Two miles down the road, the fizz of a warm Coke exploding in my nose, I spotted the derailed RL in a ditch. Rigor Mortis whooped, screeched the truck to a halt in the middle of the dust road, showering the 4.5 with clouds of dirt. It was indeed stuck. It lurched dangerously on its side, so the back axle was up in the air. The front end had ploughed into a storm drain or a donga. Two men emerged from the meagre shade of an acacia umbrella tree where they had been waiting for us.

"Gammaaaa!" yelled Hardy as he lunged off the side of the truck. "What have you done this time? Were you driving this thing?"

"It wasn't my fault, I swear it, guys," said a gaunt, harassed figure, looking very sorry for himself. He was perspiring nervously. I blinked at this apparition: a rabbit posture, thin, scrawny limbs, eyes wide with years of fear and humiliation. "Gamma?" I muttered. This was the same frail schoolboy I remembered from Churchill and from training, behaving in the same cringing way. As the dust cleared, I saw that it wasn't really Gamma, not Peter Burnett, but another clone. This look-alike adjusted thick, black-rimmed glasses, and his eyes, distorted through the lenses, looked huge and frightened, and less and less like Gamma.

"Gammaaa!" sang Rigor Mortis and Hardy in unison, drowning out his explanation. Gamma, or 'Gamma' as I should call him, flapped his arms in frustration, red in the face. "Come on, guys. Help me get this truck out." He was addressing the RAR troops who were sitting as shadows in the shade, but they did not move.

"Come on." He pointed to Rigor Mortis. "Help the boss – come on."

The four men didn't budge an inch. One was sucking a grass stem and talking loudly in Ndebele to another who laughed. One was flat on his back, napping. But when Hardy and Rigor Mortis attached the winch from the front of the 2.5 to the rear end of the 4.5, the men stood, stretched and helped push. The 2.5 strained and slipped, but eventually the 4.5 reluctantly inched out of the ditch and righted itself with a thud and a bounce. Once it was upright, the RAR troops clambered onto the back.

"Better let me drive," said Rigor Mortis. "Can't trust Gamma to do anything."

"Come off it, guys, you know it wasn't my fault," said the wheedling voice.

"This is not Gamma, this is… Gamma was…" I stuttered.

Hardy grinned. "A Gamma is a Gamma. A Mary is a Mary. They're all the same." He saw a quick look of alarm in my eyes as he said 'Mary', remembering that I too was once a Mary. In a gesture of repentance, he patted 'Gamma' on the back.

"Hey, Billy, what's this about you being injured? We brought a medic."

"Doc?" 'Gamma' stuck out a finger. "Look."

I pulled the puffy finger into the light so I could see. It was red and swollen.

"It was a scorpion, under a rock I found to put under the wheel. And you know scorpion bites, you can die from them."

The RAR men laughed, and Rigor Mortis and Hardy laughed too. Even 'Gamma' laughed. Everything 'Gamma' did or said was funny. Did he know that he was acting someone else's role, someone who had left his skin behind for him to occupy? "See how my finger is swollen and red."

"Your finger's always like that," teased Rigor Mortis, "like the rest of your body."

"Except for your willy," said Hardy, making the RAR troops howl with laughter. I took it seriously, however. I knew that scorpion bites could be deadly.

But I also knew that African scorpions often gave warning stings, conserving their venom for a second attack. It also depended on what kind of scorpion had stung him.

"Did you see the scorpion? Can you describe it?"

"It was an ant bite," suggested Rigor Mortis. "Gamma's very sensitive, you know."

"Let's see what we can do." The bite didn't look infected, but I cleaned it, put on some antihistamine cream and a bandage for good measure. Gamma was relieved. "It feels better already," he said. "Thanks, Doc."

"Hey, Doc, doesn't he also need an injection for the infection?" shouted Hardy. "No ways," said Gamma, shaking his head vigorously. "I'm not having no injection."

"Sure, you've got to," said Hardy. "Otherwise you'll grow weaker as the poison enters your blood. Can't you feel it?" Alarmed, Gamma looked at me. He was a firm believer in Authority. And I'm ashamed to say, I was torn. Should I go along with the illusion? I had in the last hour conquered B Company and become a hero. They looked expectantly at me.

"Sure, you need a jab, Gamma." I rummaged in the first-aid kit in the truck, and pulled out a large syringe and a bottle of vitamin B. I was giving them the show they wanted. The RAR troops on the truck applauded, and Rigor Mortis whooped. I was in on the joke at last, not on the outside.

"We'll hold him down, Doc," yelled Hardy, pouncing on the protesting boy who wobbled and squawked, but submitted his trusting body. I wasn't really going to go through with it, I told myself, just play along. Besides, a vitamin B jab wouldn't do any harm: it would boost his immune system. I was 'in' with these guys; I was a Vila Salazar *makonia* soldier. I had respect for a change, and power and authority.

Gamma's eyes bulged when he saw me draw the yellow liquid into the syringe. "In the arse," yelled Hardy as he pulled Gamma's pants down. I stood poised with the syringe. Gamma was white with fear, but trusting me, squeezing his eyes shut. I reacted as suddenly as if I were the one who had been bitten by the scorpion. "No," I said. "Of course he doesn't need a jab. And you should know better, you guys. What game are you playing?"

It was as if I hadn't spoken at all. They continued to wrestle Gamma into position for the injection. Rigor Mortis tried to grab the syringe from my hand to perform the deed himself, but I fought him off, and threw the syringe in the medical bag. Still they didn't take me seriously. Hardy snatched the medic's bag, and tossed it to Rigor Mortis, who swung it high above me so I had to dance and jump to get it. Even Gamma, bending down with his white behind thrust out, was laughing.

"No one touches him or the medic bag or you're on a charge!"

That stopped them. Hardy and Rigor Mortis froze, stared at me. I took the bag from Rigor Mortis and threw it on the ground. The silence was rock-hard. Hardy watched me zip up the bag and toss it onto the truck, then smiled, oily-black. "Aw, come on, Paul, we're just having a little fun." He was offering me a way out, but I stood resolute. "At someone else's expense."

"Since when have you become a… pussy?" said Hardy.

I still did not yield. Gamma was still bending over, waiting for the injection.

"Get up, Gamma. What's your real name, you're not Gamma. Who are you? How can you let them degrade you like this?"

The boy slowly stood up and pulled up his pants. He looked disappointed. Rigor Mortis stared at me through narrowed eyes. Hardy shook his head and blew out his breath. I tried to explain.

"Gamma is dead. I shot him in Vila Salazar. It was an attack, we thought he was a terrorist, in crossfire…"

I expected them to stop in their tracks and say, "Dead? Our Gamma?" But they didn't bat an eyelid. They didn't hear my confession. I tried another tack. "How would you like it if I did this to you? I'm a medic, not a practical joker…"

Now the spell was broken. They stopped grinning, but instead of asking about Gamma, the real Gamma, about what happened to our comrade from school and basic training, they stared at me stonily. After a brief silence in which I was clearly re-evaluated as a traitor, as a stick-in-the-mud, as a pussy, Rigor Mortis climbed in the truck and started the engine. Hardy and Gamma climbed into the 4.5, and I elected to sit moodily in the front cab with Rigor Mortis. Now and then, he gave me an odd glance. I had stepped outside the joke. I had made a stand. And it made me feel awful.

★ ★ ★

The spell was only broken when Rigor Mortis made another diversion on the way back, a detour across a bumpy dirt road to the rise of a hill where we could see the Bulawayo–Beitbridge road, a two-lane highway, shimmering into the far distance.

"What are we doing here?"

"The convoy passes here at this time, Doc. This is our main entertainment of the day."

When Rhodesian white civilians travelled on the roads, they now had to go in convoy. They couldn't just drive where and when they wanted. Transport between cities and towns was organised in convoys to prevent attacks by guerrillas. After horror stories of cars being shot at, occupants killed, cars stolen and plundered, the police had organised convoys to leave at six every morning, Salisbury to Bulawayo, Umtali, Fort Victoria, South Africa… Cars would register and police vans with shotgun marksmen on their roofs would patrol up and down the roads, guarding and escorting them. No one travelled on their own, it wasn't safe, especially the Fort Victoria highway. Terrorist activities occurred in the rocky hills of the Tribal Trust Land there, where the guerrilla armies of Robert Mugabe were the strongest and had claimed to have liberated certain areas, blocking off the town of Fort Victoria just as it had been in 1892. They aimed to make the country ungovernable and make the whites sweat in their *laager*.

The convoy was a dream – civilians escaping the war, escorted out of the nightmare, given a safe passage to freedom, to South Africa, to modern twentieth-century life. To Durban, to the beach, to hippydom, to free-thinking universities. How I wished I could simply step on a convoy and go AWOL, absent without leave, and never come back.

We found a prominent place near a lay-by, on a slight rise. Here we could see the road both ways to the horizon. There was a slight dip and bend where the cars would have to slow down and where we could stand on top of the vehicle and wave.

We heard the humming convoy before we saw the the glint of windscreens on the horizon. A police van came first, then – ssh, ssh, ssh – car after car, yellow, red, green, white, Peugeots, Datsuns, Renaults, Mercedes, all with families in colourful clothes going on holiday to South Africa. Children waved through the windows at us, the heroes of the bush. Rigor Mortis smiled, waved back, gave 'safe' signs to the boys, smiled at the girls. Mum, Dad, Sis, Bru, Baby. Girls, girls, girls. One car, two cars, thirteen, fourteen, a police escort plonked in every ten vehicles, one roaring up and down on the other side of the road, checking, keeping in radio contact. Dad's army with balaclavas, riding on top with an MAG swinging at every dangerous *kopje*. I looked for my Dad, but of course I knew he only patrolled on convoys in the school holidays. The police gave a thumbs-up when they saw the army: safe, my mate! This area is army controlled. Why else would these three men be standing waving with such careless abandon?

"Doc, Doc, there's a topless blonde. In that car. I saw her. She was waving and smiling at me. I saw her."

"Sure, Rigor Mortis, sure."

"No, really, I saw her. I'm not joking."

The convoy drove past at a regular speed, the cars twenty metres apart. Five minutes long: this was a big one. I stared into each intimate family circle, saw sandwiches, flasks of coffee, heard tapes of Thin Lizzy blaring, saw sunburned arms out of windows, smelt the colour of civilian life and holidays, coconut oil, sand, anticipation. Sulky teenage boys at the back, feet up against the window, eating Benny's Beef Biltong; girls reading *Fairlady* magazines, their bare arms reddening in the heat; children playing 'I spy' to pass the time: I spy with my little eye, something beginning with... S. Salisbury? Sky? Soldiers? Sick *mombes*?

Bianca had left on one of these convoys.

The last few vehicles were driven by businessmen in suits, with briefcases slung across empty passenger seats. And finally the police escort at the back. We sat in the truck, listening to the fading echoes of the vehicles. "So much for the entertainment," I said. "It makes me feel lousy."

"I know what you mean, Doc. But you're nearly out of here. How many days?"

"Thirty-one," said Hardy. "Only one more fucking month, my china."

"But didn't you see her, Doc, the topless blonde? Wasn't that worth seeing?"

"I didn't see no topless blonde," said Gamma.

"You wouldn't know a topless blonde if one sat on your prick."

On our return, we were made to recount our tale. I was stoically silent, but the others had recovered some of their wits, and the story was told with vigour and humour. Rigor Mortis told everyone how stupid Gamma had been, and Gamma laughed at his own expense. Penny's picture fluttered high on the pole, and I was still the hero, albeit an eccentric one. Hardy made up to me by bringing me a beer. "Here, Doc." After watching Phineas's antics (he acted out the scene of Gamma being bitten by the scorpion), I made excuses and returned to the medic's tent.

I found the pile of worn *Scope*s beside the *Playboy*s I had seen Hardy devouring earlier, mingled with *Reader's Digests*. I opened one and began scrutinising the pictures inside. The magazine was dated July 1977. Cathy is studying at the University of Iowa, loves swimming, athletics and walking around the house naked. Tessy pouts her lips at me and a million other watchers, then undresses to reveal a smoothly retouched body in a pink bikini, into which a million men have thrust their imaginations.

And here was *Scope*, April 1978, which boasted the 'Scandal of the School Girl Stripper' and a 'Full length poster inside of *Scope* playgirl of the month, Miss Penny Panties'. The centrefold was ripped out, of course, but there were other pictures. Here she was in a series of action shots, her back to the camera, looking over her shoulder in the classic *Scope* pose, in a see-through-but-touched-up-so-you-couldn't-see-through white dress. And here was a full-page pose, with her blonde hair blowing in a mysterious wind (a fan?), playing with her bikini strap, with pink lipstick, dangling earrings, those chipmunk cheeks rouged, the mean mouth pursed, laughing, enticing, looking at me, thinking, shall I take it off?

So she had made it. She had become a model, a dancer, a celebrity. What was next? *Vogue*? *Cosmopolitan*? *Hustler*? Good luck to her.

★ ★ ★

There was nothing to do all afternoon, just let the heat bathe us in the tent. Hardy returned after lunch, but ignored me, while I read a *Reader's Digest*, scowling fiercely, trying to defend a space I had just created for myself. I was reading how ABBA recorded 'Hole in Your Soul' in a one-off session, and had then overlaid voices and sound clips to make it professional. Then I read an article about Karen Carpenter, her voice layered 22 times on 'Yesterday Once More'. Oh, I thought naively, so she didn't naturally sing in a husky, sweet echo?

Just before two o'clock a truck arrived in camp, drove wildly up through the dusty riverbed and spread clouds of brown dust over us all. The tent flap burst open and two white soldiers, caked in dust and camouflage paint, slid a grey stretcher in for me. "Present for you, Doc."

The two men rushed outside again, before I could even react, and leaped back on the revving truck, roared back onto the main road. On the stretcher was an awkwardly placed black man in greasy overalls with slashes and holes everywhere. He was wearing an old felt trilby, and shoes that had seen better days. Trembling, I got to work at once, tripping over Hardy every time I turned, for he was anxious to help. I asked him for penicillin and a saline drip, but he was so long rummaging in the trunk that I had to get them myself. I assessed the damage, meanwhile thinking what to write in my treatment book.

The patient was an African civilian, still conscious, moaning softly. He was in a state of shock, the blood drained from his face. A bullet had torn through his abdomen, and his intestines were hanging out, soiled with dust and mud. I first set up a saline drip and gave him morphine. In two minutes the drip had drained into him and I gave another one. His face coloured, and his muscles relaxed. He no longer seemed in pain. I cut off the overalls to get to the wound, wrapped the abdomen in wet sterile cloths and tried to secure him to the stretcher so he wouldn't roll around. He stared at me with a beseeching look.

"What happened?"

"Shoot me. Do nothing," he said in English, then changed to Ndebele. "Shoot, me, do nothing." He tried to sit up, thinking he was better, because the pain was going. I pushed him gently down.

"My money," he said. "Soldiers take money."

He had been shot in the guts and he was worried about a few dollars. "Don't worry," I said. "We'll get your money back. Relax." The next step was casevac. As medics we had been trained only for emergency procedures, to secure the patient until we could get him to a hospital. There were no trucks in the centre area – they must have all been out on operations – but the Major's jeep glittered in the sun outside the ops tent. I calculated that it was an hour's drive to Bulawayo hospital. This time it would be all right. He would make it.

"Doc, we don't…" said Hardy.

I ordered him to help carry the stretcher, giving short, sharp commands. We lifted the stretcher gently, and carried it through the baking sun to the back of the jeep. It was an open flatbed, so we could simply slide the patient in. As an afterthought, I sent Hardy to speak to the Major about it and to get the keys. I would drive. I made sure that the drip was steady, strapped to an elevated side of the jeep, and that the wound was moist and clean.

Hardy puffed his way out of the tent. "The Major needs his jeep for an operation later today. We have to wait for an RL to get back. It's due this afternoon."

"We can't use the jeep?" Hardy tried to quieten me down and indicated furtively that the Major was near and could hear. "Don't shush me. Doesn't he know how urgent this is? Did you tell him it was a matter of life or death?"

"You don't know how things operate around here, Paul. For weeks, we've been…"

"I don't care how you've been doing it till now. This man needs help now, or he will die. We've got to get him to the hospital." Hardy smiled in half apology, half defiance. I turned to the patient who looked up in alarm because I had been shouting. "We take you to doctor, he fix you up, go fast in jeep." He smiled weakly.

"What's all the fuss?"

I looked up to see Viper staring at me from the opening of the ops tent. He strode over to see what I had placed on the Major's truck. He was smoking, and inhaled sharply at the sight of the dying man. "What's all the commotion, Doc? The Major is trying to rest." He cocked his thumb at the tent opening.

"Sergeant Viper." I smiled in relief. "Can you drive us to the hospital?"

He frowned. "He's pretty bad," I added. "I can't move him around, his stomach…"

Viper peered down at the blinking patient. "Why did you have to get in the way?" He shook his head and turned to me. "Crossfire. Everywhere you go in the bush, you find the inevitable *munt* in the way."

I didn't smile back.

"Listen, Doc, there's a problem here," said Viper, shifting his eyes. "I don't want to be involved in this whole thing. It's the Major. He won't allow his jeep to be used, but if we take the guy off and wait for the truck, sure, I'll take you." He looked at his watch.

I didn't budge. I stared at the Sergeant, anger rising in my throat. But I couldn't shout at him. This was my old instructor. All I could do was keep an unflinching stare on him. He flitted his eyes away, but I was solidly present; he couldn't just dismiss me. "Sergeant, if we don't get this man to the hospital soon, he's going to die, he… I'll have to make a report, I… Who will be held responsible?"

Sergeant Viper took a drag of his cigarette. "Doc, you don't have to worry about that. It will be all right, the Major will take responsibility. He makes the rules. And he has stated categorically that we cannot use his jeep. He has a big SITREP meeting in a few…"

A scream was welling up inside me, but I said nothing. The patient was in pain again. He was restless, and his wounds had opened. Thick red blood began to drip steadily on the ground and on the metal floor of the jeep. Viper frowned. "Take him off the jeep. Major's orders. If he can't go, he can't go. A few minutes won't make any difference." And with that he stomped back into the tent.

I wanted to go after him, but Hardy pulled me back. "Don't be a fool, Paul. Why take so much trouble? If they're in such a bad way, they'll die anyway…"

I pulled and strained against his arm, then fell back. I breathed out slowly. "Let's get him back to the tent." But as we retraced our steps, the drip stopped and I had to set the patient down in the dust outside the medic's tent. He looked ashen. He had understood what was happening, I thought, and his hope was withering. Or maybe he thought we were angry with him. I touched his hand and spoke gently, "I will not let them do this to you." I set up the drip again, but as we placed him in the shade of the tent, I heard the death rattle. He had stopped breathing. I gave him mouth-to-mouth; I pumped his heart; I set up another drip in his other arm, squeezed the plastic bag so the fluid gushed into his veins. "Come on, man, live. Live! Don't give up yet." I only realised I was screaming when Hardy clutched my arm and put his finger to his lips. I hit the pannier with my fist. "He could have been all right. He could have lived."

Hardy shrugged a shoulder. "Paul, it wouldn't have been wise to send him in the jeep. He would have died on the way, then we'd have made fools of ourselves sending a dead man to hospital."

At the moment of death, apparently, the soul rises out of the body and drifts tranquilly towards a tunnel of light in great peace. But how can the soul see without the organs of perception that are in the dead body below? And this was not a tranquil acceptance of death. Far from gliding along a shining white path, this man's soul must be angry, resentful, and tangled in the branches of the tree above, glaring down at me. No white angel would beckon him away. I heard singing in my ears, the wailing voices of the mourning ancestors, the dead shaming me.

I stormed off to the Major's tent. Hardy called after me. "Paul, what's got into you? You're behaving so... weird."

I pushed past Sergeant Viper who, in alarm at seeing me, tried to block my entrance. The Major was sitting on a camp stool. He wheeled around, stared at the blood dripping from my hands.

"Go and clean yourself, Doc."

But this time I was ready for him. "Was this a ricochet too? A man has just died – a man, a human being – do you know what I am saying? And I hold you directly responsible." My finger froze in the air, and I pressed my lips hard together to stop them quivering. The Major's eyes narrowed. Hardy darkened the entrance of the tent so that Madox was just a shadow. He stood, and paced towards me in three short, measured steps. I stared back at those blue eyes, and saw burning fire.

"Don't push me, Doc."

His voice was dead cold. I was on a dizzy precipice and about to fall. I mustered my remaining strength and wheeled around, turning my back on him, and walked out. Hardy tried to pull me back, but I ignored him.

"Doc," shouted the Major. I didn't see him pull out the pistol from his pocket, but I heard the shot. I don't know how close it was, but I heard the crack, and I heard the bullet thud and echo into the mopane forest nearby. It took all my will not to cringe and cower. I walked on, slowly, one foot in front of the other. When I reached the tent, I sat down and tried to calm my beating heart, listening for the Major's steps. But he did not follow me.

Two black soldiers arrived to remove the body. I sat in silence, watching them. I was still trembling and dizzy, and only now noticed that Hardy was sitting in the tent too, flicking through a *Reader's Digest*. He was thinking, what madness was this? Has Doc finally flipped his lid? He's from Vila Salazar. He's passed the final frontier, insanity.

But no: I was being myself. For the first time, I was alive. The ache that had been inside me all my life was gone, and in its place a universe was beating.

# CHAPTER NINETEEN

# AMADHLOZI

The last six months of the war were the worst. Desperate measures were taken by both sides to win or gain as much ground before the talks. Smith, bowing to the inevitable, stared into a black future and admitted that majority rule was unavoidable, yet he had to make sure it was responsible government, meaning that whites had some hand in it. If we could keep control of the military, finance and agriculture we would be OK, he said.

So he devised a plan (or someone devised a plan) to work with the so-called internal leaders, Muzorewa, Sithole and Chirau (the external leaders were the terrorists Mugabe and Nkomo). With one stroke of the pen, the AK-wielding terrorist Bishop Abel Muzorewa became a good guy, and his guerrilla army, Pfumo ReVhano, became an ally of the Rhodesian army. So too Sithole, once leader of ZANU, now ousted by Mugabe, brought his insurgents to join forces with Smith's boys to fight against the external threat of the Patriotic Front. Chirau, leader of the chiefs, now left behind by the war's usurpation of the old traditions, found a place with Smith, and with his golden chain around his neck, his inarticulate speeches, looked (poor guy, may he rest in peace) like the very running dog of the whites. It was a brilliant scheme of divide and conquer, and it nearly worked. We will have black majority rule, Smith could announce to the world. Elections – one man, one vote – will be held, and everyone will vote to choose their democratic government from these three candidates.

I missed the ceremony. I was busy fighting my own war. But on a field in KGVI Barracks, with all the army assembled, Smith arrived by helicopter, with the three stooges behind him, the Rev. Abel Muzorewa, the Rev. Ndabaningi Sithole, and the most excellent Chief Jeremiah Chirau. They were here to gain the support of the troops for the next move in social engineering, to put in place a black government that was really white underneath, a black-masked, white-skinned Zimbabwe-Rhodesia that would end all our woes. Sanctions would be lifted, the Patriotic Front would be outmanoeuvred, and we would all live happily ever after. Of course we all agreed. Whatever Smith thought best was best. Majority rule in the year, he promised.

But the war did not relent. Muzorewa was a black Smith, Sithole was a sell-out, and Chirau was a running dog on a leash (after all, the sour Voice of Zimbabwe argued, what noise does a dog makes when it barks? Chirau! Chirau!). Mugabe and Nkomo kept up the pressure. They represented the People, and the People wanted war, they said. We had unleashed a monster and now we couldn't control it.

★  ★  ★

That evening, I was still taut, waiting for another confrontation with the Major. None came. He didn't bang into the tent and point his pistol at me; he didn't order me around the camp with sandbags on my head (though that would have been a relief); he didn't call me to dress his corns or bring him tea. He knew how to play psychological war.

Instead, he sent his emissary, Viper, who, shifty-eyed, called me aside. We walked out of earshot of the others on the river bank. He lit a cigarette, offered me one and when I refused, took a deep puff of his. We both stared at the sunset gleaming on the water and listened to the riotous bird songs in the trees.

"How many days do you have to go, Doc? Hardy tells me it's twenty-nine, like him."

"Thirty."

"Then you're out of here?"

I nodded.

"What are your plans? When you demobilise?"

"Durban, to university."

He took another deep drag of the cigarette, and flicked the ash into the night. "You'll be back in Llewellin in ten days at the most. Then you bide your time in the camp hospital two, three weeks, then you'll be out of the army, and lying on the golden sands of Durban beach. Is that what you want?"

I stared at him.

"The Major's a reasonable man. He's prepared to forgive and forget."

The Major would leave me alone, and I would leave the Major alone, and everything would go well. "Think about it," he said. "Think about it."

★ ★ ★

Behind the medics' tent stood, or balanced, an enormous set of boulders, covered in patterns of orange lichen. One rock was Picasso-cubic and was perched on another grey cylinder, which in turn was impossibly balanced on a round foundation stone. The bottom rock had split. A humble *msasa* tree had wedged it apart, or had grown opportunely in the crack. Its roots showed through the grey earth, and invited me to climb. Low branches and gnarled twists and turns in its trunk helped me up. I hauled myself up what looked like a secret initiation tunnel. The lichen was luminous in the twilight. It led through a funnel of rock between two boulders, and onto a top ledge. I found myself looking down on the campsite and beyond it to the gleam of a nearby dam. I traced the lazy stream of brown mud washing down between the *kopjes* toward the Limpopo. Now I could get my bearings. There was the farmhouse we had stayed in last year. Over there was the village (see those wisps of smoke?) where I had sipped tea with the chief, and later betrayed him.

The Pastor at Hillside Baptist Fellowship had lectured us about the erroneous theory of evolution, that scientists had speculated the earth as many millions of years old. Ridiculous, scoffed Steve; it was only 6,000 years old, and the Bible proved it. If you calculated the years of the prophets back to Adam, you could determine that the earth was created on the 23 October 4004 BC at 9 a.m. But these rocks told a different story. I could see how it had happened. Slowly the molten lava had cooled, blobs of magma had hardened, then settled, then the earth had eroded away, creating a giant sculpture of alien beauty not seen anywhere on this earth. And these granite mountains captured something of the people who lived here – their spirit, their dreams, perhaps the echoes of their voices. If sounds never died out, they could still be heard if you listened carefully. And I was hearing them.

Where was Rhodes's grave, I wondered. I was ignorant of the Matopos, but I had seen pictures of World's View, of the blue horizon where you could see so far you felt small and humbled. All I saw here were thousands of small *kopjes*, all built up into giant stone fortresses. It was Mzilikazi who christened these balancing rocks the Bald Heads. For the Ndebele, it was sacred ground. I knew there were hidden places, for example, the rain shrine to Mwari; and there were sacred hills – Shumba, Shabe and Shumba Sham – so holy that to even look at them was a violation.

You're the real masters of this country, I thought. You will be here long after we've fought our stupid wars and killed each other off. You speak to me in a language, not of the Bible, but of Africa. I see you in this magnificent sunset. I hear you in the whispering trees. I saw you in the gestures of the old man who died yesterday. Perhaps I was addressing an invisible community of many gods, all those deities of the San people who lived here for forty thousand years, all the gods of the Matabele who occupied this land for a thousand years, and even the prayers of Rhodes's descendents, who were here for scarcely ninety years. I used to think of them as saints, those white people who had died and were now crowding over the balcony in heaven to observe the affairs of the world. But now I saw – I felt, I heard, I tasted, I touched – different beings around me: African spirits, perhaps what the Shona called *vadzimu*, or the Ndebele *amadhlozi*, those ancestors who were an invisible community among the living, caring for their descendents and sharing in their joys and sorrows.

But who was I to seek their presence? Who was I, a white boy, to have an African ancestor? Perhaps instead these were the whisperings of the devil, of avenging *Ngozi* spirits who had come to torment me and send me to my death. The *Ngozi*, I knew, were spirits of deceased Africans who had been greatly wronged, who wanted revenge. The African spiritual sky must be filled with the wronged spirits of these murdered people. If so, how would I ever appease such spirits?

The sun set golden and beautiful. I never want to miss another African sunset, I vowed. Watching the night close in, clutching my rifle, feeling my neck prickle at the slightest animal sound in the bushes, I felt insecure for the first time since Vila Salazar. And then another wind blew through me. No one would answer my prayers. All those desires, hopes and Bianca-dreams had simply blown away in the dust. There were no ghosts in the sky looking down on me, no God who ordered the world and counted the hairs on my head. The sky was a blue illusion, caused by atmospheric gases, and beyond that was only blackness and silence.

★  ★  ★

At the bar, Phineas was putting on a pre-supper performance. He marched up and down, saluting and shouting out commands to himself. "Phineas, wake up, you dozy Kaffir," he shouted, then leapt around and saluted. "Yessir, yessir, mister Major, sir." Then he paraded the length of the bar area with a bottle of beer as a rifle, to the delight of the applauding platoon.

"Why did you join the RAR, Phineas?"

"Ah, Corporal, it's a good life you know, food, drink, clothes, lots of money, but no women provided."

"How long have you been in the army?"

"Three years already," said Phineas. "Ah, he is a classic *boog*. No time to see *umfazis* or wives in Bulawayo."

"Three years," exclaimed Rigor Mortis. "No wonder you've gone off your rocker. Or has that VD gone to your brain?"

"Hey, here's the Doc!"

"What's up, Doc?"

"At ease, chaps," I joked. "How many days?"

"Twenty-eight!" yelled Hardy. "And you too, Doc. Twenty-eight. I can't fucking believe it. And here we are, pissing the time away in Margaritaville."

"But as soon as you're out, they zap you for camps. They give you two months and then, boom, you're back in again."

"Not me," I said. "I'm off to South Africa as soon as I'm out. Durban."

"To see Penny Panties?"

"I feel sorry for the poor buggers who signed up to go to university."

"I did that," I said. "I signed up for the University of Natal. They said they'd let me out after a year."

"And you believed them?" said Rigor Mortis.

★  ★  ★

I was woken by the revving of trucks. A red sun cut a shaft of light into my tent, sparkling the dust in the air. The energy was electric. I pulled on my Vila Salazar shirt and walked outside. The Major's jeep was the lead vehicle, and lined up behind it were five RLs, swarming with troops. Viper stood on one, issuing commands to a troop of RAR soldiers. The Major stood on top of an RL and raised a loud-hailer.

"Doc, get dressed. We need you. Someone help him with the medical pannier."

I grabbed my rifle and dragged my medical trunk outside. Rigor Mortis, the driver of the Major's jeep, obligingly drove up the tent entrance. "Jump on, Doc."

"What's going on?"

"Alpha Stick has been following a huge group of terrs and has tracked them to a village near the main road." I leaped onto the back of the jeep, and sat on the black trunk, my heart beating.

"They followed the terrs to a *gomo*. The buggers are hiding in the rocks, apparently, and they can't dislodge them."

Major Madox had found his purpose: he looked like a large wild cat panting after its prey. He leaped off the RL and dived into the passenger seat of the jeep. "Go! Go! Go!" he yelled, circling the air with his maimed hand. The vehicles set off in convoy along the dirt road. We were the lead vehicle, so I had the pleasure of watching the back of Major Madox's shaved head all the way. He was in his element, fiery-eyed, utilising everyone as parts of his beautiful machine.

At a pre-arranged rendezvous, a junction in the two dirt roads bisected by three balancing grey boulders (much like the ones on the Rhodesian banknotes), the convoy halted, and immediately a soldier in full combat gear, but with camo paint on his arms and face, stood on top of a rock, calling down at us, waving his arms. "Major, they're in the village. The whole damn lot of them. We followed them here last night from the *gomo*."

"If they think we won't attack them there, they're wrong," said the Major. "You sure there's no exit? No way they could have escaped?"

The excited troopie shook his head. The village was surrounded by rocks and high *kopjes*. Our plan was to circle it and trap the terrorists there. I say 'our' plan, but it was the Major's. I had no plan except denial. The trucks were parked in a *laager* around the village behind granite boulders, while troops poured out of the backs of the RLs and leopard-crawled into firing positions around the central compound.

I now regretted being on the lead vehicle. Instead of diving for cover, or directing operations from a safe place, the Major commanded Rigor Mortis to drive straight into the path leading to the baked brown clearing in the middle of the village. We took our place beside the eight huts which enclosed the compound. The sun was still hiding behind the low mopane trees, and cast eerie shadows through the branches onto the clearing.

There is nothing like an African dawn in a village. The grass huts blend in with the tall yellow elephant grass, the red earth is baked hard by sun, drought and pounding feet, the sun streams through dapples in the crazy *msasa* trees. Doves coo, the smell of smoking cooking fires offers its sacrifices to the sky, and the cool grey boulders look on. But this village was eerily devoid of human activity. Normally this scene would have had women clanking pots, or returning from the gurgling stream below with buckets of water, impossibly yet elegantly balanced on their heads, weaving between rocks impossibly balanced on each other. There should have been the low voices of men talking, and children running in and out of the compound, playing, laughing, crying. But we heard, saw, felt, nothing.

Once his troops were all in position, the Major stood and pulled out his loud-hailer. "*Makandangas*! We have you completely surrounded. If you surrender now, no one gets hurt. If you don't, we come in after you. This is your chance to save your village."

Major Madox's abrasive voice made no sense to me. I stared at the tyre tracks we had made into the compound, and wondered if the earth here, used to bare feet, had ever known such a strange animal as the Major's truck. I saw a crushed insect in one of the tracks, which had vainly been crossing the compound and was now curled in death. I suddenly felt pity for these absent villagers, for their vain endeavours to survive in this barren yellow Matopas area, making these frail grass huts that would be gone next year. They had nothing but grass and rocks and water and mud. Yet we were going to take what little they had away.

"Moyo, Sibanda, search the huts." The two RAR soldiers obediently skulked around the edge of the clearing and poked their rifles into the first hut. I clutched my rifle, my stomach tensing up. The two men emerged almost immediately with a man between their trained rifles, his hands on his head. He was wearing blue overalls much too big for him, and sported a scraggly Kalahari scrub beard.

"This one is a gook," called Rigor Mortis from his hiding place behind a small boulder. The Major's eyes lit up. "Where are the others?" he said. "Where are your comrades?"

I saw immediately that this man was someone whom you didn't mess with. He didn't have the cringing posture we whites expected when Africans approached us. Was it because he was a 'gook'? Or was it because he was Matabele, the proud offshoot of the Zulu people, who held their heads high, in spite of their hundred years of subjugation by the British?

"I am Chief Ngwenya."

"Where are the others?" thundered the Major. "Tell us or we blow the whole village off the map." The man, flanked by rifle muzzles, stared the Major in the eye. He didn't do what he was supposed to do – humour him, play stupid, call him *baas*.

"We have helped you," he said. "We are friends with the Rhodesian army."

The Major was myopically unaware of what I saw in this man. The chief, if that's what he was, was obviously innocent. He would never behave like this unless he was sure of himself. I wanted to nudge my commander-in-chief, and say, "He's trying to tell you something. Listen to him."

"We know they are here. You tell us or we blow your head off. Hardy?"

Hardy stood, his rifle trained on the old man.

"Sir, he can't talk to you like that," said Rigor Mortis. "He's a gook. Only gooks talk like that." The old man stared at the barrel of Hardy's gun. The Major was acting, displaying terror tactics, playing out his Matopas performance again, but Hardy didn't know this. His finger rested nervously against the trigger, eager to please the Major.

Afterwards, in my research to fill the black hole of my past, I discovered that Chief Ngwenya had not been lying; he was indeed a friend to the Rhodesian army. It seems he played devil's advocate to negotiate the survival of his village. It had been infiltrated with guerrillas, with Rhodesian troops, had been a Selous Scout base, and he had cooperated with them all: feeding the guerrillas, informing the troops (giving wrong information, of course, and playing innocent), wearing the right mask for the right occasion. He had enough credibility with the Rhodesian forces so they let him alone; he had credibility with the ZIPRA guerrillas so they left him alone, too. He had struck a deal: no guerrilla bases here. Their mothers were here, their families too. He could reason with them. He was strong enough to hold the guerrillas at bay by negotiation, by reason, by compromise. And his village had survived – until this moment.

★ ★ ★

The shot from Hardy's rifle hit the chief in the mouth, and he crumpled and fell. Hardy recoiled and the Major turned angrily on him, but at once the place lit up with machine-gun fire high in a cleft of towering granite.

"Down," yelled the Major frantically. I crouched by the wheel. I watched tracers zip into huts in purple and orange lines; I held my breath as a grenade wobbled over me and landed in the forest clump where tell-tale smoke and sparks flew; I saw soldiers leopard-crawl into positions behind trees. Next to me, the Major fired no shots at first, but once he had identified the firing position of the enemy, he clicked his FN onto automatic and blew off a whole magazine up at the boulders. The bullets ricocheted, and I was afraid they would bounce straight back at us. The huts exploded into flames, and smoke and people poured out of each one.

"They're all terrs, all damn terrs," Major Madox shouted. I saw AKs in the mob, I was sure, or ghosts of AKs, but I didn't fire a shot. I tried to bury myself in the ground, squeezing behind the large front tyre of the vehicle. I'm not part of this, I said to myself, or to any god who cared to listen to me. I burrowed as close to the earth as I could, wishing it could swallow me up, wishing I was in a Vila Salazar bunker. I lay low, the taste of soil in my mouth, a fiery lump in my throat. Fear was mixed with anger, with resentment at being caught in a trap. And this time, I wasn't fooled. *The terrs are only ghosts! You are shooting at people!*

After lying for a minute with my head in my arms, I realised that the fight was moving outwards, up through the cleft in the boulders. People lay like black blobs on the ground. And as suddenly as it had started, the firing puttered to a halt, the only sound now the crackling of fire and a high ringing sound in the sky.

"Return to base. Account for yourselves, men."

One by one the soldiers stood up from scattered positions, behind trees, rocks or in long grass, and formed a long line. Rigor Mortis waved a hat at the Major. Hardy emerged from a clump of bushes. Phineas grinned from behind the truck. 'Gamma', looking white, peeped around a tree. I stood up, too, shaking, but with the sure knowledge that there were no terrorists here at all. I had been through enough to know that we were shooting our own paranoiac reflections once again. When the grinning troopies who had radioed us from behind the *kopje* joined us, Viper stood and saluted. "All present and accounted for, sir."

"Prepare for the sweep through," the Major ordered.

Don't get me wrong. Terrorists were not a figment of our imagination. Guerrillas, insurgents, ZANLA, ZIPRA, were all very real. They raped, massacred, tortured, as we did. In the vacuum of unrestraint, all three sides allowed their lusts full play. Right now, though, the enemy was our own human nature, red in tooth and claw, our masculine propensity for violence and destruction. But this was not how the Major saw it. The enemy was out there. "Shoot anything that moves," he ordered, "otherwise we are dead."

I held defiantly back, but the Major pulled me into the line of soldiers. I knew the manoeuvre: sweep through in a line, advance, kill all in your wake, clear the area and make it safe. No one could be left out, no one could afford to miss a hiding place, or all would be in danger. With trembling FN pointing forwards, I lined up next to Gamma, Rigor Mortis, Hardy and Phineas. They trusted the Major's commands. They were grateful for training. But I dreaded what was ahead: huts burning, bushes with potential hiding places, dead bodies, or bodies pretending to be dead that might pounce and shoot once you overturned them with your toecap. I was shivering with cold. Phineas grinned at me as I nervously cocked my weapon and pretended to slot a new magazine into my rifle, as everyone else was doing. Rigor Mortis cocked his hat. Hardy, red in the face, was breathing heavily. The Major looked on in approval at his boys.

"Sweep through," came the command, and we walked forward in line across the wasteland. The shooting began again, into every likely cover, into bushes, at trees, into burning huts, at dead bodies. In my line ahead was a hut. I walked closer to it, dreading what I had to do. In my path was a dead body. A crushed *chongololo*, with his innards seeping out from under him. He was curled into a ball. I stepped around him, but to make sure he was dead (or "neutralised" as the Major put it), Phineas prodded him with his rifle muzzle, then turned him over with his foot. It was an old man, dusty, bloody, very dead.

★ ★ ★

He had lived a long life, I saw on the wrinkled face. He had lived through many indignities. He had been here when the reserves were established, and had been put in them. He had grown up, had watched the whites flourish at his expense, becoming rich and treating Africans with increasing disrespect. He was an angry young man who worked himself to old age and despair and alcoholic impotence in the mines before his lung cancer got the better of him and he was discarded to go back and die in the TTLs. But then the guerrilla war started. The *tsotsis* came and made everyone stay up all night singing revolutionary songs. In the day, the Rhodesians came and punished them. Always trouble, my life is always trouble, was his motto, and his wives would laugh at him.

★ ★ ★

Rigor Mortis was also facing a hut's yawning black mouth. He jumped in front of it, balancing on one leg, and sprayed bullets all around inside, with a panache he must have learned from Vietnam movies. I'd seen this movie before, when I was young, and here I was on the flickering newsreel myself. Now it was my turn. I knew what to expect in the hut as the darkness loomed up. I stepped over another dead body that Phineas had inadvertently rolled towards me. The Major was watching. "Shoot the bodies, you arsehole. They may be faking and hiding AKs underneath them. Doc, I'm reaching my limit with you."

I gave him an empty stare, then moved to the entrance of the hut. I took a deep breath, poked my rifle in first, gingerly, then my face. Darkness smothered me, and smoke burned my eyes and nostrils. I was supposed to shoot first, for safety, like Rigor Mortis, but I couldn't. I strained my eyes and ears to see and hear. I heard – I thought – a slight scuffling. I saw – I thought – glints of eyes. Were those pairs of eyes staring at me in silent terror? Or were they ghosts? Maybe I was seeing the whites of my own eyes in a mirror propped against the back of the hut. I clutched the rifle tighter, my finger on the trigger guard. I was terrified, more than I had ever been before. It took imagination to be as terrified as this. One bullet from a hidden terrorist and my entire life would be gone in an instant. Would I wake up on the other side? I didn't see another side now, in these immovable granite mountains. Death was the end, and religion promising me I would live on was a lie. Out loud, but softly, in my medic's voice, I said, "Just keep still and you'll be all right. Don't move. Don't do anything. Don't shoot." I stepped outside, quickly withdrawing in case an AK bullet splattered into my forehead.

"Doc?" shouted Rigor Mortis.

I shook my head. "Nothing."

"Shoot first, Paul. Don't look for trouble." But we had walked past, and the hut was now behind the line. You fool, my inner voice said, what if those are 'terrorists'? Our backs are to them; they're behind us now. They could simply step out and shoot us all in cold blood. But I couldn't have done anything else. If it was them or me, then it would have to be me. What little courage I had came from the belief that this village was not bristling with terrorists.

The line swept forward. "Doc, Doc, we need you over here." The line stopped its advance, and I stepped across to a bearded trooper crouching over a black woman who was rolling around on the ground, moaning. She had been shot in the thigh. I put my rifle down, and began to examine her. She had also been hit in the shoulder and perhaps in the chest, but she was concealing her wounds as if she were ashamed of them, curling tightly into a ball when I tried to touch her.

"Stand back, Doc!" The Major strode across the compound to see what was delaying his operation. With his boot, he pushed me aside, putting himself between me and the woman to screen me from her, then held the muzzle of his rifle against her head. "This is the only way."

"No!" It was an instant, knee-jerk reaction. I lunged at him, pulling his arm. His Uzi swung into the air, the remaining burst of fire arcing into the sky. He stopped firing, and pushed me so I fell backwards, then advanced on me, shoving me with his foot. "Doc, you are fucking dangerous."

"It's the kindest thing to do," said Rigor Mortis, as I stood and collected my weapon. I closed my eyes, unable to look at the dead woman. I tried to rewind the moment, and not be in it. I opened my eyes to see the Major with his Uzi pointed at me, as if his finger was itching to shoot me. "Watch out, Doc, watch out."

I stared at him, thinking, he's going to shoot me. But of course he wasn't; it was only another of his tricks. We continued our sweep through. A blackness crept around me, starred with white specks of light. I didn't look back at the dead woman, or at the dark entrance of the hut I had searched; I stared stonily ahead.

"Report," shouted the Major. "Body count."

"Twelve terrorist collaborators on the ground," called Viper.

"Good work, men," said the Major.

I stared down at the strewn bodies behind us. "Did you count the baby?" I said. "That makes thirteen. Shall I collect its AK too?" The Major rolled his tongue in his cheek, and his eyes twitched. "That's enough." His voice echoed in the rocky hills. I took a deep breath and said nothing, tried to disassociate myself from the dead baby, the dead woman, the dead man, the dead chief. I could hear their spirits rustle past me and see their souls smudge against the hills in flight. The Major marched towards the cleft in the rocks where the remainder of the men were gathered and were calling to us. I stood still.

"No, Major Madox, it's not enough," I shouted. Rigor Mortis placed a hand on my shoulder. "What the hell? Just forget it."

I stared at the bodies. "All dead. No job for a medic here."

"The villagers will bury them, Doc. Leave them. They're hiding in the hills. They'll come down as soon as we're gone. Leave them."

I knew what the Major hoped to find in the cleft of the boulders where we had heard the gunfire. He wanted to find ten *makandangas*, men in dirty denim jeans and shirts, bearded, with blood caked on their faces, staring blankly at the open sky. One would still clutch a wooden-butted ancient AK47; another would be sprawled on top of his RPM, the rounds wound around his blood-caked body. I would have had to admit to the Major I had been wrong: there were terrorists after all.

Without warning, the Major sprayed the cleft with bullets, as many as he could shoot in one burst, like a graffiti artist. Fired at such close range, the bullets made the granite spit white chips back at us. He wanted the rocks to be the terrorists, but I knew he also wanted them to be me.

Back at camp, Viper had a message for me: the Major wanted to see me first thing in the morning.

"You're a dead man," said Rigor Mortis. "A dead man."

CHAPTER TWENTY

# GUARDIAN OF THE UNIVERSE

When I was seven, I used to play God. Ants would cross the concrete driveway of our house (Matabele ants, red ants, black ants) and I would patrol the skies with my bomber rubber ball, and target them. I would bounce down and squish as many as three at a time, waiting for unsuspecting ant trains to get halfway across before I attacked. The glee with which I did this, and the stickiness of the rubber ball with the ant blood, made me uneasy. Yet I persisted. I kept scores of the dead; once I killed three hundred and fifty-seven ants, and their bodies were flattened in the driveway to prove it. Or, if I were in a less destructive mood, I would paint live ants with nail polish, and watch them as they went about their business, their backs Pretty Pink, or Blush Azure.

My friends were more violent. Arthur Walker shot animals with his BB gun. Thomas Johnson was reputed to tie stray cats up and cut them in half with an axe. Hank van der Westhuizen squashed frogs with his foot. Jimmy Fuller tortured flies, crickets and ants by pulling legs and wings off one at a time. Steven Swift used his catapult to kill crows, Blue Jays, Glossy Starlings and even larger birds like the Secretary Birds and Crowned Cranes that waded through our swamps (they were royal game, but that didn't stop him).

Perhaps it was the sight of a cut-in-half cat, or the limp neck of a dead Secretary Bird that moved me to repent of my bloodthirsty pastimes. At ten years old, I formed the Animal Police, fancying myself the self-styled guardian of our dumb brothers and sisters. I envisioned myself in an ambulance, painted AP, patrolling the neighbourhood and rescuing cats from the axe, birds from the pellet, and ants and beetles from the cruel hands of Jimmy Fuller. My sense of injustice was fuelled by my guilty past. Once I took down the names of hunters in my Animal Police report book (but never reported them). It was a gesture towards a better world, one in which pain was punished and cruelty banished. Even though I had enough on my plate with humans, I felt I had to take it on myself to change the cruelty of animal-on-animal violence, too. I constantly rescued birds from the cat, snakes from the ibises, and cats from the dog. My childish desire was for an ideal world, one in which animals (including human animals) did not prey on each other. Predators were an aberration of the way things were supposed to be. I would have become a vegetarian, and campaigned against hunting and inhumane treatment of animals in laboratories, had I not been distracted by my hormones and become a predatory animal myself. But now that ten-year-old self was alive again. I was ready, with all my righteous indignation and anger. Justice would be done.

★   ★   ★

It was at this point too that I began seriously to consider desertion. How sensible was it to fight a war that you knew you were losing? How honourable was it to fight for something you didn't believe in any more? Was there any Rhodesian soldier who had defected to the other side? I could not conceive of any. Was there any Rhodesian soldier who had gone AWOL and deserted? I had heard, through envious whispers of troops in training, how Steve Jackson had simply taken off on a weekend pass, boarded a plane to Durban and had never returned. Then there was Greg Barrow, who had feigned homosexuality, and had been discharged. And Misfit Me, of course. I should have gone to England, to study at the University of East Anglia when I had the chance. Rhodesian whites were leaving the country at a rate of two thousand a month. I was the rat left on a sinking ship. Or the sinking ship itself.

The convoy was my first thought; hop on the next convoy and I'll be gone. But desertion was not practical. I needed a passport. More importantly, I needed a signed letter from my company commander stating that I was either not eligible for military service or that I had fulfilled my obligation to my country at present. I had neither. No, that was the coward's way out. Today would be different. I would stand up for myself for the first time in my miserable life. Self-realisation, here we come.

★   ★   ★

The Major stood in full uniform, complete with pips, beret and combat boots. He was an officer and a gentleman. I stood on the floor in front of his desk in my Vila Salazar T-shirt, which was now a rag. I wondered how he had managed to wash and iron his clothes; but, of course, he had a batman, a servant whom he brought along with him on the trip. I held the piece of blue, red-margined paper in my hand. He stared at me, building up the thunderclouds before the storm. I knew what he was going to say. I was on a charge; I would be doubling away to the box when I returned; I was in deep shit. But I was ready for him. I didn't let him speak.

"M... M... Major Madox (it was a pity about the stutter), I am charging you with obstruction of my medical duty. This report is going straight to my CO in Llewellin Barracks, and then on up to the Commander of Llewellin and DRR." I waved the piece of paper in his face. I was conjuring up Judgement Day: the plumes on the CO's head waving in the hot Matopas breeze, the shimmering heat off the echoing rocks, the angry, sullen RAR soldiers, the ancestors assembled to judge the living and the dead. "I'm also charging you with conspiring to subvert justice, with manslaughter, and..."

I got no further. Major Madox lunged across the table and ripped the paper from my hand. I didn't quiver or cower, though I feared he would spring at my throat like a bulldog. But he did not strike me. He held the paper at arm's length to read (he did not have his glasses on), and then tore it up in three slow movements.

"You will speak only when you're spoken to," Viper said behind me. My neck muscles tightened, but I resisted the urge to turn around.

"Corporal." The Major orbited me, pacing with slow, measured steps, ending up three inches from my face. "So this is your pathetic little attempt to wriggle out of your responsibility."

"You're the one guilty of the crime, Major."

He slammed his fist on the desk. "Yes, sir, and no, sir! Is that clear?"

"Yes, sir," prompted Viper behind me, with a jab in my back to reinforce the point.

"Yes, sir."

But Major Madox was a reasonable man. He sat down, pressed his fingers together, a spider doing press-ups on a mirror. He smiled. "Perhaps you haven't noticed, but we're fighting a war. A war…" He waved his maimed left hand at the tent around him, evidence that we were fighting a war. "We're not at a Sunday afternoon tea party. There are terrorists out there – wild beasts, animals, ready to tear you apart, cut your pecker off and eat it for tea. True, eh, Sergeant?" He arched his eyebrows at Viper, who assented. He turned back to me.

"Doc, you know sweet fuck all about what we're doing here."

"You're right."

"Sir," prompted Viper.

"Sir."

Suddenly Major Madox leaped out of his camp chair, as if stung by an invisible hornet, and rushed at me. He prodded my chest with his finger. "I know you. You want us to lay down our arms and give up. Here, comrades, take over the villages, the TTLs, the country. Help yourself. Murder, maim, kill your own people. Go ahead. Over my dead fucking body!"

"I'm talking about civilians, sir."

"There are no civilians in this war, Doc." His rage made him writhe and stutter and jerk. He pulled the pistol from his holster, waved it at my nose. "Who are you, Mr Nineteen-year-old? Who designated you as guardian of the fucking universe?" I watched his red, swollen finger on the trigger guard of the gun. White flecks of spit gathered in the corners of his mouth. "I'm a fucking saint compared to some people I know. Have you seen what the Selous Scouts do in a day's work? Do I carry piano wire around in my back pocket? Do I cut the lips off suspects who don't talk and make them eat their own ears if they don't listen?"

Please God, I thought. Just one twitch of that finger and it's all over. But the moment passed. He looked at the pistol as if seeing it for the first time, shook it at me, then placed it carefully down on the table. "Corporal Williams, I'm charging you with neglect of duty. I'm charging you with obstruction of justice. I'm charging you with intent to shoot at a fellow soldier. With insubordination, you fucking cunt. I'm placing you on detention duties with immediate effect. You will report to the Sergeant first thing in the morning at oh-six-hundred hours. You will surrender your weapon. Dismissed."

★  ★  ★

Starting at oh-six-hundred hours, my life was going to be hell. I was going to suffer. I would be carrying sandbags, running on the spot, stumbling around the inside of an empty water tank until I collapsed. He was going to try to break me.

But the next morning, no one came to rouse me. At seven, I ventured a short reconnaissance around the campsite, passing the officers' tents, making sure I was not seen. Viper was fast asleep. Madox, so the guard told me, had driven off early to a SITREP meeting in Gwanda. Viper finally summoned me at midmorning. I walked into the tent, ready for anything. But Viper sat me down and offered me a cup of coffee from a metal urn. I refused.

"Doc, we've been in contact with your Company Commander, Major Brink. He informs us that you are to report back to DRR Barracks so that you can spend your last month at the camp hospital before you demobilise. The Major regrets that he can't be here for your departure, but he's arranged that you take the next transport back to Llewellin. Unfortunately, no transport is available, so we suggest that you hitch a ride on the next civilian convoy back to Bulawayo."

He scrutinised me for any signs of madness, but I had been so prepared for an attack that I was stunned into silence.

"There is one thing."

I knew what was coming.

"First, we don't want the other troops to know. It's bad for morale. We have arranged for Rigor Mortis and Philemon to take you, but no one else must know. Hardy will take over as medic until we can requisition for a replacement."

Again I said nothing. I aware of their trick, but did not know how to respond.

"Secondly, when you demob, you are free and clear of the army. That is, unless you have any outstanding complaints or grievances. Once you make any formal complaint or grievance – and this is just my personal advice, my friendly advice, because we've known each other a while now, and I know you're no fool, that you would not want to delay your demobilisation…" He hesitated, again to let me speak, or perhaps just to make sure I was aware that his advice was really a threat – "…your discharge will be indefinitely held up." He folded a letter he had been holding and placed it in my hand. "This is clearance from the Major that you are free to go, that you have no outstanding commitments to him or to B Company."

I was being blackmailed and bribed into submission. I knew that. I could have pointed an accusing finger at Viper and implicated him in the murder of five civilians. I could have become a martyr for the cause of justice. I could have torn the letter up. But of course I didn't.

★ ★ ★

DECLARATION
Army No. 111563
Name and Initials (Block capitals): WILLIAMS P.A.
Rank: T/CPL
Unit or Corps: DRR

1. I acknowledge that I have this day had my attention drawn to the more important provisions of the Secrets Act of Rhodesia.

2. I understand that the insights and truths which I have received or acquired, or to which I had had access to in the course of my military duty, is information which is covered by the provisions of the Official Secrets Act and that the unauthorised communication by me of such information to any other person after I have left the service is an offence in respect of which I may be prosecuted.

3. I understand that no atrocities occurred in the course of my military duty, nor were any civilians injured in the prosecution of my duties, and neither were any women or children raped, tortured, murdered, terrorised, or in any way harmed.

4. I declare that I have not in my possession any bitterness, hatred, malice, violent propensities to any other human beings, and that as a Rhodesian Soldier Blue, I am of sound mind and healthy body.

5. I will write no book, movie or give any true account of my experiences in the army and the two years shall be blotted out. I will be silenced. I will stammer and stutter my way through life.

Witnessed...... Staff Sgt Piggott
Signed...... PAUL WILLIAMS
Date 3/7/1978

★  ★  ★

There is still no trace of the war in Salisbury, the Sunshine City. The streets are full of shoppers, and the regular afternoon thunderstorms keep the skies clean and the grass glowing. The jacarandas are in full bloom, as are the poinsettias and the flamboyants which carpet Blakiston Avenue red. Soldiers walking down First Street arm in arm with their loved ones are a picture on a Quality Street chocolate tin.

There is no trace either of Bianca or her family. True to her word, they have indeed skedaddled off to South Africa to live happily ever after, leaving a black hole behind them. There is nothing left for me here, so I plan my escape.

★  ★  ★

Wearing my threadbare Wrangler jeans, and Lord Kitchener T-shirt, I wait for the teller to beckon me to the counter of the Air Rhodesia Office in Manica Road. I have a cheque from my father for a one-way air ticket to Durban, and have also brought with me my demob papers, my copy of Major Madox's letter, and a clearance form signed by the CO of Llewellin, the CQ stores, the hospital. The clerk whose job it is to net fleeing Rhodesian call-ups frowns at me, runs his finger down a long list and tells me to wait in an office for the officer in charge.

"Corporal Williams?" A handsome man in khakis greets me.

"Paul Williams. Call me Paul." I stand.

"I hate to break the news to you, Corporal."

"What news?"

"Where have you been, Corporal? Call-ups have been extended two years for university applicants."

"Don't try to kid me." He's joking. Break into a smile, sign the release form, and I'll be on my way. But he shakes his head and clicks his tongue.

"Two years. We have here" – he waves a letter in the air but doesn't let me read it – "your declaration that you intend to go to the University of Natal, Durban, after your military service. You signed it."

"I was specifically ordered, by my CO, by my company commander to demob. No one said anything…" My neatly calendared future crumbles beneath my feet.

"University applicants are required to do two years' continual service, and then will be exempt from camps until they have completed their degree. Therefore you will not be allowed to fly. Your demobilisation is officially cancelled. You are to report to KGVI Barracks for your next assignment immediately."

So here I am, back on the banks of Lake Kariba, staring out at the dead water, listening to the roar of another plane I missed. If this were a novel, there would be a crescendo of action, the crunch point where the protagonist's ultimate resolve is tested and he wins. Then would come the swift denouement to the satisfying ending, where all antagonists are vanquished. If it were a movie, it would follow Vreitag's triangle, or the steps of Joseph Campbell's *Hero with a Thousand Faces*. If it were an autobiography, there would at least be some moral lesson to be learned from the struggle and triumph or defeat of the hero. But it is none of these.

So herewith the anti-climax. I'm assigned to spend six months as a nondescript medic to the chaplains at KGVI Barracks. I am issued a weapon, but no rounds. I spend my time dispensing flu medicine to HQ soldiers, and injecting Propen into the buttocks of RAR soldiers.

In these final six months, four times the number of people are killed than in the previous year: two thousand five hundred and eight terrorists, three hundred and forty-five Rhodesian soldiers, three thousand civilians. Eighty thousand black civilians are left homeless. Ten thousand are crippled. There are a quarter of a million refugees. And six million people still have to say, "Yes, *baas*" to a white man at least once a day.

I remember little. Time has come to a standstill. I am occasionally sent out on assignments. I am sometimes sent to Tsanga Lodge (which harbours injured soldiers), to Umtali, to Nyanga, to Fort Victoria. The closer I get to freedom, the less free I feel. One of my last assignments is to provide medical assistance for a Christian Union camp for schoolchildren at Lake Kariba. When the children leave, I'm supposed to be on Flight 825 back to Salisbury, but my superiors have made an administrative error, so I return from the airport and wait at Kariba for the truck that will drive me back. And it is here that my story finally grinds to a halt and refuses to move forward.

★ ★ ★

Monday, September 4, 1978. *The Herald* runs the headline: VISCOUNT FROM KARIBA MISSING, and shows a picture of a blue and white Vickers Viscount, with a published a list of the names of the passengers. On Sunday night, the newspaper claims, the Captain of the Viscount sent a distress signal back to Kariba tower, saying that two starboard engines had failed.

Monday night, the news at eight. Victor Macintosh/Geoffrey Atkins/Joy Cameron-Dow/John Pank tells the war-ravaged white nation that a Viscount plane carrying 53 passengers has crashed in the Kariba area and killed 17, including the crew. The plane, however, was not brought down by enemy action; we repeat, no enemy action was involved in bringing the plane down. We also regret to inform you, however, that not only did the plane crash but – a Combined Operations Security Communique issued this afternoon says – terrorists murdered the survivors. Yes, you heard right: the plane crashed, killing seventeen people, but the survivors were massacred by terrorists.

The white population is in uproar. It's not true. It can't be true. And the cynics don't believe it either. It sounds too much like slick Rhodesian propaganda to bolster support for a dwindling war. But to prove his point the newsman/woman cuts to a clip of Nkomo's grinning face, a snippet from a BBC interview which is selectively screened on our TV (our censors don't allow us to see much – in fact, this is the first time I have ever seen Nkomo on TV). In this interview, a fat, gloating Nkomo boasts Moral Equivalence, and claims responsibility. We threw stones at it, he laughs. That's how we brought it down.

We brought that plane down, he maintains, but it is not true that we killed any survivors. The Rhodesians have been ferrying military personnel and equipment in Viscounts and we had no reason to believe that this was anything different. ZIPRA is not interested in killing civilians, but when people start using civilian aircraft, how do you know when the plane is up there? The Rhodesians should know this is a military zone. It is tragic that there has been a massive outcry in the West because white civilians have been killed. You forget that the regime kills 30 of our people a day. So the life of a black person is different from a white person? Any European child is supposed to be worth a million blacks. As far as we are concerned we were bringing down an aircraft that was being used to ferry military personnel and equipment.

He's lying, the collective voice of white Rhodesia says. No ways a *munt* could bring down a goddamn plane like that. And it was full of innocent civilians, for God's sake. Why would anyone want to gloat over that? And didn't the Minister of Transport vehemently deny that terrorists had shot down the plane?

*The Herald:* September 8. 'Investigations' confirm that the plane was brought down by a heat-seeking Soviet-made SAM-7 missile hitting the inner starboard engine. Now our righteous anger is at white heat. The Minister of Transport and Power, Bill Irvine, calls it, "An action more barbaric than anything that can be read in the annals of Genghis Khan."

September 9. The city comes to a stop this lunchtime. The funeral for the 48 civilians murdered by terrorists is held in one of the most public places in Rhodesia, the Anglican Cathedral of St. Mary and All Saints in Pioneer Square (where the white pioneers first claimed ownership of the country in 1890). About 2,000 people squeeze themselves and their anger into the cathedral, and others clog the square and block the intersections of Second Street and Union Avenue. People stand on top of *The Herald* building, others on the Treasure Trove's flat roof. There are no TV screens, but radios and loudspeakers broadcast the bitter outrage to the outside world. We are on the cusp of settlement after a bloody six-year war. A week ago, Smith was about to agree with Nkomo, isolating Mugabe, the real threat and maybe, just maybe, we had a chance to stop the war. Instead, it will take an irreversible turn for the worse. In the intransigent anger of the white mourners here, there will be no settlement.

They are making a show of it. Lines of Air Rhodesia pilots, hostesses and staff, all in uniform, are joined in solidarity by South African Airways personnel, the blue berets of the Special Air Service, and senior officers from all the important branches of Rhodesia's armed forces. The parents and relatives of the dead look oddly 'civilian' in the military parade. And, of course, in the front row we see the gaggle of politicians we know so well from the Vic Mackenzie cartoons that appear in the paper, Ian and Janet Smith, P.K. van der Byl, Bill Irvine, and other sundry hangers-on.

The sermon is pregnant with rhetorical devices that move the crowd to tears, anger and delusion. The Very Reverend John da Costa, Anglican Dean of Salisbury, blames everyone, from the church itself, to the politicians sitting in front of him, to the Western world, the World Council of Churches, the United Nations and the British government:

"This bestiality, worse than anything in recent history, stinks in the nostrils of Heaven. But are we deafened with the voice of protest from nations which call themselves 'civilised'? It seems we are not. We wait for condemnation by Dr David Owen, himself a medical doctor, trained to extend mercy and help to all in need. We listen and the silence is deafening. We listen for condemnation by the President of the United States, a man from the Bible-Baptist belt, and again the silence is deafening. We listen for condemnation by the Pope, the Chief Rabbi, the Archbishop of Canterbury, by all who love the name of God, and once again the silence is deafening."

The message is meant to be a righteous call to action. But it sounds more like an admission of defeat. Of course, no one sees the attack in the context of the many brutal assaults the Rhodesian forces have made on enemy camps, local populations and neighbouring countries. We are innocent victims, unjustly targeted. No one, I'm sure, in this crowd (except the crafty politicians) knows that only a week before the Viscount was brought down, Rhodesians used large Viscount-looking aircraft to raid Zambian camps and kill, maim, pillage and destroy.

Ian Smith walks out first, brushes away the TV cameras of the world, but before he can make his getaway, a white man behind him raises a poster: 'PM Smith – Give Nkomo a message when next you meet him secretly: Go to hell, you murdering bastard.' The crowd applauds. Smith ignores the poster and steps into his car to drive away. But when the Dean and Bishop Burrough walk past, Da Costa stops to confront the men. "This is not a political rally," he tells them. The men do not move, and when one waves his poster, insisting that its message be seen by all, Bishop Burrough tears it down and throws it to the ground.

The crowd begins to boo them. "Smith must stand down," shouts the demonstrator. "If he hasn't the guts to stand up and fight, we have." The crowd applauds him, and yells encouragement. The Dean wrings his hands and shakes his black vestments, but the man will not stop. He climbs on the stone window ledge to escape the grasping fingers of the Bishop and turns to address the crowd. "I've been fighting for this country for a long time and I'm proud of it. I'm sick and tired and there's a lot of us who feel the same way. Let's get in there and bloody well fight!"

People applaud and boo, bewildered because the West will not condemn this atrocity, bewildered because Smith is negotiating with terrorists, bewildered because they are hated so much. But most of them are saved by their belief in absolutes. How much more proof do you need that this is not a legitimate civil war against us, but a brutal attempt to return to the savagery of the Dark Continent? We have to retaliate. Bang go the carefully argued plans for reconciliation; bang goes the settlement. Smith has to fight on. He cannot back down now. How can he hope to sell us Nkomo as a partner in settlement? We want naked revenge. I say 'we' because I am one of them. I am attending my own funeral. My fellow Rhodesians and I, given sheltered employment and power and money, are at the end of the road. We are surrounded by blasphemy, treachery, unfaithfulness, doubt and despair. It is the end of our short thousand-year reign.

★  ★  ★

I finally demobilise on December 31, 1978. I say goodbye to my parents, and a month later board a plane to Durban, and leave Rhodesia forever. I have the dubious pleasure of watching the country disintegrate from a distance.

And this is how it goes down. After all the bravado, the declaration of UDI, the dream of victory, Smith concedes defeat. He sits down at Lancaster House in London and talks to the terrorists, strong-armed by South Africa, Britain and the USA. The military does all it can to stop the dam bursting. The politicians are betraying us, they cry, selling us down the river to communists and terrorists. So the attacks on bases in Mozambique, Zambia, and even Tanzania and Angola become more desperate, more daring and more absurd. Mugabe's ZANLA steps up its attacks too, so as to get full advantage at the negotiating table. The

Selous Scouts, SAS and RLI work feverishly and ruthlessly to stop them. Nkomo prepares a full-scale conventional invasion of Rhodesia. But it is all over bar the shouting.

An 'all-party' agreement is signed in December 1979. Lord Christopher Soames enters Salisbury as the British Governor and officially returns the country to colonial status. Great Britain's dominion ensures the 'peaceful' transition of power through 'free' elections held between February 14 and 18, 1980. As a result of this vote, Robert Mugabe, Enemy Number One, Terrorist Leader, is elected Prime Minister, and Zimbabwe is born.

★   ★   ★

I've dreamed of this moment. I plunge into the waves of the Indian Ocean. I clutch at the prize I have run towards. I have fought the good fight, I have finished the race, I have kept the faith. I am a straight-A student living in Durban, who swims in the sea every morning, and who has healed from the cancer of unrequited love. I sing the sun in flight; my deeds dance in a green bay; my words fork lightning.

And yet freedom eludes me. There is a glassy film in front of my face, so that I do not feel as if I am really on these beaches. I have put myself in the extreme state of unassailability. But I cannot escape my self-obliteration, or my mergence with others. I am the ballooning medic crushed under the wheels of the RL in Vila Salazar; I am the rabbit-faced boy shot by his own troops when he attacked his own image of fear; I am the soldier hit in the head by Major Madox's ricochet; I am the chief of the village who stood up to the Major's tyranny, killed by a single bullet from Craig Hardy's FN; I am a passenger on Flight 825 who died in the crash; I am a survivor massacred afterwards; I am forced to cook and eat my own lips and ears.

I have survived my own death. I am left only to bear witness. But it will take three decades and an aphasic life lived on three continents before I am able to tell my tale, and to speak of those who did not live to tell theirs.

# TWENTY-FIVE YEARS LATER

From the oval window of the Air Zimbabwe Boeing 737, Harare, Zimbabwe, in the early 2000s looks exactly like Salisbury, Rhodesia, did in 1979. My steel girder man still surveys his country from the top of the Pearl Assurance building, and the power chimneys behind the *kopje* cough up steam as they have done for the past fifty years. But the Federal Building is gone, and an American blue-glass skyscraper overshadows the Pearl building. In the east, two grey battleship buildings house Zimbabwe's administrative offices, and the penile tower with a golden cock perched on its pinnacle next to the Queen Victoria Library is the ZANU–PF headquarters. As we descend towards Harare International Airport in Epworth, I see waterways glinting silver. At this time of year, just before Christmas, I envisage Harare the Sunshine City as a green, lively place, with sprinkles of purple jacaranda flowers lining some streets, and red flamboyants still blooming down others. This is surely a flourishing, independent African country that has freed itself from the yoke of colonial slavery.

But as the plane comes down to land, I see I am mistaken. The Sunshine City looks like the aftermath of a category five hurricane. The grass is yellow (where there is any grass at all), and dust is blowing in brown clouds over the squatter camps which surround the city. Many of the politically incorrect jacarandas and flamboyants have been hacked down, and dry dongas have replaced what were once gleaming rivers.

I walk the concrete apron towards the bleached airport building, breathing in the fear, the animal sweat and smoke, the 'Africa' that wraps around my heart like cellophane. The new airport terminal is already old, the painted walls are greased by the backs of slouching airport personnel, and yawning spaces gape where there should be seating, phones, restaurants. A urine smell wafts out of the toilets.

There is no family to come home to, and most of my classmates were either killed in the war, have packed for Perth, or have settled – or is that resettled, unsettled? – in New Zealand, Canada or Great Britain. No longer are my bright young parents waving from the balcony (gin and tonic in hand), Mum with beehive hairdo (Are you hungry dear? We'll take you to the salad buffet at the Kentucky Hotel in Hatfield if you want), or Dad standing proudly, his hair Brylcreemed down, wearing a jacket and tie in this heat (he still thinks you have to dress up to go anywhere to keep up appearances in front of the natives). My parents have returned to Norwich, to the comforting See-I-Told-You-Not-To-Go wings of their Norfolk family. They are retired, stooped over, disillusioned. And though they were never Smith supporters before, during or after the war, they are now. They have managed to sell the house and all its contents, including the 1960 Cortina GX and the 1979 Datsun 120Y, for ten thousand English pounds on the black market, and escape with their seventy-year-old lives.

I shake hands with the man waiting for me. He is the estate agent who will seal the deal and turn a three-bedroom house with the sagging souls of three lives and the accumulated memories of a hundred years into cash. A caricature of himself, he wears *vellies* and safari suit and sports a V-neck tan. He calls the local black people 'non-swimmers', and his eyes bulge in exaggerated vigilance as he looks about him constantly for *tsotsis*. He is a vanishing breed, the persecuted minority, harassed by government officials wherever he goes, cigarette packet in top pocket, comb in sock, but with the arrogant assumption that he is still superior, still right, still Rhodesian. We have learned nothing.

No, you can't rent a car, he tells me. No bladdy petrol, and it's unsafe to take a taxi. "Even a Rixi taxi?" I tease? ("Don't let a ton-up spoil your hair-do; don't let a rainstorm wash you out; whatever you need transport for, Rixi's just a telephone call away.") Mr Caldwell does not smile. He hasn't smiled in years. He leads me to a rusty green Mazda 323 whose petrol tank is being guarded in the airport parking lot by his 'garden boys', ragamuffins with sticks, sitting on the curb.

We drive through the devastated ruins of my memory. Tall poles with Mugabe's face and Zimbabwe flags greet us every few hundred metres. We duck under an arch labelled 'Zimbabwe Independence 1980,' guarded by soldiers in Chinese-style uniforms and AKs casually pointed at the traffic (the first arch was blown up shortly after it was erected in 1980). We pass hundreds of destitute, ragged people who stare emptily at us from the dusty verges.

Smith must be pleased: his predictions have all come true. This country has become one of the 'certain countries to the north of us', and Robert Mugabe has joined the long list of dictators whose names we gleefully recited at school, who raped their countries and confirmed our racial prejudices about the incorrigibility of the African mind. Kloppers must be sitting in Australia gloating over another African country to add to his list: "Look at Idi Amin! Look at Kaunda! Look at Banda! Look at Nyerere! Look at Mugabe! Rhodesia (it'll never be Zimbabwe to me) was once the breadbasket of Africa – now it's a basket case! Rhodesia saves; Zimbabwe Ruins."

The Right Honorable Robert Gabriel Mugabe, President of the Republic of Zimbabwe, boasts that the final *chimurenga* has been won. But what is this victory? The country is in ruins. Sewage runs down the streets. War-veteran liberators drive in Rhodesian crocodile vehicles, point AKs at cowed residents. Even the vendors' shacks at the side of the roads have been bulldozed and demolished. Twenty thousand people have died to achieve the final liberation. *Pamberi Mugabe. Pasi Smeeth. Pasi Breetayn.*

Even Major Madox, if he is still alive, would smile. Stooped, haggard, in the prison of civilian clothes, shuffling in dismay at being left abandoned in his old age in the Africa he tried so hard to prevent, he'd clutch my arm: "Doc! Doc! You wanted us to lay down our arms and give up. You wanted the comrades to take over the villages, the TTLs, the country. You wanted them to murder, maim, kill their own people. Well, here you are. This is what you wanted. Are you happy now? Was I right or was I wrong?"

Just before my parents left Zimbabwe for good, my mother by chance met The Honourable Ex-Pry Minister, Ian Douglas Smith, at the Borrowdale Village shops. "You were right, Mr Smith," she told him. And he stooped down, gave a crooked smile and kissed her. My father also encountered him, at a bookstore where Good Old Smithy was signing copies of his fast-selling autobiography *The Great Betrayal.* My father stood at the end of a two-hour line and watched the man write two, three hundred Ian Douglas Smiths, the same signature over and over.

"Mr Smith, aren't you getting tired of signing your name? You should rest." He meant it kindly, not ironically. Smith looked up at a fellow countryman (what they now had in common were creaking bones, brittle spines and memories that played tricks on them), clapped an arthritic hand on my father's hunched back. "I never get tired of doing things for Rhodesia."

★  ★  ★

My Ian Smith is much, much younger. I haven't seen him since I was nineteen, the smooth shaved Ian Douglas at the Viscount funeral, the white man who caused all the trouble. But no one blames the whites any more except the Hysterical *Herald*, mouthpiece of ZANU–PF (Zimbabwe African National Union – Patriotic Front). The people are no longer patriots, no longer united, no longer even Zimbabweans, proud of their country or willing to fight for it. The crowds staring at me through the window of the stuttering Mazda 323 are as shrunken, as politically arthritic as Smith's bony right hand. Their yellow eyes accuse me: Why did you abandon us? Picanins chase our car, and when it stops at the traffic lights, try to pry off the hubcaps with long wires made from coat hangers.

"Christmas box, Christmas box."

"Bugger off," says my valiant escort. "Ask Mugabe for a blerry Christmas box."

Yet the city is still heartbreakingly beautiful. I love the silhouette of the *msasa* trees against the sky, the rocks bubbling out of the red clay earth. The smell of the air, the dancing of the trees above me, the blue, blue sky counterbalance the whine of the real estate agent's voice in my ear ("Bloody non-swimmers… Mugs… Price of petrol… War vets… Forex…").

The deal is done in the Meikles Hotel, which has not changed since I was a young child. We are served tea in china cups and scones with clotted cream and strawberry jam, while white-uniformed, fezzed waiters hover around our table. The only difference now is the price, which is in thousands of dollars.

In my room, Caldwell pulls out a wad of grimy pound notes from an inner coat pocket, and thwacks it on the table. I sign the document he has prepared. He has already sold the house twice over and pocketed twice the amount that we settled on, but he reminds me how fortunate I am to get anything for it these days, especially in 'Forex', as he calls British pounds, or American dollars, or any foreign currency that has not devalued 1000% in the last few years. My parents' total worth for all their labour and investment in this country stands at eleven thousand, three hundred pounds and fifty-seven pence.

The house is invisible behind walls, fences, barbed wire and glass-bottle shards, but three pine trees wave in the sky and a monkey puzzle tree stands proudly, taller than I remember. A dog barks from behind the gate which still bears my father's steady hand in Dulux white: 59 Hillside Road. I would love to walk through its rooms – Willow's room, the junk room, the lounge where Elton John's 'Your Song' made me cry. I would love to trace the nine-hole golf course I made in the garden with old Cashel Valley tins when I was eleven years old. But there is no way in. No one answers the gate, though I can hear the thumping bass of a Thomas Mapfumo song from within: *I will give you something, if you will give me something in return…*

When you are young, your parents are all-loving, all-knowing and omnipotent. When you are a teenager, they're idiots. When you are older, they are magically wise again. Not omnipotent, but wise. My parents were heroes, then fools, but now are heroes again. The dark glass of naiveté, or liberalism or scepticism, is gone, and in the clearing fog I see them as brave, imaginative, loving, steady in the face of this wave of idiocy. My mother lost everything in World War II, and my father grew up poor in that war, too. They sought a better life, made one for themselves, here in this house. They planted trees, created a garden, stood against the folly of Ian Smith, and then against the folly of Mugabe. Now they have lost everything again, their home, their sense of identity, even their Zimbabwe passports. But they've survived.

Across Samora Machel Avenue and along Helm Avenue, I follow my old path to Churchill School. The pedestrian crossing at Umtali (now Mutare) Road and Daventry Road is unchanged, but of course the road signs are all gone, used apparently to make coffin handles for the hundred of thousands of AIDS victims. It is hard to believe that these roads, small and tattered, once ran with dreams of pursued white goddesses, and that the self I am attempting to retrieve from here is a petty, insignificant one who played no role in history, except to be one of the many whites trapped in a box, thinking they were at the centre of the world. There are thirteen million people in Zimbabwe at this time, nearly three times the population of 1971. The whites constitute an irrelevant 0.1 percent. Even in 1971, with the white population at 2.5 percent, we were a tiny minority. How did we presume such significance?

The school premises look tired and worn where too many boys have trampled fields and corridors. In the drought, the once green rugby fields are dust bowls. The school is empty, so I am free to pursue my indulgent trail. Here is the blackboard on which... here is my old Latin room... here the Science lab where I had a view of the girls' playing fields every Tuesday...

What goes on here now? The piece of railway line used as a bell to summon us to class is gone, but the tree on which it was tied bears the scars of its yoke. The buildings have not been painted for twenty years, and I can peel the grey Plascon PVA paint off to expose layers of the past. There were no fences when I was at the school, but I can now detect where fences were erected to surround and protect the premises, even though the wire, pegs and posts are now gone too. At the back of the school, playing fields Garner and Benwell have been replaced with long rows of dead maize. I doubt the pupils still learn Latin, Biology and Art, but I suspect that if they have lessons at all here, they are taught Shona, Economics and Agriculture.

Nearly half my class died in the war. I don't even know who is still alive. Parker, Johnson, Hutchison, are you there? But when I push open the heavy doors of the stolid grey hall, the Honour Roll is gone. In the south entrance foyer, a square of darker paint and four screw holes reassure me that my memory is accurate. I sit on the rotten stands by the old basketball court (now a cracked maze of old tar) and close my eyes. In my head, the hymn we used to sing with gusto at the end of every term, preluding our glorious summer holidays, plays.

> *Lord, dismiss us with thy blessing, thanks for mercies past received;*
> *Pardon all, their faults confessing; time that's lost may all retrieve;*
> *May thy children, may thy children, ne'er again thy Spirit grieve.*

*Let thy father-hand be shielding all who here shall meet no more;*
*May their seed-time past be yielding year by year a richer store;*
*Those returning, those returning, make more faithful than before.*

★ ★ ★

Some hours later, I drive to a familiar neighbourhood. All the road signs to Greendale have disappeared. The precious drops of petrol in the forty-litre tank of the Mazda 323 generously provided by my host are rapidly disappearing. I park in the long elephant grass off Jameson Avenue (renamed Samora Machel Avenue after the Second *Chimurenga*, now Nothing Avenue after the Third), so that I can walk the rest of the way.

The road to her house is potholed, yet I can swear the tar is the same viscous substance I walked on in 1977. A car is rusting in the driveway, the same Datsun her parents drove – they never did get that Ford from Duly's. A dog bounds up to me at the gate, the descendant no doubt of the two who terrorised my youth.

In the bright green garden, two children play in the water sprinkler. A twelve-year-old Bianca in a sodden dress, with long wet blonde hair, squeals as she tousles with a flip-flop, which another dog is wresting from her. A blond boy, fourteen or so, leaps through the sprinkler, teasing the dog, shouting commands at his sister. When I open the gate, the children stop. Bianca stares at me with her sardonic eyes. Luke holds the dogs by their collars, so their tongues loll and their heads strain to get at me. Then the maid emerges from the shade of a tree, and calls the two children by foreign names: "Colleen! Gary! Go get your mother."

The house is even more run-down than before, but who am I to judge, I who have lived in pristine cardboard-box houses in England and the United States for twenty-five years? To have a garden like this, an acre of bleeding red poinsettias, yellow spithodia trees, purple and blue geraniums growing wild, white papery bougainvillea trellising over the front porch, to have a 3,000-square-foot house with solid red brick walls, in the United States, or England, or almost anywhere else, you'd have to be a millionaire. The pool is a green slime; it has finally become its true self. Golden flashes swim in it, and a frog watches me from a broken diving board.

A blonde woman leans against the doorway. The folded arms, the smirk, the toss of the hair tell me who she is, although in the shock of my first impression, she is an ordinary middle-aged Rhodesian housewife.

"Howdy, stranger."

We embrace awkwardly, as if we are indeed strangers.

"You haven't changed."

"Nor have you. You're just a little greyer."

This is the lie of personhood, that you remain the same throughout your whole life. Of course we are not the same people. Our bodies have regenerated cells every seven years, our thoughts have mutated, and only the illusion of our names and lying memories remains.

"Why didn't you let anyone know you were in the country? We could have had a reunion."

"It was sudden. I didn't expect to have to come back right now."

"Very bad excuse. But it's good to see you again. Come in, come in." She leads me into the dark, mouldy living room. "What have you been doing all this time? How long has it been?"

"Twenty-five years."

"No."

"It is."

"Come and have a seat. What can I get you? A cup of tea? Some orange juice?"

"Tea's great."

She disappears into the kitchen. I stroll to the mantelpiece and try to identify the people in the photographs. A solid, happy life is on display. Here's Bianca on her wedding day, white-veiled, flushed, smiling, hanging onto a handsome South African man in a tight suit. Here's her first baby. Here's her second baby, held by an aged Mrs Pennefather. Here are her two children at the Victoria Falls, peering over a ledge, held by an older Bianca, her hair tied back. There are other mementos too: a framed degree certificate, Bachelor of Arts 1982, from the University of Cape Town; a Native American dreamcatcher hanging from a nail in the middle of the wall. And dangling from the corner of a framed painting of two giraffes in a savannah landscape, a black fist, fashioned from hard wood, its thumb in a hitchhiking pose, clenching an oiled elephant-tail string.

The kettle roars in the big, open kitchen.

"Come… sit." She sits opposite me and takes a deep breath. We look at each other. Then she plunges into her life story, speaking fast, afraid of silence. She explains how she and Dave were never really happy in South Africa, and finally decided to move back to Zim in the mid-eighties. They've made a good life for themselves. They've even managed to put some money away so that if everything goes *kaput* tomorrow, they'll still be OK. Zim (the diminutive, reductive, still-OK-for-whites-Zim) is home. Their family is here, they grew up here, etc etc.

In the comfortable run-down Africa that they inhabit, there is no shadow of what will happen here soon. In a short few months, 'war vets' (men who are far too young to have fought in the war in 1978) will ravage white farms. Whites will become enemies of the state, the economy will collapse, the country will subside into a black hole. But in December 2004, Bianca still has a maid, lives in a big house, shops at Barbour's, has tea at Sam Levy's Borrowdale Village, and vacations in Nyanga, as if a revolution has not occurred, as if a war has not devastated the country, as if everyone – black and white – lives together in harmony. Life is good. Or as good as can be expected.

"We still go to Hillside Fellowship. My brother – Luke – you remember him? He's the Pastor. And me? I did my BA in Cape Town. I was a stay-at-home mom for a while, but that got boring, so I went into teaching, taught at Roosy for a while. It was so strange going back there as a teacher, seeing all those kids in uniform, just like…"

She's in mid-sentence, in the middle of my silent appraisal of her, when she brings her hands to her face and wipes her eyes. "Sorry. Sorry. Miriam?" The maid brings us tea, and the kids stumble in, looking askance at this stranger in the house who is making their mother cry. "This is Paul Williams, an old school friend of mine." Colleen and Gary collect their food and red drinks and troop outside again.

I am making her uncomfortable, so I ease into a conversation about past friends. When she pours the tea, her gesture is that of the sixteen-year-old Bianca. But what did she really look like in 1973? My present perception conflicts with my memory: back then I looked through the eyes of Romantic literature, of mystical sexual denial.

"Do you know Craig Hardy is still around? He lives around the corner in Eastlea, and is married to a sweet woman. His kids hang out with mine sometimes. We see each other at Hillside Baptist. He's a Deacon."

"A Deacon?"

"If he knew you were here, he'd really want to see you. He always wondered what happened to you. He still has that Mini Cooper, you know. Remember that…? But enough about him. I want to know about you. How long are you going to be in town?" She sits cross-legged on the couch and folds her hands self-consciously around her middle. "We all wondered what happened to you. You simply vanished off the face of the earth."

How do I answer? I could tell her how I stuttered my way through the University of Natal, following the momentum of a lost impulse, studying for a BA (a Bugger All, *nog al*). I could say, I was haunted by your image, falling in love with copies of you everywhere I went, dating and discarding, always looking for you. When I graduated, I worked in such far-flung places of the earth as England, the Middle East, the USA, searching for a way to be whole, for a place that was home. And I slowly severed – for my own survival – any feelings of patriotism for this land. I cut myself off from the things I loved, so the wound would dry up and heal. Part of it was shame; who wants to be a pariah white Rhodesian in exile after a failed war? When I saw news stories of Zimbabwe on television, I did not recognise the dust-bowl country of starving children, devastated by drought. Did I really fight in a war against these destitute people? No, I could not have been a Rhodesian soldier. Part of it was aphasia; my memories were unreliable and fantastic. Surely I did not play in a blue pool in Sinoia Caves Motel, or run through a hall of mirrors carved into the rocks at Lake McIlwaine? Surely I did not chase after a blonde girl, and then pine for her my whole life?

But I cannot say any of these things. Instead I talk about living in the USA, about doing well, teaching English at a college, being happily married with one son.

"What's America like?"

"It's not Zimbabwe. It's not Africa."

"Why don't you come back here, then? Zim? Africa? Don't you miss it?"

I stare at the pile of laundry I can see through the kitchen door, at the green pool outside the dirty windowpane, then at the dark corner of the room where the black fist hangs.

"You have no idea."

The afternoon passes quickly. We glide smoothly over the surface of our lives, careful not to be too open, too honest, or too like our past selves. Maybe we are exactly like our past selves, but we talk as if we know better now, as if the people we once were are now strangers to us. Then there is a long silence.

"You're so different now," she says.

"What do you mean?"

"You're... not so aloof."

"Aloof?"

"You were so aloof. So arrogant."

"Me?"

"No, not really." She smiles, and curls her hair around her ear with her hand, nodding her head. It is in these gestures that she most remains. Her legs are tucked under her, and her bare feet show. Finally she looks at the clock on the mantelpiece.

"Do you want to meet my husband? He finishes work at four-thirty. He should be here soon. He wants to meet you. I've told him all about you. No... you probably need to go."

"I do."

"If I'd known you were coming I would have... I'm sorry, I should have..."

She touches my arm in a twenty-five-year-old apology. Then, again without warning, she buries her face in her hands, and sobs. For a single, fleeting moment, the fog that has obscured so much of my past from view dissipates. It's in this moment that I realise that it is I who owe her an apology. The woman in front of me, covering her face with her hands, was once a girl in love with a soldier, who would not, could not, just take her in his arms. I look back and see an eighteen-year-old boy, unable to reach out beyond the codes and structures of his own habits, unable to hear the beat of another human being's heart.

"Bianca, I'm so sorry..."

"No, no. I'm glad you came." She smiles, and quickly wipes her face with the back of her hand. "It's been so good to see you. You must come to Hillside on Sunday. Luke is preaching. Craig will be there. Dave... Suzanne Rogers."

"I'm only here until tomorrow morning."

We stand. I embrace her, and hold our past in the circle of my arms. And then I let it go. As I walk down the driveway, I feel her watching me from the door. I turn once, and she waves with two fingers, her head to one side, grey-blonde hair cascading over her shoulders. With each step I take away from her, I half expect her to call me back.